THE GHETTO

THE GHETTO

Contemporary Global
Issues and Controversies

Edited by
Ray Hutchison and
Bruce D. Haynes

WESTVIEW
PRESS

A Member of the Perseus Books Group

Westview Press was founded in 1975 in Boulder, Colorado, by notable publisher and intellectual Fred Praeger. Westview Press continues to publish scholarly titles and high-quality undergraduate- and graduate-level textbooks in core social science disciplines. With books developed, written, and edited with the needs of serious nonfiction readers, professors, and students in mind, Westview Press honors its long history of publishing books that matter.

Published by Westview Press,
A Member of the Perseus Books Group

Find us on the World Wide Web at www.westviewpress.com.

Every effort has been made to secure required permissions for all text, images, maps, and other art reprinted in this volume.

Westview Press books are available at special discounts for bulk purchases in the United States by corporations, institutions, and other organizations. For more information, please contact the Special Markets Department at the Perseus Books Group, 2300 Chestnut Street, Suite 200, Philadelphia, PA 19103, call (800) 810-4145, ext. 5000, or e-mail special.markets@perseusbooks.com.

Typeset in 11 point Minion Pro by the Perseus Books Group

Library of Congress Cataloging-in-Publication Data
The ghetto : contemporary global issues and controversies /
[edited by] Ray Hutchison and Bruce D. Haynes.
    p.   cm.
  Includes bibliographical references and index.
  ISBN 978-0-8133-4503-1 (pbk. : alk. paper)—ISBN 978-0-8133-4504-8 (e-book)
1. Inner cities. 2. Sociology, Urban. I. Hutchison, Ray. II. Haynes, Bruce D., 1960–
HT156.G44 2012
307.3'366—dc23
                               2011024796

10 9 8 7 6 5 4 3 2 1

CONTENTS

INTRODUCTION   vii
Bruce D. Haynes and Ray Hutchison

1. A Janus-Faced Institution of Ethnoracial Closure: 1
   A Sociological Specification of the Ghetto
   Loïc Wacquant

2. De-spatialization and Dilution of the Ghetto: 33
   Current Trends in the United States
   Peter Marcuse

3. Toward Knowing the Iconic Ghetto   67
   Elijah Anderson

4. "You Just Don't Go Down There":
   Learning to Avoid the Ghetto in San Francisco   83
   Nikki Jones and Christina Jackson

5. In Terms of Harlem   111
   Bruce D. Haynes

6. The Spike Lee Effect: Reimagining the Ghetto   137
   for Cultural Consumption
   Sharon Zukin

7. Places of Stigma: Ghettos, Barrios, and Banlieues   159
   Ernesto Castañeda

8. On the Absence of Ghettos in Latin American Cities   191
   Alan Gilbert

9. Divided Cities: Rethinking the Ghetto
   in Light of the Brazilian Favela   225
   Brasilmar Ferreira Nunes and Leticia Veloso

10. Demonstrations at Work:
    Some Notes from Urban Africa   245
    AbdouMaliq Simone

11. From Refuge the Ghetto Is Born:
    Contemporary Figures of Heterotopias   265
    Michel Agier

12. Where Is the Chicago Ghetto?   293
    Ray Hutchison

ABOUT THE CONTRIBUTORS   327
INDEX   331

INTRODUCTION

Bruce D. Haynes, University of California, Davis
Ray Hutchison, University of Wisconsin-Green Bay

Ghetto (ghet·to), Pronunciation: /'getō, /noun (plural ghettos or ghettoes) a part of a city, especially a slum area, occupied by a minority group or groups. Historical: The Jewish quarter in a city: the Warsaw Ghetto an isolated or segregated group or area: the relative security of the gay ghetto; verb (ghettos, ghettoing, ghettoed) [with object] put in or restrict to an isolated or segregated area or group." Origin: early seventeenth century: perhaps from Italian getto "foundry" (because the first ghetto was established in 1516 on the site of a foundry in Venice), or from Italian borghetto, diminutive of borgo "borough."

Although the term *ghetto* originated in Europe and referred to the area of the city to which Jews were restricted, it has come to embody the urban spaces of marginalized groups in the United States, most notably black Americans. In American popular culture, the term has come to signify both place and mindset of ghetto-centric publications such as *150 Ways to Tell If You Are Ghetto* (Wayans, Spencer, and McCullough 1997), *Straight from the Ghetto* (Berry and Coker 1996), and the sequel *You Still Ghetto* (Berry 1998). There has even been a Broadway show, *Ghetto Klown*, written and performed by the Latin comedian John Leguizamo. In the *New York Times* bestseller *Ghettonation: A Journey into the Land of Bling and Home of the Shameless*, Cora Daniels (2008) argues that the term has morphed from a noun, denoting "overcrowded communities of filth, starvation, violence and despair," to an adjective, describing an "impoverished" mindset that embraces low expectations.

Internationally, a "ghetto culture machine" and "ghetto culture industry" helped produce and market the black ghetto as a symbol of cultural authenticity, heroic resistance, and self-determination, a viewpoint that ignores the historic processes of state and and social isolation and segregation that gave rise to ghettos. From Moscow to Monrovia, American hip hop culture and Jamaican reggae styles mix with anticolonial political struggles and local identities (Osumare 2010). In the banlieues of Paris, North African shopkeepers append the term *ghetto* to their storefront signs. In Senegal, Zimbabwe, Malawi, Kenya, Gambia, and South Africa, radio stations model their programming on the hip hop–influenced urban culture of black Americans; from Poland to Morocco, disenfranchised youth of all races use rap and reggae music to describe the deteriorating inner city.

Over the course of the twentieth century, a preoccupation with the ghetto has emerged in social science research as well, moving from historical studies of Jewish communities in New York (Thomas 1921) and Chicago (Wirth 1928) to a label meant to highlight racial segregation of the black community (Haynes 1913; Weaver 1948; Clark 1967) and finally the study of marginalized communities around the world, which inevitably are compared to and measured against the black American ghetto (Wilson 1987; Jargowsky 1997; Peach 1996, 2001; Poulsen and Johnson 2000; see also Slater 2010). Such simplistic and misleading comparisons across the Atlantic have confounded discussions. In France, violence, lawlessness, and the supposed dysfunctional culture of North African, Arab, and Muslim immigrants are conflated by politicians, social scientists, and journalists in sensational depictions of working-class banlieues (Gilbert 2011). Confrontations between suburban youths and the police have been compared to urban race riots in American cities during the 1980s and 1990s, even as scholars have argued that it is the class position of the French immigrants, modulated by their "ethnic provenance" and racial appearance that sets them apart from the native-born blacks of the United States (Wacquant 2008). Ceri Peach (1996) notes "a recurrent fear expressed by politicians, journalists, and scholars that Britain has ghettos or is developing towards the Black American Ghetto," yet the segregation of African-Caribbean immigrants or black Brits has always remained low (and has in fact has steadily declined over the past fifty years) while Asians are highly segregated (216–232).

In scholarly research the ghetto has a complicated and rich history. In the introduction to the Ghetto Symposium published in *City & Community*, we discussed the origin of the term and the evolution of social science research from the 1920s to the present (Haynes and Hutchison 2008). In this introduction, we trace the term *ghetto* from its origins in Venice through its development during the late 1800s, and consider its application over the last century by social scientists to ethnic and racial communities across the globe.

THE JEWISH GHETTO IN THE *SERENISSIMA REPUBBLICA**

During the Middle Ages and Early Modern period, the Jews of Europe held an ambiguous status within the European states and the Holy Roman Empire. On the one hand, the Church forbade Christians from "usury," or lending money to fellow Christians at interest, which was considered unclean. On the other hand, the flow of credit was central to the development of commerce and trade. Jews, who were barred from owning property and working in most trades and professions, served the crucial but reviled role of providing credit within Christian-influenced states. In fact the very role Jews played, vital to the interests of the Venetian state, was proof of their difference from Christians and their social debasement. Jews and Judaism were labeled a pariah people and religion by Max Weber and later Hannah Arendt (Swedberg 2005).

Early legends cited by scholars gave an active role to Jews in Venetian trades as early as 960 CE, but most contemporary scholars conclude that sometime around the thirteenth century they arrived in numbers in Veneto (Calimani 1988, 5). Jews had congregated unofficially in Venice in the area known as Giudecca since 1090, but their confinement to a specific area developed over the course of three centuries. A central ingredient that led to the implementation of the Venetian policy of ghettoization was the Catholic Church's Third Council of the Lateran, which decreed in 1179 that Christians should not dwell together with Jews, a vague policy that required interpretation by the numerous secular authorities throughout Christendom (Ravid 1992).** In 1221, Jews were required by edict to wear distinguishing badges and garments;

---

* Venice was formally known as *Serenìsima Repùbblica Vèneta* and was often referred to as *La Serenissima—The Most Serene Republic of Venice.*

** *In American Apartheid: Segregation and the Making of the Underclass,* Douglas Massey and Nancy Denton detail the process of ghettoization across the US that led to hypersegregated communities: the combination of racial discrimination in housing and increasing poverty.

the edict was reinforced in 1311 through the Code of Ravenna (Calimani 1988, 5, 8). Separate living quarters for Jews were established in a number of cities within the late Holy Roman Empire, including the Jewish districts in Prague (as early as 1262) and Frankfurt-am-Main (1460s), yet none would be as formally instituted as the ghetto of Venice. By the thirteenth century, the Venetian city-state had emerged as a significant trading center on the Adriatic Sea, but continuing wars with Genoa and Verona during the Crusades in the fourteenth century, followed by the devastating Black Plague, crippled the city's economy and pushed up interest rates as high as 40 percent (Calimani 1988, 5). In response, the Maggior Consiglio—the Great Council of Venice—proposed in 1356 to bring in the pawnbrokers of Mestre and Treviso to pump new credit into the economy, and by 1382 the Venetian government voted to authorize Jewish money lenders, merchants, and doctors to formally live in the city (Calimani 1988, 5). Land was granted to the Jews for a cemetery, but in 1389 the area was walled off to demarcate them as a foreign, albeit semi-permanent people. While Jews had been congregating unofficially in the city's Giudecca area since the late eleventh century, their confinement to a single, walled-in, and stigmatized space represented a new phase in their marginalization. Then, in 1424, sexual relations between Jewish men and Christian women were barred (Ravid 2001, 6).

Following the Inquisition of 1492, Venice became a magnet for Jewish refugees expelled from Spain and Portugal. In 1516 the Venetian Senate responded to this influx by directing all Jews to move to a walled enclosure, called the *Ghetto Nuovo* (New Ghetto), which was located in the *Cannaregio sestieri* (the district along the Cannaregio Canal). Gates leading into the ghetto were locked each evening at sunset and patrolled by two boats until sunrise (Davis and Ravid 2001, XII). This same legislation assigned the area adjacent to the Ghetto Nuovo, as a second ghetto, called the Ghetto Vecchio (Old Ghetto). It had once served as the city's copper and bronze foundry—referred to as the *geto* in the Venetian dialect—and was bordered by a formidable wall and fence (Ravid 2001). The very first use of the term *geto* can be traced to this senate act (Debendetti-Stow, 1992), although its etymology is still debated among scholars.

With the arrival of Tedeschi Jews (German and Italian), as well as Levantine Jews from the east (Ottoman Empire), and Ponentine Jews from the west

FIGURE 1. The Ghetto Nuovo, Venice

Source: Jacopo de' Barbari, Pianta Prospettic Della Citta, 1500.

FIGURE 2. The Ghetto Nova and Ghetto Vecchio, Cannaregio, Venice

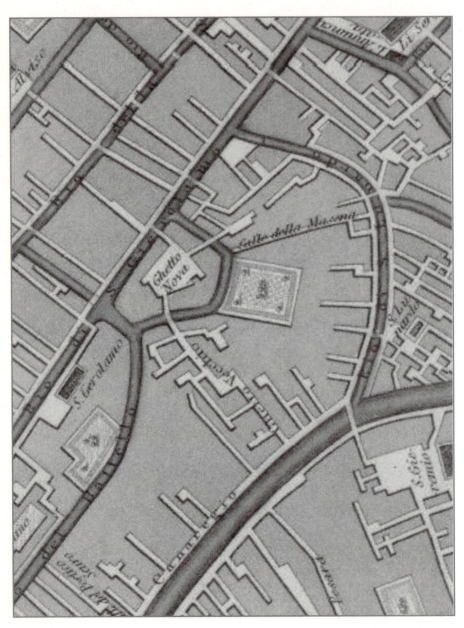

Source: Original map of Venice published by the Society for the Diffuson of Useful Knowledge, London, 1838.

(Iberian Peninsula) overcrowding became an issue. By the seventeenth century the Venetian ghetto consisted of some seven hundred households in three distinct areas, the *Ghetto Nuovo,* the *Ghetto Vecchio*, and the *Ghetto Nuovissimo* (brand new ghetto). The *Ghetto Nuovo* developed around a three-sided circular area or "campo" of store rooms, shops, and stalls that provided a central focal point for community life. This organizing strategy of settlement soon became the preferred model for other ghettos in Padua (1603) and Modena (1638) (Donatella 2001, 31).

Jews were required to pay taxes to finance the very police patrols that enforced their compliance with the nighttime curfew laws. Yet they were forbidden from owning land in the ghetto and obligated to rent, at rates one-third above the norm, from absentee owners (Ravid 2001). Each morning they would don their yellow hats (men) and scarves (women) and leave the ghetto to work or shop among Christians (Calimani 1988, 11). In exchange for a special tax levied against them, Jews were granted unique rights and protections within the walls of the ghettos to "live according to their ancestral rights." Here, a colonial structure of self-governance was maintained under the auspices of the Venetian Republic called the *Università* (Calimani 1988, 10; Malkiel 2001, 117). The Jews had their own governing body, called the Small Assembly, whose primary role was to collect taxes. Its police power was limited to establishing fines for lawbreakers, and yet was completely dependent on the Venetian state for enforcement (Malkiel 2001, 133–135).

The sociologist Richard Sennett (1994) reminds us that the essential problem of the modern city is managing the wide variety of strangers brought together in a geographic space (22). Those ascribed an inner deficiency, as debased or unclean—who carry a spoiled identity by virtue of birth—have been segregated in the modern city. Drawing on the ideas of the French postmodern theorist Michel Foucault, Sennett shows that the Christian association of the Jewish body with disease profoundly shaped urban design and structured the city during the High Middle and Early Renaissance periods; Jewish confinement signified their status as foreigners (Sennett 1994, 214). In shutting Jews behind ghetto walls, Europeans believed they were "isolating a disease" in their midst. "Christians were afraid of touching Jews: Jewish bodies were thought to carry venereal diseases as well as to contain more polluting powers. The Jewish body was unclean (215)." When Jews were blamed for an outbreak of syphilis that scourged the city in 1495–96 (following the return of sailors who had traveled with Columbus to the New World), they were ordered to wear a yellow hat *(baretta)* or scarf to replace the customary yellow badge, which was now deemed too easy to conceal (Ravid 2001). Further evidence of Jewish inferiority was found in clothing and jewelry styles favored by Jewish women. Christian women who wore jewelry were vilified as prostitutes under the Decree of 1512, which regulated their dress materials, the size and design of sleeves, fringes and ornaments, belts and headdresses, shoes and slippers, and home furnishings and bed linens (Hughes 1983).

Although the ghetto was isolated from the outside world, its walls provided the Jewish community with both security—protection from angry Christian mobs, an especially common menace during Easter season—and autonomy, giving rise to a lively Jewish arts scene and new musical styles (Bernstein 1998; Harrán 2001; Ravid 2001). Jewish culture and self-expression in the "City of the Jews" were shaped as much by the stimulating cosmopolitan environment inside the ghettos as they were by their ghettoization and isolation (Ravid 2001, 28). Five synagogues were established to accommodate the Jews of French, German (Ashkenazi), Italian, Levantine, and Sephardic (Spanish) background. Within the context of the compulsory conversion and mandatory expulsion of Jews in Spain, Portugal, and France, the Venetian ghetto (along with the ghettos of other Italian cities) constituted an intermediary space between exile and citizenship.

The Jewish ghetto in Venice is an early example of the racialization of urban space (Haynes and Hutchison 2008, 348; Hutchison 2009b). Racialization begins by stigmatizing a group for a discredited attribute—in this case, their religion—and then relegating the group, by force, to a physical space that is isolated from other areas of the city. Life inside this cloistered space becomes mysterious to outsiders, and the beliefs and behavior of the isolated are viewed with suspicion. The body itself comes to signify both disease and danger; as Sennett (1994) says, "The space of the Ghetto reinforced such beliefs about the Jewish body: behind the Ghetto's drawn bridges and closed windows, its life shut off from the sun and the water, crime and idolatry were thought to fester" (248).

Through racialization, racial meanings and identities are culturally articulated and structurally reinforced (Haynes 2001, 55); the physical body comes to signify a transcendent category of social debasement and a descriptor of group and individual identity and experience. The ghetto constitutes spacialized racialization, where racial stigma and the signification of moral difference are reinforced by the structuration of race inequality. Further, the ghetto is both racial project and process (Omi and Winant 1986). As a structural feature of modern urban life, the ghetto is an administrative strategy of state-imposed racialization, a mechanism of social control through moral debasement that serves a critical structural role by reinforcing social stratification through the signification of moral difference within the body.

The Venetian ghetto reflects the powerful dialectic of the racialization of urban space. First, although we generally view racialization as a process that occurs from the outside and has negative impacts on the groups and areas affected, the forces that create racialized spaces come from both within and outside of the ghetto. Second, while racialization of space is generally viewed as producing social inequality and therefore negative outcomes, there may be positive effects as well (Hutchison 2009b). Finally, the social stigma attached to racialized urban spaces is not static as we see historic ghetto neighborhoods transformed into tourist destinations (Hoffman 1999, 2000), as happened with the Venetian ghetto, or we see them take on new meanings (Gotham 2007; Zukin 2009, 2011).

The Jewish ghetto of Venice may be best known through William Shakespeare's *The Merchant of Venice* (performed 1597). The play likely has its origins in Edward de Vere's visit to Venice in 1575–1576, when it was fashionable for youth to complete their classical education in Greek and Latin literature with tours to Italy. Although the ghetto is not actually referenced by Shakespeare in the play, modern interpretations often depict the villain Shylock as a stereotypical hook-nosed Jewish merchant living in ghetto. Julia Pascal's 2008 production at the Arcola Theatre in London was set in the contemporary Venice ghetto, where a survivor of the Holocaust and the Warsaw ghetto confronts a group of actors and denounces the caricature of Shylock.

During the early modern era, the Venetian ghetto became a destination on the Grand Tour of the 1600s and 1700s, where young aristocrats in training, sometimes accompanied by a teacher or guardian, were expected to gain an understanding of art and architecture through their visits to Florence, Rome, and Venice (Black 1992; Redford 1996). As the Venetian ghetto became more widely known, it would attract visitors from among the growing groups of tourists coming to Venice and become a required destination for intellectuals traveling to the city. Rail travel in the 1800s would directly link Venice with cities across Europe. Davis and Marvin (2004, 216) note that by the late 1800s there were more than five thousand visitors to the city each day by train alone during the High Holy Day period (Henry James dismissed them as "trooping barbarians"; Auchard, *Italian Hours,* 1995 [1909]). After World War II, when the Jewish community itself had largely disappeared from the area, the ghetto would become one of the many tourist destinations in the city, promoted in various tour guides and in the official histories of the city. Today, the Museo Communita Ebraica in the Campo Ghetto Nuevo offers a tour of what was the ghetto with visits to three of the historic synagogues, while other tourist packages offer guided tours of the ghetto "in the footsteps of Shylock" to connect us back with *The Merchant of Venice.* Although most tourists to Venice go to see the famous canals, St. Mark's, or the Rialto, the ghetto holds the allure of an off-the-beaten-path destination, and there is an official map of the ghetto in English, Japanese, and other languages available at most tourist offices (Hutchison 2009a).

By the late medieval period, specific Jewish quarters developed in Prague, Frankfurt-am-Main, and Mainz, and by the 1700s separate Jewish areas were created in Kraków, Warsaw, Vilnius, Lublin, and other Polish cities. The Roman ghetto, established by Pope Paul IV in 1555, was legally abolished in 1798 during the Roman Republic—an event celebrated by the planting of the "tree of liberty" in the Piazza della Scole—only to be reinstituted once the papacy regained control the following year. In fact Jews would be required to reside in ghettos until the papal states were overthrown in 1870. In "The Jewish Question," Bruno Bauer (1844) argued that the emancipation of Jews represented the demise of Judaism and Jewish customs, while Karl Marx (1844) suggested that the question of Jewish emancipation revealed a weakness of bourgeois liberalism because real political emancipation first required true social emancipation (Hall et al. 2010, 681). By this time, rising anti-Semitism across much of Europe, culminating in the Dreyfus Affair in France, had pushed Jews to emigrate to England and the United States. The migrant stream would turn into a flood when *pogroms* were directed against Jews in the Russian Empire in the years 1881 through 1884, and again from 1903 to 1906.

THE JEWISH GHETTOS OF LONDON AND NEW YORK

By the late nineteenth century, the Jewish population in the East London neighborhoods had swelled to more than 140,000, spawning a thriving Jewish culture that many compared to the earlier European ghettos. In 1894, a London correspondent for the *American Hebrew* magazine wrote: "We are in the centre of Spitalfields in the heart of the Jewish quarter. All about is Jewish! Men with beards, others clean-shaven of face. Women with shitels or lint, girls gaudily dressed, boys in corduroy suits of the Jews' Free School—all Jewish. Posters in Yiddish, some religious, some socialistic, bills in crude colors, notices of rooms to let in the same tongue. Patois in the ear and in the eye, the tone, the habit, the idea is foreign."

The term ghetto was romanticized by a number of Jewish immigrant writers, like Israel Zangwill (1865–1926), the politically active author of *Children of the Ghetto* (1892), *Ghetto Tragedies* (1893), *Dreamers of the Ghetto* (1898), and *Ghetto Comedies* (1907). Zangwill, whose parents had immigrated to England from Eastern Europe, drew upon his experiences growing up in London's East End. He likened the nineteenth-century immigrant ghetto to a zone of transition, a "crossroads between tradition and modernity," and used the term *ghetto culture* to describe the way of life of the Old Country (see Nahshon 2005).

Abraham Cahan (1860–1951), a Jewish refugee from Lithuania who settled in New York, depicted the struggles of an Eastern Europe immigrant adjusting to a new life on the Lower East Side. Cahan went on to become the first editor of the *Jewish Daily Forward (Forverts),* a socialist Yiddish-language daily that advocated for Jewish immigrants in the city. Still, the negative stereotypes of Jewish immigrants were propagated by many non-Jewish writers. Hutchins Hapgood, a journalist who worked with Cahan at the *New York Commercial Advertiser*, wrote a series of articles about Yiddish New York for the *Atlantic Monthly* and other magazines between 1898 and 1902. His sketches of immigrant types and personalities were compiled in *The Spirit of the Ghetto: Studies of the Jewish Quarter of New York* (1902). In its preface, he writes: "The Jewish quarter of New York is generally supposed to be a place of poverty, dirt, ignorance, and immorality—the seat of the sweatshop, the tenement house, where 'red-lights' sparkle at night, where the people are queer and repulsive. Well-

to-do persons visit the 'Ghetto' merely from motives of curiosity or philanthropy; writers treat of it 'sociologically,' as of a place in crying need of
improvement."

The Lower East Side and other Jewish neighborhoods in New York City
are described by W. I. Thomas in *Old World Traits Transplanted,* one of the early
classic social science studies written in the United States (1921). At the time
the Jewish population had reached 1,500,000 (one-quarter of the city's total
population, and a larger population than in any other city in the world) and
was strongly concentrated on a ghetto on the Lower East Side. Thomas wrote
that life in the New York City ghetto was not a new experience because most
immigrants had come from the ghettos of various European cities. Many
spoke Yiddish in addition to their national language, while cultural differences between the native and foreign-born Jews, as well as prejudice from
other ethnic groups, affected both institutional life and interpersonal relationships. A later analysis of the 1910 census reveals that mother tongue, national origin, and race were central factors shaping segregation across groups,
despite demographic and socioeconomic controls, and that robust segregation measures existed for a number of groups, although most markedly for
Jews and blacks (White et al. 1994, 203). And yet while anti-Semitism was
on the rise in Britain, France, Germany, and Russia, anti-Semitism faded in
the United States. Jews would claim membership as whites (Caucasian) and
be legally granted full rights and privileges. Before long, more prosperous
Jews were moving to other neighborhoods, and the ghetto began to lose its
hold. Although the largest Jewish population was located in New York City,
the Jewish community in Chicago was growing rapidly during this same
period and experiencing many of the same transitions that were noted in
New York.

LOUIS WIRTH AND THE CHICAGO
SOCIOLOGICAL TRADITION ON THE GHETTO

Louis Wirth, the well-known Chicago School sociologist, is often cited as the
most important scholar to write about the Jewish ghetto. His research on Jewish immigrants in Chicago, culminating in the seminal book *The Ghetto*
(1928), shaped a generation of scholarship. However, Wirth provides an in-

complete view of Jewish historical development, tracing immigration from the ghetto of Frankfurt-am-Main to the Chicago ghetto (Maxwell Street), regarding the new ghetto as an area of second settlement (he even referred to it as "Deutschland"). In fact, most American Jews had immigrated from Central and Eastern Europe, not Germany, and lived in small towns and villages known as *shtetls*, rather than large cosmopolitan centers like Frankfurt. Although Wirth had also depicted most of the early Jewish immigrants as Orthodox, already by the 1880s some two hundred Reform congregations had been founded in America, in contrast to only a dozen Orthodox congregations.

Wirth's study was not the first sociological examination of the Chicago ghetto: the subject already was well established by the time Manuel Zeublin contributed a chapter titled "The Chicago Ghetto" to the *Hull House Maps and Papers* (1895). Interestingly, although Hull House—the famous Chicago settlement house founded by Jane Addams—was located just a few blocks from the Jewish ghetto along Maxwell Street, it had little contact with local Jews. Zeublin's chapter noted that in 1895 the dispersal of the earlier ghetto was already well under way, and that some areas had seen an increase of black households. Some thirty years later, Maurice Krout noted "a rapid dissolution of social ties in the Ghetto," an encroachment of business and industry into the residential area of the ghetto (described as the most densely settled area of the city), and fewer than half of the population being foreign-born at the time of his study (1926).

This background is important, because Wirth's description of the Chicago community in *The Ghetto* follows these earlier studies, and also builds on many of the themes presented in Thomas's *Old World Traits Transplanted*: life in the ghetto was not a new experience for the Jewish immigrants coming from the European cities, and that those who could afford to quickly fled to other areas. For both scholars, the ghetto was similar to other ethnic settlements where first-generation immigrants lived and over time became assimilated and economically mobile. Like Wirth, Thomas (1921) traced the movement of mostly German Jews from Maxwell Street into the area of second settlement North Lawndale ("Deutschland") throughout the 1910s and 1920s. By 1960 the west side neighborhoods had been largely abandoned, as secular and religious Jews moved into the north side suburbs. A second generation of scholars would refer to these affluent suburban areas as "Gilded Ghettos" (Kramer and Leventman 1961; Rose 1969; Rose 1977).

Consequently, Wirth's description of the ghetto should be understood within the broader context of neighborhood succession in the city:

> The occupation of this area by the Jews, it seems, is merely a passing phase of a long process of succession in which one population group has been crowded out by another. There is, however, an unmistakable regularity in this process. In the course of the growth of the city and the invasion of the slums by new groups of immigrants there has resulted a constancy of association between Jews and other ethnic groups. Each racial and cultural group tends to settle in that part of the city which, from the point of view of the rents, standards of living, accessibility, and tolerance, makes the reproduction of Old World life easier. . . . The Jews have successively replaced the Germans, the Irish, and the Bohemians, and have themselves been displaced by the Poles and Lithuanians, the Italians, the Greeks, and Turks, and finally the Negro. . . . The latest invasion of the ghetto by the Negro is of more than passing interest. The Negro, like the immigrant, is segregated in the city into a racial colony; economic factors, race prejudice, and cultural difference combine to set him apart. [68]

Wirth notes that his research is concerned with the "natural history" of the ghetto and should serve as a model for the acculturation of other groups: "Viewed from this angle the study of the ghetto is likely to throw light on a number of related phenomena, such as the origin of segregated areas and the development of local communities in general; for while the ghetto is, strictly speaking, a Jewish institution, there are forms of ghettos that concern not only Jews. Our cities contain Little Sicilies, Little Polands, Chinatowns, and Black Belts. There are Bohemias and Hobohemias, slums and Gold Coasts, vice areas and Rialtos in every metropolitan communities" (58).

Wirth has often been critiqued for suggesting that all immigrant groups would follow the Jewish model, moving through similar stages of neighborhood succession and assimilation (a critique echoed in several chapters in this volume as well). In fact, both Wirth and his colleague Roberts Ezra Park distinguished the settlements of immigrant ethnic populations from the racial colonies of non-white groups: "The slum includes also the areas of first settlement to which the immigrants inevitably gravitate before they have their places in the larger environment. The racial 'ghettos,' which now shelter and set part from the rest of the community Negroes and Chinese as they once sheltered and segregated Jews, are invariably located in the slum. The Jewish ghetto still exists, but the slum, so far as the Jew is concerned, is at present only an area of first settlement. Negroes and Chinese, on the other hand, still find it difficult to live beyond the pale" (Park 1927).

A student of George Simmel, Park worked with Burgess to map the city, demarcating the Black Belt with a solid black rectangle that ran north-south from the Chicago Loop. The term "Black Belt" was originally used to describe areas of the Deep South where African Americans were concentrated following the expansion of cotton production in the 1830s. It was a relatively polite term to refer to Negro residential areas; in fact, until 1962 the U.S. Board on Geographic Names included in its official record of geographic sites hundreds of towns, streams, mountains, hills, valleys, brooks, and swimming holes with such names as "Nigger," "Nigger Creek," and "Nigger Gulch." In Chicago, the Black Belt encompassed the Federal Street slum, an area of older, dilapidated housing to which African Americans had been confined following the Chicago race riots.

St. Clair Drake and Horace Cayton's 1945 classic *Black Metropolis*, a study of the famous South Side neighborhood Bronzeville, offers a rich description of the African-American community at the end of the Great Depression, with ethnographic sources documenting the lifestyles of the black middle class and the everyday life of the lower class. Social differences between older, established families and newcomers, as well as between social classes, corresponded closely with spatial segregation within the community: the lower class lived in the oldest areas along 22nd Street and the Federal Street slum, while the black middle class had moved into neighborhoods including Woodlawn. It is notable that Drake and Cayton name an entire chapter "The Black Ghetto." In their use of the term ghetto, they broke with traditional Chicago School scholars who had defined it as an area of voluntary first settlement leading toward assimilation. Their definition aligned with that of black social scientists like Du Bois (1903), Haynes (1913), and Johnson (1943), who distinguished the black ghetto, "which becomes increasingly more concentrated" from the "colonies that tend to break up." The black ghetto is "primarily the result of white people's attitudes towards having Negroes as neighbors," especially middle-class whites who, through the imposition of restrictive residential covenants, limited black mobility in the city (Drake and Cayton 1945, 174).

In 1948, Robert Weaver, who would later become the first secretary of the U.S. Department of Housing and Urban Development, conducted research that foreshadowed contemporary scholarship on the impact of restrictive covenants and state policies like the Home Owners Loan Corporation (HOLC) in shaping Negro segregation patterns. Appropriately titled *The Negro Ghetto* (1948), Weaver's study was the first comprehensive analysis of housing segregation in American cities. Weaver noted that Chicago was "leading the way" toward segregation patterns and identified restrictive covenants as "the villain" (1944) that had structured four general patterns of ghetto formation:

A single, central Black Belt extending into surrounding areas not yet completely colored but rapidly becoming so. This distribution is found in a part of New York City . . . Newark, Columbus, Buffalo, Atlantic City, Toledo, and Milwaukee.

Two or more Black Belts, one of which is in the center of the city and the principal are of Negro concentration and from which expansion is occurring into surrounding areas. This is the pattern of Chicago . . . Detroit, Cincinnati, and Indianapolis.

Several major Black Belts and many minor Black Belts, all of which are expanding into surrounding areas. This is more characteristic of border cities like Washington, Baltimore, and even St. Louis than of urban communities in the north, yet Philadelphia follows this arrangement.

A single large Black Belt expanding into surrounding areas and one or more smaller area of higher Negro concentration. Cleveland, Pittsburgh (to a modified degree), Los Angeles, Boston, and Dayton belong in the group that follows this pattern. [100]

He further explained that "ghetto patterns of residence are of recent origins in this Nation. They were initiated, perpetuated, and popularized by certain institutions" responsive to special interests with strong motives of "special economic advantage."

Although early scholars viewed ghettos as a phenomenon of local generis, by the middle of the twentieth century, scholars began to focus their attention on one "certain institution" in Weaver's analysis: the federal government. In *The Making of the Second Ghetto,* Arnold Hirsch argues that a second Chicago ghetto, which lasted from 1933 to 1968, was distinguished from earlier segregation patterns in that it arose in the context of federally funded high-rise public housing. Yet it's the impact of Weaver's work that remains undeniable. The preface to his second edition (1957) summarizes the new conceptualization: "When The Negro Ghetto was published [1948], there had been occasional references to black ghettos. The use of the term "Negro ghetto," however, was almost unprecedented. Today the concept of the Negro ghetto is accepted in the literature on racial relations. It has become the symbol of involuntary residential segregation and the deprivations that harass the occupants of these enclaves of urban America."

Gilbert Osofsky's landmark study *Harlem: The Making of a Ghetto* (1963, 1968) set the agenda for "a new generation of scholarship on African American communities." He identified "second class Citizenship," poor quality schools, segregated labor markets, violence against blacks, and congested-slum (poverty) conditions as the key sources of the "enduring" ghetto. Scholars like Allan Spear, the author of *Black Chicago: The Making of a Negro Ghetto* (1967) and Kenneth Kusner, author of *A Ghetto Takes Shape: Black Cleveland 1870–1930* (1976), made important contributions, but it was Kenneth Clarke's *Dark Ghetto* (1967) that stressed the role of power in the creation and maintenance of the black ghetto and described its psychological and sociological impact on African Americans: "The ghetto is ferment, paradox, conflict, and dilemma. Yet within its pervasive pathology exists a surprising human resilience. The ghetto is hope, it is despair, it is churches and bars. It is aspiration for change, and it is apathy. It is vibrancy, it is stagnation. It is courage, and it is defeatism. It is cooperation and concern, and it is suspicion, competitiveness, and rejection. It is the surge toward assimilation, and it is alienation and withdrawal within the protective walls of the ghetto" (11–12).

By the time *Dark Ghetto* was published, the term ghetto had become widely associated with black people and black culture, and was used to describe virtually all African-American communities in and out of the city. In the absence of a thick detailed description of African-American life and culture, many social scientists linked certain social behaviors, such as welfare dependency, crime, and sexual promiscuity, to the black urban poor and suggested that they were symptomatic of a pathological ghetto "culture" (Moynihan 1963; Wilson 1987).

Some scholars came to characterize entire inner cities as ghettos and used the term to refer to schools and other institutions in the urban core. But a number of scholars began criticizing the very concept of the ghetto. Karl Rasmussen (1968) argued that from Nazi reinvention of the Warsaw Ghetto to the Black Ghetto of Watts in South Central Los Angeles, the term is "axiomatic," "ambiguous," and "emotional" and has become an offensive and useless analytical term (282). And while he concurred that the black ghetto is an urban neighborhood created by imposed spatial boundaries of a "socio-cultural homogeneous minority" excluded from complete social acceptance and "dumped into a walled area," he also believed that its residents shared "different" values that reveal "a 'ghetto mentality' characterized by an excessive parochial attitude" (Rassmusen 1968, 282–283). It was not long before this concept of parochialism was used to extend the term ghetto to "voluntary" self-segregated communities and indeed any cloistered community: William Partridge's *The Hippie Ghetto* (1985), Kim England's *Suburban Pink Collar Ghettos* (1993), Charles and Grusky's *Occupational Ghettos* (2004), and Jessie O'Neill's *The Golden Ghetto: The Psychology of Affluence* (1997).

CONTEMPORARY URBAN THEORY AND THE GHETTO

Despite strongly contested meanings, the term ghetto continues to be used as descriptor (of physical space) and analytical concept (to explain observed outcomes) in contemporary urban research. Social scientists have further obfuscated the issue by invoking the term as a catchall to explain poverty, segregation, and social organization in both African-American and "minority" communities across the globe. Too often minority communities are labeled with the same negative characteristics used to stigmatize black ghettos.

The ghetto concept sheds light on the lack of a unified theory of cities. In an attempt to make order out of chaos, urban scholars developed a nomenclature embedded in various "schools of thought" in which the Chicago School of Sociology figures prominently.

Michael Dear (Dear and Flusty 1997, 1998) argues that the traditional city form, as represented by the modern industrial metropolis of Chicago, along with Ernest W. Burgess's model of concentric zones, assimilation, and "invasion and succession," is being replaced by a postmodern urban environment characterized by increased polarization and fragmentation. Dear and associates in Southern California posited the "Los Angeles" school as a counter to the famed Chicago School of Urban Sociology, and a seventy-five-year-old debate over the effectiveness of ecological models to examine the ghetto as a feature of modern cities. The Los Angeles scholars also drew important attention to the field's preoccupation with Chicago as representative of the processes governing urban growth more generally (Dear 2002).

Arguably the best known research on the Chicago ghetto is the work of William Julius Wilson. His most widely read works, *The Truly Disadvantaged: The Inner City, the Underclass, and Public Policy* (1987) and *When Work Disappears* (1996), are based on research grounded in the neighborhoods that make up Chicago's South Side. Consistent with the Chicago School orientation, Wilson studies poverty in cities and argues that class has become more dominant in shaping the life chances of blacks. But with Wilson we find a more deliberate use of the term ghetto. He maintains that in the post–civil rights era, the central challenge facing the ghetto poor is lack of economic opportunity, not spatial marginality from race discrimination per se. Wilson's ghetto, like Wirth's, is in part a cultural phenomenon, defined by the social characteristics of individuals who live there.

For nearly two decades, Berkeley scholar Loïc Wacquant has taken issue with Wilson's argument, maintaining that: "To say that they are ghettos because they are poor is to reverse social and historical causation: it is because they were and are ghettos that joblessness and misery are unusually acute and persistent in them" (Wacquant 1997, 343). Wacquant has utilized the ghetto concept as a pivotal theoretical component of his research strategy on social marginality and exclusion, developing a model of advanced urban marginality based on research he conducted between 1987 and 1991 in Chicago's Black Belt and France's "Red Belt." Wacquant treats these areas as ideal types in order to highlight processes of institutionalized spatial confinement and control during a period of industrial decline, state retrenchment, and media hysteria about minority youth. One key difference between the French banlieue and the American ghetto, he argues, was the American withdrawal of key resources, which contributed to the ghetto's deterioration and necessitated the rise of a penal system to manage the urban underclass (Wacquant 2001).

Wacquant places the institution of the prison in historical sequence following slavery and the ghetto, and argues that these "peculiar institutions" have defined the black experience in America. In fact, as the penal management system replaces the social welfare system as a mechanism of social control in an environment of industrial decline and deregulated wage-labor markets, the traditional ghetto becomes more like a prison and the prison becomes more like the ghetto, eventually making the latter obsolete (2001). The ghetto becomes a central place for "sociopolitical struggles" and political mobilization against white domination in the city, a viewpoint consistent with Omi and Winant's (1986) understanding of racial projects.

Wacquant's critique wrenched discussions on the ghetto away from the urban poverty discourse and connected the term back to its original meaning—the formal segregation of stigmatized groups supported by institutional structures. At the same time, relying on the historic Black Belt as the single case on which to build a theory raised questions of whether Chicago was representative of general urban processes and the Chicago School's model with its ecological focus on the ghetto as a stage in the assimilation process. And by focusing on the city of Chicago during the traumatic period of urban decline in the 1980s, Wacquant reproduced iconic images and sensationalist tropes, calling it a "brutish" place full of "mugging," "wilding," and "drive-bys" (Wacquant 2008).

As soon as we leave the confines of the Chicago Black Belt, nothing quite looks the same (Nobles 2010). In New York City, blacks were never as poor, isolated from jobs, or segregated from whites as in Chicago (Beveridge 2011). Although Wacquant famously argues that there are many banlieues but just one ghetto, Small (2008) notes that there is no single urban policy or housing program at the national level, but rather state and local programs that attempt to ensure a diversity of urban neighborhoods. When we turn our attention to the Latinos in America, scholars have tended to use the term *barrio* in a way that closely parallels ghetto, while areas believed to be the result of voluntary segregation, like Chinatowns, are generally called "ethnic enclaves" (Gans 2008).

When we turn our attention to the European, Asian, African, and South American contexts, do similar processes of social exclusion produce comparable results across contemporary societies? Are the stigmatized territories of Rio de Janeiro's Morro de Providencia *favela*, the *barriadas* of Lima, the ranchos of Venezuela, the squatters of Mumbai, the shantytowns of South Africa, the slums of Lagos, the banlieues of France, or the villa miserias, slums, and kampongs across the globe similar to the ghetto? (See Caldiera 2009; Christopher 2005; Guillaume 2001; Olivera 1996; Perlman 2010.) In *The World Is a Ghetto: Race and Democracy Since World War Two*, Howard Winant (2002) discusses how race drives modernity and the modern world system, particularly in the United States, South Africa, Brazil, and Europe—but he largely ignores the spatial dimensions of the ghetto. And in his indictment of post-1978 "neoliberal globalization," Mike Davis argues in *Planet of Slums* (2006) that global cities have become dumping grounds for an expanding "informal working class" that is marginally employed, overlaps with a slum population (178). Could the proliferation of dollar-a-day *rickshawalas*, low-wage pedi-cabs, and the privatization of toilets in Ghana and New York City be the harbingers of the urban landscape of the twenty-first century (189)?

THE GHETTO: CONTEMPORARY GLOBAL ISSUES

Our strategy for structuring *The Ghetto: Contemporary Global Issues and Controversies* is to provide a context for debate among scholars who have forged analytical and empirical projects around the concept of the "ghetto," and to seek insights from the tensions, inconsistencies, and overlaps between them. As the title of this volume suggests, our intent is to move the discussion from the specifics of the American ghetto, which may or may not be relevant to understanding residential and social isolation in other countries, to a more general consideration of marginalized urban spaces and peoples around the globe. We invited a group of internationally renowned scholars to engage in a constructive dialogue about the meaning and usefulness of the term ghetto in social science research. The chapters that follow reveal that despite their appearance under different political and economic regimes, these spaces share important characteristics: concentrated poverty, unemployment, and social exclusion.

We asked contributors to consider the following questions: What is the meaning of the term *ghetto*? Is the formation and later dissolution of the Jewish ghetto an appropriate model for understanding the experience of other ethnic or racial populations (see Marcuse 1997, 1998, 2002)? Does the concept have scholarly utility, or is it simply an overused colloquialism? Does the ghetto arise from normative ecological or structural processes of urban regions, or is it the consequence of social conflict and government policy (Hirsch 1983,

Massey 1990, Massey and Denton 1993, Gotham 2000)? Can we draw a relevant distinction between voluntary and involuntary processes of spatial isolation and segregation (Gans 2008)? Has the term become an offensive oversimplification of the social relations and conditions of social exclusion? Is there a single model of the ghetto that can be applied to all cities (see Small 2007, 2008)?

We begin with selections from several prominent scholars in the urban field. In Chapter One, Loïc Wacquant refers to the ghetto as a "Janus-faced" institution: a two-faced instrument of group power. He reiterates his contention that spatial isolation operates as "an instrument of closure and control" and continues developing a model of the ghetto that emphasizes the dimensions of economic extraction and marginalization as well as social exclusion and stigmatization, directly challenging two widespread assumptions that have come to dominate social sciences: (1) the ghetto is a "natural area" with a "natural history" of settlement as Louis Wirth understood it to be, and (2) the ghetto can be reduced to the characteristics of poverty.

Peter Marcuse has also argued that the classic ghetto was the result of the involuntary spatial segregation of a group that stands in a "subordinate political and social relationship to its surrounding society" (1997, 2005). Marcuse emphasizes the difference between racial segregation (creation of ghetto), that is, "segregation based on race," and what he calls "market segregation," segregating people of lower-income households into "class ghettos" (2005). In Chapter Two, "De-spacialization and Dilution of the Ghetto," Marcuse details the disappearance of the "hard ghetto" and the "de-ghettoization of space" and outlines the construction of what he terms the new "softer" forms of social control that are no longer concerned with traditional racial exclusion and are focused more on containing and maintaining class inequality. Marcuse views the shift to mass incarceration of poor black men as a form of "spatialized oppression" that stems from particular manifestations of colonial relationships and that serves to neutralize resistance. Thus his definition of the "hard" ghetto as spatial, racial, institutional, and state implemented does not contradict Wacquant's notion that the institutional ghetto requires spatial confinement and social control, yet it does suggest that Wacquant's argument misses important demographic changes that have taken place in urban ghettos since 1990, particularly the deconcentration of poverty as the poor move toward the suburbs. Nevertheless, Marcuse concurs with Wacquant's argument that the prison now serves as surrogate ghetto, the central mechanism of control after 1996, which "attenuates the control function of the ghetto."

Urban ethnographer Elijah Anderson writes about place but harkens back to Du Bois through his familiar focus on present-day Philadelphia, where there are few economic opportunities and much to be feared on the street (Anderson 2006). Anderson's first ethnographic work, *A Place on the Corner,* was a study of streetcorner life at a local carryout on Chicago's South Side. But it was Anderson's *Streetwise: Race, Class, and Change in an Urban Community* (1990) and *Code of the Streets: Decency, Violence, and the Moral Life of the Inner City* (1999), books that document the life of the urban poor in Philadelphia, that have become his trademark. In *The Cosmopolitan Canopy* (2011), Anderson describes a new racially and ethnically diverse urban environment where various social, cultural, and racial groups leave their various ethnic enclaves and come together in a civil exchange in neutral public spaces like museums, parks, universities, train terminals, and hybrid institutions like Barnes & Nobel or Starbucks. But the canopy can be ruptured by a "nigger moment," "a time in the life of every African American when he or she is powerfully reminded of his or her putative place as a black person. . . . Emotions flood over the victim as this middle-class, cosmopolitan-oriented black person is humiliated and shown that he or she is, before anything else, a racially circumscribed black person after all" (2004, 253).

And in Chapter Three of this volume, "Toward Knowing the Iconic Ghetto," Anderson argues that the impact of the stigmatized iconic black ghetto—the "imagined ghetto"—affects all those within and those outside its borders. He writes, "The ascription of 'ghetto' to all black Americans has saddled the group with a provisional social rank revealing how the upwardly mobile deploy strategies from their tool kit to escape their racial stigma—which works to distance them from the ghetto and its people." Anderson identifies the public imagination and the media as sources that stigmatize all blacks regardless of class position, conflating ideas of race with bad people and places.

Nikki Jones and Christina Jackson strike a similar tone in Chapter Four, "'You Just Don't Go Down There': Learning to Avoid the Ghetto in San Francisco," in which they examine how social isolation in the Lower Fillmore neighborhood of San Francisco is exacerbated by "discursive redlining": routinely warning people to avoid those persons perceived to be dangerous in public spaces, especially young black men believed to come from the ghetto. Jones and Jackson show that even though the ghetto may not be confined to specific urban space, its reputation carries a commonly acknowledged image and symbolic power that influence everyday life and decision making.

In Chapter Five, Bruce Haynes reflects on fact and fiction about the Harlem community of his youth. Haynes has written about state and real estate practices shaping racialization and suburban development (2001), but here turns his attention toward detailing the view from within the iconic community of Harlem, New York, in which he grew up. Haynes details the context of a middle-class African-American life and demonstrates the ways in which culture, history, class, and race intersect to shape the public imagination.

Known for her award-winning research on the changing urban landscape, gentrification, arts and economic development, Sharon Zukin (2010) begs the question in her provocatively titled chapter "Why Harlem Is Not a Ghetto," in which she argues that through public policy (Hope VI), gentrification, economic development, and demographic changes, the "authenticity" of the neighborhood has been co-opted. Even earlier, Zukin (1998) had argued that the "place identity of racial ghettos" might be up for grabs as state redevelopment programs like Hope VI and an influx of capital investment reshaped experiences on the street. In Chapter Six of this volume, "The Spike Lee Effect: Reimagining the Ghetto for Cultural Consumption," Zukin returns to the theme that gentrification, tourism, and empowerment zones have led to a reimagining of the stigmatized "Dark Ghetto" that characterized Harlem and Bedford-Stuyvesant, and have made these communities desirable "comparative advantages" for middle- and upper-class home ownership. For Zukin, commercial redevelopment, gentrification, and a reimagined real estate market have actually transformed historic Ghetto spaces into "non-ghettos."

In *Cities of the South*, Drieskens, Mermier, and Wimmen (2007) note that the urban and suburban experience varies greatly from country to country. Among the poorest sections of the global society, the marginalized spaces of the inner city and the inherited poverty of the nineteenth- and twentieth-century urban slum have been superseded by the suburbanization of poverty and racial segregation, and the proliferation of the shantytown and the favela. These are largely unplanned settlements, just as the poorest areas of the Victorian city were the unplanned residue and residuum of urbanization and industrialisation. The gated community is an increasingly common expression of residential segregation in many parts of the world, where a variety of income groups corral themselves away from the threat of crime. Many of the largest gated communities are built exclusively for the wealthiest in society, but this pattern is not restricted to North America. The pattern can be identified in new elite residential areas across the world, in particular the Global South. Wealthy areas often exist side-by-side with much poorer suburban settlements, raising conflicts over unequal access to resources as the middle-class withdraw from the civic and financial functioning of town and city (Roitman 2005).

Ethnographer Ernesto Castañeda has studied international migration, transnationalism, and economic development in New York City, Paris, Barcelona, and in communities in Algeria, Mexico, and Morocco. His essay "Transnacionalismo, Asimilación, Multiculturalismo, en Perspectiva Comprada" (2010) compares Latino and Muslim immigrants in the United States and Europe by analyzing the contexts of reception and the resulting political inclusion of immigrants and minorities. Casteñada (2009) argues that the ghetto and banlieue are symbolically distinct yet analytically similar: "In the United States the word *suburb* carries a positive connotation associated with private property, middle-class ease, low-density population, and an overall high quality of life. In contrast, the immediate connotation of the French *banlieue* and its inhabitants, the *banlieuesards*, is one of overcrowded public housing, people of color, new immigrants, and crime. It is something closer to the stereotype of the ghetto in America, but although there are important differences, what is common in both cases is the association between categorical inequality, exclusion from the labor market, and social boundaries resulting in residential segregation."

In Chapter Seven, "Places of Stigma: Ghettos, Barrios, and Banlieues," Casteñada explores the creation of marginalized spaces in the contemporary city, and deconstructs the myths of the Chicago ghetto and the urban-rural divide that underlies much urban studies and confounds our ability to understand contemporary developments like the French banlieues. He presents a strong argument against the isolated case study, and sets out to study immigrants across the Parisian urban region. Casteñada notes that "banlieues are an integral part of Paris because much of its business, work, and daily life are done there, behind the scenes, in the backstage of the banlieue, without which the Parisian front stage could not hold up. Thus one cannot talk about the Parisian banlieue without talking about Paris, and in the same way one cannot talk about Paris without taking its banlieue into account." It is striking that while one cannot discuss the American city without talking about the ghetto, it is not because of the ghetto's centrality to business and work in the city, though an interdependent relationship does exist between ghetto and city. Casteñada maintains that if the term ghetto is not applicable in France, then "it would be only because it lacks the historical equivalent of an African American population but this does not mean that present social boundaries against stigmatized groups are not also inscribed in space, mind, and as speech in the word *banlieue*."

Alan Gilbert, Professor Emeritus at University College London, is well known for his research on urbanization, housing, and poverty in Latin America and South Africa. He has long been interested in the spread of social marginalization and poverty and the impact of globalization on Latin America. He argues that poverty is no longer confined to poor countries. Neoliberalism, combined with globalization, has generated inequality and poverty everywhere. Gilbert has also cautioned scholars about the return of extreme thinking about slum dwellers (2010), and about the very use of the word slum: "The new millennium has seen the return of the word 'slum' with all of its inglorious associations. With the launch of the 'cities without slums' initiative in 1999, the UN reintroduced this dangerous word into the habitat vocabulary." The use of the word, he warns, will create many myths about poor people that have been discredited by many years of careful research (Gilbert 2007, 697).

His chapter here, "On the Absence of Ghettos in Latin American Cities," presents us with a comprehensive demographic overview of the countries and major cities of Latin America, the most heavily urbanized region of the world, and notes that: "If the ghetto is defined as a spatially confined area containing a racial or ethnic minority, then there are very few ghettos in Latin American cities. And, if we adopt Wacquant's (2004, 2) more sophisticated requirement that the 'four constituent elements of the ghetto' are 'stigma, constraint, spatial confinement, and institutional encasement,'—then there are rather few anywhere. Perhaps that is why, to my recollection, over forty years I have never heard the term *gueto* used by a Latin American."

The reason for the lack of a racial ghetto (as defined by Wacquant) include the distinctive racial structure of Latin American societies, in which social class weighs more heavily than does racial background; the fact that in many cities where black populations are heavily concentrated they are also the majority; and most importantly, the extremely high levels of poverty in Latin

American countries, which make the poor the majority of the urban and nonurban populations. Gilbert's discussion of the cloistered neighborhoods of the rich parallels earlier discussions of "(voluntary) clustering" (Marcuse 2005) and "voluntary segregation" (Gans 2008). Gilbert's discussion of marginality demonstrates the need for "new ways of thinking about the poor and their relationship to society and the economy at large. . . . We are unlikely to return to any kind of belief in the 'culture of poverty', 'ruralization' and 'overurbanization', but no doubt some academic or—these days—some journalist will produce an apocalyptic new interpretation of the situation of the poor."

Brasilmar Ferreira Nunes and Leticia Veloso, from the Universidade Federal Fluminense in São Paolo, present us in Chapter Nine with further possibilities for understanding marginalization in Latin America. They have published numerous studies on urban issues in Brazil, including studies of urban planning, urban space, and heterogeneity (Nunes) and children and youth, poverty, and violence (Veloso). Nunes's two books on Brasila have presented "the construction of the everyday" and the "embodied fantasy" of the capital city. Veloso's research interests are reflected by her continuing ethnographic fieldwork for a comparative study of youth, violence, and rights in urban space in São Paolo and Glasgow (Scotland). Veloso discusses the development of the Brazilian favela in a recent chapter titled "The Pacification of Favelas in Rio de Janeiro" (Veloso 2010). Her work reminds us that even the poorest favelas are products of suburbanization, and also that they have close and complicated relationships, both socially and spatially, with other suburban working-class neighborhoods. Veloso also describes the limitations of a North American approach to studying urban development that emphasizes a city-suburb duality rather than the more nuanced patterns where working-class and lower-class neighborhoods share suburban space in many Brazilian cities. Both of these points mesh nicely with what Castañeda presents in his discussion of the banlieue.

Nunes and Veloso note that the comparison of the favela and the ghetto may offer important insights as to their historical development and current predicament: while they are very different phenomena, the fact that "both are marginalized urban spaces with a long history in their *respective* societies allows for this comparative exercise." The favela arose as a marginal space where economically and socially excluded individuals were collected because of the rapid migration from rural areas during the period of industrial growth.

The ethnic composition of favelas has always diversified, and segregation has its roots in economic marginality. "In this sense, the question of stigma does not appear, at first, as strongly as in the American ghetto, at least in terms of race or ethnicity, for neither is the main marker of difference for *favela* residents. To the contrary, the *favela* is, first and foremost, a place inhabited by the poor in the city, that is, it is the very space of a poverty that has, over the centuries, proven itself to be structural in Brazilian society. In this form of poverty, race and ethnicity are still important, but they are not the sole marker of exclusion; probably not even the key one."

Although racial stigma may be less intense in Brazil, a casual visit to Rio de Janeiro's famed City of God and the Copacabana beaches reveals a clear relationship between space and race, and that class alone does not explain social segregation. In Recife, Salvador Fortaleza, and Belem, white exposure to non-whites is similar to the U.S. and the city of Salvador actually approximates the level of segregation in Chicago, the most extreme U.S. city (Telles 2004, 205). For Nunes and Veloso, it is the high level of poverty that has produced the favela in Latin America, and it is different in significant ways from the American ghetto. In her earlier work Veloso (2010) describes *compulsory closeness* in the Brazilian city, a process characterized by "a series of parameters of distance and proximity that are relative rather than absolute, and are produced by ambiguous strategies of separation and proximity different from those documented in other metropolises."

AbdouMaliq Simone, an urbanist who teaches at Goldsmith's College in London, has worked for a number of African NGOs, municipal governments, regional institutions, and universities in Khartoum, Ghana, Western Cape, and Johannesburg. Trained as a sociologist, his research uses case studies that uncover the informal economies and social networks—what he calls "provisional networks"—by which most of Africa's urban dwellers procure basic goods and services. In *For the City Yet to Come: Changing African Life in Four Cities* (2004) Simone examines provisional networks in Pikine, a large suburb of Dakar, Senegal; in Winterveld, a neighborhood on the edge of Pretoria, South Africa; in Douala, Cameroon; and among Africans seeking work in Jeddah, Saudi Arabia.

In *City Life from Dakar to Jakarta*, his most recent book, Simone (2010) challenges the commonplace view among governments and urban planners that Africa's metropolises are failed cities, unable to provide even basic services.

He develops the important concept of *cityness*: "Cityness refers to the city as a thing in the making. No matter how hard analysts and policy makers might try, practices of inhabiting a city are so diverse and change so quickly that they cannot easily be channeled into clearly defined uses of space and resources or patterns of social interchange. In other words, at the heart of city life is the capacity for its different people, spaces, activities, and things to interact in ways that exceed any attempt to regulate them" (2–4).

In Chapter Ten, "Demonstrations at Work: Some Notes from Urban Africa," Simone follows a "crew of guys" in Kasa-Vubu, a centrally located district in Kinshasa (Congo), on their daily efforts to forge networks and cash in on the provisional networks that make daily life possible. The group styles themselves after the Bloods (the Los Angeles street gang), with red bandanas and some level of knowledge about the gang. Simone notes that it is hard to tell when the work really begins or even what it is: "The most intense activity seems to occur in the late afternoon in the intersection of various satisfactions and apprehensions. Some are relieved to have made more than they anticipated and can look forward to treating their friends to a beer. Others have barely sold or made anything and are reluctant to return home. There are those who will hide from creditors and those who will under-count the day's receipts. And some will bundle what they have left with the surplus of others and try quickly to pass off the package deal to those who roam the markets at this hour looking for last-minute bargains." It is the motion of urban life, and the ebb and flow of everyday life, that creates and re-creates cityness. It is challenging to think what our picture of the ghetto, banlieue, favela, and other marginalized spaces might look like if we were to take forward the ideas and methodologies presented in this chapter, and by Michel Agier in the next, to study other countries.

Michel Agier, director of the Institute of Research for Development (IRD) at L'Ecole des Hautes Etudes en Sciences Sociales, Paris, has long been interested in the issues raised in our volume, beginning with his work on the banlieues, shantytowns, and favelas of the developing world published in 1994 as *L'invention de la ville: banlieues, townships, invasions et favelas*. He has studied refugee camps for nearly a decade, publishing *On the Margins of the World: The Refugee Experience Today* in 2008 and *Managing the Undesirables* in 2011. As he notes in *On the Margins of the World*, some 50 million persons are the victims of forced relocation caused by wars and violence on all continents around the world. He argues that entire countries are being created from the refugee settlements of fleeing Afghans from the war against terrorism, displaced Colombians from the drug wars and political violence, deported Congolese from the ongoing racial conflicts in that country, Iraqis fleeing the violence of the post-Sadam era, and Chechens, Somalis, and Sudanese who have borne witness to wars, massacres, and terror. In a recent article Agier (2009, 855) wrote: "There is indeed an urban form that has arisen during the history of Palestinian refugees, the result of the 'ghettoization' of the camps (in the sense of a relative spatial, socio-legal, cultural, and political enclosure), a form of ghetto that encourages the refugees to leave the camps if they wish to rise socially or else transform them by developing an informal economy, but that also encourages them to locate their identity as victims of the *Naqba* (the 1948 exodus) and their expectation of return."

In Chapter Eleven, "From Refuge the Ghetto Is Born," Agier reports on how people reconstruct their identities after being forced into exile or regrouped into refugee camps. The camps are both "the emblem of the social condition created by the coupling of war with humanitarian action, the site where it is constructed in the most elaborate manner, as a life kept at a distance from the ordinary social and political world, and the experimentation of the large-scale segregations that are being established on a planetary scale." The refugee camps are intended as temporary protection from an increasingly chaotic political world, but have become a semipermanent feature of the urban landscape. As residents build shelters and organizations set up distribution systems, and as children are born and raised and schooled in the camps, these spaces on the perimeter of the world morph into settlements and towns that Agier describes as city-camps. Deemed as undesirables within the host country, the refugees are kept apart and out of sight, and are marked by dislocation and waiting. Some would argue that they are not unlike the residents of ghettos, banileues, and favelas.

In the volume's final chapter, "Where Is the Chicago Ghetto?" Ray Hutchison returns to Chicago and draws on the long history of scholarship on the African-American community, beginning with Johnson's *The Negro in Chicago*, Frazier's *The Negro Family in Chicago*, and Drake and Cayton's *Black Metropolis,* and continuing on to Wilson, Wacquant, Pattillo, and others to describe the changing perceptions of Chicago's black ghetto. Notable in this chapter is Ernest Burgess's original sketch for the "chart" that would be published in *The Growth of the City*.

Surprisingly, the original diagram showed *two* Black Belts in the city, and included an Arts District in the area adjacent to the Black Belt. Hutchison questions Burgess's decision to include just one Black Belt and remove the Arts District from the map that would become the template for subsequent scholarship about the Chicago ghetto. By following the movement of the African-American population across the city and studying both the mappings and descriptions of neighborhood areas employed in these studies, he confronts the debate between Wilson and Pattillo over the definition of the ghetto: should the ghetto be defined by concentrated poverty, or is it better defined as contiguous neighborhoods of black settlement?

Hutchison's mapping reveals a problem with Pattillo's definition of the ghetto as contiguous neighborhoods of black settlement: African-American neighborhoods snake across the entire South Side of the city into the south suburbs and older industrial communities in northern Indiana. Eschewing the use of ghetto to circumscribe such a vast area, he draws on his earlier discussion of the Fourth World to describe the emerging urban landscape of the twenty-first century. Hutchison reprises that the ghetto is everywhere and nowhere simultaneously:

> It would seem that the ghetto is nowhere—with respect to those areas identified in the urban landscape of the iconic ghetto of the late twentieth century—and everywhere at the same time. Academic scholarship has compared favelas in Brazil and neighborhoods in the United Kingdom and shantytowns in Africa to "the American ghetto" and too often has labeled these marginalized urban spaces as ghetto-like or perhaps even real ghettos when in fact they have independent origins rooted in earlier colonial regimes and systems of economic discrimination. Popular culture has created yet another version of the American ghetto and exported the sights, sounds, and physical culture to the corners of the earth—the ghetto is everywhere even as we try to dismantle the systems of urban apartheid that created the American ghetto and subjected generations of African Americans to conditions rivaling those of urban slums in many developing nations. Dismantling the folk concept of the ghetto may prove even more difficult.

The formerly iconic Jewish ghetto of yesteryear has been replaced by the iconic black ghetto of the twentieth-first century. The ghetto and "the hood" have become synonymous with the poorest and most desperate. When the famed Robert Taylor Homes were destroyed, 60 percent of its residents were poor, but nearly 100 percent of them were black; there are deep contradictions and collateral damage created by spatial isolation along lines of race/ethnicity and class (Venkatesh 2000; Haynes 2001). And although broad segments of many historic black ghettos have reached new extremes of marginality and alienation, many housing projects have been destroyed and their populations relocated through government programs like Hope VI over the past decade (Venkatesh 2000).

We have no crystal ball that tells us what the future will hold for cities across the globe, but the scale of spatial confinement appears to parallel population growth and continued urbanization. The Venetian ghetto's population numbered in the thousands; today's urban ghettos easily reach 250,000. In the post–Great Recession era of austerity measures, continued growth of neoliberal policies, and new forms and manifestations of spatial marginality around the globe, just who will inhabit the ghetto of the twenty-first century remains an open and contested question.

The pages that follow initiate the discussion.

References

Agier, M. 1994. *L'invention de la ville: banlieues, townships, invasions et favelas*. Paris: Editions des Archives Contemporaines.

———. 2007. "From Refugee Camps to the Invention of Cities." In B. Direskens, F. Mermier, and H. Wimmen, H. (eds.), *Cities of the South*. London: Saqi Books.

———. 2008. *On the Margins of the World: The Refugee Experience Today*. New York: John Wiley.

———. 2009. "The Ghetto, the Hyperghetto, and the Fragmentation of the World." *International Journal of Urban and Regional Research* 33, 3 (September): 854–857.

———. 2011. *Managing the Undesirables: Refugee Camps and Humanitarian Government*. New York: John Wiley.

Anderson, E. 1976. *A Place on the Corner*. Chicago: University of Chicago Press

———. 1990. *Streetwise: Race, Class, and Change in an Urban Community*. Chicago: University of Chicago Press

———. 1999. *Code of the Street: Decency, Violence, and the Moral Life of the Inner City*. New York: W.W. Norton and Co.

———. 2004. "The Cosmopolitan Canopy." *Annals of the American Academy of Political and Social Science* 595, 1 (September): 14–31.

Arrizabalaga, J., J. Henderson, and R. French. 1997. *The Great Pox: The French Disease in Renaissance Europe*. New Haven: Yale University Press.

Auchard, J. ed. 1995 [1909]. *Henry James: Italian Hours*. New York: Penguin.

Baur, B. 1843. *Die Judenfrage (On the Jewish Question)*. Brunswick.

Berry, B. 1998. *You Still Ghetto*. New York: St. Martin's Press.

Berry, B., and J. Coker. 1996. *Sckraight from the Ghetto: You Know You're Ghetto If. . . .* New York: Macmillan.

Bernstein, J. A. 1998. *Music Printing in Renaissance Venice: the Scotto Press, 1539–1572*. Cambridge: Oxford University Press.

Beveridge, A. 2011. "Commonalities and Contrasts in the Development of Major United States Urban Areas: A Spatial and Temporal Analysis from 1910 to 2000." In M. P. Gutmann et al. (eds.), *Navigating Time and Space in Population Studies, International Studies in Population* 9: 185–216.

Black, J. 2003. *Italy and the Grand Tour*. Princeton: Princeton University Press.

Bond, M. R. 2008. *Jim Crow Nostalgia: Reconstructing Race in Bronzeville*. Minneapolis: University of Minnesota Press.

Bryce-Laporte, S. 1968. *The Conceptualization of the American Slave Plantation as a Total Institution*. Los Angeles: University of California

Cahan, A. 1896. *Yekl: a Tale of the New York Ghetto*. New York: Appleton.

Caldiera, T. P. R. 2000. *City of Walls: Crime, Segregation, and Citizenship in São Paulo*. Berkeley: University of California Press. (Originally published in 2000 as Cidade de muros: crime, segregação e violência em São Paulo).

Calimani, R. 1988. *The Ghetto of Venice*. Milan, Italy: Rusconi.

Castañeda, E. 2009. "Banlieue." In *Encyclopedia of Urban Studies*, Ray Hutchison (ed). Thousand Oaks, Calif.: Sage Publications.

———. 2010. Transnacionalismo, asimilación, multiculturalismo, en perspectiva comparada." In Marcela González (ed.), *7 Buenos Aires*: Prometeo Press.

Charles, M., and D. B. Grusky. 2005. *Occupational Ghettos: The Worldwide Segregation of Women and Men*. Stanford: Stanford University Press.

Clark, K. 1967. *Dark Ghetto:Dilemas of Social Power*. New York: Harper & Row.

Cressey, P. F. 1938. "Population Succession in Chicago, 1898–1930." *American Journal of Sociology*, 44, no. 1 (July): 59–69.

Daniels, C. 2007. *Ghettonation: A Journey into the Land of Bling and Home of the Shameless*. New York: Random House.

Davis, M. 2006. *Planet of Slums*. New York: Verso Press.

Davis, R. C., and R. Benjamin. 2001. *The Jews of Early Modern Venice*. Baltimore: Johns Hopkins University Press.

Davis, R. C., and G. R. Marvin. 2004. *Venice, the Tourist Maze: A Cultural Critique of the World's Most Touristed City*. Berkeley: University of California Press.

Dear, M., and S. Flusty. 1998 "Postmodern Urbanism." *Annals of the Association of American Geographers* 88(1): 50–72.

———. 1997. "The Iron Lotus: Los Angeles and Postmodern Urbanism." *Annals of the American Academy of Political and Social Science* 551(1): 151–163.

Drake, S. C., and H. Cayton. 1945. *Black Metropolis*. Chicago: University of Chicago Press.

Drieskens, B., F. Mermier, and H. Wimmen, eds. 2007. *Cities of the South: Citizenship and Exclusion in the 21st Century*. Beirut: SAQI.

Du Bois, W. E. B. 1899. *The Philadelphia Negro: A Social Study*. Philadelphia: The University of Pennsylvania Press.

Elliott, J. R., and M. Sims. 2001. "Ghettos and Barrios: The Impact of Neighborhood Poverty and Race on Job Matching Among Blacks and Latinos." *Social Problems* 48: 341–361.

England, K. V. L. 1993. *Suburban Pink Collar Ghettos: The Spatial Entrapment of Women?* London: Blackwell. England.

Frazier, E. F. 1932. *The Negro Family in Chicago.* Chicago: University of Chicago Press

Gans, H. J. 2008. "Involuntary Segregation and the Ghetto: Disconnecting Process and Place." *City & Community* 7(4): 353–357.Gilbert, A. G. 2007. "Inequality and Why it Matters." *Geography Compass* 1(3): 422–447.

Gilbert, A. 2007. "The Return of the Slum: Does Language Matter?" *International Journal of Urban and Regional Research* 31(4): 697–713.

Gilbert, A. G. 2007. "Inequality and Why It Matters." *Geography Compass* 1(3): 442–447.

———. 2009. "Extreme Thinking About Slums and Slum Dwellers: A Critique." 2009. *SAIS Review* 29(1): 35–48.

Gotham, K. 2000. "Urban Space, Restrictive Covenants, and the Origin of Racial Residential Segregation in a U.S. City, 1900–1950." *International Journal of Urban and Regional Research* 24, no. 3: 616–633.

———. 2002. *Race, Real Estate, and Uneven Development: The Kansas City Experience, 1900–2000.* Albany: State University of New York.

———. 2007. *Authentic New Orleans: Tourism, Culture, and Race in the Big Easy.* New York: New York University Press.

Gottreich, E. B. 2006. *The Mellah of Marrakesh: Jewish and Muslim Space in Morocco's Red City.* Bloomington: Indiana University Press.

Hall, J., et al. 2010. *Handbook of Cultural Sociology.* New York: Routledge.

Hapgood, H. 1902. *The Spirit of the Ghetto: Studies of the Jewish Quarter of New York.*

Harrán, D. 1989. "Tradition and Innovation in Jewish Music of the Later Renaissance." *Journal of Musicology* 7: 107–130.

———. 1998. "'Dum Recordaremur Sion': Music in the Life and Thought of the Venetian Rabbi Leon Modena (1571–1648)." AJS *Review,* 23, no. 1: 17–61. (Association for Jewish Studies)

———. 2001. "Jewish Musical Culture." In R. C. Davis and B. Ravid, *The Jews of Early Modern Venice.* Baltimore: Johns Hopkins Univeristy Press.

Haynes, B. 2001. *Red Lines, Black Spaces: The Politics of Race and Space in a Black Middle-Class Suburb.* New Haven: Yale University Press.

Haynes, B., and R. Hutchison. 2008. "The Ghetto: Origins, History, and Discourse," *City & Community.*

Haynes, G. E. 1913. "Conditions Among Negroes in the Cities." *Annals of the American Academy of Political and Social Science* 49: 105–119.

Hayden, D. 2003. *Pox: Genius, Madness, and the Mysteries of Syphilis.* New York: Basic Books.

Hirsch, A. R. 1983. *Making the Second Ghetto: Race and Housing in Chicago, 1940–1960.* Chicago: University of Chicago Press.

Hoffman, L. 2003. "Revalorizing the Inner City: Tourism and Regulation in Harlem." In *L. M. Hoffman,* S. S. Fainstein, and D. R. Judd (eds.) *Cities and Visitors: Regulating People, Markets, and City Space.* New York: Wiley-Blackwell.

———. 1999. *Tourism and the Revitalization of Harlem.* In Ray Hutchison (ed.) *Constructions of Urban Space (Research in Urban Sociology, Volume 5).* Bingley, U.K.: Emerald Group Publishing.

Hughes, D. O. 1984. "Sumptuary Law and Social Relations in Renaissance Italy." In J. Bossy (ed.), *Disputes and Settlements*. New York: Cambridge University Press.

Hutchison, R. 2009a. "Ghetto." In *The Encyclopedia of Urban Studies*. Thousand Oaks, Calif.: Sage Publications.

———. 2009b. "Racialization." In *The Encyclopedia of Urban Studies*. Thousand Oaks, Calif.: Sage Publications.

Jargowsky, P. A. 1997. *Poverty and Place: Ghettos, Barrios, and the American City*. New York: Russell Sage.

Johnson, C. S. 1943. *Patterns of Negro Segregation*. New York: Harper Brothers.

Kelley, R. D. G. 2004. "Looking for the 'Real' Nigga: Social Scientists Construct the Ghetto." In M. Forman and M. Anthony (eds.), *That's the Joint!: The Hip-Hop Studies Reader*. New York: Routledge.

Kramer, J. R., and S. Leventman. 1961. *Children of the Gilded Ghetto: Conflict Resolutions of Three Generations of American Jews*. New Haven: Yale University Press.

Krout, M. A. 1926. "A Community in Flux: The Chicago Ghetto Re-Surveyed." *Social Forces*, 5 (2): 273–282.

Kusmer, K. L. 1976. *A Ghetto Takes Shape: Black Cleveland 1870–1930*. Urbana: University of Illinois Press.

———. 1998. "Space over Time: The Changing Position of the Black Ghetto in the United States." *Journal of Housing and the Built Environment* 13(1): 7–23.

———. 1997. "The Enclave, the Citadel, and the Ghetto: What Has Changed in the Post-Fordist U.S. City." *Urban Affairs Review* 33(2): 228–264.

"London's Jewry." 1894, September 7. *American Hebrew*, p. 557.

Massey, D. S. 1990. "American Apartheid: Segregation and the Making of the Underclass." *American Journal of Sociology* 96: 329–357.

Massey, D. S., and N. Denton. 1993. *American Apartheid: Segregation and the Making of the Underclass*. Albany: SUNY Press.

Moynihan, D. P. 1965, March. "The Negro Family: The Case for National Action." Office of Policy Planning and Research, United States Department of Labor.

Nahshon, E. 2005. *From the Ghetto to the Melting Pot: Israel Zangwill's Jewish Plays*. Detroit: Wayne State University Press.

Nobles, M. 2010. "Here a Ghetto, There a Ghetto: The Value and Peril of Comparative Study." *Urban Geography* 21(2): 158–161.

Olivares, N. D. S. 1996. "Favelas and Ghettos: Race and Class in Rio de Janeiro and New York City." *Latin American Perspectives* 91(23): 71–89.

Omi, M., and H. Winant. 1986. *Racial Formation in the United States from the 1960s to the 1990s*. New York: Routledge.

O'Neil, J. 1997. *The Guilded Ghetto: The Psychology of Affluence*. Milwaukee: The Affluenza Project.

Osofsky, G. 1968. "The Enduring Ghetto." *The Journal of American History* 55(2): 243–255.

———. 1963. *Harlem: The Making of a Ghetto: Negro New York, 1890–1930*. New York: Harper & Row.

Osumare, H. 2010. "Motherland Hip-Hop: Connective Marginality and African American Youth Culture in Senegal and Kenya." In M. Diouf and I. K. Nwankwo (eds.), *Rhythms of the Afro-Atlantic World: Rituals and Remembrances*. Ann Arbor: University of Michigan Press.

Park, R. E. 1927. "Editor's Preface." In Frederic M. Thrasher, *The Gang: A Study of 1,313 Gangs in Chicago*. Chicago: University of Chicago Press.

Partridge, W. L. 1973. *The Hippie Ghetto: The Natural Evolution of a Subculture*. New York: Holt, Rinehart, and Winston.

Pattillo, M. 2003. "Extending the Boundaries and Definition of the Ghetto." *Ethnic and Racial Studies* 26: 1046–1057.

Peach, C. 1996. "Does Britain Have Ghettos?" *Transactions of the Institute of British Geographers*, 21, no. 1: 216–235.

———. 2001. "Sleepwalking into Ghettoisation? The British Debate over Segregation." In Karen Schönwälder (ed.), *Residential Segregation and the Integration of Immigrants: Britain, the Netherlands and Sweden*. Discussion Paper Nr. SP IV 2007–602. Berlin: Social Science Research Center.

———. 2007. *Black on the Block: The Politics of Race and Class in the City*. Chicago: University of Chicago Press.

Perlman, J. E. 2006. "The Metamorphosis of Marginality: Four Generations in the Favelas of Rio de Janeiro." *Annals of the American Academy of Political and Social Sciences* 606 (July): 154–177.

Poulsen, M. F., and R. J. Johnston. 2000. "The Ghetto Model and Ethnic Concentration in Australian Cities." *Urban Geography*, 21 (1): 26–44.

Rasmussen, K. R. 1968. "The Multi-Ordered Urban Area: A Ghetto." *Phylon* 29(3): 282–290.

Ravid, B. 1988. "The Establishment of the Ghetto Nuovissimo of Venice." In *Jews in Italy: Studies Dedicated to the Memory of U. Cassuto*, edited by H. Beinart. Jerusalem: Magnes Press, Hebrew University.

———. 2001 "The Venetian Government and the Jews." In R. C. Davis and B. Ravid (eds.), *The Jews of Early Modern Venice*. Baltimore: Johns Hopkins University Press.

———. 1997. "Christian Travelers in the Ghetto of Venice: Some Preliminary Observations." In *Between History and Literature, Studies in Honor of Isaac Barzilay*, edited by Stanley Nash. Tel-Aviv: Hakibbutz Hameuchad.

———. 1993. "New Light on the Ghetto of Venice." In *Shlomo Simor/sohn Jubilee Volume: Studies on the History of the Jews in the Middle Ages and Renaissance Period*, edited by D. Carpi et al. Tel Aviv: Tel Aviv University.

———. 1992. "From Geographical Reality to Historiographical Symbol: The Odyssey of the Word *Ghetto*." In *Essential Papers on Jewish Culture in Renaissance and Baroque Italy*, edited by D. B. Ruderman. New York: New York University Press.

Redford, B. 1996. *Venice and the Grand Tour*. New Haven: Yale University Press.

Roitman, S. 2010. "The Changing Image of Suburban Areas in Latin America and the Role of the Local Government." In M. Clapson and R. Hutchison, *Suburbanization in a Global World*. Bingley, UK: Emerald Group Publishing.

Rose, P. I. 1969. *The Ghetto and Beyond: Essays on Jewish Life in America*. New York: Random House.

Ruderman, D. B. 1992. *Preachers of the Italian Ghetto*. Berkeley: University of California Press.

Sennet, R. 1994. "The Fear of Touching: The Jewish Ghetto in Renaissance Europe." In *Flesh and Stone: The Body and the City in Western Civilization*. New York: W. W. Norton.

Simone, A. M. 2004. *For the City Yet to Come: Changing African Life in Four Cities*. Durham, N.C.: Duke University Press.

———. 2010. *City Life from Jakarta to Dakar: Movements at the Crossroads*. New York: Routledge.

Slater, T. 2010. "Ghetto Blasting: On Loïc Wacquant's Urban Outcasts." *Urban Geography* 31(2): 162–168.

Small, M. L. 2008. "Four Reasons to Abandon the Idea of 'The Ghetto.'" *City & Community* 7(4): 389–398.

Spear, A. H. 1967. *Black Chicago: The Making of a Negro Ghetto, 1890–1920*. Chicago: University of Chicago Press.

Telles, E. 2004. *Race in Another America: The Significance of Skin Color in Brazil*. Princeton, N.J.: Princeton University Press.

Thomas, W. I. 1921. *Old World Traits Transplanted*. New York: Henry Holt. (Originally published with authorship credited to R. E. Park and H. Miller.)

Veloso, L. 2010. "Governing Heterogeneity in the Context of 'Compulsory Closeness': The 'Pacification' of Favelas." In M. Clapson and R. Hutchison (eds.), *Suburbanization in Global Society (Research in Urban Sociology, Vol. 10)*. Bingley, United Kingdom: Emerald Group Publishing Ltd.

Venkatesh, S. 2000. *American Project: The Rise and Fall of a Modern Ghetto*. Cambridge, Mass.: Harvard University Press.

Wacquant, L. 1996. "The Rise of Advanced Marginality: Notes on Its Nature and Implementation." *Acta Sociologogica* 39: 121–139.

———. 2002. *Urban Outcasts: A Comparative Sociology of Advanced Marginality*. Cambridge: Polity Press.

———. 2007. *Urban Outcasts*. Cambridge, MA: Harvard University Press.

Warfield, D., and Hamm. 1901. *Ghetto Silhouettes*. New York: James Pott & Company.

Wayans, S., C. Spencer, and S. McCullough. 1997. *150 Ways to Tell If You Are Ghetto*. New York: Dell.

Weaver, R. C. 1948. *The Negro Ghetto*. New York: Harcourt and Brace.

———. 1959. *The Negro Ghetto* (2nd ed.). New York: Russell & Russell.

Wilson, W. J. 1987. *The Truly Disadvantaged*. Chicago: University of Chicago Press.

———. 2003. *When Work Disappears*. New York: Random House.

Winant, H. 2002. *The World Is a Ghetto: Race and Democracy Since World War Two*. New York: Basic Books.

Wirth, L. 1928. *The Ghetto*. Chicago: University of Chicago Press.

Zangwill, I. 1892. *Children of the Ghetto*. Philadelphia: Jewish Publication Society.

———. 1893. *Ghetto Tragedies*. London: McClure & Co.

———. 1898. *Dreamers of the Ghetto*. New York: Harper & Brothers.

———. 1907. *Ghetto Comedies*. New York: The Macmillan Company.

Zeublin, C. 1895. "The Chicago Ghetto." *In Hull-House Maps and Papers: A Presentation of Nationalities and Wages in a Congested District of Chicago, Together with Comments and Essays on Problems Growing Out of the Social Condition*. New York: Thomas Y. Crowell.

Zukin, S. 2009. *Naked City: The Death and Life of Authentic Urban Places*. New York: Oxford University Press.

———. 2011. "Reconstructing the Authenticity of Place." *Theory and Society* 40(2): 161–165.

✦ ✦ ✦

CHAPTER 1

A Janus-Faced Institution of Ethnoracial Closure: A Sociological Specification of the Ghetto

Loïc Wacquant

*The scientific mind must form itself
by continually reforming itself.*

—Gaston Bachelard, *Psychanalyse de l'esprit scientifique* (1938)

It is a paradox that, while the social sciences have made extensive use of "ghetto" as a *descriptive term*, they have failed to forge a robust *analytical concept* of the same. In the historiography of the Jewish diaspora in early modern Europe and under Nazism, the sociology of the black American experience in the twentieth-century metropolis, and the anthropology of ethnic outcasts in East Asia and Africa—its three traditional domains of application—the term *ghetto* variously denotes a bounded urban ward, a web of group-specific institutions, and a cultural and cognitive constellation (values, mind-set, or mentality) entailing the socio-moral isolation of a stigmatized category as well as the systematic truncation of the life space and life chances of its members. But none of these strands of research has taken the trouble to specify what makes a ghetto *qua* social form, which of its features are constitutive and which are derivative, as they have, at each epoch, taken for granted and adopted the *folk concept* extant in the society under examination.

This explains that the notion, appearing self-evident, does not figure in most dictionaries of social science.[1] It is also why, after decades of employing the word, sociologists remain vague, inconsistent, and conflicted about its core meaning, perimeter of empirical pertinence, and theoretical import. The recent "Symposium on the Ghetto" organized by *City & Community* in the wake of Mario Small's critique of the central theses of my book *Urban Outcasts* richly documents the myriad observational anomalies and analytic troubles spawned by the unreflective derivation of social-scientific from ordinary constructs (Haynes and Hutchison 2008). These troubles are not resolved but redoubled when the composite U.S. imagery of the (black) ghetto (after its collapse) gets transported to western Europe and Latin America, and they are trebled when scholars attempt cross-national comparisons of patterns of urban marginality and/or ethnoracial inequality based on the national common sense of their home societies as to the meaning of "the ghetto."[2] This debate vividly demonstrates that the ghetto is not a *contested concept* à la Gallie (1956) so much as a *confused conception* that comes short of the level of analytic specificity, coherence, and parsimony minimally required of a scientific notion.

This chapter clears up this confusion by constructing a rigorous sociological concept of the ghetto as a spatially based implement of ethnoracial closure. After spotlighting the semantic instability and slippage of the notion in American culture and scholarship, I extract the structural and functional similarities presented by three canonical instances of the phenomenon: the Jewish ghetto of Renaissance Europe, the black American ghetto of the Fordist United States, and the reserved districts of the Burakumin in post-Tokugawa Japan. Against thin *gradational* conceptions based on rates (of ethnic dissimilarity, spatial concentration, poverty, and so on), which prove promiscuous and prone to metaphorical bleeding, as well as inchoate, I elaborate a thick *relational* conception of the ghetto as a socio-spatial institution geared to the twin mission of isolating and exploiting a dishonored category. So much to say that the ghetto results not from ecological dynamics but from the inscription in space of a material and symbolic *power asymmetry*, as revealed by the recurrent role of collective violence in establishing as well as challenging ethnoracial confinement. Next, I unscramble the connections between ghettoization, segregation, and poverty and articulate an ideal-typical opposition between ghetto and ethnic cluster with which to carry out measured comparisons of the fates of various stigmatized populations and places in different cities, societies, and epochs. This points to the role of the ghetto as organizational shield and cultural crucible for the production of a unified but tainted identity that furthers resistance and eventually revolt against seclusion. I conclude by proposing that the ghetto is best analogized not with districts of dereliction (which confuses ethnoracial seclusion with extraneous issues of class, deprivation, and deviance) but with other devices for the forcible containment of tainted categories, such as the prison, the reservation, and the camp.

A FUZZY AND EVOLVING NOTION

A brief recapitulation of the strange career of "the ghetto" in American society and social science, which has dominated inquiry into the topic both quantitatively and thematically, suffices to illustrate its semantic instability and dependency on the whims and worries of urban rulers. For the past century, the range and contents of the term have successively expanded and contracted in keeping with how political and intellectual elites have viewed the vexed nexus of ethnicity and poverty in the city (Ward 1989).

At first, in the closing decades of the nineteenth century, the "ghetto" designated residential concentrations of European Jews in the Atlantic seaports and was clearly distinguished from the "slum" as an area of housing blight and social pathology (Lubove 1963). The notion dilated during the Progressive era to encompass all inner-city districts wherein exotic newcomers gathered— namely, lower-class immigrants from the southeastern regions of Europe and African Americans fleeing the Jim Crow regime of racial terrorism in the U.S. South. Expressing upper-class worries over whether these groups could or should assimilate into the predominant Anglo-Saxon pattern of the country, the notion referred then to the intersection between the ethnic neighborhood and the slum, where segregation was believed to combine with physical disrepair and overcrowding to exacerbate urban ills such as criminality, family breakdown, and pauperism and thwart participation in national life. This conception was given scientific authority by the ecological paradigm of the emerging Chicago School of Urban Sociology. In his classic book *The Ghetto*, Louis Wirth (1928, 6) assimilates to the Jewish ghetto of medieval Europe the "Little Sicilies, Little Polands, Chinatowns, and Black Belts in our large cities," along with the "vice areas" hosting deviant types such as hobos, bohemians, and prostitutes. All of them are said to be "natural areas" born of the universal desire of different groups to "preserve their peculiar cultural forms," and each fulfills a specialized "function" in the broader urban organism.[3] This is what one may call *Wirth's error*: confounding the mechanisms of socio-spatial seclusion visited upon African Americans and upon European immigrants by conflating two urban forms with antinomic architectures and effects, the ghetto and the ethnic cluster. This initial error enabled the ecological paradigm to thrive even as the urbanization of African Americans blatantly contradicted its core propositions (Wacquant 1998). It would be repeated cyclically for decades and persistently obfuscate the specificity of ghettoization as an exclusive type of enclosure.

The notion contracted rapidly after World War II under the press of the civil rights movement to signify mainly the compact and congested enclaves to which African Americans were forcibly relegated as they migrated into the industrial centers of the North. The growth of a "Black Metropolis in the womb of the white" wherein Negroes evolved distinct and parallel institutions to compensate for and shield themselves from unflinching exclusion by whites (Drake and Cayton 1945/1993) contrasted sharply with the smooth residential dispersal of European Americans of foreign stock. And the mounting political mobilization of blacks against continued caste subordination made their reserved territory a central site and stake of sociopolitical struggles in the city as well as a springboard for collective action against white rule. Writing at the acme of the black uprisings of the 1960s, Kenneth Clark (1965, 11) made this relationship of ethnoracial subordination epicentral to his dissection of the *Dark Ghetto* and its woes: "America has contributed to the concept of the ghetto the restriction of persons to a special area and the limiting of their freedom of choice on the basis of skin color. The dark ghetto's invisible walls have been erected by the white society, by those who have power." This diagnosis was confirmed by the Kerner Commission (1968/1989, 2), a bipartisan task force appointed by President Johnson whose official report on the "civil disorders" that rocked the American metropolis famously warned that, because of white racial intransigence, America was "moving toward two societies, one black, one white—separate and unequal."[4]

But over the ensuing two decades, the dark ghetto collapsed and devolved into a barren territory of dread and dissolution, due to deindustrialization and state policies of welfare reduction and urban retrenchment. As racial domination grew more diffuse and diffracted through a class prism, the category was displaced by the duet formed by the geographic euphemism of "inner city" and the neologism of "underclass," defined as the substratum of ghetto residents plagued by acute joblessness, social isolation, and antisocial behaviors (Wilson 1987). By the 1990s, the neutralization of the "ghetto" in policy-oriented research culminated in the outright expurgation of any mention of race and power to redefine it as any tract of extreme poverty ("containing over 40% of residents living under the federal poverty line"), irrespective of population and institutional makeup, in effect dissolving the ghetto back into the slum and rehabilitating the folk conception of the early twentieth century (Jargowsky 1997).[5] This paradoxical "deracialization" of a notion initially fashioned, and until then deployed, to capture ethnoracial partition in the city resulted from the combination of the crumbling of the historic dark ghetto of the industrial era and the correlative political censorship of race in policy-oriented research after the ebbing of the civil rights movement. This "gutting of the ghetto" (Wacquant 2002) was then taken one step further by the rash proposal to abandon the notion altogether, instead of clarifying it, on grounds that it cannot capture the complexity, heterogeneity, and fluidity of "poor black neighborhoods" in the United States (Small 2009)—as if ghettoization were a flat and static synonym for impoverishment, occurred only in the United States, and could not encompass, or partake of, a fluid and differentiated urban formation.

Meanwhile, the term was extended to the study of the distinctive sociocultural patterns elaborated by homosexuals in the cities of advanced societies "in response to both stigma and gay liberation" after the Stonewall riots (Levine 1979, 31). It has also made a spectacular return across western Europe in heated scholarly and policy debates over the links between postcolonial immigration, postindustrial economic restructuring, and spatial dualization as the fear of the "Americanization" of the metropolis swept the continent (Musterd, Murie, and Kesteloot 2006; Schierup, Hansen, and Castles 2006). That European social scientists took to invoking "the ghetto" to stress the growing potency and specificity of ethnoracial division in their countries just when their American colleagues were busy extirpating race from the same notion is an irony that seems only to further muddle its meaning. Yet one can extract out of these varied literatures common threads and recurrent properties to *construct* a *relational concept* of the ghetto as an *instrument of closure and control* that clears up most of the confusion surrounding it and turns it into a powerful tool for the social analysis of ethnoracial domination and urban inequality. For this it suffices to return to the historical inception of the word and of the phenomenon it depicted in Renaissance Venice.

A JANUS-FACED INSTITUTION OF
ETHNIC CLOSURE AND CONTROL

Coined by derivation from the Italian *giudecca, borghetto*, or *gietto* (or from the German *gitter* or the Talmudic Hebrew *get*—the etymology is disputed), the word *ghetto* initially referred to the forced consignment of Jews to special districts by the city's political and religious authorities. In medieval Europe, Jews were commonly allotted quarters wherein they resided, administered their own affairs, and followed their customs. Such quarters were granted or sold as a privilege to attract them into the towns and principalities for which they fulfilled key roles as money-lenders, tax collectors, and long-distance tradesmen. But between the thirteenth and sixteenth centuries, in the wake of the upheavals caused by the Crusades, favor gradually turned into compulsion (Stow 1992). In 1516 the Senate of Venice ordered all Jews rounded up into the *Ghetto Nuovo*, an abandoned foundry on an isolated island enclosed by two high walls whose outer windows and doors were sealed while watchmen stood guard on its two bridges and patrolled the adjacent canals by boat (Curiel and Cooperman 1990). Jews were henceforth allowed to come out to pursue their occupations by day, but they had to wear a distinctive garb that made them readily recognizable and return inside the gates before sunset on pain of severe punishment. These measures were designed as an alternative to expulsion to enable the city-state to reap the economic benefits brought by the presence of Jews (including rents, special taxes, and forced levies) while protecting its Christian residents from contaminating contact with bodies perceived as unclean and dangerously sensual, as carriers of syphilis and vectors of heresy, in addition to bearing the taint of moneymaking through usury, which the Catholic Church equated with prostitution (Sennett 1994, 224).

As this Venetian model spread in cities throughout Europe and around the Mediterranean rim (Johnson 1987, 235–245),[6] territorial fixation and seclusion led, on the one hand, to overcrowding, housing deterioration, and impoverishment as well as excess morbidity and mortality and, on the other, to institutional flowering and cultural consolidation as urban Jews responded to multiplying civic and occupational restrictions by knitting a dense web of group-specific organizations that served as so many instruments of collective succor and solidarity, from markets and business associations to charity and mutual aid societies, to places of religious worship and scholarship. The *Judenstadt* of Prague, Europe's largest ghetto in the eighteenth century, even had its own city hall, the *Rathaus*, emblem of the relative autonomy and communal strength of its residents, and its synagogues were entrusted with not only the spiritual stewardship but also the administrative and judicial oversight of its population. Social life in the Jewish ghetto was turned inward and verged "on overorganization" (Wirth 1928), so that it reinforced both integration within and isolation from without.

One can detect in this inaugural moment the four constituent elements of the ghetto, namely, (i) *stigma*, (ii) *constraint*, (iii) *spatial confinement*, and (iv) *institutional parallelism*. The ghetto is a social-organizational device that employs space to reconcile two antinomic functions: (1) to maximize the material profits extracted out of a category deemed defiled and defiling, and (2) to minimize intimate contact with its members so as to avert the threat of symbolic corrosion and contagion they are believed to carry. If the target population did not serve an essential economic function, it could be kept out of the city or expelled from it—as Jews had been periodically in medieval history. If that same group were not irremediably tainted, it would simply be exploited and allowed to mingle in the city in accordance with its position in the division of labor. It is the conflictive combination of economic value and symbolic danger that made handling Jews problematic and spurred the invention of the ghetto.

These same four building blocks and the same dual rationale of *economic extraction cum social ostracization* governed the genesis, structure, and functioning of the African American ghetto in the Fordist metropolis during the half-century after World War I. Blacks were actively recruited into northern cities of the United States at the outbreak of World War I because their unskilled labor was indispensable to the industries that formed the backbone of a factory economy fed by booming military production but starved of hands by the interruption of European migration (Marks 1989). Yet there was no question of them mixing and consorting with whites, who regarded them as inherently vile, congenitally inferior, and shorn of ethnic honor owing to the stain of slavery.[7] As blacks moved in from the South in the millions, white hostility increased and patterns of discrimination and segregation that had hitherto been informal and inconsistent hardened in housing, schooling, and public accommodations and were extended to the economy and polity (Spear 1968; Osofsky 1971). African Americans were forcibly funneled into reserved districts that quickly turned homogeneously black as they expanded and consolidated. They had no choice but to seek refuge inside the bounded perimeter of the Black Belt and to endeavor to develop in it a network of separate institutions to procure the basic needs of the castaway community. Thus arose a duplicate city anchored by black churches and newspapers, black block clubs and lodges, black schools and businesses, and black political and civic associations, nested at the core of the white metropolis yet sealed from it by an impassable fence built of custom, legal suasion, economic discrimination (by realtors, banks, and the state), and violence, as manifested in the beatings, firebombings, and riots that checked those who dared to stray across the color line.

This forced institutional parallelism predicated on enveloping and inflexible spatial seclusion—not extreme poverty, housing blight, cultural difference, or mere residential separation—is what has distinguished African Americans from every other group in U.S. history, as noted by leading students of the black urban experience, from W. E. B. Du Bois and E. Franklin Frazier to Drake and Cayton, to Kenneth Clark and Oliver Cox (Wacquant 1998). It also characterizes the trajectory of the Burakumin in the Japanese city after the close of the Tokugawa era (Hane 1982). As the lineal descendants of the *eta* and *hinin*, two categories locked out of the fourfold estate order of feudal Japan (composed of warriors, peasants, artisans, and merchants), the Burakumin were untouchables in the eyes of the Buddhist and Shinto religions.[8] As a result, they suffered centuries of virulent prejudice, discrimination, segregation, and violence that kept them cloistered in social and physical space. By the nineteenth century, they were legally confined from sundown to sunup in out-of-the-way hamlets (*buraku*) that were omitted from official maps, they were obliged to wear a yellow collar and walk barefoot, they were expected to drop on their hands and knees when addressing commoners, and they could be killed virtually without sanction. Crucially, the Burakumin were barred from entering shrines and temples, and they were restricted to wedding solely among themselves, based on the belief that the filth of their ancestors was indelible and communicated by blood. Although they are phenotypically indistinguishable from other Japanese, they can be identified through the marriage registries established and diffused during the Meiji era (1868–1912), as well as by their patronym and place of provenance or residence.

The Burakumin were officially emancipated in 1871, but as they moved into cities they were funneled against their will into notorious neighborhoods near garbage dumps, crematoria, jails, and slaughterhouses that were widely viewed as nests of criminality and immorality. There they were barred from industrial employment and locked in low-paying and dirty jobs, sent to separate schools, and compelled to remain largely endogamous (DeVos and Wagatsuma 1966), effectively leading constricted lives encased by a network of parallel and inferior institutions. By the late 1970s, according to the Burakumin Defense League, they were estimated to number three million, trapped in six thousand buraku districts in some one thousand cities across the main island, with strong concentrations in the Kyoto region. After a full decade of vigorous programs of affirmative action launched in 1969, one-fifth of the Burakumin were still employed as butchers, shoemakers, and in the leather trades, and over one-half worked as street sweepers, trash collectors, and public works employees. As a result, their rates of poverty, welfare receipt, and mortality stood far above the national average (Sabouret 1983).

Spread over three continents and five centuries, the Jewish, African American, and Burakumin cases demonstrate that the ghetto is not, *pace* Wirth (1928, 284–285), a "natural area" arising via environmental adaptation governed by a biotic logic "akin to the competitive cooperation that underlies the plant community." The mistake of the early Chicago School here consisted in falsely "converting history into natural history" and passing ghettoization off as "a manifestation of human nature" virtually coterminous with "the history of migration" (Wirth 1928, 285), when it is a highly peculiar form of urbanization warped by asymmetric relations of power between ethnoracial groupings (based on descent): a special form of *collective violence concretized in urban space*. That ghettoization is *not* an "uncontrolled and undesigned" process, as Robert E. Park asserted in his preface to *The Ghetto* (Wirth 1928, viii), became especially visible after World War II in the United States when the black American ghetto was reconstructed from the top down, and its shelf life extended by another quarter-century, through state policies of public housing, urban renewal, and suburban economic development intended to bolster the rigid spatial and social separation of blacks from whites (Hirsch 1983/1998). It is even more glaring in the instance of the "caste cities" built by colonial powers to inscribe in space the hierarchical ethnic organization of their overseas possessions, such as Rabat under French rule over Morocco and Cape Town after the passage of the Group Areas Acts under the apartheid regime of South Africa (Abu-Lughod 1980; Western 1981).[9]

Recognizing that it is a product and instrument of group power makes it possible to appreciate that, in its full-fledged form, the ghetto is a *Janus-faced institution*: It plays opposite roles for the two collectives it binds in a relation of asymmetric dependency. For the dominant category, its rationale is to *confine and control*, which translates into what Max Weber (1920/1978) calls the "exclusionary closure" of the subordinate category. For the latter, however, it is a *protective and integrative device* insofar as it relieves its members from constant contact with the dominant and fosters consociation and community-building within the constricted sphere of intercourse it creates. Enforced isolation from the outside leads to the intensification of social exchange and cultural sharing inside. Ghettos are the product of a mobile and tensionful dialectic of external hostility and internal affinity that expresses itself as ambivalence at the level of collective consciousness. Thus, although European Jews consistently protested relegation within their outcast districts, they were nonetheless deeply attached to them and appreciative of the relative security they afforded and the special forms of collective life they supported: Frankfurt's ghetto in the eighteenth century was "not just the scene of confinement and persecution but a place where Jews were entirely, supremely, at home" (Gay 1992, 67). Similarly, black Americans took pride in having "erected a community in their own image" even as they resented the fact that they had done so under duress as a result of unyielding white exclusion aimed at warding off the specter of "social equality," that is, sexual mixing (Drake and Cayton 1945/1993, 115).

Acknowledging the double-sidedness of the ghetto spotlights its role as organizational matrix and symbolic incubator for the production of a "spoiled identity" in Erving Goffman's (1963) sense of the term. For the ghetto is not only the concrete means and materialization of ethnoracial domination

"I Love Harlem Because It Belongs to Me"

The sentiment of being "home" inside the ghetto, in a protected and protecting space, is expressed with verve in the narration of the daily foibles of Jesse B. Semple, or Simple, the character created by the poet Langston Hughes (1957, 20–21) to give voice to the aspirations of urban black Americans at the midcentury point. Thus, he exclaims about Harlem:

> "It's so full of Negroes, I feel like I got protection."—"From what?"—"From white folks," said Simple. "I like Harlem because it belongs to me. . . . You say the houses ain't mine. Well, the sidewalk is—and don't you push me off. The cops don't even say, "Move on," hardly no more. They learned something from them Harlem riots. . . . Here I ain't scared to vote—that's another thing I like about Harlem. . . .[1] Folks is friendly in Harlem. I feel like I got the world in a jug and the stopper in my hand! So drink a toast to Harlem!"

Note

1. In 1935 and 1943, the residents of Harlem rose up against racial exclusion made unbearable by the economic collapse of the Great Crisis (cf. Greenberg 1991).

through the spatial segmentation of the city; it is also a site of intense cultural production and a potent *collective identity machine* in its own right. It helps to incrustate and elaborate the very division of which it is the expression in two complementary and mutually reinforcing ways. First, the ghetto sharpens the boundary between the outcast category and the surrounding population by deepening the sociocultural chasm between them: It renders its residents objectively and subjectively more dissimilar from other urban dwellers by submitting them to unique conditionings, so that the patterns of cognition and conduct they fashion have every chance of being perceived by outsiders as singular, exotic, even "aberrant" (Sennett 1994, 244; Wilson 1987, 7–8), which feeds prejudicial beliefs about them.

Next, the ghetto is a cultural combustion engine that melts divisions among the confined population and fuels its collective pride even as it entrenches the stigma that hovers over it. Spatial and institutional entrapment deflects class differences and corrodes cultural distinctions within the relegated ethnoracial category. Thus, Christian ostracism welded Ashkenazic and Sephardic Jews under an overarching Jewish identity such that they evolved a common "social type" and "state of mind" across the ghettos of Europe (Wirth 1928, 71–88; 1956/1964). Similarly, America's dark ghetto accelerated the sociosymbolic amalgamation of mulattoes and Negroes into a single unified "race" and turned racial consciousness into a mass phenomenon fueling community mobilization against continued caste exclusion (Drake and Cayton 1945/1993, 390).

Yet this unified identity cannot but be stamped with ambivalence, as it remains tainted by the very fact that ghettoization proclaims what Weber (1918/1978) called the "negative evaluation of honor" assigned to the group confined. It is therefore wont to foster among its members sentiments of self-doubt and self-hatred, dissimulation of one's origin through "passing," the pernicious derogation of one's kind, and even fantastical identification with the dominant (Clark 1965, 63–67).[10] The ghetto is home, but it remains an inferior home, built under duress, that exists at the order and sufferance of the dominant. Its residents know that, as it were, in their bones.

DISENTANGLING POVERTY, SEGREGATION, AND ETHNIC CLUSTERING

Articulating the concept of ghetto as socio-spatial mechanism of ethnoracial closure makes it possible to disentangle the relationship between ghettoization, urban poverty, and segregation and thence to clarify the structural and functional differences between ghettos and ethnic neighborhoods. I tackle each of these questions in turn.

1. Poverty is a derivative and variable characteristic of ghettos.

The fact that many ghettos have historically been places of endemic and often acute misery owing to the paucity of space, the density of settlement, and the economic restrictions and statutory maltreatment of their residents does not imply that a ghetto is necessarily a place of destitution, nor that it is uniformly deprived. Indeed, the very opposite is true: Ghettos have more often than not been vectors of economic amelioration, even as they imposed multifarious restrictions on their residents. The *Judengasse* of Frankfurt, instituted in 1490 and abolished in 1811, went through periods of prosperity no less than penury, and it contained sectors of extraordinary opulence as court Jews helped the city become a vibrant center of trade and finance; part of its glamour to this day comes from it being the ancestral home of the Rothschild dynasty (Wirth 1928, ch. 4). Being forced to dwell within the walled compound of the *mellah* did not prevent the Jews of Marrakech from thriving economically: Many of its business leaders were renowned throughout Morocco for their wealth (Gottreich 2006, 102–105). Turning to the United States, James Weldon Johnson (1930/1981, 4) insisted that the Harlem of the 1930s was "not a slum or a fringe" but the "cultural capital" of black America, a place where "the Negro's advantages and opportunities are greater than in any other place in the country." Similarly, Chicago's "Bronzeville" at the mid-twentieth-century point not only was far more prosperous than the southern black communities from which its residents had migrated but harbored the largest and most affluent African American bourgeoisie of its era (Drake and Cayton 1945/1993).

The ghetto arises through the *double assignation of category to territory and territory to category* and therefore purports to contain the gamut of classes evolved by the confined group. It follows that, to the degree that this group experiences socioeconomic dispersion, its reserved district offers extensive avenues for economic betterment and upward mobility in its internal social order. Indeed, in the case of African Americans, ghettoization, class differentiation, and collective enrichment proceeded apace: In addition to allowing the conversion of peasants into industrial workers, the rise and consolidation of the ghetto fostered the growth of a black middle class of business owners, professionals, politicians, teachers, and preachers servicing a captive clientele of lower-class coethnics that the dispersed rural communities of the South could have never sustained.[11] Whether a ghetto is poor or not, and to what degree, depends on the overall economic standing of the category it cloisters, its distribution in the division of labor, and on extraneous factors such as demography, ecology, state policies, and the shape of the surrounding economy.

Conversely, not all dispossessed and dilapidated urban districts are ghettos—and if they are such, it is not by dint of their level of deprivation. Declining white neighborhoods in the deindustrializing cities of the U.S. Midwest and the British Midlands, depressed rural towns of the former East Germany and southern Italy, and the disreputable *villas miserias* of greater Buenos Aires at the close of the twentieth century are territories of working-class demotion and decomposition, not ethnic containers dedicated to maintaining an outcast group in a relationship of seclusive subordination (see the case of Buenos Aires dissected by Auyero 2000). They are not ghettos other than in a purely metaphorical sense, no matter how impoverished and how isolated their residents may be. If extreme rates of concentrated poverty breeding social isolation sufficed to make a ghetto, as argued by William Julius Wilson (1996), then the backcountry of Alabama, Native American reservations, large chunks of the former Soviet Union, and most Third World cities would be gargantuan ghettos. More curiously still, by that definition neither Venice's *Ghetto Nuovo* nor Chicago's Bronzeville at the peak of their historical development would be ghettos![12]

The *favelas* of the Brazilian metropolis are often portrayed as segregated dens of dereliction and disorganization, overrun by drugs and violence, but upon close observation they turn out to be variegated working-class wards with finely stratified webs of ties to industry and to the wealthy districts for which they supply household service labor. They display considerable variety in levels of segregation and situations of collective "socioeconomic vulnerability" (Marques and Torres 2005; see also Kowarick 2009). As in the *ranchos* of Venezuela and the *poblaciones* of Chile, families that dwell in these squatter settlements span the color continuum and have extensive genealogical bonds to higher-income households; they are "not socially and culturally marginal, but stigmatized and excluded from a closed class system" (Perlman 1976, 195; see also Zaluar and Alvito 1998). In any case, neither their poverty rate nor the mix of functions they fulfill in the metropolis, from viable reservoir of labor power to warehouse for the rejects of "regressive deindustrialization," would qualify them as ghettos. The same demonstration applies to the *ciudad perdida* in Mexico, the *cantagril* in Uruguay, and the *pueblo jóven* in Peru (Wacquant 2008a, 7–12; 2008b).[13]

Given that not all ghettos are poor and not all poor areas are (inside) ghettos, one cannot collapse the analysis of ghettoization into the study of slums, impoverished estates, and assorted districts of dispossession in the city. This conflation is precisely the mistake committed by those European observers who, smitten with a vague and emotive vision of the black American ghetto as a territory of urban dissolution and social dread—that is, with the barren *vestiges* of the dark ghetto *after its implosion* at the close of the 1960s—conclude that "ghettoization" has struck the lower-class zones of the urban periphery of Europe as a result of rising unemployment, immigrant segregation, and festering delinquency, or, worse, because they adopt the fleeting impressions of their residents who think of themselves as "ghetto" since this is how depressed and defamed neighborhoods are now publicly labeled in public debate.

2. All ghettos are segregated, but not all segregated areas are ghettos.

The select boroughs of the West of Paris, the exclusive upper-class suburbs of Boston, Berne, or Berlin, and the "gated communities" that have mushroomed in global cities such as Milan, Miami, São Paulo, and Cape Town are monotonous in terms of wealth, income, occupation, and, very often, ethnicity, but they are not for all that ghettos. Segregation in them is entirely voluntary and elective, and for that very reason it is neither all-inclusive nor perpetual. Fortified enclaves of luxury package "security, seclusion, social homogeneity, amenities, and services" to enable bourgeois families to escape what they perceive as "the chaos, dirt, and danger of the city" (Caldeira 2000, 264–265). These islands of privilege serve to enhance, not curtail, the life chances and protect the lifestyles of their residents, and they radiate a positive aura of distinction (Low 2004), not a sense of infamy and dread. In terms of their causal dynamics, structure, and function, they are the very antithesis of the ghetto. To call them such, as with variations on the expression "gilded ghetto," invites confusion and stretches the semantics of the term to the point of meaninglessness.[14]

This indicates that residential segregation is a necessary but not a sufficient condition for ghettoization. For a ghetto to emerge, spatial confinement must first be *imposed and all-encompassing*; then it must be overlaid with a distinct and *duplicative set of institutions* enabling the population thus cloistered to reproduce itself within its assigned perimeter. If blacks are the only ethnic category to be "hypersegregated" in American society (Massey and Denton 1993), it is because they are the only community in that country for which involuntary segregation, assignment to a reserved territory, and organizational parallelism have combined to entrap them in a separate and inferior social cosmos of their own, which in turn bolstered their residential isolation, as well as enforced their extreme marital isolation, virtually unique in the world among major ethnic groups (Patterson 1998).

That even forcible segregation at the bottom of the urban order does not mechanically produce ghettos is demonstrated by the fate of the declining lower-class *banlieues* of France after the mid-1970s. Although they have been

---

"The Ghetto" Comes to France: How "Everyday Usage" Drowns Out Sociology

Didier Lapeyronnie's (2007) thick book on the alleged coalescence of the "urban ghetto" in France announces a study of "segregation, violence and poverty" in that country but contains not a shred of data and no analysis on these trends and their overlap. Instead, it uses the word *ghetto* as a loose synonym for declining lower-class estates branded as such by journalists and by some of their residents (who themselves have learned the label from the media). The notion then inexplicably devolves into a subjective concept pertaining to lifestyle, self-conception, and "the shared feeling of having been betrayed" by dominant institutions:

> The term ghetto belongs to the everyday vocabulary of the banlieue [lower-class periphery]. It is used to designate a difficult social or personal situation, even a psychological situation stamped by disorder, poverty, and sometimes violence. It is not necessarily associated with urban segregation and confinement in a territorial sense. . . . Many residents can be of the ghetto without living in the ghetto. They can live it partially, as a function of moments and interactions. . . . By following this everyday usage, we understand the ghetto to be a dimension of individual and collective behaviors. . . . The ghetto is not a situation, it is a category of action in an array of social relations. . . . We shall seek to evaluate and to define the ghetto as a function of its effects on the self-construction effected by its residents, as a function of the capacity of individuals to name themselves and to assert an "I," to establish or not a positive relationship to self. . . . We shall seek the truth, or rather the truths, of the ghetto,

[continues]

widely described and disparaged as "ghettos" in public discourse, and their inhabitants share a vivid feeling of being cast out in a "penalized space" suffused with boredom, anguish, and despair (Pétonnet 1982), relegation in these depressed concentrations of public housing laid fallow at the urban periphery is based first on class and only secondarily on ethnicity, and it is remarkably impermanent. Proof is that the residents who move up the class structure typically move out of the neighborhood—so much so that the rate

[continued]

in the words and in the reflections of its residents. [Lapeyronnie 2007, 22–23, 24, 26]

Characterizing the ghetto as a matter of subjective orientation, "a psychological situation stamped by disorder, poverty, and sometimes violence," is both incoherent and inconsistent with the established conceptual usage of the term. By that definition, neither the Jewish ghetto of Venice nor the black ghetto of Chicago in their full bloom would be ghettos; any population invoking the idiom of the ghetto is *eo ipso* ghettoized; and consequently the simple remedy to ghettoization is for the residents of lower-class districts to change their representations of themselves. Not to mention that French citizens residing outside the country's "sensitive neighborhoods" who feel "betrayed" by leading institutions would be surprised to discover that, unbeknownst to them, they "live the ghetto."

Echoing Lapeyronnie (on whose views he relies), *Le Monde* journalist Luc Bronner in his sensationalist book titled *The Law of the Ghetto* (2007) provides a selective account of street delinquency and a long litany of clashes between unemployed youths and the police in a few banlieues brashly labeled *ghettos* because of the shock value of the term to describe territories of "social, political, and economic violence": "We must dare this term which so frightens the Republic" to describe "our Gomorra" (Bronner 2007, 249, 23). When the so-called law of the ghetto denotes the imprint of low-grade criminality, the flourishing of an informal economy, and assorted urban disorders, we know we have reached the point where the word has been emptied of any sociological meaning to serve as an ordinary *categoreme*, a term of accusation and alarm, pertaining not to social science but public polemic, that serves only to sell books and to fuel the spiral of stigmatization enmeshing the impoverished districts of the urban periphery.

of geographic mobility among the households of "sensitive neighborhoods" surpasses the national average (Observatoire des Zones Urbaines Sensibles 2005). As a result, these degraded districts are culturally heterogeneous, typically harboring a mix of native French families with immigrants from three to six dozen nationalities. And their inhabitants suffer not from institutional duplication and enclosure but, on the contrary, from the lack of an ingrown organizational structure capable of sustaining them in the absence of gainful employment and adequate public services. Like the German *Problemquartier*, the Dutch *krottenwijk*, and the British "sink estates," France's deteriorating *banlieues* are, sociologically speaking, *anti-ghettos* (Wacquant 2008a).

The Anti-Ghettos of Western Europe and the Roma Exception

If and when an urban district turns into a ghetto, it should display five mutually reinforcing properties resulting from the reciprocal assignation of category and territory: (1) growing ethnic homogeneity, (2) increased encompassment of the target population, (3) rising organizational density, (4) the production and adoption of a collective identity, and (5) impermeable boundaries. On all five dimensions, the formerly industrial *banlieues* of France harboring rising shares of immigrants have been *moving steadily away from the pattern of the ghetto* (Wacquant 2008b).

Over the past thirty years, these defamed districts have become more diverse in their ethnic composition; the proportion of all foreigners living in them has stagnated or decreased (depending on geographic location and national provenance); and they have lost most of the dense web of organizations that they harbored at the bloom of the age of the industrial "Red Belt." Most strikingly, notwithstanding political campaigns periodically denouncing "multiculturalism" and the media obsession with "Islamicization," these districts have failed to spawn a collective idiom and vision that would unify their residents on grounds of ethnicity, nationality, religion, or postcolonial status.[1] Lastly, families experiencing upward mobility, whether through education, employment, or entrepreneurship, have crossed the boundaries of these districts in droves to move up the ladder of neighborhoods and diffuse in the metropolitan space. With national variations and regional twists, this French pattern of a multilevel drift *antithetical to ghettoization*

[continues]

[continued]

fits the trajectories of most immigrant "minorities" throughout western Europe (Hartog and Zorlu 2009; Musterd and Kempen 2009; Peach 2009).

The French analysts who, caught in the political mood and fed by swirling media rumor, bemoan the morphing of the declining working-class districts of the urban periphery into fearsome "immigrant ghettos" wed conceptual confusion and historical amnesia (see, for example, Lapeyronnie 2007; Mucchielli and Le Goaziou 2007). First, they conflate territories of dereliction (marked by increased unemployment, the deterioration of the housing stock, and the devalorization of their public image) with ethnic segmentation, and they mistake mere segregation, produced by the conjoint press of class and ethnonational origin, for territorial assignation and institutional parallelism—whose absence is then obfuscated by the hazy and sulfurous category of "communautarianism," or by the invocation of the loose journalistic category of "Muslim communities" that exists only in the worried minds of outsiders. Next, they conveniently forget that ethnically marked populations issued from the former colonies were notably *more* segregated spatially and *more* isolated socially (in terms of social ties, marital unions, and institutional participation) in the 1960s and 1970s than they are today. A half-century ago, these immigrants lived separated lives tightly encased in the peripheral sectors of the secondary labor market and in the parallel institutions of the shantytowns (*bidonvilles*) and reserved housing compounds of the Société Nationale de Construction de Logements pour les Travailleurs (SONACOTRA), the state agency entrusted with housing workers migrating from the Maghrib (Sayad and Dupuy 1995; Bernardot 1999). Indeed, in sharp contraposition to the black American hyperghetto, it is the growing *mixing* of native and immigrant populations at the bottom of the structure of classes and places and the correlative *closing* of social distance and disparities between them in the context of the decomposition of traditional "working-class territories" that are the source of the xenophobic tensions and conflicts that stamp these urban zones (Wacquant 2008a).

If there is one category whose experience deviates sharply from this pattern to veer toward ghettoization, it is the Roma of eastern Europe. This population of 3 to 5 million, dispersed mostly across Romania, Bulgaria, Hungary, Czechoslovakia, and the Balkans, has long been marginalized in both monoethnic rural villages and urban districts combining the four structural components of stigma, constraint, spatial enclosure, and institutional parallelism. After the collapse of the Soviet empire, the destruction of the safety net and the abrupt social polarization wrought by the market economy have

[continues]

[continued]

reactivated anti-Roma prejudice (as a "criminal race"), animosity, and discrimination, and territorial fixation has flared anew as Gypsies sank into unemployment and destitution (Gheorghe 1991). But there are also counter-tendencies: Many Romas have passed undetected among the non-Gypsy population while others have experienced upward class mobility against the backdrop of a fuzzy ethnic hierarchy enforced with variable stringency in the different nations. Overall, class and country prove to be stronger determinants of the trajectory of Gypsies than race and space (Ladányi and Szelényi 2006). Nonetheless, the controversial policy of the Berlusconi government to reinstitute state-run camps to corral Gypsies on the outskirts of Italian cities and the heinous campaign of destruction of "illegal Rom encampments" launched by President Nicolas Sarkozy in France in the summer of 2010 to curry favor with electors of the far right are there to remind us that the Roma remain prime candidates for the (re)activation of sociospatial enclosure even in western Europe.[2]

Notes

1. Identification based on territory, often cited as a ground for ethnogenesis among lower-class immigrant youths, turns out to be weak: It is defensive, situational, and labile; it is closely linked to life cycle; and it evaporates upon entry into the labor market or migration out of the neighborhood (Lepoutre 1997).

2. The prototype Rom "village" of Castel Romano outside of Rome, home to some eight hundred Gypsies, with its prefabricated huts laid out in a grid and surrounded by a high metal fence patrolled around the clock by a special police force, and the subjection of its residents to a special census and fingerprinting are strongly redolent of the early modern Italian ghetto (see Marinaro 2009; Calame 2010).

3. Ghettos and ethnic neighborhoods sport divergent structures and serve opposite functions.

Moving beyond a gradational perspective to scrutinize the peculiar patterning of social relations within the ghetto as well as between it and the surrounding city throws into sharp relief the differences between the ghetto and the ethnic clusters or immigrant neighborhoods such as those newcomers to the metropolis have formed in countless countries. The foreign "colonies" of interwar Chicago that Robert Park, Ernest Burgess, and Louis Wirth—and after them the liberal tradition of assimilationist sociology and historiography (Miller 1992)—

mistook for so many white "ghettos" were scattered and mobile constellations born of cultural affinity and occupational concentration, more so than prejudice and discrimination. Segregation in them was partial and porous, a product of immigrant solidarity and ethnic attraction instead of being rigidly imposed by sustained out-group hostility. Consequently, residential separation was neither uniformly nor rigidly visited upon these groups: In 1930, when the all-black Bronzeville harbored 92 percent of the city's African American population, Chicago's Little Ireland was "an ethnic hodgepodge" of twenty-five nationalities composed of only one-third Irish persons and containing a paltry 3 percent of the city's denizens of Irish ancestry. The eleven dispersed districts making up Little Italy were 46 percent Italian and contained just under one-half of Chicagoans of Italian origin. Thus, both of these clusters were ethnically plural and monolithically white, and both contained a minority of the population supposedly ghettoized in them (Philpott 1978, 141–145).

This pattern was not unique to Chicago but repeated itself in every major industrial center of the Midwest and Northeast of the United States. For instance, the typical Italian immigrant to Philadelphia in 1930 resided among "14 percent other Italian immigrants, 38 percent Italian stock, 23 percent all foreign born persons and 57 percent all foreign stock" (Herschberg et al. 1981, 200). Except for marginal and local peculiarities, there were no white "ethnic" neighborhoods in the American metropolis wherein members of one European community were thoroughly isolated from native whites and monopolized space and local institutions to the exclusion of urbanites of other national origins (Warner and Burke 1969). What is more, the distinctive institutions of European immigrant enclaves were turned outward: They operated to facilitate adjustment to the novel environment of the U.S. metropolis. They neither replicated the organizations of the country of origin nor perpetuated social isolation and cultural distinctiveness. And so they typically waned within two generations as their users gained access to their American counterparts and climbed up the class order and the corresponding ladder of places (Nelli 1970). All of which is in sharp contrast with the immutable racial exclusivity and enduring institutional alterity of the Black Belt. This Chicago illustration dramatizes the fact that the immigrant neighborhood and the ghetto serve diametrically opposed functions: The one is a springboard for *assimilation* via cultural learning and social-cum-spatial mobility, and the other is a material and symbolic isolation ward geared toward *dissimilation.* The former is best figured by a bridge, the latter by a wall.[15]

FROM SHIELD TO SWORD

It is fruitful, then, to think of *ghetto and ethnic cluster as two ideal-typical configurations situated at opposite ends* of the homological continua of constraint and choice, entrapment and self-protection, exclusivity and heterogeneity, encompassment and dispersal, inward and outward orientations, and rigidity and fluidity, along which various populations (themselves differently marked) can be pegged or travel over time depending on the intensity with which the forces of stigma, constraint, spatial confinement, and institutional parallelism impinge upon them and coalesce with one another. We can then shift the analysis from the ghetto as a topographic object, a static state, to *ghettoization* as a socio-spatial dynamic, a *multilevel process* liable to empirical specification and measurement. A population that formed mobile clusters out of cultural affinity and inconsistent hostility can find itself subjected to stringent ostracization and territorial fixation such that it evolves permanent sites for comprehensive seclusion: Such was the experience of Jews in early modern Europe and of African Americans in the northern metropolis of the United States at the dawn of the Fordist era as they shifted from segregation to ghettoization.

Conversely, ghettoization can be attenuated to the point where, through gradual erosion of, and disjunction between, its spatial, social, and mental boundaries, the ghetto devolves into an elective ethnic concentration operating as a springboard for structural integration and/or cultural assimilation into the broader social formation. This describes well the trajectory of the Chinatowns of the United States from the early to the late twentieth century (Zhou 1992) and the status of the Cuban immigrant enclave of Miami, which fostered integration through biculturalism after the Mariel exodus of 1980 (Portes and Stepick 1993). It also characterizes the "Kimchee Towns" in which Koreans converged in the metropolitan areas of Japan, which sport a blend of features making them a hybrid of ghetto and ethnic cluster (DeVos and Chung 1981): They are places of infamy that first arose through enmity and constraint, but over the years their population has become ethnically mixed; residential mingling has in turn enabled Koreans to socialize and intermarry with Japanese neighbors as well as obtain Japanese citizenship through naturalization.

This analytic schema allows one to assess the degree to which a given urban configuration approximates one or the other pure type and on what dimension(s). Thus, the so-called gay ghetto is more aptly characterized as a "quasi-ethnic community," since "most gay persons can 'pass' and need not be confined to interacting with their 'own kind'" and none are forced to reside in the areas of visible concentration of gay institutions based on their sexual orientation (Murray 1979, 169). Indeed, the vast majority of gays do not live in, or even patronize, these districts, which are local clusters of commercial establishments and public spaces catering to the preferences of gays in matters of consumption and sociability. Their degree of closure, mutual orientation, and collective organization are highly variable and often contested, both without and within the gay district, as illustrated by the case of Le Marais in Paris (Sibalis 2004).

The double-sidedness of the ghetto as *sword* (for the dominant) and *shield* (for the subordinate) implies that, to the degree that its institutional completeness and autonomy are abridged, its protective role is diminished and risks being swamped by its exclusionary modality. In situations in which its residents cease to be of economic value to the controlling group, extraction evaporates and no longer balances out ostracization. Ethnoracial encapsulation can then escalate to the point where the ghetto morphs into an apparatus merely to warehouse the spoiled and supernumerary population, as a staging ground for its expulsion, or as a springboard for the ultimate form of ostracization, namely, physical annihilation.

The first scenario fits the evolution of America's "Black Metropolis" after the peaking of the civil rights movement in the mid-1960s. Having lost its role as a reservoir of unskilled labor power, the dark ghetto crashed and broke down into a dual socio-spatial structure composed of (i) the *hyperghetto*, entrapping the marginal fractions of the black working class in the barren perimeter of the historic ghetto; and (ii) the *black middle-class satellites* that burgeoned at the latter's periphery in the areas left vacant by white out-migration, where the growing African American bourgeoisie achieved spatial and social distance from its lower-class brethren (Wacquant 2008a, 51–52, 117–118). The hyperghetto is a novel socio-spatial configuration, doubly segregated by race and

class, devoid of economic function, and thus stripped of the communal institutions that used to provide succor to its inhabitants. These institutions have
been replaced by the social control institutions of the state (increasingly staffed
by the black middle class), and in particular by the booming prison and its
disciplinary tentacles. As the authorities turned from the social welfare to the
penal regulation of racialized marginality in the city, the hyperghetto became
deeply penetrated by and symbiotically linked to the hypertrophied carceral
system of the United States via the triple relationship of structural homology,
functional surrogacy, and cultural fusion (Wacquant 2011). The second and
third scenarios, wherein the ghetto devolves into a means of radical ostracization, were those implemented by Nazi Germany when it revived the *Juden-
ghetto* between 1939 and 1944, first, to impoverish and concentrate Jews with
a view toward relocation, and later, after mass deportation turned out to be
impractical, to funnel them toward extermination camps as part of the "final
solution" (Friedman 1980; Browning 1986).

The unchecked intensification of its exclusionary thrust attendant upon
the loss of its shielding capacity suggests that the ghetto might be most profitably studied not by analogy with urban slums, lower-class districts, and immigrant enclaves but alongside the reservation, the camp, and the prison, as
belonging to a broader genus of institutions for the *forced confinement of dispossessed and dishonored groups*.[16] It is not by happenstance that the Bridewell
of London (1555), the Zuchthaus of Amsterdam (1654), and the Hospital
général of Paris (1656), designed to instill the discipline of wage work in va-
grants, beggars, and criminals via incarceration, were invented around the
same time as the Jewish ghetto. It is not by coincidence that today's sprawling
refugee camps in Sierra Leone, Sri Lanka, and the occupied territories of Palestine and the Gaza Strip look ever more like a cross between the ghettos of
early modern Europe and gigantic gulags (Agier 2008; Rozelier 2007), and
that retention camps for unlawful immigrants have mushroomed throughout
Europe as the European Union has moved to treating transnational pere-
grination from the Global South as a matter of material security and ethnonational status (Le Cour Grandmaison, Lhuilier, and Valluy 2007).

A robust analytic concept of the ghetto as an organizational device for
the spatial enclosure and control of a stigmatized group offers a way out of
the semantic morass and empirical confusion created by the unreflective adop-

tion of the shifting folk notions of the same among political and intellectual elites. It allows us not only to describe, differentiate, and explain the diverse urban forms developed by tainted populations as they come into the city without falling into the many traps set by the metaphorical and rhetorical usages of "the ghetto." By spotlighting the tangled nexus of space, power, and dishonor, it also gives us the means to grasp the structural and functional kinship between the ghetto, the prison, and the camp just as the state managers of the advanced societies are increasingly resorting to borders, walls, and bounded districts as the means to define, confine, and control problem categories.

Notes

1. Remarkably, *ghetto* receives no entry in the nineteen-volume *International Encyclopedia of the Social and Behavioral Sciences* published in the United States just as the country was being shaken to its core by a wave of ghetto riots (Sills and Merton 1968). Even specialized dictionaries of racial and ethnic studies give the notion short shrift: Definitions in them are typically short, limited to the mention of ethnic segregation in space and to a descriptive denotation of particular ghettos (those of the Jewish and black diasporas).

2. An extended argument in favor of epistemological rupture as the only viable solution to the "demarcation problem" in the comparative sociology of urban marginality is Wacquant (2008a, 7–12, 135–162, 233–235, 272–276).

3. A useful analytic survey of the works of the Chicago School on this front is Hannerz (1969); a cutting critique of the biotic naturalism of Park, Burgess, and Wirth is in Logan and Molotch (1987, ch. 1).

4. This formula was intended as an inverted echo of the Supreme Court decision *Plessy v. Ferguson* (1896), which proclaimed racial segregation congruent with the country's Constitution, provided that the dual institutional tracks thus spawned be "separate but equal" (which they never were, not surprisingly since the same court studiously omitted to specify any criteria of equality or the means to bring it about). This ruling provided the juridical basis for the establishment of six decades of legal segregation in the United States, until the 1954 decision *Brown v. Board of Education* found that racial separation by itself implies an inegality that violates constitutional principles. That decision points to the pivotal role of the state in the (un)making of the black ghetto and of ethnoracial domination more generally.

5. At the same time, the ostensibly deracialized conception of the ghetto as a district of widespread destitution kept the focus squarely on the African American (sub)proletariat by adopting as its operational cutoff point the bureaucratic category of a census tract with a 40 percent poverty rate, which coincidentally ensured its *empirical overlap* with the remnants of the historic Black Belt. Like the discovery of the "underclass" a decade earlier, this conceptual move validated the special worries of state elites about the management of black marginality in the inner city while eliding the latter's roots in ethnoracial domination and regressive state policies.

6. A functional variant arose with the ghetto of Rome, which was founded in 1555 on the banks of the Tiber and abolished in 1870. It purported to foster the religious conversion and cultural dissolution of Jews, but it ended up having the opposite effects and it did not diffuse geographically (Stow 2001).

7. The following disquisition on the "Negro character" published in the journal of the Hyde Park Property Owners' Association (cited in Spear 1968, 220) captures the tenor of the view of African Americans held by white Chicagoans at the close of the Great War: "There is nothing in the make-up of a Negro, physically or mentally, which should induce anyone to welcome him as a neighbor. The best of them are insanitary. . . . Ruin alone follows their path. They are proud as peacocks, but have nothing of the peacock's beauty. . . . Niggers are undesirable neighbors and entirely irresponsible and vicious."

8. The *eta* ("filth eternal") were permanent and hereditary pariahs descended from the occupational guilds tainted by the handling of death, blood, leather, and armor. The *hinin* ("nonhuman") were temporary and nonhereditary pariahs tainted by criminal punishment (typically banishment for ten to twenty years). The exact origins, composition, and evolving status of the Burakumin are the objects of fierce debates in Japanese historiography in relation with contemporary political battles and policy alternatives (Neary 2003), and the topic continues to be as sulfurous as the category.

9. Colonial societies form a vast yet largely uncharted domain for the comparative study of the dynamics and forms of ghettoization for three reasons. First, in their settler variant, they were "geographic" social formations, predicated on land spoliation, close control of the circulation of goods and people, and the rigid regimentation of space. Second, they were founded on sharp, stiff, and salient ethnoracial divisions that were projected onto the spatial organization of the city. Lastly, urban forms were major vehicles for social engineering and identity crafting in the colony. For illustrations, see the complementary studies of French dominions by Wright (1991) and Çelik (1997).

10. The phenomenon of "passing" among the Burakumin is an explosive question in the historical sociology and politics of Japan's "invisible race" (Neary 2003). An abiding sense of disgrace born of the internalization of stigma is a prevalent theme in the autobiographies of Burakumin activists (see, for example, Hane 1982, 163–171).

11. The ghetto of Chicago thus produced the country's first black national newspaper, *The Chicago Defender*, whose owner, Robert S. Abbott, was also the city's first black millionaire (Spear 1968, 165–167).

12. Another anomaly generated by the income-based (re)definition of the ghetto is the following: The same neighborhood, harboring the same population and institutions and fulfilling the same functions in the metropolitan system, would alternately become a ghetto and cease being one with wide variations of its poverty rate caused by cyclical fluctuations of the economy. This conception not only leaves out the canonical cases of the ghetto; by making ghettoization a derivative property of economic inequality and income distribution, it also fails utterly to identify a distinctive socio-spatial form.

13. There are at least three major interlinked reasons why ghettos did not emerge in Latin American cities, a fact attested by Gilbert (1998; Gilbert, this volume). First, the countries with significant dishonored populations (descendants of African slaves and native peasants) have evolved gradational systems of ethnoracial classification based on phenotype and a host of

sociocultural variables, as opposed to categorical systems based on descent (as defined Jews in Europe and blacks in the United States), resulting in fuzzy and porous ethnic boundaries. Second, and correlatively, they sport low and inconsistent patterns of residential segregation, and solid segregation is a necessary stepping-stone to ghettoization. Third, Latin American states have spawned sharply asymmetric conceptions of citizenship, but they have typically not given legal imprimatur to ethnoracial classification and discrimination.

14. Pinçon and Pinçon's (2007) dissection of the dense web of associations, clubs, and councils through which the upper crust of the French bourgeoisie bulwarks its secluded spaces (exclusive urban enclaves, parks and castles, beaches and gardens) shows that the "ghettos of the gotha" are no ghettos. This catchy coinage makes for good marketing copy but muddies the sociological waters.

15. For full documentation of the sharp divergence between the black ghetto and the "colonies" formed by European immigrants (Jews from eastern countries, Poles, Italians, and the Irish) in the first half of the twentieth century in the United States, see Lieberson (1980), Bodnar, Simon, and Weber (1982), Zunz (1986), and Gerstle (2001, esp. ch. 5). Workers of Belgian, Italian, Polish, and Iberian provenance underwent a very similar process of spatial diffusion via class incorporation in the French industrial cities of the first half of the twentieth century in spite of being subjected to virulent xenophobia and widespread collective violence during phases of economic turmoil (Noiriel 1988). Over the past quarter-century, postcolonial migrants have been following a germane trajectory in cities throughout Europe, characterized by low to moderate segregation from nationals and stagnant to decreasing spatial concentration (Musterd 2005).

16. Wacquant (2010) sketches an analytic framework that brings together into a single model forms of socio-spatial seclusion at the top (gated communities, upper-class districts) and at the bottom (slum, ethnic cluster, ghetto, prison), as well as urban and rural forms (among which figure preserves, reservations, and camps).

References

Abu-Lughod, Janet L. 1980. *Rabat: Urban Apartheid in Morocco.* Princeton, N.J.: Princeton University Press.

Agier, Michel. 2008. *Gérer les indésirables. Des camps de réfugiés au gouvernement humanitaire.* Paris: Flammarion. (Published in English as *Managing the Undesirables: Refugee Camps and Humanitarian Government.* London: Polity, 2011.)

Auyero, Javier. 2000. *Poor People's Politics: Peronist Survival Networks and the Legacy of Evita.* Durham, N.C.: Duke University Press.

Bernardot, Marc. 1999. "Chronique d'une institution. la 'Sonacotra' (1956–1976)" ("Chronicle of an institution: The 'Sonacotra' [1956–1976]"). *Sociétés contemporaines* 33–34: 39–58.

Bodnar, John, Roger Simon, and Michael P. Weber. 1982. *Lives of Their Own: Blacks, Italians, and Poles in Pittsburgh.* Urbana: University of Illinois Press.

Bronner, Luc. 2007. *La Loi du ghetto. Enquête dans les banlieues françaises* [The Law of the Ghetto: A Foray into the French banlieues]. Paris: Calmann-Lévy.

Browning, Christopher R. 1986. "Nazi Ghettoization Policy in Poland, 1939–1941." *Central European History* 19, no. 4: 343–368.

Calame, Jon. 2010. "The Roma of Rome: Heirs to the Ghetto System." *The Design Observer* (December). Available at http://places.designobserver.com.

Caldeira, Teresa. 2000. *City of Walls: Crime, Segregation, and Citizenship in São Paulo.* Berkeley and Los Angeles: University of California Press.

Çelik, Zeynep. 1997. *Urban Forms and Colonial Confrontations: Algiers Under French Rule.* Berkeley and Los Angeles: University of California Press.

Clark, Kenneth B. 1965. *Dark Ghetto: Dilemmas of Social Power.* New York: Harper.

Curiel, Roberta, and Bernard Dov Cooperman. 1990. *The Ghetto of Venice.* New York: Rizzoli.

DeVos, George, and Deakyun Chung. 1981. "Community Life in a Korean Ghetto." In *Koreans in Japan: Ethnic Conflict and Accommodation,* edited by Changsoo Lee and George DeVos. Berkeley and Los Angeles: University of California Press.

DeVos, George, and Hiroshi Wagatsuma, eds. 1966. *Japan's Invisible Race: Caste in Culture and Personality.* Berkeley and Los Angeles: University of California Press.

Drake, St. Clair, and Horace R. Cayton. 1993. *Black Metropolis: A Study of Negro Life in a Northern City.* Chicago: University of Chicago Press. (Originally published in 1945.)

Friedman, Philip. 1980. "The Jewish Ghettos of the Nazi Era." In *Roads to Extinction: Essays on the Holocaust.* New York: Jewish Publication Society of America, pp. 59–87.

Gallie, W. B. 1956. "Essentially Contested Concepts." *Proceedings of the Aristotelian Society* 56: 167–198.

Gay, Ruth. 1992. *The Jews of Germany: A Historical Portrait.* New Haven, Conn.: Yale University Press.

Gerstle, Gary. 2001. *American Crucible: Race and Nation in the Twentieth Century.* Princeton, N.J.: Princeton University Press.

Gheorghe, Nicolae. 1991. "Roma-Gypsy Ethnicity in Eastern Europe." *Social Research* 58, no. 4 (Winter): 829–844.

Gilbert, Alan. 1998. *The Latin American City.* New York: Monthly Review Press.

Goffman, Erving. 1963. *Stigma: Notes on the Management of Spoiled Identity.* New York: Simon & Schuster.

Gottreich, Emily. 2006. *The Mellah of Marrakesh: Jewish and Muslim Space in Morocco's Red City.* Bloomington: Indiana University Press.

Greenberg, Cheryl Lynn. 1991. *Or Does It Explode? Black Harlem in the Great Depression.* New York: Oxford University Press.

Hane, Mikiso. 1982. *Peasants, Rebels, and Outcastes: The Underside of Modern Japan.* New York: Pantheon.

Hannerz, Ulf. 1969. *Soulside: Inquiries into Ghetto Culture and Community.* New York: Columbia University Press.

Hartog, Joop, and Aslan Zorlu. 2009. "Ethnic Segregation in the Netherlands: An Analysis at Neighborhood Level." *International Journal of Manpower* 30, nos. 1–2: 15–25.

Haynes, Bruce, and Ray Hutchison, eds. 2008. "The Ghetto: Origins, History, Discourse." *City & Community* 7, no. 4 (December): 347–398.

Herschberg, Theodore, et al. 1981. *Philadelphia: Work, Space, Family, and Group Experience in the Nineteenth Century.* New York: Oxford University Press.

Hirsch, Arnold. 1998. *Making the Second Ghetto: Race and Housing in Chicago 1940–1970.* Chicago: University of Chicago Press. (Originally published in 1983 by Cambridge University Press.)

Hughes, Langston. 1957. *Simple Stakes a Claim*. New York: Harcourt Brace Jovanovich.

Jargowsky, Paul A. 1997. *Poverty and Place: Ghettos, Barrios, and the American City*. New York: Russell Sage Foundation.

Johnson, James Weldon. 1981. *Black Manhattan*. New York: Da Capo. (Originally published in 1930.)

Johnson, Paul. 1987. *A History of the Jews*. New York: HarperPerennial.

Kerner Commission. 1989. *The Kerner Report: The 1968 Report of the National Advisory Commission on Civil Disorders*. New York: Pantheon. (Originally published in 1968.)

Kowarick, Lúcio. 2009. *Viver em risco. Sobre a vulnerabilidade socioeconômica e civil* (*Living at risk: On socioeconomic and civil vulnerability*). São Paulo: Editora 34.

Ladányi, Janos, and Ivan Szelényi. 2006. *Patterns of Exclusion: Constructing Gypsy Ethnicity and the Making of an Underclass in Transitional Societies of Europe*. New York: Columbia University Press.

Lapeyronnie, Didier. 2007. *Ghetto urbain. Ségrégation, violence, pauvreté en France aujourd'hui* (*Urban ghetto: Segregation, violence, and poverty in France today*). Paris: Robert Laffont.

Le Cour Grandmaison, Oliver, Gilles Lhuilier, and Jérome Valluy, eds. 2007. *Le Retour des camps: Sangatte, Lampedusa, Guantanamo* (*The Return of the camps: Sangatte, Lampedusa, Guantánamo*). Paris: Autrement.

Lepoutre, David. 1997. *Coeur de banlieue. Codes, rites et langages* (*Heart of the banlieue: Codes, rites, and languages*). Paris: Odile Jacob.

Levine, Martin P. 1979. "Gay Ghetto." *Journal of Homosexuality* 4, no. 4 (Summer): 363–377. Reprinted in expanded form as "'YMCA': The Social Organization of Gay Male Life," in *Gay Macho: The Life and Death of the Homosexual Clone*. New York: New York University Press.

Lieberson, Stanley. 1980. *A Piece of the Pie: Blacks and White Immigrants Since 1880*. Berkeley and Los Angeles: University of California Press.

Logan, John R., and Harvey L. Molotch. 1987. *Urban Fortunes: The Political Economy of Place*. Berkeley and Los Angeles: University of California Press.

Low, Setha, M. 2004. *Behind the Gates: Life, Security, and the Pursuit of Happiness in Fortress America*. New York: Routledge.

Lubove, Roy. 1963. *The Progressives and the Slums: Tenement House Reform in New York City, 1890–1917*. Pittsburgh: University of Pittsburgh Press.

Marinaro, Isabella Clough. 2009. "Between Surveillance and Exile: Biopolitics and the Roma in Italy." *Bulletin of Italian Politics* 1, no. 2: 265–287.

Marks, Carol. 1989. *Farewell—We're Good and Gone: The Great Black Migration*. Bloomington: Indiana University Press.

Marques, Eduardo, and Haroldo Torres. 2005. *São Paulo. segregação, pobreza e desigualdades sociais* (*São Paulo: Segregation, poverty, and social inequalities*). São Paulo: Editora do Senac.

Massey, Douglas, and Nancy Denton. 1993. *American Apartheid: Segregation and the Making of the Underclass*. Cambridge, Mass.: Harvard University Press.

Miller, Z. L. 1992. "Pluralism, Chicago School Style: Louis Wirth, the Ghetto, the City, and Integration." *Journal of Urban History* 18, no. 3: 251–279.

Mucchielli, Laurent, and Véronique Le Goaziou. 2007. *Quand les banlieues brûlent. Retour sur les émeutes de novembre 2005* (*When the banlieues are burning: On the riots of November 2005*). Paris: La Découverte.

Murray, Stephen O. 1979. "The Institutional Elaboration of a Quasi-Ethnic Community." *International Review of Modern Sociology* 9 (July): 165–177.

Musterd, Sako. 2005. "Social and Ethnic Segregation in Europe: Levels, Causes, and Effects." *Journal of Urban Affairs* 27, no. 3: 331–348.

Musterd, Sako, and Ronald van Kempen. 2009. "Segregation and Housing of Minority Ethnic Groups in Western European Cities." *Tijdschrift voor Economische en Sociale Geografie* 100, no. 4: 559–566.

Musterd, Sako, Alan Murie, and Christian Kesteloot, eds. 2006. *Neighbourhoods of Poverty: Urban Social Exclusion and Integration in Europe.* London: Palgrave.

Neary, Ian. 2003. "Burakumin at the End of History." *Social Research* 70, no. 1: 269–294.

Nelli, Humbert S. 1970. *Italians in Chicago: A Study in Ethnic Mobility.* New York: Oxford University Press.

Noiriel, Gérard. 1988. *Le Creuset français.* Paris: Seuil. (Published in English as *The French Melting Pot*, Ithaca, N.Y.: Cornell University Press, 1996.)

Observatoire des Zones Urbaines Sensibles. 2005. *Rapport 2005* (2005 Annual Report). Paris: Délégation interministérielle à la ville.

Osofsky, Gilbert. 1971. *Harlem: The Making of a Ghetto—Negro New York, 1890–1930.* 2nd ed. New York: Harper & Row.

Patterson, Orlando. 1998. "Broken Bloodlines." In *Rituals of Blood: Consequences of Slavery in Two American Centuries.* New York: Basic/Civitas Books.

Peach, Ceri. 2009. "Slippery Segregation: Discovering or Manufacturing Ghettos?" *Journal of Ethnic and Migration Studies* 35 (November): 1381–1395.

Perlman, Janice. 1976. *The Myth of Marginality: Urban Poverty and Politics in Rio de Janeiro.* Berkeley and Los Angeles: University of California Press.

Pétonnet, Colette. 1982. *Espaces habités. Ethnologie des banlieues* (*Inhabited spaces: The Ethnology of the banlieue*). Paris: Galilée.

Philpott, Thomas Lee. 1978. *The Slum and the Ghetto: Neighborhood Deterioration and Middle-Class Reform, Chicago, 1880–1930.* New York: Oxford University Press.

Pinçon, Monique, and Michel Pinçon. 2007. *Les Ghettos du gotha. Comment la bourgeoisie défend ses espaces* (*The Ghettos of the Gotha: How the bourgeoisie defends its spaces*). Paris: Seuil.

Portes, Alejandro, and Alex Stepick. 1993. *City on the Edge: The Transformation of Miami.* Berkeley and Los Angeles: University of California Press.

Rozelier, Muriel. 2007. *Naplouse Palestine. Chroniques du ghetto* (*Nablus Palestine: Chronicles of the ghetto*). Paris: Presses de la Renaissance.

Sabouret, Jean-François. 1983. *L'Autre Japon. les Burakumin* (*The Other Japan: The Burakumin*). Paris: Éditions Maspéro.

Sayad, Abdelmalek, and Éliane Dupuy. 1995. *Un Nanterre algérien, terre de bidonvilles* (*Algerian Nanterre, a Land of slums*). Paris: Éditions Autrement.

Schierup, Carl-Ulrik, Peo Hansen, and Stephen Castles. 2006. *Migration, Citizenship, and the European Welfare State: A European Dilemma.* Oxford: Oxford University Press.

Sennett, Richard. 1994. "Fear of Touching." In *Flesh and Stone: The Body and the City in Western Civilization.* New York: W. W. Norton.

Sibalis, Michael. 2004. "Urban Space and Homosexuality: The Example of the Marais, Paris's 'Gay Ghetto.'" *Urban Studies* 41, no. 9 (August): 1739–1758.

Sills, David, and Robert Merton, eds. 1968. *International Encyclopedia of the Social Sciences.* New York: Free Press.

Small, Mario. 2009. "Four Reasons to Abandon the Idea of 'the Ghetto.'" *City & Community* 7, no. 4 (December): 389–398.

Spear, Allan H. 1968. *Black Chicago: The Making of a Negro Ghetto, 1890–1920.* Chicago: University of Chicago Press.

Stow, Kenneth R. 1992. *Alienated Minority: The Jews of Medieval Latin Europe.* Cambridge, Mass.: Harvard University Press.

————. 2001. *Theater of Acculturation: The Roman Ghetto in the Sixteenth Century.* Seattle: University of Washington Press.

Wacquant, Loïc. 1998. "'A Black City Within the White': Revisiting America's Dark Ghetto." *Black Renaissance* 2, no. 1: 141–151.

————. 2002. "Gutting the Ghetto: Political Censorship and Conceptual Retrenchment in the American Debate on Urban Destitution." In *Globalization and the New City: Migrants, Minorities, and Urban Transformations in Comparative Perspective*, edited by Malcolm Cross and Robert Moore. Basingstoke, UK: Palgrave.

————. 2008a. *Urban Outcasts: A Comparative Sociology of Advanced Marginality.* Cambridge: Polity Press.

————. 2008b. "Ghettos and Anti-Ghettos: An Anatomy of the New Urban Poverty." *Thesis Eleven* 94 (August): 113–118.

————. 2010. "Designing Urban Seclusion in the Twenty-First Century." *Perspecta: The Yale Architectural Journal* 43: 165–178.

————. 2011. *Deadly Symbiosis: Race and the Rise of the Penal State.* Cambridge: Polity Press.

Ward, David. 1989. *Poverty, Ethnicity, and the American City, 1840–1925.* Cambridge: Cambridge University Press.

Warner, Sam Bass, Jr., and Colin B. Burke. 1969. "Cultural Change and the Ghetto." *Journal of Contemporary History* 4 (October): 173–187.

Weber, Max. 1978. *Economy and Society,* 2 vols., edited by Guenter Roth and Claus Wittich. Berkeley and Los Angeles: University of California Press. (Originally published in 1918–1920.)

Western, John. 1981. *Outcast Cape Town.* Minneapolis: University of Minnesota Press.

Wilson, William Julius. 1987. *The Truly Disadvantaged: The Inner City, the Underclass, and Public Policy.* Chicago: University of Chicago Press.

————. 1996. *When Work Disappears: The World of the New Urban Poor.* New York: Knopf.

Wirth, Louis. 1928. *The Ghetto.* Chicago: University of Chicago Press.

————. 1964. "The Ghetto." In *On Cities and Social Life*, edited by Albert J. Reiss Jr. Chicago: University of Chicago Press. (Originally published in 1956.)

Wright, Gwendolyn. 1991. *The Politics of Design in French Urban Colonialism.* Chicago: University of Chicago Press.

Zaluar, Alba, and Marcos Alvito, eds. 1998. *Um século de favela* (*A Century of favelas*). Rio de Janeiro: Fundação Getúlio Vargas Editora.

Zhou, Min. 1992. *Chinatown: The Socioeconomic Potential of an Urban Enclave.* Philadelphia: Temple University Press.

Zunz, Olivier. 1986. *The Changing Face of Inequality: Urbanization, Urban Development, and Immigrants in Detroit, 1880–1920.* Chicago: University of Chicago Press.

CHAPTER 2

De-spacialization and Dilution of the Ghetto: Current Trends in the United States

Peter Marcuse

Three intertwined processes will determine the future of what is generically called the ghetto:

1. *The de-spatialization of the ghetto: the replacement of space by other mechanisms for accomplishing the results that ghettos have historically achieved.* Ghettos, as conceptualized and defined in this chapter, have historically used spatial confinement to buttress social control and economic exploitation of those thus confined. The contention here is that such control and exploitation continue, but that spatial confinement today plays a much more limited role in maintaining it and is being replaced by essentially nonspatial forms of control, ranging from the criminal justice system to welfare policies to co-optation and "inclusion."

2. *The dilution of the ghetto; the replacement of the users of the space occupied by ghettos by other users and uses.* Most ghettos occupy space close to central economic activities in cities but are kept separate by physical walls or legal and social boundaries. Yet that space is valuable, and as its use for other purposes becomes more and more attractive the ghetto is (functionally) diluted, by processes ranging from urban renewal and gentrification to social inclusion and de-concentration.

3. *The marketization of the social control function of space.* Public policies have historically played a critical role in the maintenance of ghettos.

Economic pressures reflecting short-term and private economic interests, ranging from real estate ownership to a status premium in the constitution of effective residential demand, to employment policies seeking to take advantage of cheap and accessible labor, crisscross broader economic and political state policies, sometimes reinforcing, sometimes undercutting their avowed purposes, but shifting the mechanism from formal policies to informal market mechanisms.

Underlying these three ghetto-specific processes are three broader issues that this chapter deals with only as background to the directly ghetto-related urban consequences of these shifts.

1. *Relations of power.* Changes in the inequalities of power and resources among groups (class, ethnic, racial, gender-defined) with conflicts over the production and distribution of the benefits and costs of the economic system as a whole. The literature here is substantial, and the broad outlines of increasing inequality as it disproportionately affects minorities are generally known.

2. *Conflicts over the use and control of space in the city as a whole.* The dynamic is that of an ongoing contest over the use and control of the space of the city—over who has the right to the city—between, on the one hand, those who want to use it for profit and for the social control necessary to permit profit to be maximized and, on the other hand, those who depend on the city to provide the shelter and facilities and access they need for a normal life. In the contest between those who see the city as a source of exchange value and those who value the city for its human use, power has shifted in favor of the former. And of course many are caught in the middle. The process of gentrification reflects the complex outcome.

3. *Macroeconomic and demographic shifts.* The shift from manufacturing to services in production, technological advances in transportation and communication, immigration, occupational changes among minority groups, and globalization are all influential factors. The growth of a substantial African American middle class is directly relevant to the evolution of the ghetto.

These developments call for a new taxonomy of the generic *ghetto*, which might run somewhat as follows:

A *dispersed or de-spatializing ghetto*, located a distance from the central business district, often in the suburbs; less racially concentrated, more middle-class, but with residents still discriminated against economically and socially in a variety of forms, and sometimes limited in extent by state actions.

A *hard ghetto*, spatially concentrated by relatively rigid economic behaviors in other parts of the metropolitan area and singled out for special treatment by governmental actions; lower income; widely perceived as socially dangerous and in need of strict control; stigmatized; the classic stereotype of the ghetto.

A *weak or gentrifying diluted ghetto*, still significantly racially concentrated in the spaces of the older hard ghetto; more diverse and more middle- and upper-middle-class; disproportionately found in globalizing cities; prime sites of gentrification.

An *abandoned ghetto*, the space of some former hard ghettos, abandoned by both the market and the state; often the location of older public housing; often with high vacancies, substandard physical housing, and inadequate services and public facilities; disproportionately found in de-globalizing cities.

The evolving pattern suggests the virtual disappearance of the *hard ghetto*, though not the disappearance of the *weak ghetto*, which is maintained by continuing segregationist racism and a reaction of solidarity built on the enclave aspect of spatial identity. The disappearance of the hard ghetto should not by any means suggest the disappearance of racial discrimination, domination, and exploitation. It only means that racism's effect—the continuing inequality within and outside our cities—is now achieved with less emphasis on spatial boundaries. Controls imposed on the earlier victims of the hard ghetto are now imposed outside as well as inside the weak ghetto—for example, criminal justice controls—and within the weak ghetto displacement of some poorer victims and the opening opportunities for their middle-class counterparts have changed the physical and social characteristics.

To phrase the point most broadly: Every society uses mechanisms of social control to maintain its basic structures of power and its arrangements for the distribution of the resources of society. The World Social Forum's charter speaks of social problems using two terms that are relevant to the discussion of the ghetto: "the problems of *exclusion* and *social inequality* that the process of capitalist globalization with its racist, sexist and environmentally destructive dimensions is creating internationally and within countries."[1]

I take *exclusion* to mean "exclusion from equal or fair participation in the benefits of organized society" and to include, for example, spatial exclusion, as with ghetto walls. I take *social inequality* to refer to a wide range of structural conditions that support such exclusion by other means, for example, political domination, legal structures, and market mechanisms. The central theme here, then, is that the ghetto's role in achieving exclusion by spatial means is diminishing and the sophisticated use of other means of control is increasingly taking its place. Space continues to play a key role in the playing out of relations of power, but insofar as the hard ghetto is concerned, its role is changing.[2] This is what I mean by *de-spatializing*. By *dilution* I mean that the role of space in today's weak ghetto is likewise changing, specifically in the weakening of the spatial social control function, which is less concerned with exclusion but continues to play a role in maintaining social inequality.

Within that framework, the argument of this chapter is that there has been a significant change in the uses of space in the city—and particularly the space occupied by ghettos—in the last ten years or so in two major regards: (1) the *neutralization* of the ghetto, that is, the perception that the potential for resistance by the ghetto's segregated residents has been eroded and is now controllable by "softer" techniques than those that rely on the spatial containment of the historic ghetto, and (2) the *gentrification* of the ghetto, which is to say, changes in the forms and relations of work and production that have led to a polarization of incomes and occupations in which the business community has expressed its spatial desires by claiming land that historically has been occupied by poorer people and members of minority groups. The ghetto is diluted when these changes are overlaid by the process of gentrification. Whether the "ghetto" is subsequently disappearing, changing its character, or being diluted is a matter of definition; by whatever definition, it has changed, and in ways that include each of these characterizations.

In the context of current debates, the position here is that the historic ghetto has not "disappeared," as an exaggerated reading of Sharon Zukin's chapter on Harlem or as some of Camillo Vergara's work might, for instance, suggest.[3] Nor would I argue that the ghetto has become more "excluded" or "marginalized," as some readings of Loïc Wacquant's work might suggest, or that it has simply changed in density or demographics, as contributions to the "Community & City" listserv might lead one to believe. What has changed since around 1995 is the handling of the ghetto by public policy and the market to attempt to shape a neutralized and diluted ghetto, with different and softer forms of social control but essentially the same set of relations of exploitation and domination as before—the term *weak* here being somewhat misleading in that, while some aspects of the ghetto are indeed less harsh and demonstratively oppressive, at least one key aspect, the role of the police and the criminal justice system, is only spatially soft.

In using New York City as the example of these tendencies, no claim is made that New York City is typical of all cities or that all ghettos follow the pattern there; the claim is rather that these two tendencies, gentrification and neutralization, are to be found to a widely varying extent in most cities in the United States and the Western world—indeed, gentrification may be found in cities throughout the world. Gentrification takes place depending on the location of a ghetto and the economy of the city in which it is located; de-spatialization takes place depending on the militancy of the residents of that ghetto.

The argument here not only is confined to cities like New York with similar patterns of ghettoization, ghetto policies, and gentrification but explicitly is not made as a general description of the relation of space to oppression around the world today. While there is a tendency to the neutralization of certain residential spatially based forms of resistance to oppression and— viz., workers' quaters—public spaces remain central arenas of conflict. But that tendency varies enormously from place to place, country to country, city to city, time to time. David Harvey suggests how broad some of the pattern may be when he speaks of the likelihood that in the future high-rise business clusters will loom where today the favelas cover the hillsides near central Rio de Janeiro. That would be a striking extension of some of the tendencies commented on here, but I think in the immediate future talk of the de-spatialization of oppression is a minor theme in most of the Third

World, including both its megacities and its less globalizing cities. Squatter settlements, not all racialized but all representing the uses of space to reinforce oppression, spatialized oppression, remains the predominant pattern, and the concern for resistance has not been neutralized in most of them; the citadels in the city and the gated communities of the dominant classes within and outside the cities, and the squatter settlements outside them, represent the (temporary?) relations of power in the contest for the right to the city for most of the world today.

Further the dynamics of spatialized oppression can work themselves out very differently where colonial relations are involved. Oren Yiftachel (personal communication with the author) makes the point sharply by pointing to the effect of the wall between Israel and the West Bank:

> The Israeli/Palestinian case raises a very important theoretical perspective about segregation and ghettoization. The liberal context in which western scholars work, particularly in North America, lends itself to a focus on immigration and the capitalist property system as the main "sources" of urban segregation. In other parts of the world, however, where nationalist and colonialist projects are still at full flight, intermeshed as they are with other social forces, segregation is often an expression, and a tool, of politics of identity in a most profound, essentialising manner. Hence what I call "homeland ethnicities" act differently in their spatial politics to minorities in the west. This throws a new light on the issue of segregation, quite different to the host-immigrant-integration relations typical to western settings. There is a theoretical issue here beyond Israel/Palestine.

Likewise, no claim is made that these are new tendencies; rather, gentrification is the continuation of an old pattern. As David Harvey has commented, it is startling the extent to which descriptions of Manchester in the middle of the nineteenth century could be applied with little change to its parallel cities in the twenty-first. De-spatialization, however, is a relatively new phenomenon, and while the choice to focus on the last decade is necessarily arbitrary, the tendency has crystallized remarkably in that period. What persists is oppression, as defined later in this chapter. It may be a de-spatialized oppression with a significant neutralization of resistance, but it is oppression nevertheless.[4] This is perhaps the most important point: If the spatialized nature of oppression is changing—if, say, indices of dissimilarity are falling in various cities—that does not mean that the level of oppression and discrimination against minority groups is falling. It remains for social scientists, political leaders, and activists to examine closely just what is changing and what is not and to direct their efforts at remedying those injustices, both new and old, both spatial and nonspatial, that endure today.

KEY CONCEPTS

A number of terms used here, often in different ways, require definition.[5] The term *ghetto* can be used in many different ways, and no one of them is "correct." (Although there is one incorrect way: To speak of an "elite ghetto," or a "ghetto of the rich," deprives the term of any possible social meaning.) But precisely because the term has been used in so many different ways, it is important to be clear about how it is used here.

Generically, in many discussions a ghetto is simply the space in which a large portion of a subordinated, usually racially defined group is located. More specifically, *a ghetto should be defined as a bounded area of spatial concentration of an oppressed group, defined by an ascribed identity, in which the confinement is used for the purpose of social control over and economic subordination of the resident population.* Thus, a ghetto is (1) a space created by (2) relations of power, and (3) used for oppression and control. The ghetto is created by dominant forces that separate and limit—other than simply through the private market—an oppressed population group that is externally defined as racial or ethnic or foreign, held to be inferior by the dominant society, and treated as such; residence within the ghetto is used to stigmatize and de-limit the opportunities of its residents and help control their conduct. Its function is to facilitate the exploitation and control of a group thus defined. The extent of concentration may vary widely, and given areas may have the social characteristics of a ghetto to a greater or lesser extent. Thus, it is useful to distinguish among the various forms of the ghetto, as outlined above, recognizing that these forms lie along a spectrum, with the historic Jewish ghetto at the hard, involuntary end and the weak ghetto, with only survivals of the social control characteristics of the hard ghetto, at the voluntary end.

A *hard ghetto* is a ghetto in which the spatial confinement is legally established, implemented by force of law, and used as a primary tool of social

control. Typically almost all of the members of the group are confined within
its defined space. It is the classic Jewish ghetto of history, whose epitome was
the Jewish ghetto of Warsaw under fascism: Walled in, oppressed, and exploited
for their labor, its residents were treated as subhuman in every way. Solidarity
may indeed be a by-product of the hard ghetto, but not because anyone voluntarily moves there.[6] The hard ghetto is significantly reinforced by state
action—explicitly in earlier history, less explicitly today.

Thus, in the view taken here, the hard ghetto is primarily a *spatialized
method of social control.*[7]

A *weak ghetto* is a pattern in which a group defined by an ascribed identity
is oppressed and finds itself spatially clustered, although not legally thus confined,
as a result of inequalities of power and subject to social controls not exercised
primarily by its spatial concentration. A weak ghetto historically has two sets of
characteristics, one typical also of a hard ghetto, the other typical of an enclave.
It remains an area of spatial concentration of members of a group historically
subject to discrimination, domination, and exploitation, but it also fosters the
development of solidarity and resistance. Further, because a weak ghetto can leak
out of its area of primary spatial concentration to a significant extent, increasing
numbers of the target group may live outside of that area. Thus, many scholarly
discussions that use quantitative and mapping techniques to describe levels of
segregation take a high level of clustering of a given population to be synonymous with ghetto creation, although any high level of clustering can theoretically
be consistent with a hard ghetto, a weak ghetto, or an enclave and most likely
shares some aspects of each, although in critically different proportions.

The weak ghetto is a ghetto created largely by the operations of the private
market in housing. It responds both to racial prejudice within the housing industry and among residents and to inequalities in the distribution of incomes.
In the weak ghetto the social control function of the hard ghetto plays a less
and less important role. We might speak of the weak ghetto as a diluted hard
ghetto without walls of exclusion—or as a *social ghetto* or a *market ghetto.*

An *enclave* is an area of spatial concentration in which members of a particular population group, self-defined by ethnicity or religion or otherwise,
use their spatial concentration to enhance solidarity and protect and enhance
their economic, social, political, and cultural development. Any area with the
predominant characteristics of either a ghetto or an enclave inevitably has
some of the characteristics of the other.[8]

Ghettoization is the process of creating and maintaining ghettos, as generically defined. The term is used regardless of whether the ghettos in question are spatial, or weak if functional, or in transition. *Hard ghettoization* is the central process that defines hard ghettos, focusing on their legal control function; it may also be a lingering component (or, as argued here, a declining component) of weak ghettos.

The term *segregation* should not be used to describe any finding of spatial concentration, but only when that concentration results from the imposition of spatial ghettoization. The better term for spatial concentration itself is *clustering*, which can be used to cover hard ghettos, weak ghettos, enclaves, affinity communities, and various other patterns.

Ghetto population is an unscientific term that deserves further discussion than is possible here. In general, as here used, it refers to those who would classically have been residents of the hard ghetto: very disproportionately poor, unemployed, African American, and residing in single-parent households. The issue of the segregation and ghetto formation of other population groups is not dealt with here.

De-spatialization is the movement toward dispersion of the population of the ghetto—that is, moving parts of the ghetto population out of the ghetto—while retaining its control functions in a less concentrated spatial setting.

Dilution of the ghetto is the movement toward gilding the ghetto—retaining its spatial characteristics but softening their control functions. Dilution aims at changing the living conditions of the ghetto population and making the ghetto's space available to others, i.e., gentrification.

Marketization, as here used, is the shift in the importance of state policies as an instrument for dealing with the ghetto and the control of ghetto populations in favor of the sanctioned operation of the private market. This shift from the political sphere to the economic sphere signals not so much direct privatization of public actions as the withdrawal of the state from certain policies and their replacement by an expansion of the role of private market forces, as in the decline of urban renewal and the rise of gentrification.

Definitions are neither right nor wrong; rather, their validity is measured by the extent to which they are useful for analytic purposes and for purposes of policy determination. The definitions used here are intended to highlight the relational character of the ghetto: It cannot be understood without examining the relation between the inside and the outside of the ghetto, the forces that create it, and the forces that resist its creation or respond to its creation by developing enclaves.[9] Definitions along these lines are essential for clarity of understanding and policy formulation and to distinguish desired from undesired elements. For policy purposes, they avoid legitimating ghettos as equivalent to the enclaves of solidarity that immigrants form and further avoid looking at ghettos as simple consequences of the market, with unequal income distribution as their sole cause.

The definitions suggested here may cause problems of measurement and create some difficulties in empirical application. A definition that simply measures levels of residential concentration—examining their relationship to variables of race, ethnicity, income, and so on—is easier to use and permits easier comparison over time and across cities or countries. But we should not choose the definition of a concept for analytic purposes simply because it is easy to quantify or test empirically. The definition here suggested can in fact be handled empirically, even if the exact borderline in measurement needed for many of its terms must inevitably be arbitrary in empirical work.

I believe the definition of the ghetto offered here is substantially the definition implicitly used in the classic understanding of the term *ghetto*, although fudging the distinction between the hard and the weak ghetto.[10] It is in any event the definition used in this chapter. And definitions make a difference: Under these definitions, Harlem and Soweto, it is here argued, are gradually shifting from spatial to weak ghettos, but Gaza is firmly a spatial one. The overall level of ghettoization or segregation in a society should not be measured simply through an index of dissimilarity or similar indexes, which are essentially generic measures of clustering and separation, and factors such as high levels of incarceration, which might otherwise contribute to reducing the scale of a ghetto by removing some of its members, would deepen its harsher characteristics instead.

THE DEVELOPMENT OF THE GHETTO IN THE UNITED STATES

What has happened to the ghetto in the last two decades needs to be seen as part of the longer historical development of the ghetto in the United States. Multiple strands in that history, roughly rising in importance sequentially over time, can be separated out. Each is summarized here only briefly because each is basically well known and has been extensively studied elsewhere.[11] The focus here is on specifically new developments in the last two decades. The historical process is as follows:[12]

1. Exploitation of a particular population group
2. Legitimation of that oppression by the branding of that group as inferior (racism)
3. Use of space to control resistance (the advent of the hard ghetto)
4. Resistance to oppression (the solidarity of the ghetto)
5. Resistance in the ghetto (the shift from solidarity to explosion)
6. Domination of the group through force in the hard ghetto (oppression)
7. Shifting demands for the use of space for gentrification (dilution)
8. Development of alternative methods of control (dispersion, de-spatialization)
9. Survival of the weak ghetto (racism, marketization)

I then look at the ghetto as it exists today, highlight the shifting role of space, and examine what has happened to the populations of the ghetto as its nature and spatial structure have changed.

The Exploitation of a Particular Population Group

The history of the ghetto starts, of course, with the exploitation of one group by another: of black slaves by white slave-owners. An extensive literature details the benefits of such discrimination to dominant groups and is not recapitulated here. The themes run from the obvious exploitation of slaves to the exploitation in the labor market of groups kept from resources of education and wealth by economic discrimination; to the divisions produced among those who generally resist exploitation in the workplace; to the profit made from limited access to housing, health care, and other necessities of everyday life. Segregation reinforces this exploitation, and is part of the discrimination underlying it, through exclusion of the targeted group from public benefits, economic isolation, stigmatization, division in the workplace, and so on. And ghettoization, to the extent that it creates communities of cheap and inferior housing quality and infrastructure, reduces the costs of the maintenance of a workforce ("the social reproduction of labor"), thus contributing significantly and directly to profit by making lower wages possible and securing a cheap reservoir of un-employed but employable labor available when needed.

Exploitation, in any of these forms, requires legitimation. Racism pro-vides it.

The Legitimation of Oppression by the Branding of a Group as Inferior: Racism

Racism and prejudice are essential parts of the constitution of the ghetto, both in our definition and, I believe, as the term has historically generally been used. This was true of the Jewish ghettos of the Middle Ages, it is true of certain im-migrant ghettos in Western Europe (Turkish workers in Germany, Indonesians in the Netherlands, Pakistanis in Britain), and it is certainly central for African Americans in the United States. This relational aspect of the ghetto is harder to capture empirically than are quantitative demographic definitions, such as that given by Douglas Massey and Nancy Denton: "A ghetto is a set of neigh-borhoods that are exclusively inhabited by members of one group, within which virtually all members of that group live."[13]

That definition picks up one key component of every ghetto: It is a spa-tially separate area. The definition has difficulties, but most importantly, it ignores the quality of the relationship between the members of that group and the rest of the city.[14] The relationship of ascribed inferiority applies both to the residents of the ghetto and to the space they occupy. The term *ghetto* is often equated, however, in the media and in popular discourse, with the place of residence of a resident minority. Thus, we see references to a ghetto of movie stars in Beverly Hills or of the elderly in retirement communities; those residing within Washington's Beltway could be considered a ghetto, or the rich in Scars-dale. But such usage distorts what the word could usefully mean. It is the im-putation of inferiority—and specifically racism—that distinguishes the ghetto with which we are here concerned from other uses of the term.

Exploitation, then, in any of its forms, even if legitimated for the dominant society, provokes resistance by those being exploited. If a group is systematically oppressed and exploited, we may expect resistance, and the spatialized con-finement of the oppressed and exploited group is one way in which that re-sistance may be contained.

The Use of Space to Control Resistance: The Advent of the Hard Ghetto

The use of the ghetto—spatial confinement in a defined area in which social control may be readily exercised—is one way of containing such resistance. It was developed in the United States primarily after the end of slavery rather than during it. (Slave quarters may be considered a form of ghetto, but their spatial relationship to the outside was essentially different from that of the succeeding ghetto, and they were primarily rural.) Urban ghettos were not a significant factor even in most southern towns before the Civil War and the Emancipation Proclamation; they increased in size and number, in both the South and the North, as other forms of legal and physical control weakened.[15]

Resistance to Oppression: The Solidarity of the Ghetto

Paradoxically, the spatializing of the ghetto, while it enhanced control by those outside, also strengthened resistance by those on the inside. For ghettos are not spaces suffering from disorganization and lacking "social capital"—a bastard phrase[16]—or without cohesion, leadership, and so on.

The evidence is by now clear. Simply in order to survive, ghetto residents have developed complex patterns of mutual support that are critical to life and astounding in their complexity.[17] Such cohesion, as well as the resistance it supports, has two origins: the positive cultural history of the group being subordinated, and the resistance by members of that group to the subordination to which they are subject. This dual-rooted solidarity is parallel to the solidarity that underlies enclave formation, and thus every ghetto has aspects of an enclave as well. The ghetto and the enclave are in tension with each other, and their coexistence is almost inevitable. Indeed, high levels of ghettoization and strong solidarity may well accompany each other. Thus, Henry Louis Gates Jr., for instance, writes:

> The Harlem Renaissance . . . occurred precisely as Harlem was turning into the great American slum. The death rate was 42 percent higher than in other parts of the city. . . . Four times as many people died from tuberculosis as in the white population. The unemployment rate . . . was 50 percent. [Even so,] James Weldon Johnson . . . wrote *Black Manhattan* to create the fiction of Harlem as a model of civility and black bourgeois respectability, rather than

as an example of the most heinous effects of urban economic exploitation and residential segregation . . . the valorization of black rhythm, spontaneity, laughter, sensuality . . . contrasted starkly with Harlem's squalor, environmental or structural limitations upon individual choices such as those finally depicted in Wright's *Native Son* (1940).[18]

It is not surprising that segregation encounters resistance, that residents of a ghetto band together in solidarity to counteract the subordination to which they are being subjected, and that cultural resources are tied into such resistance.[19] The forms taken by that resistance, however, are very much subject to the historical context in which ghetto residents find themselves. In the immediate post–World War II period, the growing civil rights movement focused on the elimination of the constrictions of the ghetto and on the opening of the suburbs to their residents. But that movement in the urban centers, however successful legally, proceeded slowly and was largely thwarted by what is here called the marketization of the ghetto: the real estate industry's foot-dragging, buttressed by reliance on the racism it saw among buyers in the market.

Resistance in the Ghetto: From Solidarity to Explosion

The period after World War II was a period of heightened aspirations for blacks, stemming in part from the ideological and political nature of the fight against fascism and the need for workers in the munitions industries and in the army. Legal channels for resistance seemed to be open: legislation was passed, commissions were appointed, and supportive groups were formed.[20] The slow pace of reform and perhaps the relative prosperity led to the civil rights movement, which used militancy to accelerate legal redress. But change was tortuously slow, and militancy erupted into riots and revolts on the streets of the most prominent ghettos in the United States. The urban unrest in the ghettos in the 1970s—prominently in Newark, in Watts in Los Angeles, and then in cities throughout the country—was met with new efforts at control.[21]

A sense of the post-riot setting is provided in Alex Cockburn's summary:

Forty years ago the topic of slums was a lot hotter in the United States than it is now. The Cold War was on, and Soviet propaganda could make hay with

America's urban riots in the mid-1960s. The Black Panthers organized armed patrols, set up free schoolchildren's breakfast programmes and formed alliances with such urban gangs as Chicago's Blackstone Rangers. American radicals started organizing in the ghettos. In 1966 Malcolm X—the man who really frightened America's ruling orders—was assassinated, perhaps with police connivance, in New York. Amid the uprisings that followed Martin Luther King's murder on April 4, 1968 the young Panther leader Bobby Hutton was gunned down by Oakland cops, having surrendered after a police onslaught on the house he was living in. In December of the following year the Chicago cops, with FBI assistance, murdered Panther leader Fred Hampton in his bed. It was open season on the Black Panthers, many of whom were killed. Spiro Agnew, Nixon's vice president, advised a sense of distance from urban policy: "If you've seen one city slum you've seen them all," he nonchalantly declared.[22]

Those using these tactics saw the control of the ghetto as a matter of maintaining "law and order," which they saw as threatened in the ghetto; reimposition of law and order was required by any means necessary, including physical force. Force was imposed in part under color of laws that did not explicitly speak of the ghetto but that clearly had a heavily disproportionate effect on the ghetto—everything from the Rockefeller drug laws to the extreme concentration of arrests, incarcerations, and justice system supervision of residents of the ghetto.[23] But these efforts ran into significant roadblocks, both because of failing effectiveness and, perhaps even more so, because of the strong reaction of the civil rights movement and the ghetto residents themselves. The reactions to Rodney King's manhandling by the police in Los Angeles may be the best symbolic evidence of that failure.

CURRENT PATTERNS OF CONTROL: DE-SPATIALIZATION AND DILUTION[24]

The Latest Stage: Shifting Patterns of Policy and Reaction

The failures of control through hardening of the ghetto led to the latest stage in efforts at control of the ghetto. These efforts highlighted the importance of two policies that had their origins many years earlier after the end of World War II, gaining in strength after 1965 and coalescing in the aftermath of the Rodney King arrest in 1992: de-spatialization and dilution. This latest stage is not so much the beginning of something new as a significant shift in the emphasis of public policy and its spatial consequences. As the importance of dilution and de-spatialization increased, the policy of hardening the ghetto continued at a reduced level alongside them, not so much contradicting them as operating in a reduced and more sophisticated manner. Given a continuation of the trends of de-spatialization and dilution, ultimately the hard ghetto will become an anachronism, because it is coupled with other pressures for movement in the same direction, including gentrification and civil rights pressures for dispersion of the ghetto population and the development of other, marketized means of social control of the de-ghettoized population.[24]

Thus, three patterns developed side by side: (1) continued ghettolike control of the ghetto populations within the ghetto; (2) increased movement of ghetto populations from the ghetto to outside it, including the suburbs; and (3) dilution and "upgrading" of the spaces that constituted the ghetto.

The development of these patterns can be traced over time. The permanent concerns about controlling resistance to the exploitation and domination represented by the ghetto shifted dramatically after 1965 from a hard to a conciliatory approach: The Voting Rights Act of 1965 was a conciliatory effort to head off violent resistance, but the Watts riots of 1965 suggested it did not go far enough.[25] The Kerner Commission report,[26] issued by the bipartisan task force appointed by President Lyndon Johnson to investigate the "civil disorders" of that time, explicitly identified "growing concentrations of impoverished Negroes in our major cities, creating a growing crisis of deteriorating facilities and services and unmet human needs," as a key issue and resulted in programs of subsidized housing targeted at low-income residents, the Civil Rights Act of 1968, and the War on Poverty. But as the ghettos cooled down force was also used to put down disturbances, and with the Nixon administration the soft approach of the civil rights era gave way to increasing neglect and then repression. Howard Zinn asks (after a passage describing the killing of Black Panther leader Fred Hampton in Chicago in 1969), "Was the government turning to murder and terror because the concessions . . . were not working?"[27]

Certainly the government was turning to more forcible measures to control the ghettos. Zinn partially answers his own question:

> Was the black population—hemmed into the ghetto, divided by the growth of a middle class, decimated by poverty, attacked by the government, driven into conflict with whites—under control? Surely, in the mid-seventies, there was not great black movement under way. Yet, a new black consciousness had been born and was still alive.[28]

No one knew what was to be expected, so the governmental response was two-sided: repression on the one hand, concession on the other, the balance between them fluctuating somewhat with electoral results, economic conjunctures, and international events. *Repression* took many forms—from the official violence of the sheriff's department of Oakland, California, to the assassination of Black Panthers by federal officials in Chicago, to unofficial police brutality throughout the country, to much milder forms of the same in more "sophisticated" jurisdictions, such as racial profiling and punitive criminal legislation like the Rockefeller drug laws. *Concession*, like *repression*, is actually too broad a term to use for a time when policy was shifting as to which groups among those potentially active in resistance should be offered concessions and the kind of concessions that would be made to each. At the height of the War on Poverty, many groups took empowerment seriously and looked at the poorest and most militant as being among the appropriate beneficiaries of the program. They saw a shift of power in their direction as an appropriate goal. As time progressed, however, that approach, under the ideological onslaught of people like Daniel Patrick Moynihan, came to be considered a "misunderstanding," and finally it was sharply withdrawn.[29] The War on Poverty became a program that did not empower the poor but rather gave the middle range of the poor a step up the ladder into the middle class. Antipoverty policy reflected fluctuations not only in the form of repression but also in the extent and targeting of concessions. Under Reagan and the two Bushes, and indeed under Carter as well as Clinton, the concessions of the earlier decades that had dealt with the militants and might have strengthened their effectiveness were slowly eroded.

Empowerment zones, which may be analogized to the social city programs in some German cities and policies of "social inclusion" throughout the

European Union, were aimed at improving conditions in the ghetto, fostering entrepreneurship within its confines, and subsidizing job creation within it for its residents. Nevertheless, "the whole approach to economic development [represented by the empowerment zone legislation] is more likely softly to reinforce the ghetto than to break down its hard walls."[30]

The two most government-favored housing policies today are housing vouchers and the Low-Income Housing Tax Credit (LIHTC) program, both of which effectively reinforce segregation and represent a victory of marketization over dedicated affirmative public action. Housing vouchers support concentration in the ghetto because landlords in the private market inevitably use them only where they provide greater and steadier rental income than could otherwise be obtained—thus they are used largely if not exclusively in the ghetto. Tax credits contribute to marketization because the LIHTC statute gives preference to private developments in low-income neighborhoods— which are, of course, disproportionately minority.

Thus, there has been a steady if uneven movement from the idea of "empowering" ghetto residents and reducing the extent of their subordination, to the limited aim of assuaging the worst features of the ghettos, supporting some dilution of their sharp and potentially dangerous concentrations of minority households while creating smaller concentrations in the suburbs and leaving the weakened ghetto alone.[31] Meanwhile, police repression has continued, both at a more sophisticated and carefully targeted level within the ghetto and at an increasing pace in society as a whole.

Loïc Wacquant, in *Urban Outcasts*, reaffirmed his judgments from earlier papers as to the increasing scope of the hard ghetto.[32] Yet quantitatively, ghettoization, to the extent it is a spatial concept, is not increasing—nor is the spatial concentration of the very poor increasing. Using the standard of the population living in places (census tracts) in which more than 40 percent of the residents are below the poverty level ("high-poverty places"), that figure declined from 8,545,000 in 1990 to 7,033,000 in 2000, and it may be continuing to decline.[33] Nor is the concentration as heavily found in central cities as it once was: The suburban poor outnumbered the central-city poor by 1 million by 2000, and the percentage of the poor living in high-poverty areas declined from 30 percent in 1990 to 19 percent in 2000. *Ghetto* and *high-poverty area* are, of course, not synonymous terms, but there is surely substantial overlap between them. In Chicago, where Wacquant did much work in the early 1990s, poverty became steadily more concentrated from 1980 (nine community areas) to 1990 (eleven areas); by 2000, however, it had fallen to six areas. In 1990 six areas had poverty rates over 50 percent; in 2000 only one did. The title of the study reporting these results is "The Deconcentration of Poverty in Chicago: 1990–2000."[34] Perhaps Wacquant will examine more recent developments and consider how they might fit into his overall framework. In the last chapter, he does quote a 2004 figure, but only to downplay its significance: "In 1994, the Census Bureau reported that the American poverty rate had risen to a ten-year high of 15.1 percent," despite robust economic expansion. But then he notes in parentheses, "(in 2004, there [was] still . . . a poverty rate of 13 percent)."[35] Quite a drop, but taken as evidence of no change.

Anecdotal evidence supports a finding of change, at least in New York City:

> Bronx Borough President Adolfo Carrion Jr. released his latest development report today. The report shows that the Bronx continues to experience unprecedented economic growth. Just last month alone over 150 million dollars was invested in residential, institutional and commercial development throughout the borough and 75 new addresses were issued in the Bronx. "Through smart investments we have changed the story of [the] Bronx," stated Borough President Adolfo Carrion. "These developments represent jobs and homeownership opportunities for the Bronx. I have always said that the best social program is a job and that homeownership builds stronger communities."

New York City is not, of course, representative of all cities, but the point here is to emphasize a trend and pattern of change, not to suggest a wholesale rupture with the past.

So the spatial aspect of the ghetto has changed; racialized oppression continues to exist, but in spatially more differentiated form.[36] Has resistance, and the need for control, changed? Wacquant writes, in a chapter based on a paper from 1993:

> The question facing First World countries at the threshold of the new millennium is whether their polities have the capacity to prevent the further contraction and fragmentation of the sphere of citizenship fuelled by the desocialization of labour. . . . Failing which, we may witness not only continued

urban disorder, collective violence and ethnoracial conflict (actual or imagined) at the heart of the advanced societies, but a protracted process of societal fission and a capillary ramification of inequalities and insecurities at the bottom of the order of classes and places.[37]

He may be right about inequalities and insecurities, but I do not believe that the evidence supports "continued urban disorder" or "collective violence," or even continued ethnoracial conflict, at least not in the African American community. And in any event, the dominant elements in government and the business community have not acted as if they were worried about handling urban disorder or collective violence—certainly not in the Bush years.

Further, the self-confidence of those dominant elements and of the two Bush administrations and their supporters seems to have increased since 1992, as the relations of power that keep them in their positions have changed. There has been a steady decline in labor union membership, and the liberal wing of the Democratic Party is barely functional. Issues of immigration reform have been made very divisive, and the "War on Terror" has muted criticism of basic policy.[38] An arrogance in which stupidity plays no small role pervades the highest levels of governance. Thus, even if a threat of disorder continued to exist, those self-confidently in power might feel readily able to handle it with no need to adopt directly repressive measures.

Against the background of the events outlined here, which changed significantly the extent of the concern of dominant groups about resistance from the ghetto, a set of new developments in the treatment of the ghetto has emerged. These developments can be characterized as aimed at neutralizing the ghetto. In the following discussion, it is not suggested that they were a deliberately coordinated set of policies that some dominant interests thought out and put in place to serve their purposes. They are seen rather as a set of independent developments that are mutually reinforcing, that are separately supported by very similar and often identical groups, including government at all levels, and that in practice go in a single direction—neutralizing the ghetto.[39]

The Redundancy of the Hard Ghetto: De-spatialization

In 1996 Loïc Wacquant found evidence that the Chicago ghetto was likely to explode.[40] Even earlier, in the 1960s, the Kerner Commission had seen a nation divided and unequal, in which riots were an understandable consequence of inequality and division. Wacquant saw that constellation of factors continuing into the 1990s. But today evidence suggests a change: Fear of protest and riots has abated and can no longer be used to support arguments for the type of harsh controls and police repression of the Nixon and Giuliani eras. The spatialization of control that takes place in a hard ghetto is no longer a priority.

While no one could have known it in advance, what has become clear over the years is the simple fact that, since the 1992 Rodney King riots, there has not been a major disturbance in any U.S. city. With this tapering off of fears of ghetto uprisings, a new phase in the development of the space of the ghetto in the United States may be taking place. Wacquant has trenchantly characterized the new social order as "the penal state" and written of the prison as a "surrogate ghetto."[41] The evidence recounted by Wacquant and others of the astonishingly high rate of incarceration in the United States and the broad sweep of control exercised by the criminal justice system is convincing.

Violent disorder of the type that is widely expected to accompany ghetto riots and that represents the form of resistance most feared by dominant groups is likely to involve disproportionately those from groups with prior strained relations with the police. Today members of those groups are vastly overrepresented in the prison population: incarceration, which has become a major phenomenon in the ghettos, has always been a measure of social control, but now occurs on an unprecedented scale:

> African Americans and Latinos comprise about half the population of the city, but account for 91 percent of those in jail. In 2006, half of all police stops were of African Americans, 29 percent were of Latinos and 11 percent were of whites. The report says that this occurred despite the fact that "white suspects were 70 percent more likely than black suspects to have a weapon."[42]

The rates of incarceration in the United States are so high that they undoubtedly affect the nature of collective responses—of resistance—in the ghetto.

It is intriguing to compare what is happening within the ghetto in the United States to how anti-immigrant practices are playing out in some countries in Europe.

The spatial distantiation of immigrants the support of which helped leaders like Sarkozy to get elected is increasingly at odds with economic realities. . . . Construction and cleaning companies say that they cannot get enough legal workers to fill the available jobs. The employers' federation of the restaurant and hotel business has called for the legalization of 50,000 workers in that field alone. . . . Every time Caussade [owner of a famous café] advertises a job in the paper, only Africans and Sri Lankans respond. . . . "Even French high school dropouts don't want the jobs we offer," [said the head of human resources of . . . a company in Marseille that provides cleaning services]. Stephane Vallet of Bouygues, the construction company, concurred.[43]

The threat of deportation is simply no longer needed to keep Algerians and Sri Lankans in line, and the reality of deportation is affirmatively harmful to the profit-driven economy by rendering unavailable a labor pool willing to work for low wages and under poor conditions. The parallel to the controversy about illegal immigration in the United States is clear. Less obvious, but I believe equally true, is the parallel to ghettoization in the United States. As the threat of riots has receded and African Americans have become perceived as needed in the labor pool to fill both the lowest-wage jobs and, increasingly, lower-middle-wage jobs, confining this desirable labor force in ghettos becomes counterproductive. The scapegoating of a minority group has shifted to "illegal" immigrant workers. Moreover, ghettoization gets in the way of other policies desired by those in power, specifically gentrification, as discussed later in this chapter. The ghetto has been neutralized as a threat, if not made entirely redundant. The penal system has permitted the replacement of the hard ghetto by the weak ghetto—a de-spatialization of the control function of the ghetto.

Margit Mayer and others have traced this phenomenon in the "Social City" policies of Germany and the European Union.[44]

Dilution of the Ghetto: Shifting Demands for the Use of Space

Thus, the space occupied by the historic ghetto in the United States has changed; its control function has been attenuated and its racial and ethnic characteristics modified. These changes have combined to alter the space of the ghetto, in a complex process, from its hard form to its weaker form. There have also been changes in those who reside in the ghetto: To the members of what are often referred to here as "ghetto populations"—in whom class and race, poverty and ethnicity, are sharply combined—have been added newcomers, gentrifiers, who may be either African American or white.

The demographic aspect of this process of dilution is statistically complex. It comprises changes in patterns such as:

1. Increases in the number and proportion of the classic ghetto populations (defined by race/ethnicity and class/income) moving out of the ghetto (de-spatialization)
2. A decline in the proportion of the classic ghetto populations residing within the ghetto
3. An increase in the number and proportion of non-ghetto populations residing in the ghetto
4. Movement in and out of the ghetto of "pioneers"—such as students, artists, and immigrants
5. Changes in the spatial boundaries of the ghetto and the areas of residence outside the ghetto occupied by ghetto populations and non-ghetto populations.

Because the results of the 2010 census are just being released as this is written, it would be foolhardy to try to pin down these patterns in detail here; excellent work is being done, however, that will be very enlightening when completed.[45] That work may, of course, disprove or require modification of the hypotheses put forward here, but I believe that in broad terms these patterns will remain roughly the same as they have been since about 1992. The current economic crisis will also have consequences for these patterns, and short-term and long-term trends will be hard to dissociate. We need to wait and see.

The physical characteristics of the ghetto are changing with the movement from the hard to the weak ghetto. Abandonment was an early step in the process.[46] Slum clearance and redevelopment preceded abandonment in the restructuring of space in the cities, and the development of megaprojects in the market with public assistance is the latest large-scale orchestration of spatial change in which ghetto residents are evicted and ghettos diluted.

The function of controlling the ghetto population has been retained in the weak ghetto, but by other, less spatially circumscribed means. One is the set of welfare and employment programs linked to the welfare-to-work policies. The downward trend began with the welfare reforms and welfare-to-work legislation of 1996 and the parallel implementation of new local welfare policies by the Giuliani administration in New York City and local governments in other cities, and it continued during a period of growth in local employment. The city's welfare initiatives included intensive screening of new applicants, work requirements, and the use of job placement firms to aggressively push recipients into the paid workforce. These local initiatives were reinforced by reforms of state and federal welfare policies. The combined effect of these policy changes and local job growth in New York was a 60 percent reduction in the city's public assistance caseload between 1995 and 2001.[47] The net effect is to use the pressure of poverty to enforce compliance with principles of order, "good" citizenship, and hard work and subordination to market principles as guides in everyday life.[48]

Gentrification needs to be singled out as a key contributing factor, one whose long-term importance is fairly well established.[49] The ongoing gentrification of portions of Harlem has two consequences. First, as the process of displacement and replacement advances, poorer residents disappear and are replaced by middle- and upper-income people who, though largely of the same color, are of quite different class. Thus, the number of poorer residents is reduced. Second, the in-movement of the gentrifiers—most of whom in Harlem are lawyers, stock brokers, and other professionals—adds a new element to the population mix, changing the identification of Harlem from poor black ghetto to middle- to upper-class black enclave. Over time that may be the most profound change of all: As one group is excluded, a different group is included.[50]

The structural changes that account for gentrification have been extensively studied.[51] A key work is by Neil Smith, who builds on substantial earlier work, both his own and that of others, to consider the direct link between gentrification and ghettoization, abandonment, and subsequently globalization.[52] Not all historical ghettos are located in places desired by gentrifiers; thus, the impact of gentrification on ghetto impairment is not uniform. The more global the city, generally, the greater the pressures of gentrification. Where it exists, gentrification is of major concern to residents. More importantly, gentrification is intimately connected with broader social and economic changes, such as the shift from manufacturing to service employment, the globalization of control functions, the growing importance of financial activities, and the polarization along income, occupational, educational, and wealth lines. These changes are ongoing and international, so that the pressures of gentrification on the ghetto are also going to be ongoing and supra-local in origin.

The impact of gentrification on the ghettos where it takes place is two-sided. On the one hand, it is welcomed by certain groups: The higher the incomes of residents, and the more professional and managerial their occupations, the more welcome it is.[53] The weakening of the ghetto is self-reinforcing. For the earlier resident ghetto population, on the other hand, gentrification means displacement.[54] In places where globalization, high technology, and financialization are well advanced, and where a ghetto, with a stock of readily convertible housing, is located within easy access to the central business district, gentrification has been a major factor and a key component in dilution of the ghetto. In some places—for instance, where empowerment zone programs have been implemented—public policies may contribute both to upgrading (thus diluting) and to displacement (thus de-spacialization). De-ghettoization and dilution reinforce each other in the changes they produce in the ghetto.

The portrayal of the ghetto as an "undiscovered market," in the enthusiastically received phrase of Michael Porter, represents a further step toward changing the nature of the ghetto, one that would make life in the ghetto a tributary serving the mainstream of economic activity in the city.[55] The unspoken but firm assumption is that ghetto residents should behave just like all other city residents, peacefully subordinating themselves to the market and rejecting the idea that they are in any way being differently treated from others or that collective action would advance their interests better than increased market presence. When an "Initiative for a Competitive Inner City" proclaims a $122 billion retail market in U.S. inner cities and forms an "Inner City Economic Forum" for the "revitalization of America's inner cities to create jobs, income and wealth for inner city residents,"[56] it is clear that "'inner city' [is] a catch phrase for 'ghetto.'"[57] In this case, improvement of the ghetto is the goal—not dispersion, not opening opportunities outside the ghetto, not opening opportunities in the broader economy for ghetto residents, but rather sustaining the ghetto as ghetto and making it more palatable for its residents—soft segregation.

The push for expanding homeownership has a similar effect on the residents of the weak ghetto and certainly on its former residents now in the dispersed or de-spatialized ghettos of the suburbs. The subprime mortgage market has attracted much attention recently, but one aspect needs emphasis here. It has long been official public policy, going back to the days of Herbert Hoover's Commission on Home Ownership, to press homeownership on lower-income households. The argument has been that owning a home makes a person responsible, law-abiding, productive, and well behaved. In more recent years, federal programs have specifically extended support for low-down-payment mortgages to households of limited income and restricted credit, including options for making initially low payments that rise as, presumably, the household's income rises. Ghetto residents are an obvious focus of such policies. As a recent account phrases it: "Lenders have targeted the most vulnerable—black and Latino borrowers have been twice as likely to receive subprime loans as whites; female homeowners, thirty percent more likely than male; black women, five times more likely than white men."[58]

The residents of Harlem are clearly affected by these policies.[59] Some may be induced to purchase a home within Harlem, while others may be encouraged to move out. No good geographically focused studies are yet available to document the patterns, but the changes these policies produce are likely to alter permanently the relationship of more middle-income Harlem residents to their community.

The mild push for tourism development in Harlem further helps in diluting the ghetto. Harlem has become a stop for tourist buses in New York City and is being promoted as a tourist destination for its unique "cultural characteristics."[60] Small businesses, boutiques selling African-style clothing, soul food restaurants, arts production capitalizing on Harlem's artistic legacy—all are geared toward bringing the community into the New York City scene, but at a limited level. Where the push goes further, supporting the construction of a modern high-rise hotel and condominiums at the corner of 125th Street and Park Avenue, the result is likely to provide low-level employment in the low-paid "hospitality industry" to some Harlem residents, but to displace others through secondary displacement caused by the increase in property values in the neighborhood. The ghetto is to become less and less ghettolike, even though selected aspects of its solidaristic history, purged of any hint of oppression or exploitation, are held out as acceptable and even noteworthy parts of the city.

Finally, a well-known political and social process affects the nature of the weak ghetto: co-optation. Co-optation of militant leadership and organizations is nothing new. In the years of the War on Poverty, it was a topic of constant discussion: Was the shift of many organizations from militant advocacy to efficient service provision a result of funding by those who might be the targets of critical advocacy? Was the shift a form of selling out? Indeed, is there not a tension for an individual between working for collective advancement and taking opportunities for individual advancement—especially when the latter is ceaselessly touted as stemming from the entrepreneurship that propels individuals up the ladder of achievement?

In a period when the possibility of collective advancement and radical social change appears remote and funding for such efforts, certainly from neoliberal governments, is drying up, the lure of individual action for individual betterment is strong, and it is being substantially fostered by limited public programs. The "empowerment" of empowerment zones, for instance, means simply successful private business activity. Private firms and charities largely support the most established minority group organizations. In Chicago, for instance, Wal-Mart is making a $1 million grant to the Congressional Black Caucus Foundation, a $5 million grant to the National Urban League, and a $1.5 million grant to the United Negro College Fund.[61]

Thus, the pull is strong and growing stronger for the most ambitious and entrepreneurial of the residents of the ghetto to improve themselves and move out, or perhaps switch sides in the gentrification debate within the community.

The Survival of the Weak Ghetto: Marketization

Underlying the changes within the weak ghetto are two forces: the state and the market. We have mentioned policies such as the empowerment zone programs that build on the traditions of the War on Poverty, community development policies, and the kind of public policies for inclusion that are more developed in Europe and are ably described by Margit Mayer.[62] More important, certainly in the United States, is the operation of the market. Real estate price changes and the operations of the speculative housing market inevitably stratify city residents based on social position, on income and wealth, and, heavily, on racial attitudes. The widespread survival of racial prejudice and the resulting discrimination, although perhaps declining and perhaps moderated by some elements of public policy, strongly influences who lives where and fundamentally controls the opportunities of ghetto residents.

> In rental markets [in New York City, testers of discrimination showed that] whites were consistently favored over blacks in 21.6% of tests, while non-Hispanic whites were consistently favored over Hispanics in 25.7% of tests. In sales, whites were consistently favored over blacks in 17.0% of tests; and non-Hispanic whites were consistently favored over Hispanics in 19.7% of tests.[63]

The operation of racism may be less visible today because it is so closely tied to the operation of "normal" market forces. For instance, it underlies the construction of gated communities—high-income residential towers overwhelmingly white-occupied, with security protecting entry, citadels whose residents never need to be in contact with the everyday life of the city where they live and work, in which those of a different color are already a majority.

The survival of the weak ghetto can be attributed in large part to this marketization of the allocation of housing.

CONCLUSION

To what extent are there African American ghettos today in the United States?

Sharon Zukin has recently argued, I think correctly, that Harlem as a traditional hard ghetto is disappearing.[64] This is Harlem as a ghetto generically spatially defined, Harlem as regarded by the dominant outside world. It is in fact true of the direction in which Harlem as hard ghetto is rapidly moving. Has the attenuation of the Harlem hard ghetto changed the living conditions of most African Americans in New York City? There is substantial evidence that the answer is no.[65] Despite the changes in Harlem and other changes summarized in this chapter, things have not improved for ghetto residents.[66] The ghetto may have been de-spatialized, its former space de-ghettoized and marketized, but in the words of an early student, the problems once concentrated there have just been moved around, not solved.

Notes

1. World Social Forum, "Charter of Principles," June 8, 2002, paragraph 11, available at: http://www.forumsocialmundial.org.br/main.php?id_menu=4&cd_language=2.

2. There is an extensive discussion in academic circles about the role of space, with some seeing spatial justice as the critical element in social justice (for example, Ed Soja, *Seeking Spatial Justice* [Minneapolis: University of Minnesota Press, 2010]), and others seeing it as an essential constitution of social justice but exploring how it is created and enforced by broader mechanisms of urbanization (Henri Lefebvre, *The Urban Revolution*, foreword by Neil Smith, translated by Robert Bononno [1970; reprint, Minneapolis: University of Minnesota Press, 2003]) and capitalism (David Harvey, *Social Justice and the City* [Baltimore: Johns Hopkins University Press, 1973]). I am more inclined to the latter view and have preliminarily stated my position in "Spatial Justice: Derivative but Causal of Social Injustice" ("La Justice spatiale: À la fois résultante et cause de l'injustice sociale," translated into French by Sonia Lehman-Frisch, *Espace et Justice* 1 [September 2009], available at: http://jssj.org/05.php#d), but going into the more theoretical discussion would be a distraction from the main points being made here.

3. Camilo José Vergara, *The New American Ghetto* (New Brunswick, N.J.: Rutgers University Press, 1995), for instance, traces a different form of the physical disappearance of the spaces that had been the ghetto.

4. Whether oppression is de-racialized as well is a matter not reviewed in this chapter. I suspect that, partially because of the trends described here, and even more because of immigration and the large-scale and deep oppression of immigrants, the relative oppression of African Americans has been moderated. A contrary logic would suggest that the more intense oppression of immigrants has intensified the oppression of African Americans as well, owing to competitive pressures in the labor market; studies indicate a real downward pressure on the wages of workers from the widespread use of immigrant labor (Krugman). But the comprehensive study that would permit a careful judgment of this issue as not yet been done, to my knowledge.

5. My definition of *ghetto* has been developed over a number of years and could undoubtedly be refined further. Its most recent full incarnation appears in Peter Marcuse, "Enclaves Yes, Ghettos No," in *Desegregating the City*, edited by David P. Varady (Albany: State University of New York Press, 2005), and most recently I have used it in "Putting Space in Its Place: Reassessing the Spatiality of the Ghetto and Advanced Marginality," *City* 11, no. 3 (December 2007): 378–383. This issue of *City* also discusses the work of Loïc Wacquant and has other relevant contributions. *Ghetto* has been even further defined in discussions on the CUSS listserv, many of the contributions to which I found helpful for the formulation of the definitions in this chapter.

6. I must make a personal confession: I have just seen the documentary *Shoah*, considered by many the greatest documentary film ever made. Its depiction of life and death in the Jewish ghetto of Warsaw between 1940 and 1943 is indelible, and only with difficulty can one consider it in abstract terms. The powerful book whose details on that ghetto are used in the film is Jan Karski, *Story of a Secret State* (Boston: Houghton Mifflin, 1944).

7. Later in the chapter I discuss the parallels to the use of anti-immigration patterns and legislation as a nonspatial but strikingly similar method of social control.

8. The term *enclave* has historically also been used to describe the areas in which imperial countries established their quarters in the colonies—for instance, an imperial British enclave

in Canton—and I tried to take this into account in "Enclaves Yes, Ghettos No," by distinguishing between enclaves of solidarity and enclaves of exclusion. Thus, gated communities are enclaves, much as Chinatowns and many other immigrant communities are enclaves, but of quite a different sort from exclusionary or imperial enclaves. I would welcome suggestions of alternative terms that capture this distinction. The colonial relationship might lead to the interesting conception of a native population, although a majority of the population, being ghettoized because of its exclusion from the imperial enclave.

9. Ghetto formation is not an openly acknowledged or explicit policy in any country today, as it was in the Jewish ghettos of the Middle Ages and in South Africa under apartheid. Legally speaking, one is held to "intend" the foreseeable consequences of one's acts, and in this sense large-lot zoning, for example, would be considered intentional ghetto formation. But in everyday usage, individuals supporting large-lot zoning may vigorously deny having any intent to assist in ghetto formation, and politically it seems to me more useful not to push the point of intent and instead to go along with the idea that an unintended but inevitable consequence of large-lot zoning is that it supports ghetto formation and to argue against it on that ground.

10. The sometimes contentious discussion on the ISA Community & Urban Sociology Section (CUSS) listserv by and large accepts such a definition in practice.

11. The best account I know of that focuses on the major developments essential to the history of the ghetto in the United States is Howard Zinn, *A People's History of the United States, 1492–Present* (1980; reprint, New York: Harper Perennial Modern Classics, 1980), to which I refer the reader for background on the history of the ghetto in the United States. For an excellent history of the use of the term internationally, see Anthony W. Schuman, "Ghetto: A Word and Its Usage Through the Twentieth Century," available at: http://74.125.155.132/scholar?q=cache:ZE6_448OnqYJ:scholar.google.com/+tony+schuman+ghetto&hl=en&as_sdt=0,33.

12. For my own earlier work along these lines, see Peter Marcuse, "The Enclave, the Citadel, and the Ghetto: What Has Changed in the Post-Fordist U.S. City," *Urban Affairs Review* 33, no. 2 (November 1997): 228–264, and "Ghetto," in *Encyclopedia of Community*, vol. 2, edited by Karen Christensen and I. David Levinson (Thousand Oaks, Calif.: Sage Publications, 2003), pp. 547–551, with further references.

13. Douglas S. Massey and Nancy A. Denton, *American Apartheid: Segregation and the Making of the Underclass* (Cambridge, Mass.: Harvard University Press, 1993), p. 1819. I cite Massey and Denton somewhat unfairly, for their discussion of the ghetto and its formation is extraordinarily valuable and much more sophisticated than the quote suggests. Presumably "set of neighborhoods" might mean "set of ghettos," and the unit that contains "all members of that group" is ambiguous, but in application these points could be clarified.

14. *Neighborhood* remains undefined in Massey and Denton's formulation. The problem is important not only for purposes of measurement—changing the scale of the unit, the neighborhood, substantially changes the results of the index of dissimilarity, for instance—but also substantively. Ronald van Kempen (personal communication with the author), for instance, raises the question of what to call a situation where Chinese make up only 10 percent of a given neighborhood, but all Chinese in the city live in that neighborhood. That certainly sounds like an exclusion of Chinese from all other neighborhoods, and I would be surprised if looking at "neighborhood" on a smaller scale did not reveal an area in which Chinese were the large majority.

15. The history is outlined in more detail in Peter Marcuse and Ronald van Kempen, *Of States and Cities: The Partitioning of Urban Space* (Oxford: Oxford University Press, 2002).

16. Margit Mayer, "Urban Social Movements in an Era of Globalisation," in *Urban Movements in a Globalising World*, edited by Pierre Hamel, Henri Lustiger-Thaler, and Margit Mayer (London: Routledge, 2000), pp. 141–156, and Margit Mayer, "The 'Right to the City' in the Context of Shifting Mottos of Urban Social Movements," *City* 13, nos. 2–3 (June–September 2009): 361–374.

17. The point is one of the "pernicious premises" addressed by Loïc Wacquant in "Advanced Marginality in the City: Notes on Its Nature and Policy Implications," notes for experts' meeting (Paris: OECD, March 1994), and supported by extensive empirical work by sociologists such as Katherine S. Newman, *No Shame in My Game: The Working Poor in the Inner City* (New York: Vintage Books, 1999) and Sudhir Vankatesh, *Gang Leader for a Day* (London: Penguin Press, 2008).

18. Henry Louis Gates Jr., "Harlem on Our Minds," *Critical Inquiry* 24, no. 1 (Autumn 1997): 11.

19. In an interesting wrinkle on the ghetto-enclave discussion, the criticism by Frances Fox Piven of efforts tending toward the dissolution of the ghetto in the name of opening the suburbs might be read as an argument that the enclave value of the spatial concentration of blacks outweighs the negatives of its ghetto character. See Frances F. Piven and Richard A. Cloward, "Desegregated Housing: Who Pays for the Reformer's Ideal?" *The New Republic*, December 17, 1966, p. 20.

20. Zinn, *A People's History,* pp. 449ff.

21. *Riot* is a disputed term. Many see the events of this period as forms of rebellion, and some have the same view of the unrest after the murder of Martin Luther King Jr. and the police beating of Rodney King in Los Angeles. They were certainly seen as such by many of the proponents of taking harsh repressive measures to control them. *Riot* is used here only for the convenience of using the more widely used term.

22. Alex Cockburn, "Rogue Projects," *New Left Review* 50 (March–April 2008): 139–144.

23. Laura Kurgan, in studio work, has dramatically demonstrated the spatial effects of criminal justice policies by mapping the locations in which arrests are made and the locations to which the incarcerated are returned on release.

24. I neglect in this discussion the growing importance of the growth of the Hispanic population and immigration from Latin America. To some extent Hispanics have been victimized in ways analogous to the victimization of African Americans in U.S. cities, partly through their confinement to the same or similar ghettos and partially through the penal system. New Hispanic concentrations with strong characteristics of enclaves as well as ghettos have been created. See Mike Davis's provocative discussion, *Magical Urbanism: Latinos Reinvent the U.S. City* (London: Verso, 2000). While there are significant differences between the positions of African Americans and Hispanics in regard to segregation and discrimination (see Massey and Denton, *American Apartheid*), I do not believe that issue affects the argument being made here.

25. Zinn, *A People's History*, pp. 458ff.

26. U.S. Kerner Commission, *Report of the National Advisory Commission on Civil Disorders* (Washington, D.C.: U.S. Government Printing Office, 1968).

27. Zinn, *A People's History*, p. 463.

28. Ibid., p. 467.

29. See Daniel Patrick Moynihan, "Maximum Feasible Misunderstanding," which plays on the War on Poverty's official "maximum feasible participation of the poor," and Frances Fox Piven's blistering response (see Piven and Cloward, "Desegregated Housing").

30. See Peter Marcuse, "Federal Urban Programs as Multicultural Planning: The Empowerment Zone Approach," in *Urban Planning in a Multicultural Society*, edited by Michael Burayidi (Westport, Conn.: Praeger, 2000), pp. 225–234, for a detailed analysis of the empowerment zone legislation and its history.

31. See the comprehensive analysis of the data on federal-assisted housing by Lance Freeman, *Siting Affordable Housing: Location and Neighborhood Trends of Low-Income Housing Tax Credit Developments in the 1990s* (Washington, D.C.: Brookings Institutions, Center on Urban and Metropolitan Policy, March 2004).

32. Loïc Wacquant, *Urban Outcasts* (Cambridge, U.K.: Polity Press, 2007). For a wide-ranging discussion of Wacquant's book, see *City* 11, no. 3 (December 2007), which includes, among other relevant articles, my own "Putting Space in Its Place."

33. George Galster, "Consequences from the Redistribution of Urban Poverty During the 1990s: A Cautionary Tale," *Economic Development Quarterly* 19 (2005): 119.

34. John F. McDonald, "The Deconcentration of Poverty in Chicago: 1990–2000," *Urban Studies* 41, no. 11 (October 2004): 2119–2120.

35. Wacquant, *Urban Outcasts*, p. 265.

36. "A study conducted by the Association of Community Organizations for Reform Now, or ACORN, which was released last year, found that 21 percent of property owners in New York City have properties available that meet the federally funded program's rental limits, but less than 50 percent of them actually accept tenants with Section 8." See Courtney Gross, "Stated Meeting: Housing Discrimination," *Gotham Gazette*, February 4, 2008, http://www.gotham gazette.com/article/searchlight/20080204/203/2423.

37. Wacquant, *Urban Outcasts*, p. 38.

38. See Stephen Graham, ed., *Cities, War, and Terrorism: Towards an Urban Geopolitics* (Malden, MA: Blackwell, 2004), and Peter Marcuse, "The Threat of Terrorism After 9/11: Security or Safety" (2006).

39. A detailed analysis of these "dominant forces"—what groups they belong to, how they are constituted, how they act, and to what extent they act together—would be extremely useful. Growth machine approaches, regime theory, traditional Marxist class analysis, power elite discussions, and analyses of "the state" are all relevant, and empirical work focused on the particular policies described here would be very rewarding.

40. Wacquant, *Urban Outcasts*.

41. Loïc Wacquant, *Punishing the Poor: The Neoliberal Government of Social Insecurity* (2004; reprint, Durham, N.C.: Duke University Press, 2009).

42. Urban Justice Center, Human Rights Project.

43. Kagtrin Bennhold, "Clandestine Workers Stand Up in French Protests," *International Herald Tribune*, May 9, 2008, pp. 1, 8.

44. See also my own discussion of those in "The Down Side Dangers in the Social City Program: Contradictory Potentials in German Social Policy," *German Politics and Society* 24, no. 4 (Winter 2006).

45. Specifically, the excellent work of John Logan and his group at Brown University and of Andrew Beveridge and his group at Queens College in New York.

46. See Peter Marcuse, "Gentrification, Abandonment, and Displacement: Connections, Causes, and Policy Responses in New York City," *Journal of Urban and Contemporary Law* 28 (1985), reprinted in revised form as "Gentrification, Abandonment, and Displacement: The Linkages in New York City," in *Gentrification of the City*, edited by Neil Smith and Peter Williams (Boston: Allen and Unwin, 1986), pp. 153–177, and in *The Gentrification Reader*, edited by Loretta Lees, Tom Slater, and Elvin Wyly (London: Routledge, 2010), pp. 333–348.

47. New York City Independent Budget Office, "Most Food Stamp Recipients No Longer Also Welfare Recipients" (fiscal brief), January 2008.

48. See the parallel critique of EU social integration policies in Mayer, "Urban Social Movements," and Mayer, "The 'Right to the City.'"

49. See the pioneering work of Neil Smith, Damaris Rose, Tmo Slater, Elvin Wyle, and Daniel J. Hammel, most of which, along with other key writings, are in Loretta Lees, Tom Slater, and Elvin Wyly, eds., *The Gentrification Reader* (Oxford: Routledge), 2010.

50. See the discussion of the difference between an enclave and a ghetto in Marcuse, "Enclaves Yes, Ghettos No."

51. My own summary assessment of that research appears in "Gentrification and Social Research—Its Uses (and Not)" (draft).

52. See Neil Smith and Peter Williams, eds., *Gentrification and the City*, which includes Peter Marcuse, "Gentrification, Abandonment, and Displacement"; Neil Smith, "New Globalism, New Urbanism: Gentrification as Global Urban Strategy," *Antipode* (2002): 427–450.

53. Many of those interviewed in Lance Freeman's study *There Goes the 'Hood: Views of Gentrification from the Ground Up* (Philadelphia: Temple University Press) reflect that point of view.

54. For a trenchant summary of some issues with that research, see Tom Slater, "The Eviction of Critical Perspectives from Gentrification Research," *International Journal of Urban and Regional Research,* 2006, 30(4), 737–757.

55. Michael E. Porter, "The Competitive Advantage of the Inner City," *Harvard Business Review* (May–June 1995).

56. "The Inner City Economic Forum is the country's most influential network focused on inner-city business development. . . . The Forum includes leaders from every discipline that contributes to business success, urban wealth creation, and job creation in the inner city." See ICIC's website: http://www.icic.org/urban-economic-development/inner-city-economic-forum/

57. Xavier de Souza Briggs, e-mail to the author, February 4, 2008.

58. Max Fraser, "Subprime Obama," *The Nation*, February 11, 2008, http://www.thenation.com/article/subprime-obama. Limited data on the spatiality of subprime foreclosures appears in Ford Fessenden and Gerri Hirshey, "The American Dream Foreclosed," *New York Times*, October 14, 2007.

59. On the strongly racialized nature of the problem, see Katrina Vanden Heuvel, "Where Did the Water Come In?" *The Nation*, February 20, 2008, http://www.thenation.com/blog/where -did-water-come.

60. See the detailed discussion in Susan S. Fainstein and Dennis Judd, eds., *The Tourist City* (New Haven: Yale University Press, 1999), and in Johannes Novy's doctoral dissertation, Columbia University, which includes a comparison with a parallel development in Kreusberg, Berlin.

61. James Thindwa, "Where Is the Dream? Black Progressives Face Challenges in Organizing," *Black Agenda Report*, February 12, 2008, http://www.blackagendareport.com/category/african

-america/black-radio. Thindwa goes so far as to speak of "the flight of many black leaders from the progressive agenda of the civil rights era" and points out that in 2006 one black pastor on Chicago's South Side "turned out 1,000 community members to rally against a City Council living wage bill." This is in the face of simultaneous "community disorganization and disengagement, high rates of incarceration, joblessness, school dropouts, student indebtedness and family disorganization."

62. Mayer, "Urban Social Movements"; Mayer, "The 'Right to the City.'"

63. Urban Justice Center, Human Rights Project, "Race Realities in New York City" (NYC CERD Shadow Report), December 2007, http://www.hrpujc.org/documents/RaceRealities_001.pdf, p. xxxv.

64. Sharon Zukin, *Naked City: The Death and Life of Authentic Urban Places.* New York: Oxford University Press, 2009.

65. See Urban Justice Center, Human Rights Project, "Race Realities in New York City."

66. On the one side are the improvements attributable to welfare-to-work programs. On the other side, however, staggering levels of incarceration (which Wacquant and many other critics have properly called attention to) and grossly disproportionate unemployment, health, housing quality, and education statistics can all be marshaled to illustrate the point.

CHAPTER 3

✦ ✦ ✦

Toward Knowing
the Iconic Ghetto
Elijah Anderson

For contemporary Americans, both black and white, the word *ghetto* has generally come to be associated with black people, powerfully referring to the areas in which blacks have become concentrated over time; in popular parlance it is "the black side of town," or "the 'hood." To blacks and whites alike, the meaning of the term is almost always pejorative. For outsiders, the ghetto is more often imagined than directly experienced—imagined as impoverished, chaotic, lawless, drug-infested, and ruled by violence. Over the years this imagined ghetto has become an icon, a kind of polestar by which all blacks are measured. Relations outside the ghetto between blacks and whites have become complicated by this salience (see Winant 2002). The history of racism in America, along with the ascription of "ghetto" to people with black skin, has worked to saddle blacks with a provisional status, and those who have become upwardly mobile often develop interactional strategies to escape this stigma—in the quest for decent treatment from those they encounter outside the ghetto, they manage their identities, often distancing themselves from the ghetto and its image, if not from its people (see Goffman 1963; Anderson 1999, 2011).

Note: This chapter is adapted from my essay "The Iconic Ghetto" (forthcoming, 2012) and builds on the ethnographic fieldwork and analysis previously published in *Streetwise* (1990), *Code of the Street* (Anderson 1999), *Against the Wall* (Anderson 2008), and *The Cosmopolitan Canopy* (Anderson 2011).

As outsiders, blacks and whites alike for the most part act with caution when they encounter strangers with black skin who seem to be from the ghetto. For the power of the ghetto image, embodied in the mark of color, makes all black people suspect, makes them people "with something to prove," as they venture forth in the wider society.

Long regarded as the home of black people treated as second-class citizens, the ghetto community has always provided support and social nurturance in a setting apart from the dominant society, with its own social system of checks and balances, its own distinctive social order. During the 1960s, when the civil rights movement culminated in rioting in urban black ghettos, these fearsome conflagrations seared in the minds of Americans the stereotypical image of the black ghetto as synonymous with disorder, trouble, and urban distress, if not rebellion (*Report of the National Advisory Commission*, 1968). This public image was powerfully underscored in 1992 when riots were ignited in Los Angeles by the acquittal of the police officers charged in the beating of Rodney King. And popular media and newspaper reports reinforced this image of the black ghetto as a place where disorder, senseless crime, and mayhem are common.

As the industrial base of the American economy changes from manufacturing to service and high technology in the context of an increasingly global economy, dislocation spreads and workers with limited marketable skills bear the brunt, facing persistent joblessness. Great numbers of people find it increasingly difficult to make effective adjustments to these changes.

Moreover, the relatively low-paying service jobs that do become available often fail to pay a living wage. The resulting poverty is best described as "structural." As the wider economy fails these citizens, they cope the best way they know, relying on whatever forms of capital they can summon. As they go about meeting the demands of getting a living, or simple survival, their coping strategies, legal and illegal, are often dramatized in the public media, which is inclined to put forth the most sensational and negative image of the community, effectively racializing their efforts to cope with the effects of economic distress.

In this context, when such scenarios are witnessed, discussed, and at times experienced by residents of the wider society themselves, empathy is limited. Not only do black ghetto residents face long-standing prejudice, but they develop a peculiar negative capital, or even the exacerbation of their individual stigma. As they compete with others who do not have the disadvantage of being associated with the ghetto, gainful employment becomes further out of their reach.

As omnipresent unflattering pictures of the ghetto abound, the actual workings of the inner-city economy—but particularly the media reports of it—make many residents of the wider society both curious and fearful of "dangerous" black people. This chapter explores the actual workings of the ghetto economy that contribute to this public image that so powerfully fuels stereotypes and prejudice about the present-day black ghetto.

THE WORKINGS OF THE GHETTO ECONOMY

The inner-city economy at "ground zero" of the ghetto rests essentially on three prongs: (1) low-wage, casualized jobs that offer little continuity of employment and few if any benefits; (2) welfare payments, including Temporary Assistance for Needy Families (TANF), food stamps, and other government transfer programs; and (3) the informal economy, which encompasses (a) legal activities carried on outside the marketplace, such as bartering labor and goods among friends and relatives, (b) semilegal activities, such as small businesses operated out of the home under the radar of regulation, and (c) illegal activities, such as drug dealing, prostitution, and street crime (see Anderson 1999).

Until recently, poor black people have relied for subsistence on all three ways of gaining income simultaneously (see Valentine 1980; Stack 1997). For example, welfare payments and earnings from employment not only supplement one another but provide capital and consumers for informal businesses, such as braiding hair, washing cars, or watching children. Within the community, money circulates. But if any one of the three elements of the ghetto economy is unproductive or fails to deliver financial resources, individuals are pressed to rely on the remaining two. In this context, members of families, households, and neighborhoods engage in nonmarket exchanges, borrowing and lending and, in the process, transferring and transforming these resources. As individuals obtain money from one or more of these sources, it further circulates throughout the inner-city community.

Everyday life in the inner-city ghetto is characterized by a great number of interpersonal transactions. But these transactions are carried on largely without the benefit of civil law. The civil law in the community has eroded as the police, the justice system, and the municipal authorities have lost credibility—not to mention that the poor tend not to sue others. Street justice has filled this void: To get along, one must often campaign for and develop a reservoir of "street credibility," or sometimes simply a "decent," respectable reputation. Very often, one gains leverage in the settling of interpersonal disputes through a willingness to place one's body in the gap or to engage in violence. The complex attitudes implicit in such scenarios, and the actions stemming from them, account for the historically high rates of violence and homocide presently characterizing so many isolated and impoverished black ghetto communities.

With the recent drastic reductions in welfare payments and the latest contractions in job opportunities for less educated workers, many inner-city residents increasingly rely on the informal economy: the more desperate people become, the more this economy becomes characterized by criminality and violence.

The reality of daily life for too many young black men in areas of concentrated poverty revolves around simply meeting the challenge of "staying alive." To avoid being killed as they navigate their way in public within the disfranchised community, they acquire personas with a street-toughened edge. This image becomes generalized, supporting the negative stereotype that has become a master status of the black man throughout white society (see Hughes 1944; Anderson 1990). Employers often reject young black male applicants on this basis, further undermining their prospects for legitimate employment (see Kirschenman and Neckermann 1991). Joblessness has deeper ramifications that feed on themselves, leading many young men to rationalize their involvement in the illegal, and often violent, underground economy (see Anderson 1980, 1999; Venkatesh 2009).

At the same time that elected leaders have made major cuts in the safety net, including welfare and other social supports, poor people must compete more fiercely for low-paying jobs and scarce resources with new immigrants to the United States as well as indirectly with poor working people around the globe. Thus, globalization has completed what suburbanization and deindustrialization began. When corporations send their manufacturing operations to other places that offer plentiful supplies of low-wage labor, now including China and India as well as the U.S. South and West, Mexico, and the Asian Pacific region, even more jobs leave Philadelphia and other industrial centers, creating a powerful employment vacuum. And inner-city black men have many competitors for the relatively few jobs that do exist. Black women may have an advantage in customer service positions; immigrants may get a foothold in key employment niches. For the truly disadvantaged, especially high school dropouts or men with criminal records, jobs are very difficult to obtain (Pager 2003a, 2003b, 2007).

The "end of welfare as we know it" coincided with a brief period of unusual expansion in the labor market, fueling the illusion that most people would be able to move from welfare to work, but the recessions that followed have deepened the effects of these structural shifts, and joblessness and distress are now widespread. Under these conditions, the informal underground economy expands to pick up the slack. For the most deperate, this third prong of the economy has become increasingly salient. More and more people engage in various irregular exchanges, as well as hustling, and, at times, outright street crime in order to survive.

The jobs held by people living in the inner city qualify them as the working poor. They toil as night watchmen, janitors, office cleaners, street sweepers, dishwashers, construction laborers, car washers, landscapers, fast-food workers, nurse's aides, office assistants, and domestic workers. Most of the available jobs pay little and provide few if any benefits.

These ghetto residents are often the first casualties in an economic downturn, such as the current "Great Recession," which encourages their participation in the informal economy. Despite the fluctuating national employment rate, conditions in many inner-city black neighborhoods generally fail to improve, with the impact felt most acutely by uneducated young black men (see Mincy 2006). And a great many people who do find employment remain impoverished even while working. In these circumstances, the "neighborhood effects" of concentrated poverty described by William Julius Wilson (1987) become ever more salient, exacerbating local problems.

In the inner-city ghetto community, money earned is quickly spent, and many people walk the streets almost broke. One common scenario begins with a man receiving a paycheck from a legitimate employer. Since, like many inner-city residents, he may not have a bank account, he likely cashes his paycheck at a "cash exchange," which charges exorbitant fees. Often he then goes from the cash exchange to the corner tavern for "a taste," a drink of liquor with friends. Typically, the man has accumulated debts to associates on the corner that he must repay when he sees them or answer to the lender. His debts have accumulated in part because his earnings are insufficient to cover all his expenses between paychecks; he must often borrow money from friends to make ends meet. Through the week before payday, men can be heard soliciting others to "let me hold ten [borrow ten dollars] until Friday." When payday comes, if the debt is not paid, the lender's sense of self-respect may be on the line; arguments and altercations leading to outright violence may ensue over the money owed. When a debtor is observed using the money for something other than repaying his debt, the lender can feel disrespected, or "dissed." He may then need to "set the debtor straight," to communicate his feelings of disrespect. And if the debt is not paid promptly enough, the lender is not likely to extend credit again. This informal economic system has built-in sanctions, including arguments that can lead to altercations and violence.

The third element of the ghetto economy, the irregular component, includes many irregular business ventures that fall close to the blurry line between legality and criminality. For example, a party host might sell dinner platters for six or seven dollars. People routinely gamble on card games; a minimum stake of twenty or thirty dollars a person may be required, and the game goes on all evening, with people joining in and dropping out. People organize other forms of gambling in their homes, in the backrooms of barbershops and bars, or on the street.

Among the most desperate ghetto residents, illegal activities include dogfights, cockfights, dice games, robbery, burglary, fencing, dealing drugs, and "loan sharking." On the legal side are various interpersonal accommodations, such as the barter system, which works through the exchange of goods and services. For example, a person repairs a neighbor's car on the weekend, helps paint someone's steps, performs a plumbing job, or styles someone's hair, but takes no money for any of this work; rather, he or she waits to be paid back with a favor in the future (see Anderson 1999). Mothers routinely trade child care in the same manner. Legal gambling, in the form of the state lottery, is also highly popular.

Marginal forms of work merge into the informal economy: freelancers may work on their own, doing odd jobs or engaging in petty entrepreneurship as street vendors or working for someone else, most notably at the local car wash. This sector of the economy, where relations are informal and characterized by age-related peer groups, family relationships, and personal connections, is reminiscent of the marginal urban economies in developing or underdeveloped nations.

Crime, in various low-level forms, has taken up some of the slack left by the termination of government transfer payments and the contraction of wage earning from legitimate jobs. Illegal activities supply some income to the neighborhood. With such pressures, men can now be overheard in barbershops and bars saying such things as, "I'm gon' get mine somehow," and "Somebody's gon' pay me." These allusions to street crime made by men who appear to be peaceful do at times get acted out. It is hard to quantify such impressionistic evidence, but an observer gains a clear sense of the high frustration levels in the community.

Although many people are managing to adjust, many others become frustrated, develop short fuses, and are easily aroused to anger. The Korean grocers who have opened stores in otherwise all-black neighborhoods appear to be bearing the brunt of this frustration. Not only are they of a different ethnic group and national origin, but they appear to be making money off the black community. To be sure, many Korean proprietors are solicitous of local people and employ them in visible positions, but enmity can build, and occasionally this tension mounts to the point that a clerk is killed in a robbery of the family's grocery store. There is an observable connection between frustration levels and the number of robberies and assaults occurring on the streets. When frustration levels are high, the potential for violence rises.

In these circumstances, informal social transactions become an increasingly common way to survive. But, as previously indicated, these exchanges are made essentially without the benefit of civil law. In the local community, the civil law and its agents have limited credibility, and over time confidence in the law has eroded. Street justice fills this void, becoming an important principle of local status relations, and matters of reputation or street credibility become all the more important, serving as a form of social coin. But "street cred" cannot be obtained once and for all; it is high maintenance and must be nurtured, husbanded, and replenished from time to time. Strikingly, it is replenished most effectively not by talk and recriminations, but through actual deeds, which must be performed repeatedly to earn the desired effect: respect. Certain inner-city residents are always looking for opportunities to develop and have others validate their street credibility. In these circumstances, the constant need to address shows of disrespect creates a stimulus for interpersonal violence.

The peculiar forms of social capital and regulation that develop in the isolated inner-city community—street justice and street credibility—not only sustain the drug trade but exacerbate its violence and extend its reach. Residing in areas of concentrated poverty in which hustling and crime flourish, poor inner-city males often observe opportunities for making money just outside their homes. In the inner-city community, drugs are everywhere, as the illegal enterprise moves in where the wider economy has failed local residents. Desperate young men, who cannot avoid confronting the drug network, often seize the economic opportunities made available by the drug trade and the remunerative street crime that accompanies it.

Although the dominant society fears the violence of alienated young people, the inner-city neighborhood itself suffers the greatest harm at their hands. In response to persistent structural poverty, failures of public policy, and intensifying joblessness, the irregular economy expands, but its fallout is violent crime perpetrated primarily by desperate young males.

Many alienated and otherwise idle youths enter the drug trade voluntarily, motivated by a street culture that places a premium on material objects, such as new sneakers, gold chains, and leather jackets, which function as signs of status and may help a man win the attentions of young women and prestige among his peers. For many of these young people, participating in the drug trade becomes a strong bid for financial success. And such aspirations for well-being exist alongside a desperate desire for "street cred."

In Philadelphia, the drug trade is organized hierarchically in terms of "top dogs," "middle dogs," and "low dogs" (Anderson 1990, 1999), similar to a pyramid scheme. The top dogs, who are believed to make the most money, operate essentially as drug "kingpins," but to local residents they are mostly invisible, known largely in the abstract or as urban legends. As aging "baby daddies," "homeboys," brothers, cousins, nephews, and sons, the middle dogs are more visible and often have an everyday presence in the community. Ranging in age from twenty-five to thirty-five, they visit the local street corner carryouts, clubs, barbershops, and car washes and drive around the neighborhood in flashy "rides"—a Lexus, Mercedes, or BMW—that attest to their financial success and draw the attention of youthful wannabes. As they "do their business" and make their rounds of the local ghetto neighborhoods, they also are on the lookout, or even the outright hunt, for young recruits to the trade. Their most likely prospects are financially strapped young boys in need of self-esteem. Typically, such boys lack a "decent" and strong father figure or other adult male presence in their lives. But the draw of the street and the promise of "fast money" are so powerful that boys from even the most intact families can become attracted and taken in.

Upon spotting vulnerable boys, sometimes as young as thirteen or fourteen, the middle dogs often seek to cultivate them and turn them into "low dogs." By showing them attention, the middle dogs overtly or subtly court the boys, perhaps by letting them "hold" (borrow) a few dollars or by performing other small financial favors for them. Or they may assign a task to the boy—something as simple as serving as a lookout on the corner. With each completed task, a test is passed and a bond is struck between the young boy and the middle dog and mutual confidence grows. As their relationship develops, the middle dog "lets" the boy do incrementally larger tasks, with each completed one earning more trust.

Eventually, the young boy wants to "step up to the plate" and show that he is "ready"—that is, to prove that any degree of faith shown him by the middle dog was justified and not misplaced. In time the little tasks turn into "odd jobs" for which the boy might be paid, a process that encourages dependence while bonding the boy to the middle dog. At times, after benefiting from the occasional largesse of the middle dog, the young boy may use his credit and build up a debt that becomes ever harder to repay. As the young boy becomes increasingly dependent on this relationship, his street credibility is ever more strongly tied to his job performance as evaluated by the middle dog.

This hierarchical relationship has elements of coercion as well as seduction, given the differences in age and power between the middle dog and the young boys. When directly approached by an older man to work for him, a boy may be flattered, but he may also take the offer as a threat, and then after discovering that the man is a real dealer, he may feel intimidated, believing that it is too risky not to work for the man and that refusing to do so might put his life in danger. But with the promise of "living large," with ready money and enhanced street credibility, why not? To seal the deal and initiate him into the drug trade, the middle dog may offer the young boy a "package" to hold, or even a corner from which to sell drugs. As the dilemma crystallizes, the boy can feel deeply anxious, but may find it easier to comply with the wishes of the middle dog than to refuse.

The stage is now set for the boy to become a full-fledged low dog in the local drug trade. Consummating his new status, he stands on the corner "holding" or selling drugs to passersby, day and night, typically making drug transactions that involve handling large sums of cash. In the neighborhood and on the streets, the boy is now "clocking," which means that the middle dog has "fronted" him drugs to sell, often on consignment. But it also means that the young boy has taken on the burden of a drug bill, a promissory note that must be paid, either in money or by the return of the unsold product.

If the youth is unable to meet his account, his very life may be on the line. These debts can easily grow to unwieldy proportions, since "interest" rates of fifty cents on the dollar are not uncommon. If the boy borrows money from a dealer and fails to repay in the allotted time, a middle dog may allow him to repay by working in the trade. Failure to collect on a debt jeopardizes the middle dog's street credibility, leading him to exact payment in some form, through physical harm or even assassination.

Making matters worse, conditions of endemic poverty have encouraged the emergence of "stickup" boys who roam the ghetto streets looking for money or drugs and robbing the low dogs who stand on the corner selling drugs. If a boy is robbed and cannot account for his drugs by producing the right amount of cash, he may be told by his middle dog: "If you don't pay up, you have twenty-four hours to live." Under pressure to come up with the money on short notice, the boy may well resort to robbery and other forms of street crime. Before scores can be settled, several people may die. Violence and counterviolence have a place in many transactions. With the erosion of civil law, street justice becomes one of the few ways of mediating disputes and street credibility becomes the coin, for both expressive and instrumental reasons.

In these circumstances, for his own sense of security, the young boy becomes highly motivated to "get himself a gun." Acquiring a weapon begins largely as a matter of personal defense. Typically, the gun is seen as standing between the young dealer and his own death. He must be prepared to defend what is his, be it money, drugs, or street credibility. From his experience of the streets, he knows that respect on the street is a must, and that his very life depends on having it.

Possession of a gun provides instant street credibility. And guns are readily available; young boys beg, borrow, rent, and steal them. Once he has a weapon, the boy often carries it, and when he does not he sometimes adopts elaborate ruses in order to present himself as "strapped," including a hunched or labored style of walking that, for those who are streetwise, sends the unmistakable message "I'm packing." Through the multifarious drug transactions that "go down" on the corner, the young boy becomes involved in a web of social and financial relations that are essentially regulated not by civil law but by a "code of the street" (Anderson 1999) in which street credibility becomes all the more critical to his survival. Arguments can arise from almost anywhere at any time, and the boy must be prepared to deal with them. For protection, he carries his "piece" to the multiplex, to Mickey D's, to his girlfriend's house, sometimes even to school—or to any "staging area" where trouble might arise and beefs might be settled.

This almost insatiable need for street credibility, reinforced by a "code of silence" that prohibits and punishes "snitching," contributes powerfully to the high murder rate that Philadelphia and other cities are presently experiencing. A root cause is persistent urban poverty, which leaves no clear way to acquire money other than by engaging in this criminal, violent dimension of the underground economy.

As indicated by this account, young black men face extreme disadvantages just by living in areas of concentrated urban poverty. Yet most families in inner-city communities—even those who are most impoverished—hold "decent" or mainstream values, but they are under extreme pressure in the neighborhood. When venturing outside their homes, they are required to deal with the "street element," and to do so, many of these folks will present themselves as "street"—or at least as people capable of "getting ignorant" if they need to. Culturally, they understand that shows of decency are taken as signs of weakness, and this will not "get you much on the street." They try to socialize their children to have decent values, while understanding full well that the open display of these values can be dangerous, calling the children's street credibility into question. Thus, youth from decent families of the ghetto must learn to code-switch, and in the process they very often develop an exquisite ability to tell "what time it is" and to behave accordingly.

In the ghetto, the police are often viewed as highly selective in carrying out their duties. When they are called, residents complain that they often arrive late, and then sometimes abuse "the very people who called them." Residents report being called "out of my name, cussed at, and disrespected." Generally, the chief complaint is that the police are often arbitrary in their approach to the community. As one young man explained:

The police don't respond to gun calls. Take 'em five hours to get there [to the scene] for that. But you call and tell 'em that somebody on the corner sellin' a bag of weed, here they come, fifty cars deep. But you tell 'em somebody layin' on the ground dying, been shot four times, it takes the cops four hours to get there for that!

But in the community, police officers guard the entrances and hallways of the local schools. And if a youth is involved in an altercation, or almost any serious disruption, he seldom goes directly to the principal's office but is often handcuffed on the spot. His name is entered into a computer database as someone who has violated the law, so he gets an instant record.

Meanwhile, his neighborhood peer group smokes marijuana cigarettes or blunts, experimenting with mind-dulling drugs. By the time black males get out of school and approach the job market, many of them cannot pass the background check or the drug test. The employer then has a ready excuse not to hire dark-skinned young males, typically discriminating in favor of immigrants or young people from the suburbs.

The life course of the young black male in the inner city is shaped by the concentration of poverty in an isolated, segregated community. In this racially circumscribed environment, his contacts with the wider society are limited, and he has limited exposure to role models not in his situation. Instead, the black youth sees others who are similarly situated and naturally identifies with them; they likely become his most important reference group. This limited experience and perspective work to shape his orientation and, ultimately, his outlook on life, its possibilities and limitations. In the company of peers, he strives to fit in. To be sure, a large part of his worldview is a function of the real world in which he must survive and function every day. Typically his home life is female-centric; he lives with his mother, perhaps along with his grandmother or an aunt, but not with a father. The men in his life are his brothers and cousins, occasionally an uncle or a grandfather. Seldom does he have the positive and direct influence of a father who lives nearby and stays in touch. When a father figure is present, he is rarely an effective and positive role model, a lack that is largely a function, both directly and indirectly, of the absence of family-sustaining jobs and opportunity that would inspire and reinforce a positive view of the future. And because of this, youth more often than not emerge and grow up without a strong sense of connection with mainstream society and the wider culture.

The persistent issue for so many young people is that of not having enough money. The whole community is in the pit of poverty, and it seems like there is never enough money for anyone. Residents require this money for the bare necessities of everyday life, to be sure, but for many it also becomes important to obtain money so that they can acquire the trinkets that are so important for enhancing social identity: the gold bracelet or neck chain, the iPod, the jacket, and the sneakers. The oversized white T-shirt worn over pants that hang well below the waist is a part of the urban uniform. It makes one suddenly presentable, and at three, four, or five dollars, it is relatively inexpensive. The local youth culture is highly competitive, and pervaded by envy and jealousy; young people often feel an intense need to show themselves to be "better than" the next person. Hence, there exists a preoccupation with status and ranking in local peer groups. Expensive and flashy accessories make a clear and positive impression. Dress becomes a visible sign of belonging and status. But by the same token, wearing worn-out clothes or going about unkempt has major social costs, thereby setting in motion an emphasis on material things defined as symbols of status in the local culture.

Additionally, many young men acquire spending money from their mothers or uncles, or they borrow from one another; a few have part-time jobs. But if respectable money is not forthcoming, a certain urgency comes over many of these boys, and they become vulnerable to the street ethic of chasing "fast" money. When some quickly become ensnared in the fast life, their example beckons to others. In these circumstances, a boy can become increasingly alienated; often shortsighted and confused, he is "out there" doing what he feels he must do to survive. Survival is not simply a matter of need or subsistence, however, but also of status. So powerful are these "needs" that they work to "justify" a range of unsavory activities, from sticking someone up, or snatching a pocketbook, to "picking up a package." Hustling can become a way of life, but there are consequences when things go awry—as they almost always do eventually. Violence culminating in jail or death is the common result. Young black people at ground zero know full well the fatal consequences of resorting to these expedients, but they seldom see any alternative.

Like soldiers in a war zone, young men become preoccupied with simply staying alive, and then go about adopting the attitudes and postures that survival on the streets requires. It is with this orientation that the maturing inner-city male approaches the world inside the ghetto, including the institutions there that interface with the wider society: schools, churches, stores, the police, the criminal justice system.

It is a cruel irony that even the black residents who somehow powerfully resist the crushing economic and social forces at play in the ghetto and live "decent" lives are victimized by those forces anyway when they step outside the ghetto into the larger society.

When black strangers, particularly males, actually appear outside the ghetto in public, depending on their presentation of self, those whom they encounter become anxious to make quick sense of them, to determine whether they are friend or foe, peaceful or dangerous. Given the stereotypical image of "the iconic ghetto," the person from the wider society is inclined at first blush to associate the black person with the ghetto, his bearing, his dress, and his presumed position notwithstanding. From this position, the black person is saddled with a provisional status. Those encountering a black person size up that individual, including the symbols he or she displays, in an instant and are either put at ease or perhaps even more alarmed.

The burden is placed squarely on the black person to demonstrate that he is not crime-prone but law-abiding, civil, and nonthreatening. In addition, he must show that he is a "normal" person entitled to trust, that he has full person status—or that he does not smell, that he is not stupid, lower class, or ignorant, that he is at least okay. But this is a strong challenge in part because those whom the black person encounters and would impress have something to prove themselves. Hence, they have reason to form a low opinion of the black person, if only to place themselves above him. Strikingly, the evidence against the most negative assessments is always questionable, mainly because of the lingering context of racial segregation within which the reputation of the iconic ghetto rests. Thus, those encountering a black person outside the ghetto are most often not easily impressed. During such split-second encounters, each person usually goes on about his business, and simple distance is validated and maintained.

Because of the power of the ghetto image, it follows the person with black skin, hovering about him like a shadow and making him vulnerable to further marginalization. The ghetto is viewed and imagined as a highly undesirable place to be, and anyone who is from such a place or associated with such a place by skin color and phenotype is first and foremost viewed as lower class, "no account," or déclassé by those of the wider society, including perhaps increasing numbers of blacks themselves, who may harbor such attitudes simply out of some need to defend or protect themselves socially. However, the negative stereotype applies with particular force to black males, who are often misunderstood, feared, and profiled as potentially violent criminals whenever they present themselves in public. The more "ghetto" they appear, the more scrutiny they attract. In worst-case scenarios, the police are summoned and the black person, no matter how high his putative position, is reminded emphatically of his provisional status—that he is an "other," an outsider, someone who at best commands a limited degree of trust, status, and respect.

Though prejudiced whites who may be as committed as ever to containing the ghetto are inclined to marginalize those blacks who appear among them, this may not be easy as it once was, given the recent changes in the status of blacks, including the highly successful civil rights movement that was followed by a racial incorporation process that has resulted in a subsequent opening up of the American occupational structure with implications for other institutions. A wide diversity of people are now present in so many public and quasi-public spaces of the city, if not in formerly distinct racial and ethnic enclaves throughout the city.

Yet in the imagination of most everyone, the iconic black ghetto persists as "the place where the blacks live," defying the fact that "the ghetto" is generally not so absolutely black as before; many recent colored immigrants now call it home. Moreover, black people today are of every social class, reside almost anywhere throughout the city, and are thus capable of being taken as "anyone." As this positive process advances, now including growing numbers of colored immigrants who take their own places as professionals as well as working people, the urban mosaic becomes ever more complex. As the urban environment becomes ever more pluralistic and the veneer of racial civility spreads, a profound stigma persists, embodied ultimately in black skin and manifested in the iconic black ghetto.

References

Anderson, Elijah. 1978. *A Place on the Corner: A Study of Black Street Corner Men*. Chicago: University of Chicago Press.

————. 1980. "Some Observations on Youth Employment." In *Youth Employment and Public Policy*, edited by Bernard Anderson and Isabel Sawbill. Englewood Cliffs, N.J.: Prentice-Hall.

———. 1990. *Streetwise: Race, Class, and Change in an Urban Community.* Chicago: University of Chicago Press.

———. 1999. *Code of the Street.* New York: W. W. Norton.

———. ed. 2008. *Against the Wall: Poor, Young, Black, and Male.* Philadelphia: University of Pennsylvania Press.

———. 2011. *The Cosmopolitan Canopy: Race and Civility in Everyday Life.* New York: W. W. Norton.

———. Forthcoming, 2012. "The Iconic Ghetto." *Annals of the American Academy of Political and Social Science.*

Drake, St. Clair, and Horace Cayton. 1993. *Black Metropolis: A Study of Negro Life in a Northern City.* Chicago: University of Chicago Press.

Du Bois, W. E. B. 1996. *The Philadelphia Negro.* Philadelphia: University of Pennsylvania Press.

Goffman, Erving. 1963. *Stigma: The Management of Spoiled Identity.* Englewood Cliffs, N.J.: Prentice-Hall.

Hughes, Everett C. "Dilemmas and Contradictions of Status," *American Journal of Sociology* 50(1945): 353–359

Kirschenman, Joleen, and Kathryn Neckermann. 1991. "'We'd Like to Hire Them But . . .': Race in the Minds of Employers." In *The Urban Underclass,* edited by Christopher Jencks and Paul E. Peterson. New York: Sage Publications.

Massey, Douglas, and Nancy Denton. 1993. *American Apartheid: Segregation and the Making of the Underclass.* Cambridge: Harvard University Press.

Mincy, Ronald, ed. 2006. *Black Men Left Behind.* Washington: Urban Institute Press.

Pager, Devah. 2003a. "Blacks and Ex-Cons Need Not Apply." *Contexts* 2, no. 4: 58–59.

———. 2003b. "The Mark of a Criminal Record." *American Journal of Sociology* 108, no. 5: 937–975.

———. 2005. "Walking the Talk: What Employers Say Versus What They Do." *American Sociological Review* 70, no. 3: 355–380.

Report of the National Advisory Commission on Civil Disorders, or *The Kerner Commission Report.* 1968. Washington, D.C.: Government Printing Office.

Stack, Carol. 1997. *All Our Kin: Survival Strategies in the Black Community.* New York: Basic Books.

Valentine, Betty Lou. 1980. *Hustling and Other Hard Work.* New York: Free Press.

Venkatesh, Suhir Alladi. 2009. *Off the Books: The Underground Economy of the Urban Poor.* Cambridge, Mass.: Harvard University Press.

Wilson, William Julius. 1987. *The Truly Disadvantaged: The Inner City, the Underclass, and Public Policy.* Chicago: University of Chicago Press.

Winant, Howard. 2002. *The World Is a Ghetto: Race and Democracy Since World War II.* New York: Basic Books.

Wirth, Louis. 1928. *The Ghetto.* Chicago: University of Chicago Press.

CHAPTER 4

✦ ✦ ✦

"You Just Don't Go Down There": Learning to Avoid the Ghetto in San Francisco

Nikki Jones and Christina Jackson

More and more people are moving to cities, and in some of them the new urban migrants are younger and whiter than city-dwellers of a previous generation. As the demographics of metropolitan areas continue to change, middle-class urban migrants become more likely to live in close proximity to people of another class position. The challenges associated with these changes have been documented in the literature on gentrification. In this chapter, we look at the ways in which newcomers learn to navigate their new homes, drawing on field research conducted by the first author over a five-year period, including thirty months of continuous residence in the Western Addition, a historically black neighborhood in San Francisco.[1] We begin with a vignette from her ethnographic account of that experience.

> Lukas is the owner of a small bed-and-breakfast in San Francisco.[2] I was a frequent guest at his inn during the two years before I moved to the Western Addition, a historically black neighborhood in San Francisco. Sometimes people refer to the area as "the Fillmore," but when they are discussing the most troubled parts of the neighborhood, especially the places frequented by low-income African American residents, they are more likely to use the

83

term "Western Addition" (or "the Lower Fillmore"—we use the terms inter-changeably in this chapter). A German immigrant with broad shoulders, white hair, and a thick lingering accent, Lukas arrived in the city in the 1960s. The Western Addition was dangerous, he tells me, like many other urban areas at the time. A lot of people left the city, he says, but not him: "We love the city."[3] One morning, over a small breakfast of orange juice, coffee, and a fluffy croissant, Lukas offers a brief oral history of his time in the neighbor-hood. He tells me how difficult it was to get bank financing to purchase and restore homes when he did it back in the late 1960s and early 1970s. Up until about ten years ago, he says, the entire area was "redlined." Banks would not give loans to buy houses in the Western Addition, he says. He could not get a loan for his house when he bought it back then. The mortgage lenders could not be direct about what they were doing—no one said, "We are not giving loans to blacks," who made up much of the Western Addition's population at the time. After World War II, migrants from the South had swelled the African American population in the Western Addition from 4,000 to 40,000, and it would remain high into the 1970s (Day and Abraham 1993). (See Figure 4.1.) In response, Lukas continues, the banks redlined the entire area, making it nearly impossible for anyone to get a loan to purchase the crumbling Vic-torian homes that are now a fixture of San Francisco's architectural history.

Lukas also tells me about the impact on the neighborhood of the urban redevelopment carried out by the Department of Housing and Urban De-velopment (HUD). HUD cleared the land of all structures and then left the land razed for years before building new structures. In the intervening time, neighborhood residents planted vegetable gardens in the empty lots—an eighty-acre vegetable garden, Lukas laughs. In the 1980s, during the second phase of urban renewal in the neighborhood, the vegetable gardens were re-placed by the Fillmore Center apartment complex, where I lived for two and a half years.

Lukas says that, for many people, the name "Western Addition" still means, "Don't go there." He explains: "If I picked up the telephone when people called and asked where we were located and I told them right away, 'The Western Addition,' they wouldn't make the reservation. So instead I say, 'Alamo Square.' They ask if it is near Fisherman's Wharf, a popular tourist at-traction in the city. 'No,' I say. 'It's near Alamo Square.'" Near the end of our conversation, Lukas makes what I would eventually discover is a distinction commonly made by locals to distinguish the neighborhood's "great" location in the heart of the city from its bad reputation: "It's a great location, right in the middle of the city. I have never been in a traffic jam," he says. "I could be—Polk, Van Ness, Gough—all traffic jams. Not here." I nod in agreement.[4]

The Western Addition has not been officially redlined in the ways described by Lukas for several decades. In fact, the discriminatory housing practices that he describes were made illegal by historic civil rights legislation (Wilson 2009). Yet observations of daily life in the neighborhood reveal that people remain reluctant to spend time in the area. They generally acknowledge that the neighborhood is situated in a great location, but lament its reputation as a bad neighborhood because of its struggles with crime and dramatic episodes of violence. Lukas is aware that the neighborhood's spatial identity encourages people to avoid it, so he describes the location of his inn as within the boundaries of an adjacent neighborhood.

LEARNING TO AVOID THE GHETTO IN SAN FRANCISCO

In this chapter, we draw on field research conducted in the Western Addition to explain how the neighborhood is constructed as a bad neighborhood in ordinary conversations and the consequences of this construction for neighborhood residents. These conversations reveal a practice of *discursive redlining*: informal, talk-based declarations or warnings that discourage newcomers and outsiders from making interpersonal investments in certain parts of the city. Discursive redlining can be observed in conversations on popular review websites or in face-to-face encounters.[5] Often, these warnings are accomplished without making an explicit reference to race. Instead, the practice of discursive redlining relies on the use of racially coded terms like *ghetto* to describe certain people or places as potentially problematic.[6] "The most powerfully imagined neighborhood is the iconic black ghetto or the 'hood," Elijah Anderson writes in *The Cosmopolitan Canopy* (2011). Such areas are "often associated in the minds of outsiders with poverty, crime, and violence." This idea of the ghetto, which in reality is a "figment of the imagination of those with little or no direct experience with the ghetto or contact with those who live there," shapes how black people are treated in "spaces outside the ghetto" (Anderson 2011, 29). The practice of discursive redlining reveals how understandings of the ghetto shape newcomers' perceptions of their neighbors, especially black residents, *within* an area that is now seen by some as "a ghetto on the rise" (Beveridge 2008, 364).

Discursive redlining is distinct from the official redlining of the past in at least two ways. First, discursive redlining operates apart from the type of legal lending restrictions that created the suburbs and the ghetto, since restrictions that would prohibit making financial investments in neighborhoods with a substantial percentage of African Americans no longer exist. In fact, for most of the 2000s, financial advisers were far more likely to encourage a range of actors—banks, developers, first-time homeowners—to invest in an area like the Western Addition. Second, and in contrast to institutional redlining, which warned people away from making substantial *economic* investments in a neighborhood, like buying a home, discursive redlining discourages outsiders and newcomers from making *interpersonal* investments, like dining at a local restaurant or spending time at a café in the area. The consequences of discursive redlining are likely to be felt most by those seen as the most problematic by others, like young black men who hang out on street corners in the neighborhood.

THE BLACK COMMUNITY IN SAN FRANCISCO

Much of the literature on urban poverty focuses on postindustrial cities in the Midwest or northeastern cities like Philadelphia. In recent years, Chicago's South Side has served as the site for a number of significant studies on the black ghetto (Small 2008). In contrast, there are relatively few studies that focus on the black experience in the West, and perhaps especially in San Francisco. Yet the unique history of blacks in San Francisco makes it an ideal site to study the black urban experience, especially the experience of African Americans in the later stages of the Great Migration and the process of ghettoization (see, for example, Broussard 1993).

Prior to World War II, the Fillmore neighborhood was home to much of the city's black community, including a number of black professionals (Daniels 1980). The relatively small black community shared space in the Fillmore with Irish, Jewish, and Japanese residents. The neighborhood's composition changed dramatically after the start of the war. African Americans, especially those from states like Arkansas, Louisiana, and Texas, were recruited to join the war effort (Johnson 1944). African American workers who arrived en masse in the 1940s found crowded but affordable housing in the Fillmore, where they rented rooms in the homes of Japanese residents who had been sent to internment camps by the U.S. government following the start of the war. Once in the city, black migrant workers took up jobs in the war industry and related services, including bars, restaurants, and jazz clubs. The Fillmore became a cultural hub for African Americans during the wartime period (Jackson 2010). This new set of locals would come to describe the area as "the Harlem of the West."[7]

San Francisco's "Negro Problem"

The city's new black population created a social problem for government officials and city elites: "For the first time in the city's history, white San Franciscans would have to adjust to a large black community" (Broussard 1993, 142). In some corners of the city, the response of San Franciscans to this new pattern of migration was characterized by tolerance and ambivalence. In other areas, the response to the city's changing demographics mirrored the discriminatory practices of local officials in other cities. In the area of housing, for example, racial lines were drawn as homeowners used restrictive covenants to prevent the sale of homes to African Americans (Broussard 1993).

The arrival of African American workers in the Bay Area also created a problem for racially segregated industries, including the military and defense contractors. Racial discrimination in industries tied to the war effort was prohibited after President Franklin D. Roosevelt, who was influenced by civil rights activists like Bayard Rustin and A. Philip Randolph, issued Executive Order 8802. As ordered by the president, the federal Fair Employment Practices Commission declared that "there shall be no discrimination in the employment of workers in defense industries or government because of race, creed, color, or national origin" (Collins 2001, 273). The executive order opened up skilled and semiskilled training opportunities in the defense industry for black migrants in the Bay Area (Fusfeld and Bates 1984). The integration of African Americans into previously restricted workplaces improved the social and economic well-being of black migrants during the war.

Despite the contributions of African Americans to the war effort, some Navy officials viewed the mass migration of African Americans to the area surrounding the shipyard, and the increase in Negro personnel generally, as a problem. The Navy officially addressed this new problem in conference proceedings, memos, and booklets. In a transcript from a 1943 "Conference with Regard to Negro Personnel," an admiral explained the situation quite frankly: "We are faced with a problem—a very serious problem—in connection with our naval enlisted personnel and that is the introduction into the District of the large numbers of Negro personnel. . . . The order has come now and it isn't a question of whether anybody likes it or not" (U.S. Navy 1943).

From the perspective of Navy officials, black migration disrupted the military's social order. As the admiral's comments suggest, Navy officials embraced the increase in African American personnel and integration somewhat grudgingly. Despite this initial reluctance, the Navy began to churn out black workers for the war industry. By 1943 the Navy had trained over 100,000 blacks in shipbuilding, aircraft repair, and machinery. In 1945 Hunter's Point shipyard was the largest in the world: At peak production, it employed 18,235 workers over three shifts per day (Lomax 1972). Many other African Americans found work in the cottage industries that catered to a population of young black migrants with some money to spend, including the burgeoning jazz scene in the Fillmore.

As in other urban industrial centers, the fate of black workers would turn after the end of the war. In San Francisco, African Americans were largely let go from wartime jobs, but remained excluded from other employment opportunities in the city. More than one city official had hoped that African Americans would leave the city at the end of the war, but many stayed. As Arthur Hippler (1974, 14) writes: "The presence of thousands of semiskilled and unskilled black shipyard workers who had been laid off immediately after the war and who stayed on in San Francisco represented what city officials considered a civic problem." Like other cities confronted with a large African American population in the postwar period, San Francisco's city officials hoped to solve this "civic problem" through "cheap public housing and welfare." This would prove to be an inadequate solution.

Before 1940, there had been no black ghetto in San Francisco. In the Fillmore, African Americans lived in an integrated neighborhood and attended integrated schools. The spatial identity of the Fillmore changed dramatically following World War II. By the late 1940s, the Fillmore was largely considered by middle-class whites and blacks a "cesspool of crime and vice" (Broussard 1993, 231–233). In the 1950s, the process of ghettoization quickened. The Fillmore would become the sort of place described by Herbert Gans (2008, 353) as a "place to which subjects or victims of the involuntary segregation process are sent." The Fillmore would become a ghetto.

The Fillmore After the War

Since the end of World War II, the Fillmore neighborhood has followed a trajectory similar to that of many distressed inner-city neighborhoods across the country. In the decades following the war, urban planners and government officials officially categorized the places where poor black people lived as "slums." This official definition was consequential for neighborhood residents (Bellush and Hausknecht 1967; Geron et al. 2001; Hartman 2002; Lai 2006). Once slums were officially defined as the problem, then institutional solutions were developed to remove the slums from the city (Hartman 2002). The practice of slum removal mirrored the practices used in other industrial centers. Older housing units were destroyed and replaced by public housing projects and other apartment developments. As was the case in Harlem, New York, "the new developments did not come close to housing the same number of people" (Beveridge 2008, 361).

During the first phase of urban renewal, large portions of the Fillmore neighborhood were razed and replaced by federally subsidized housing projects. The neighborhood was also split in two by a cornerstone of the first wave of redevelopment: Geary Boulevard. The construction of the boulevard, designed to ease the commute of downtown workers to the city's quickly developing suburbs, would cut through the heart of the black Fillmore. As Lukas alludes to in the opening vignette, many lots in the neighborhood would lie vacant for years. In the wake of urban renewal, the Fillmore neighborhood's African American population would decline substantially—as would the city's.

As economic conditions worsened across the country, the Fillmore neighborhood would also face challenges similar to those of other inner-city neighborhoods. The lingering history of these challenges continues to shape the spatial identity of the Fillmore. Dislocation from the mainstream

FIGURE 4.1. Black Population in San Francisco, 1940–2009

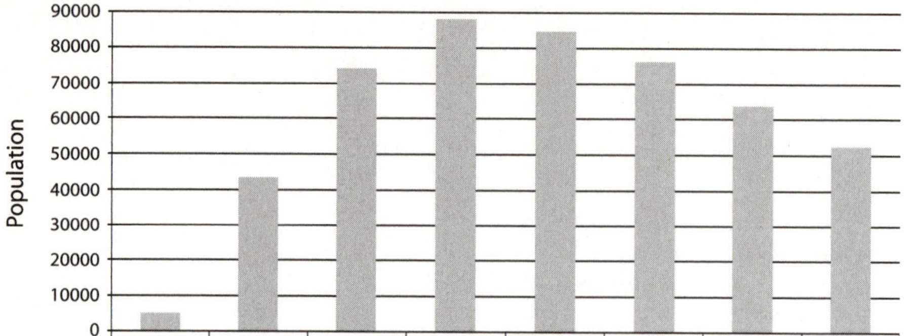

Population	1940	1950	1960	1970	1980	1990	2000	2009
Population	4846	43,502	74,382	88,343	84,857	76,343	64,070	52,342

Source: Unfinished Agenda, US Census 2010.

economy and the deep entrenchment of poverty have exacerbated the neighborhood's isolation from the rest of the city. The neighborhood has faced an increase in crime, rapidly deteriorating schools, and an increase in drug trafficking and the violence associated with the drug trade (Anderson 1999; Massey and Denton 1993; Wilson 1980, 1987, 1996). Today, in the minds of many who are familiar with the city—including the residents of the nearby and gentrifying Lower Pacific Heights and Alamo Square neighborhoods and the smaller Japantown neighborhood—the Western Addition is largely defined as a bad neighborhood marked by crime and violence. Newspaper reports of shootings and gang activity regularly reinforce such assumptions (Martin 2006; Van Derbeken 2005; Van Derbeken and Lagos 2006).

The Fillmore Today: A Ghetto on the Rise?

Like a number of other historically black neighborhoods in the country, the Fillmore is experiencing a new phase of renewal. Parts of the neighborhood may still fit the definition of a ghetto in that there remain areas in which low-income African American live in high concentrations, but like New York's Harlem and the "U Street Corridor" in Washington, D.C., it is also "on the rise" (Beveridge 2008, 364). Markers of the neighborhood's renewal (or demise, depending on whom you ask) are visible to newcomers: a Magic Johnson's Starbucks, a remodeled Safeway grocery store, and, perhaps the most symbolic, the Fillmore Heritage Center, which opened in 2007. The center includes a jazz history museum, a jazz club, and eighty condominium units, twelve of which were slated to sell at under market rates.

The Fillmore Heritage Center sits across the street from one of the most visible symbols of the second wave of urban redevelopment: the Fillmore Center. The Fillmore Center's efforts to attract a new market of residents, along with other new projects in the area, are slowly pushing the boundaries of the Lower Pacific Heights area into the Lower Fillmore. As a result, the boundaries around what is commonly considered the most troubled parts of the Lower Fillmore—especially the federally subsidized housing complexes on Eddy Street, which runs perpendicular to Fillmore Street—are becoming harder. With this pending encroachment, daily interactions between newcomers and longtime residents can sometimes be tense, especially in public forums. But longtime residents also cite the presence of newcomers, especially white newcomers, as a sign that the neighborhood is changing, for good or for bad. People with business stakes in the neighborhood appear to be more open to this sort of neighborhood change, even if it means a change in the demographic composition of the area, but some longtime residents view the changes as the last nail in the coffin of the historically black Fillmore neighborhood.

These changes have also encouraged a new sort of interactional trouble for newcomers to the neighborhood. In the recent past, much of the area below Geary Boulevard was a "no-go" zone, an area identified by residents and outsiders as one that only outcasts of society would live in because of its violence, deprivation, and perceived immorality (Wacquant 1999). This avoidance was not altogether unreasonable in the 1980s. Eric, a key respondent in my field research, explained to me that during this time a group of young men—the "red light bandits"—would target white drivers stopped at red lights in the neighborhood. Since the 1990s, however, and especially during the first decade of the new millennium, much of the violence has turned inward. In the Western Addition, black youth, especially young black men, are the most frequent targets of lethal violence.

The concentration of this sort of crime and violence has been a long-standing problem for local residents, but it presents a different problem for newcomers to the area, especially those who are unfamiliar with the neighborhood's terrain and its people. Newcomers may be unaccustomed with urban life, or they may have expectations of safety that are challenged by their surroundings. Their efforts to warn others away from problematic people or places in their new neighborhood reflect a preoccupation with a fear of crime and victimization that has come to order the lives of many middle-class people:

> The everyday lives of middle-class families [have] been transformed not so much by crime itself, as by "fear of crime." For middle-class families, choices such as where to live, where to work, and where to send children to school are made with increasing reference to the perceived risk of crime. (Simon 2007, 6)

It is in this context that discursive redlining emerges as an everyday practice. Newcomers and outsiders to the neighborhood teach each other, through direct and indirect warnings, about where the danger is and how to avoid it. They learn how to avoid the ghetto.

DISCURSIVE REDLINING AND THE SOCIAL CONSTRUCTION OF THE GHETTO

Whether it's women sharing lunch "up the hill" in Pacific Heights, hotel workers in nearby neighborhoods, or real estate workers eager to attract new residents to the neighborhood, there are many people instructing others in how to navigate the Western Addition. Some people warn friends to avoid the area altogether, while others make suggestions about how to avoid the most problematic sections of the neighborhood. These warnings often draw on anecdotal evidence lifted from newspaper reports or secondhand accounts passed along from a friend or family member. Embedded in this instruction is a warning about the danger that lies in what is widely known as a poor, black neighborhood. The crudest versions of these warnings can be found on websites like Yelp, which newcomers to the area often use to find reviews of potential housing. Despite an advertising campaign that billed the complex as "luxury apartments," the Fillmore Center, where the first author lived for thirty months from 2007 to 2009, generally received low ratings (three stars or less). The public postings that generate ratings of the center illustrate the common discursive elements that appear in conversations about the Western Addition.

"The Neighborhood Is Ghetto"

The online conversation about the Fillmore Center is framed by the same distinction that Lukas makes in the opening vignette: Although some reviewers highlight the center's convenient location ("I like going everywhere in the city, and this is probably the most central location to the core neighborhoods in the city"), others focus on the bad neighborhood that surrounds it. "Apart from the fact that the projects are close by, the location overall is good," notes one reviewer (Urban D., May 8, 2009). "The location is excellent," says another (Amber P., October 23, 2009), "although admittedly if you live in one of the buildings further down towards Turk you might not be as big of a fan of your surrounding 'hood."

These comments demonstrate that, for some, the neighborhood's good location is tainted by its proximity to a federally subsidized housing complex. Reviewers never use explicit racial references in their postings, but they do rely on racially coded language, using terms like *ghetto*.[8] In the thirty-four postings, the term *ghetto* is used thirteen times.[9]

Ghetto is a term that is no longer used solely to refer to a geographically bound place. Inner-city residents use the term to make distinctions among the "value orientations" of their neighbors.[10] Community members use these distinctions as a basis for understanding, interpreting, and predicting their own and others' actions, attitudes, and behaviors, especially when it comes to interpersonal violence (Anderson 1999; Blokland 2008, 372; Jones 2010, 9). The term is now widely used by individuals outside of the inner city, including people whose understanding of "the ghetto" is largely shaped by popular culture, especially commercial hip-hop music.

In the online reviews, the word *ghetto* is mentioned over a dozen times. At times it is used to describe the area surrounding the Fillmore Center. Jerome F., for example, uses the term to distinguish between the interior of the Fillmore Center, which he describes as "nice," and the area surrounding the apartment complex: "The complex interior is nice, but the building . . . is surrounded by ghetto-projects and the associated dwellers, crack heads, and a plethora of shady characters" (June 19, 2008). It is clear what *ghetto* means to Jerome F.: "ghetto-projects and the associated dwellers." His post is one of the few that provides such an explicit definition of *ghetto*. In most of the postings where *ghetto* appears, the term is used to describe essential characteristics of the surrounding area: In other words, the area is not described, as it is in Jerome F.'s posting, as *a ghetto*, but as *ghetto*. *Ghetto* is used in this way, for example, in G.G.'s post from June 25, 2007: "I agree with the other reviewers: this place is heinously ghetto!" When used by these online reviewers as an adjective, *ghetto* provides a shorthand and color-blind description of the essential character of the people and places that "surround" the Fillmore Center.

What is it that makes the area surrounding the Fillmore "ghetto"? The postings suggest that it is not just the presence of federally subsidized housing complexes—or "projects," in the words of Jerome F.—but also the perceived threat of exposure to violence and personal injury. For example, when listing a "con" of living in the Fillmore Center, W.D. writes: "1. The neighborhood is ghetto. You have to cross over Geary [the boulevard constructed for commuters] for decent restaurants and *safety*" (November 16, 2007, emphasis mine). The following remarks from Miss K. also reveal the relationship between ghetto and perceptions of safety. The place is ghetto, her post suggests, because it is marked by danger, crime, and violence. It is an especially strong warning in that it mentions not only the danger surrounding the area but also how that danger penetrates the physical boundaries of the Fillmore Center:

> did i mention this area is dangerous? they have security on premises and cameras everywhere but obviously they need it. my friend knows someone who got held up at gunpoint in the elevator. many cars have been broken into in the garage. and not too long ago, someone got shot in the safeway parking lot across the street. jazz district, my ass. we live in the ghettos baby! truth be told, i felt safer (ok, less scared) in my boy's old tenderloin hood. (February 20, 2007)

In this post, Miss K. provides the sort of secondhand account of violent victimization that might otherwise be passed along during a conversation among friends in a café. This disclosure acts as a warning. The message to readers of this review is clear, perhaps especially to children from middle-class families whose choices about where to live are often made with "reference to the perceived risk of crime" (Simon 2007, 6).

Not all of the Fillmore Center's reviews are negative. Some reviewers even challenge the definition of the surrounding area (or at least some parts of it) as ghetto. However, their postings do not entirely disrupt the framing of the surrounding area as ghetto but instead dispute the degree to which this is the case. On December 18, 2008, Mollie S. writes:

> i totally disagree with all the reviews posted here. . . . Yes, some of the neighborhood is ghetto . . . but right across the street there's Yoshi's and the Kabuki Theater and some other awesome Jazz Clubs, and walking up Fillmore Street toward Pac Heights is really pleasant. I'm a girl, and I walk to Safeway at night by myself quite a bit and have never experienced any problems. It's not the best area, but it's up-and-coming, and let's face it: San Francisco is a CITY. At least you aren't living in the Tenderloin.

Brad D. had this to say on January 10, 2008:

> Ok, from the comments I keep reading I have to say that yet again I continue to be amazed by my "friends and neighbors" in SF. I live in the Fillmore Center. I moved here last year on a moment's notice after a short stint in sunnier climes, and 15 years living in London and New York. Yes, there is a lot of public housing around us, yes there are some interesting characters in the parking lot at Safeway, but this is hardly ghetto living.

Several common themes emerge from reading these postings side by side, including, as already noted, the distinction between the good location and the bad neighborhood. Commenting on the good location, reviewers note that it not only sits in the center of the city but is easily accessible to public transportation. Yet the neighborhood and especially the people who live on the borders of the Fillmore Center (who have lived there for generations) and the places they frequent, like the Safeway (the only grocery store in the area since another that catered to the black community closed down), are represented as "ghetto." These postings do not seem to refer to the ghetto as "place." Instead, they use the term *ghetto* as an adjective. These postings suggest that the neighborhood is bad because of the people—the poor black people—who live in the nearby projects and make up much of "Baby Compton."

These postings are also largely ahistorical: They reflect an ignorance of not only the ghetto as a product of structural circumstances but also the particular history of the neighborhood. The declarations and complaints in these postings ignore the institutional history of the neighborhood. The Fillmore Center apartments were a product of one of the largest redevelopment projects in the country, as were the nearby "projects," yet the postings reflect an ignorance of how the problems that "surround" them are connected to the monumental mismanagement of the area by the San Francisco Redevelopment Agency or the dramatic shifts in the economy that isolated generations of African Americans from the mainstream economy. The ghetto is not represented as a "place to which subjects or victims of the involuntary segregation process are sent" (Gans 2008, 353). Neither is it represented as a consequence of the city's failure to adequately address its "Negro problem" in the wake of World War II. Rather, the online conversation suggests that a concentration of certain types of people and behaviors in an area is what makes a place ghetto. The consequence of this framing of the problem is obvious. If it is the people who *make* a place ghetto, then the ghetto is no longer the problem to be solved. Instead, the people and the places they frequent are identified as the problem. The solution is to avoid the people or, in time, remove them from the area (Beckett and Herbert 2010).

Avoiding the Ghetto: Face-to-Face Warnings

It is possible that the anonymity of the Internet encourages the practice of discursive redlining (although people do sometimes post their names and pictures alongside their reviews), but discursive redlining is not restricted to online conversations. In this section, we offer a final illustration of discursive redlining. As in the online conversations, everyday conversations reveal an effort to educate newcomers about the problematic areas in the neighborhood by reconstructing the spatial identity of the Western Addition—as demonstrated in this field note of June 18, 2006 (from the first author's fieldwork in San Francisco):

> My partner and I noticed signs advertising the Alamo Square Condos the last time we were driving through the neighborhood together, but we didn't

stop in then. Today, we follow the signs posted on sidewalks near Alamo Square, an area that is technically in the Western Addition. We are staying at an inn that borders the square. The condos are just down the street, a couple of blocks off of Fillmore Street. The signs advertising units for sale lead us into a small office area. Several white professionals who look to be in their mid-thirties are at work inside. A few desks are crowded into the small front office area. Another desk sits off in the back. A poster that hangs above the desks displays a variety of floor plans: studios, 1-, 2-, and 3-bedroom units. Two women who are sitting at a desk greet us after we step into the office. I announce that we are interested in looking at what's for sale. One of the women grabs a clipboard and asks for some information. After we provide the information, a sales representative takes us on a tour of the complex.

The buildings that make up the complex reflect the Victorian-style architecture that now characterizes San Francisco. I ask when the complex was built. "1999," the sales rep says. She explains that owners leased the units for five years and are now selling the units as condominiums. The interiors of the units have been gutted and now reflect the most recent design trends: New stainless steel kitchen appliances, granite countertops, and tiled bathroom floors have been installed in each of the units. Each unit we see is about 700 square feet. The starting price for a unit on the ground floor: $535,000. This price does not include any of the possible upgrades available to buyers. The first unit we see has a small patio off the bedroom that opens onto an interior courtyard with a large fountain. Two-story, two- and three-bedroom townhouse-style units are located on the third level of the complex. We look at a unit on the second floor. It is slightly smaller than the unit on the first floor and doesn't have a patio. It doesn't come with the standard maple floor that we saw in the downstairs unit either. Starting price: $519,000. As we look around the unit, the sales rep tells us that the area is great—easy access to so much of the city. As we finish up our tour, she asks us if we'd like to talk to the Wells Fargo mortgage representative. We agree to do so.

The mortgage representative is enthusiastic. At times, she comes across as slightly aggressive in her pitch. She reviews the incentives that are being offered to buyers: Sellers are paying the first two years of the HOA [home owners' association] fee. This is about $10,000 in savings she says. She then takes us to her office in the back room. We take a seat as she begins to work through some numbers. She asks a series of questions: Which units were we looking at? How much are we interested in putting down? 10%, I say. 10% down would mean a first mortgage of $415,000 at 6.35% interest, she explains. This would translate into a $2,205 monthly payment. The second mortgage, she explains, would cover the additional 10% down at an interest rate of about 8%. That would add another $375 to your monthly payment. Property taxes that are payable every six months would average about $480 per month. The HOA fee is $350 per month. The monthly expense of living in the advertised Alamo Square Neighborhood: $4,310 per month.

Near the end of her pitch, the mortgage rep hands us a brochure shaped like a picket fence: "Alamo Square: Welcome to the Neighborhood." A trio of pictures is arranged vertically. One picture is of the famous Painted Ladies, the Victorian homes that are San Francisco landmarks, that are just a short walk away. Another picture is of a smiling young white woman with her dog at a park. The last picture is of two hands clasped in a handshake: One of the hands is brown the other white. The mortgage rep writes the prices of each unit we looked at on the brochure. When I turn the brochure over I notice a final picture of a middle-class professional African American couple.

With the formal pitch now over, the mortgage rep shifts into informal conversation. She tells us that she used to live in this neighborhood, but now lives in Bernal Heights, "where all the lesbians with kids live." We got priced out of the Castro, where the boys [a reference to gay men] are, she tells us, and couldn't afford Noe Valley, where lesbians used to go, so we went to Bernal Heights. It's great. Kids everywhere. It was great living in this neighborhood too, she says. Great bus lines. She then adds, while motioning her thumb over her shoulder toward the direction of Fillmore Street: "You just don't go down there."

Decades ago, it was far more likely that young professionals like us would have been discouraged from purchasing a home anywhere within the boundaries of the Western Addition. It would have been difficult to get one mortgage to purchase a home in the neighborhood, much less two mortgages on the same property. By 2006, times have changed. The mortgage representative doesn't warn us away from purchasing a home within the neighborhood's boundaries. In fact, the mortgage rep provides a rather aggressive pitch for purchasing a home in the area (a home that we could not afford—a harbinger of the economic crisis to come).

In her pitch, the mortgage rep also employs the common good location–bad neighborhood distinction used in the online conversations. She offers some instruction on how to avoid the more troubled parts of the neighborhood: "Just don't go down there." Her warning does not refer to race explicitly, but it is racially coded language. She offers this warning after a series of neighborhood descriptions that made explicit reference to the types of people who lived there. Her descriptions of the specific neighborhoods in the city suggest that each neighborhood belongs to a particular group of people. The Castro is where the "boys" (gay men) are. Noe Valley is where the lesbians used to go. Yet she stops short of identifying who lives "down there," even though it is generally known that low-income and working-class blacks live down there. Here the omission leaves a space for us to fill in—a space that is often filled with stereotypes of poor, black people.

This is another way in which the practice of discursive redlining is different from the overtly racist practices of urban planners and mortgage lenders in earlier periods. In those times, racial restrictions were officially written into policies and practices. Now, in the postracial color-blind era, race is not used explicitly. Instead, the reference to "down there" stands in for race and class and is used to discourage people from spending time in specific areas of the city, especially those with higher concentrations of low-income African Americans. The accumulation of these warnings over time solidifies the spatial identity of the Western Addition as ghetto and discourages newcomers from making substantial interpersonal investments in this area.

Avoidance and Isolation: Young Black Men in the Western Addition

The mortgage rep did not know that the first author, as a field researcher, would deliberately spend a good deal of time "down there." She would come to know residents who were, as they often said with pride, "born and raised in the Fillmore." She would also interact with young men who were seen by outsiders, newcomers, and some longtime residents as the most troublesome young men in the neighborhood. In San Francisco, perhaps nobody is viewed as more dangerous than the poor, young, black male.[11] Viewed from a distance, these young men appear to reinforce widely circulated stereotypes about urban black youth: The "young ghetto male's self-presentation is often consciously off-putting or 'thuggish,' a 'master status' that overpowers positive qualities"

(Anderson 2008, 3). Implicit in the instruction to avoid certain areas of the Fillmore is the warning to avoid the poor, young, black men who live there. These warnings contribute to the process of ghettoization: "The very space of the city becomes identified with the stigmatized; persons living outside of the Ghetto view the behavior and beliefs of those inside the Ghetto with suspicion and their bodies as dangerous" (Haynes and Hutchison 2008, 348). The media also contribute to the public identity of black men in the city. Newspaper articles refer to black assailants as "thugs," and targeted policing practices officially, and quite publicly, define groups of young men as gangsters. As a consequence, young black men in the Western Addition felt the brunt of the calls for increased police surveillance. Together, these patterned avoidance practices and police surveillance practices that targeted young black men reconstruct not only "the ghetto," but also poor, young, black men *as* ghetto.[12]

The interpersonal consequences of these patterned avoidance strategies are significant. Such practices exacerbate the social distance between young men and their neighbors: "People—black as well as white—necessarily avoid him, and through their avoidance behavior teach him that he is an outsider in his own society" (Anderson 2008, 6). During a 2008 conversation at a local cheese steak shop, I asked a small group of young men about how they thought others viewed them. These young men, who had grown up in the housing complex referred to as "the projects" by some Fillmore Center reviewers, often congregated on a street corner that was visible to Fillmore Center residents. Their friends had been victims of the violence commonly associated with the area. A gang injunction that included young men from their housing complex was introduced in the neighborhood in 2007.[13] We were meeting in 2008 to discuss what life was like after the injunction. One of the young men named on the injunction joined the conversation.

The gang injunction issued by the city attorney had received a good deal of coverage from the press and was also a topic of conversation in the neighborhood. I asked the small group how they thought the injunction shaped people's perceptions of them.

"Do you think it changed how people look at you in the neighborhood?" I asked. Tre, a twenty-one-year-old, said that he thought that the injunction did not change perceptions among people who had known them for much of their lives, but that it did change how housing security and other outsiders saw them. In general, he thought that the gang injunction helped to "paint a picture [of young men] from the outside looking in," including other young men not named on the gang injunction. "From the inside looking out," he said, "the people who know us already know. They know what we do, you know what I'm sayin'? Old lady might come, she got a cart full of groceries, we goin' help her. She don't even have to ask. We gon' come help her. Period. Somebody need help getting in the gate, anything. We gon' automatically help, know what I'm sayin'?"

Elaborating, he added, "So they paint a picture from the outside looking in so people who is on the outside looking in could think that we these bad people, gangs."

Tre was aware of the message that media coverage and targeted policing strategies send to outsiders, many of whom already avoid the neighborhood and the young men who live there. As Anderson (2008, 19) describes it in *Against the Wall: Poor, Young, Black, and Male*: "Every newspaper or television story that associates a young black man with a violent crime sends a message to everyone that reinforces the stereotype of class: the dark-skinned inner-city male who is to be closely watched, feared, not trusted and employed only as a last resort." In the Fillmore, young men routinely were "closely watched" by police and were often seen as suspicious or dangerous by their neighbors. The degree to which young men understood how others perceived them was also revealed during a conversation that included young men from a set on the other side of Fillmore Street. Near the beginning of the conversation, I posed a question similar to the one I had asked of the young men gathered at the cheese steak shop.

"I would like to ask you how you think other people in the neighborhood generally think about you. Do you think they generally have a positive feeling? Do you think they stereotype you?" I asked.

"People in the neighborhood you said?" one young man asked.

"Yeah. What do you think? Do you live in this neighborhood?"

"Yeah," he said. "Some people look at us in a positive way and then some people don't."

"And so if you are thinking about who those 'some people' are, who are some people that think about you in a positive way?" I asked.

In his response to my question, the young man made a distinction similar to the one made by Tre. People who knew the young men knew that they were not one-dimensional stereotypes. It was the people who did not know them who were likely to think of them in negative ways.

People who know you look at you in a positive way, he explained. He added, "Most people that don't know you don't look at you positively."

This young man's comments reveal an appreciation of his position in the postindustrial city (Anderson 2008). His comments also reveal his own under-standing that, in the minds of many people, he was no more than a stereotype—he was a problem.

Later in the conversation, a young father who was named on the recent gang injunction validated his peer's assessment:

> People that don't know us might think negative about us. People that do know us, certain peoples, like our friends' mothers, probably think positive of us. They probably don't always think that we do positive stuff, but they probably think that we want to get away and, you know, and don't always want to be around this, so I think they think positive about us.

Like the young man who spoke before him, this young father's comments reveal an appreciation of the consequences of social isolation, which is a defining characteristic of ghettoization. People who knew them knew that they might not always do "positive stuff," but they also knew that these young men had a range of hopes and dreams. They might have presented themselves as tough or thuggish on the block, but they might also have wanted to "get away" and escape the tough circumstances in which they were coming of age. To understand this, the young men suggested, people needed to get to know them, but that was not likely when so many people were actively working to avoid them.

Negative perceptions about young black men are held not only by outsiders and newcomers to the area but also by some of their neighbors. A comment from one mother who joined the conversation highlights the layers of negative perceptions that young black men confront in their daily lives. In response to my question about perceptions, she responded: "Everybody out here, everybody out here look at them bad." She continued:

> I'm not lying. They look at them bad and, you know, I have a son that's out here with them as well, but if you don't know them, you will never know any-

thing about them. You know, like, I see them every day, and I know that they are not always up to no-good. I mean every kid is mischievous. Nobody is perfect, even the parents. Nobody is perfect. But if you don't take the time to get to know the person, or get to know your neighborhood, you will always think that something bad is going on. Always.

As in the comments from the young men, this mother's comment highlights a consequence of social isolation, even for people who live in close physical proximity to the young men in the neighborhood. From a distance, only the most problematic qualities of the young men are apparent. People who do not know the young men may see their public presentation-of-self or their behavior as reinforcing widely held beliefs about poor, young, black men. Some of this behavior is likely to cause real trouble in the neighborhood, especially violence, but people are likely to see this trouble not as a consequence of structural circumstances, but solely as a consequence of the behavior of problematic people within the neighborhood. From this perspective, the danger does not lie in the ghetto as a historically constructed space, but in the bodies of the young black men who live there. People instruct others to avoid the places where poor, young, black men congregate—"down there"—and in doing so reinforce the social distance that defines the ghetto: "If you don't take the time to get to know the person, or get to know your neighborhood, you will always think that something bad is going on. Always."

The Social Consequences of Patterned Avoidance

It is not uncommon for people who live in neighborhoods like the Fillmore to develop strategies to navigate potential threats to their well-being. In her analysis of how inner-city adolescent girls navigate the "difficult and often unpredictable inner-city terrain" (Jones 2010, 53), the first author writes that these girls develop a set of "situated survival strategies: patterned forms of interpersonal interaction, and routine or ritualized activities oriented around a concern for their personal well-being." The two main strategies she describes are "situational avoidance" and "relational isolation":

The concept of situational avoidance captures all the work teenaged girls do to avoid social settings that pose a threat to their well-being and situations in which potential conflicts might arise. . . . The concept of relational isolation illuminates the work girls do to isolate themselves from close friendships. . . . By avoiding close friendships, girls can reduce the likelihood of their involvement in a physical conflict. (Jones 2010, 54)

In some ways, the practice of discursive redlining is similar to the set of survival strategies often developed by inner-city youth, but there are also significant differences between the two strategies. In particular, the practice of discursive redlining encourages a set of avoidance strategies that are much less nuanced than the strategies commonly used by inner-city residents (Anderson 2011; Jones 2010). Instead of avoiding troublesome corners in the neighborhood, for example, people who practice discursive redlining warn others—typically others whom they perceive to be like themselves in class or status position—to avoid certain parts of the neighborhood *entirely*.

Discursive redlining also discourages newcomers to the neighborhood from building relationships with a wide swath of people who live in the nearby federally subsidized housing complexes, but especially the young black men who are often seen as the most problematic residents in the area. In doing so, people are warned away from making the kind of interpersonal investments in the neighborhood that, according to many researchers, are important factors in combating the crime and violence that plague the neighborhood. In the end, these patterns of generalized avoidance provide tacit support for institutional policies and practices that systematically remove or displace problematic people from the neighborhood.

DISCURSIVE REDLINING AND THE SOCIAL (RE)CONSTRUCTION OF THE GHETTO

In *Culture and Civility in San Francisco,* Howard Becker and Irving Louis Horowitz highlight the lack of conceptual clarity in planners' definitions of areas as "slums" and the consequences of such definitions for urban residents:

> Thus when we confront the problem of slums and urban renewal, we send for the planner and the bulldozer. But the lives of urban residents are not determined by the number or newness of buildings. *The character of their relationships with one another and the outside world does that.* Planners

and technocrats typically ignore those relationships, and their influence in shaping what people want, in constructing solutions. They define "slums" impersonally . . . and fail to see how an awakened group conscious can turn a "slum" into a "ghetto," and a rise in moral repute turn a ghetto into a "neighborhood." (Becker and Horowitz 1971, 40, our emphasis)

The practice of discursive redlining, and especially the use of the term *ghetto*, tells us a good deal about the contemporary relationship between people who live in the Fillmore and the outside world. The people and places that surround the Fillmore Center are largely seen as a problem to be avoided or removed. As is often the case, the assessments made by newcomers lack the sophistication of the distinctions made by inner-city residents in the neighborhood (Anderson 2008; Jones 2010), yet they are still consequential for patterns of inclusion and exclusion. Longtime Fillmore residents, especially those who are seen as the most problematic, are aware of how people view them, especially young black men. These patterns of avoidance and young men's awareness of how they are perceived by newcomers exacerbate the social distance between the two groups. This social distance can make it more difficult for locals to make use of the social capital that newcomers may bring to neighborhoods in transition.

Although discursive redlining is a practice that is embedded in everyday interactions, it can lead to serious institutional consequences. The online reviews and the face-to-face warnings described in this chapter encourage an ahistorical sense of the ghetto as a problem. Embedded in the warnings is an understanding of the ghetto not as a place but rather, as Elijah Anderson puts it, as something that people carry with them, whether they want to or not. The online conversation about the Fillmore Center uses *ghetto* as an adjective to refer to the essential and problematic qualities of places and people. These types of conversations also suggest that the ghetto is carried in the adolescent bodies of poor black youth, who are seen by others as "thugs" or "ghetto chicks." This perspective reinforces the basest stereotypes about black people and erases the experiences of longtime residents in the neighborhood, including residents who take some pride in being "born and raised" in the Fillmore.

Framing the problem of the ghetto as a problem of the moral or behavioral qualities of a particular class of people has serious consequences for neighborhood change. In the recent past, scholars argued that addressing power relationships was instrumental to changing the conditions of the ghetto: "In order to change the conditions of the ghetto, residents needed to change the power dynamic between ghetto residents and the majority society outside the confines of its 'invisible wall'" (Haynes and Hutchison 2008, 351). Such an understanding reflects an appreciation of the relational and institutional dimensions of the problem. Herbert Gans (2008, 356) explains this relationship in a recent comment on the ghetto: "Even in the very poorest areas, the deleterious effects of poverty are not caused by the neighborhood, but by institutions, most of them outside the neighborhood, that initiate or perpetuate poverty and conditions associated with it." People who practice discursive redlining do not identify crime or violence as *institutional* problems or as symptoms of a city's failure to incorporate African Americans into economic and civic life in the postwar era (Anderson 2008). Instead, discursive redlining suggests that it is the people, their bodies, and their behaviors that are the problem. The sorts of solutions that follow this conceptualization of the problem are obvious: patterned avoidance or systematic removal.

From Ghetto to Neighborhood

In the mid-twentieth century, the problem was officially defined as "slums," and slums were, in turn, removed. Today the problem is defined both officially and in everyday talk as the people, and it is the problematic people, especially young black men in public spaces, who are the target of removal efforts. The practice of discursive redlining sets the stage for targeted policing practices and criminal-civil hybrids like gang injunctions, which have the consequence (unintended or otherwise) of encouraging the displacement of young men and their families from the neighborhood through eviction, incarceration, or mandatory exclusion (for example, stay-away orders as a condition of probation). In short, when newcomers to an area think of the ghetto as something that *people carry with them*, then institutionalized efforts to get rid of the ghetto are naturally tied to getting rid of the people who are seen *as* ghetto.

Discursive redlining is a key mechanism in the reproduction of a neighborhood's spatial identity and can have an indirect effect on people's willingness to make economic and interpersonal investments in a transitioning neighborhood like the Fillmore. Identifying the interactional mechanisms by which people are warned away from the Western Addition is important not only because doing so reveals how inequality is reproduced, but also because doing so identifies potential sites for intervention. Recent efforts to combat the concentration of poverty encourage just the sort of housing patterns that are becoming more evident in the Fillmore. But the presence of mixed-income housing does not necessarily mean that the ghetto will disappear. Instead, understandings of what "ghetto" means may shift from a type of place to a quality of a people, as appears to be the case in the Fillmore. In this context, daily interactions, especially in cities that offer few spaces for people to gather under cosmopolitan canopies (Anderson 2008, 2011), are likely to exacerbate the social isolation of longtime residents and newcomers.

Contemporary urban renewal efforts are focused primarily on the deconcentration of poverty. Yet today's class of ghetto scholars and urban planners should pay serious attention to the character of the *relationships* that develop in the newly configured ghetto. The character of these relationships will play a key role in determining whether places that were largely seen as ghettos in the twentieth century will become neighborhoods in the twenty-first century.

Notes

1. The first author lived in the area for about a month in 2004 and two months in 2005, then returned several times a year until taking up primary residence there for the next two and a half years, from July 2007 to December 2009. She ended formal data collection for this ethnographic project in 2010. Her research was supported by an award from the William T. Grant Foundation.

2. All names are pseudonyms.

3. Field note entry, July 12, 2005.

4. Field note entry, November 3, 2005.

5. After reviewing thirty-four postings for this analysis, the first author created a database of the reviews, manually open-coded to generate a coding scheme, and then completed focused line-by-line coding using dedoose, a qualitative analysis web-based software program. She retains an archived copy of the reviews in her files (last accessed April 9, 2010).

6. This practice is distinct from the situated survival strategies (Jones 2010) used by residents of distressed urban neighborhoods to avoid areas and groups of people that are likely to attract violence.

7. For a pictorial history of the Fillmore's jazz scene, see Pepin and Watts (2006).

8. A search for the term *black* on the website turned up zero references, but the common usage of terms like *ghetto* and *'hood* makes it clear that the Western Addition is a place where poor black people live and that this fact is *the* problem with the neighborhood.

9. See Yelp, "The Fillmore Center (Apartments)," http://www.yelp.com/biz/fillmore-center
-apartments-san-francisco?rpp=40&sort_by=date_desc (accessed April 4, 2010). Eleven (Urban
D., Willie A., Mollie S., Jerome F., Max A., Brad D., W.D., Summer D., G.G., Miss K., and James
D.) use the term *ghetto* in their postings on the Fillmore Center.

10. Bruce Haynes and Ray Hutchison (2008, 352) discuss the migration of the word *ghetto*
from popular culture into academic research. The term *ghetto* is now used to refer to speech,
dress, or behavior.

11. This image is paralleled only by the image of the gang-affiliated Latino adolescent male.

12. Elijah Anderson (2008, 7) writes: "The black male may 'put white people off' just by being
black, and the younger he is and the more 'ghetto' he looks, the more distrust he engenders."

13. A gang injunction is a civil injunction that restricts the behavior of the individuals named
on the injunction within a geographically defined area.

References

Anderson, Elijah. 1999. *Code of the Street: Decency, Violence, and the Moral Life of the Inner
City.* New York: W. W. Norton.

———. 2008. *Against the Wall: Poor, Young, Black, and Male.* Philadelphia: University of Pennsylvania Press.

———. 2011. *The Cosmopolitan Canopy: Race and Civility in Everyday Life.* New York: W. W.
Norton.

Becker, Howard, and Irving Louis Horowitz. 1971. *Culture and Civility in San Francisco.* New
Brunswick, N.J.: Transaction.

Beckett, Katherine, and Steve Herbert. 2010. "Penal Boundaries: Banishment and the Expansion
of Punishment." *Law and Social Inquiry* 35, no. 1: 1–38.

Bellush, Jewel, and Murray Hausknecht, eds. 1967. *Urban Renewal: People, Politics, and Planning.*
Garden City, N.Y.: Anchor Books/Doubleday.

Beveridge, Andrew. 2008. "A Century of Harlem in New York City: Some Notes on Migration,
Consolidation, Segregation, and Recent Development." *City & Community* 7, no. 4: 358–
365.

Blokland, Talja. 2008. "From the Outside Looking In: A "European" Perspective on the *Ghetto*."
City & Community 7, no. 4: 372–377.

Broussard, Albert. 1993. *Black San Francisco: The Struggle for Racial Equality in the West, 1900–
1954.* Lawrence: University of Kansas Press.

Collins, William J. 2001. "Race, Roosevelt, and Wartime Production: Fair Employment in World
War II Labor Markets." *American Economic Review* 91, no.1 (March): 272–286.

Daniels, Douglass Henry. 1980. *Pioneer Urbanites: A Social and Cultural History of Black San
Francisco.* Philadelphia: Temple University Press.

Day, Noel A., and Zenophon Abraham. 1993. "The Unfinished Agenda: The Economic Status
of African Americans in San Francisco, 1964–1990." San Francisco: Human Rights Commission of San Francisco, Committee on African American Parity.

Fusfeld, Daniel, and Timothy Bates. 1984. *The Political Economy of the Urban Ghetto.* Carbondale:
Southern Illinois University Press.

Gans, Herbert J. 2008. "Involuntary Segregation and the Ghetto: Disconnecting Process and Place." *City & Community* 7, no. 4: 353–357.

Geron, Kim, Enrique de la Cruz, Leland Saito, and Jaideep Singh. 2001. "Asian Pacific Americans' Social Movements and Interest Groups." *PS: Political Science and Politics* 34, no. 3: 618–624.

Hartman, Chester. 2002. *City for Sale: The Transformation of San Francisco.* Berkeley and Los Angeles: University of California Press.

Haynes, Bruce, and Ray Hutchison. 2008. "The Ghetto: Origins, History, Discourse." *City & Community* 7, no. 4: 347–352.

Hippler, Arthur E. 1974. *Hunter's Point: A Black Ghetto.* New York: Basic Books.

Jackson, Christina. 2010. "Black Flight from San Francisco: How Race, Community, and Politics Shape Urban Policy." MA thesis, University of California–Santa Barbara.

Johnson, Charles S. 1944. *The Negro War Worker in San Francisco: A Local Self-Survey.* San Francisco: American Missionary Association.

Jones, Nikki. 2010. *Between Good and Ghetto: African American Girls and Inner City Violence.* New Brunswick, N.J.: Rutgers University Press.

Lai, Clement. 2006. "Between 'Blight' and a New World: Urban Renewal, Political Mobilization, and the Production of Spatial Scale." ISSC Fellows working papers. Berkeley, Calif.: Institute for the Study of Social Change.

Lomax, Aleena. 1972. "The View from Hunter's Point." *San Francisco Examiner*, March 20.

Martin, A. 2006. "Slain Community Center Worker Had Criminal Record." *San Francisco Examiner*, April 29–30.

Massey, Douglas, and Nancy Denton. 1993. *American Apartheid: Segregation and the Making of the Underclass.* Cambridge, Mass.: Harvard University Press.

Pepin, Elizabeth, and Lewis Watts. 2006. *Harlem of the West: The San Francisco Fillmore Jazz Era.* San Francisco: Chronicle Books.

Simon, Jonathan. 2007. *Governing Through Crime: How the War on Crime Transformed American Democracy.* New York: Oxford University Press.

Small, Mario Luis. 2008. "Four Reasons to Abandon the Idea of 'the Ghetto.'" *City & Community* 7, no. 4: 389–398.

U.S. Navy. 1943. "Conference with Regard to Negro Personnel." Memo from Capt. Hinkamp, October 6, 1943. Fifth Naval District Headquarters. Norfolk, Va.: National Archives.

Van Derbeken, Jaxon. 2005. "More Delays, More Killings." *San Francisco Chronicle*, December 21.

Van Derbeken, Jaxon, and Marisa Lagos. 2006. "Gym Shooting Victim Was on Probation: Hired to Work with Kids, He Had a Felony Assault Conviction." *San Francisco Chronicle*, April 29.

Wacquant, Loïc. 1999. "Urban Marginality in the Coming Millennium." *Urban Studies* 36, no. 10: 1639–1647.

Wilson, William Julius. 1980. *The Declining Significance of Race: Blacks and Changing American Institutions.* Chicago: University of Chicago Press.

———. 1987. *The Truly Disadvantaged: The Inner City, the Underclass, and Public Policy.* Chicago: University of Chicago Press.

———. 1996. *When Work Disappears: The World of the New Urban Poor.* New York: Vintage Books.

———. 2009. *More Than Just Black: Being Black and Poor in the Inner City.* New York: W. W. Norton.

CHAPTER 5

✦ ✦ ✦

In Terms
of Harlem
Bruce D. Haynes

For nearly a century Harlem has come to signify black space—culturally, physically, metaphorically—in the consciousness of people across the globe. The name alone conjures both place and idea—a symbolic boundary between civility and mayhem, the archetypical black ghetto characterized by urban decay, poverty, crime, drugs, delinquency, and death, a stand-in for every ghetto in America. As soul singer Bobby Womack put it in the title song of the 1972 film *Across 110th Street*, "Every city you find the same thing goin' down, Harlem is the capital of any ghetto town!" Some evoke its name as a badge of authenticity, others as the new Greenwich Village.

Harlem is neither of these. Nor is it a single residential neighborhood. As a youngster, I came to know Harlem as a sprawling group of contiguous neighborhoods above 110th Street where colored folks lived, loved, and labored. What looked to outsiders like one giant black belt was actually subdivided into numerous identifiable spaces: Harlem Heights and Harlem's Valley, Mount Morris Park, Striver's Row, Riverside Drive, Spanish Harlem, Morningside Heights, and our own neighborhood—the area around City College often clumped with Sugar Hill but officially known as West Inwood—Washington Heights (New York City Landmarks Preservation Commission 2001). Some neighborhoods had multiple names: Spanish Harlem is also known locally as El Barrio and East Harlem.

My Harlem was roller-skating in Riverside Park with my two brothers and playing stickball with my dad at the handball courts. It was Mr. Softie ice cream trucks on sweltering summer days and elders doling wisdom from their stoops on balmy summer evenings. A place where even underemployed men wore a shirt and tie on Sunday mornings and where we echoed Stokely Carmichael's call for "Black Power" and, later, shouted "I'm Black and I'm Proud!" from the fire escapes and rooftops! But that was the 1960s, long before the North River sewage treatment plant transformed Riverside Park into a noxious soup, pushing asthma rates up five times the national average (Sze 2007, 81).

Harlem was the YMCA and the Schomburg Center for Research in Black Culture on 135th Street—the original cultural and commercial hub of Harlem. And it was most definitely 125th Street—the epicenter of black culture, commerce, and politics, the place where Harlem's hipsters and hustlers, its immigrants and migrants, the marginally employed and the stable middle class all converged. Moorish Science Muslims, Black Hebrew Israelites, and Black Jews preached side by side with Baptists, Methodists, and Seventh-Day Adventists. Immigrants from Senegal, the Ivory Coast, and Ethiopia mingled with Jamaicans, Trinidadians, and Guyanese. In *Black Manhattan* (1930/1991), James Weldon Johnson reported that newcomers to the area did not remain mere "Harlem Negroes" but became New Yorkers. Today people are still becoming New Yorkers as new immigrants and their children inherit the city (Kasinitz et al. 2006; Kasinitz et al. 2008). Similar spaces in the postindustrial urban landscape are described as "cosmopolitan canopies" where diverse social, cultural, and racial groups come together to conduct business and social life (Anderson 2004, 14).

Strolling down 125th Street, we'd pass corner preachers and street hawkers and inhale the smell of fresh watermelons brought all the way up from the Carolinas and sold from the backs of large trucks along Madison Avenue. Early in the day, we'd take our place in the long queue outside Georgie's Bakery, where folks in the know flocked for the city's best glazed doughnuts. Cigarettes, too, were brought from the Carolinas, where Big Tobacco kept taxes low. In Harlem, you could purchase a single cigarette at a newsstand or penny candy store for a dime and a carton of Benson and Hedges 100s—my mother's brand—for half-price. Like most Harlem women, my mother came to 125th Street for the cocoa-butter hair products and cosmetics that could be found only in stores that catered to a black clientele. My brothers and I came to rummage through the 45s and record albums at Bobby's Happy House, where the latest Wilson Pickett or Supremes blasted onto the street, or the Record Shack, whose owner, South African ex-patriot Sikhulu Shange, cried out for support of black-owned businesses after the 1964 riots. Others, like my oldest brother, George, came for knowledge and culture, both to be found at the National Memorial African Book Store (dubbed "The House of Common Sense and Proper Propaganda"), said to contain the largest collection of books about blacks in the world—that is, next to the Schomburg.

But that was only one part of Harlem—the Valley—and a long stretch from our five-thousand-square-foot limestone row house in the Heights and the majestic Convent Avenue Baptist Church just down the street. (On March 26, 1968, at this one-hundred-year-old neo-Gothic marble structure, Dr. Martin Luther King Jr. gave his last New York address, just nine days before his assassination.) Commerce in the Heights was concentrated along 145th Street from Broadway down to Lenox and between 140th and 147th Streets along Broadway, St. Nicholas, and Amsterdam Avenues. Here streets were dotted with small clothing and hardware stores that bore the names of their Italian and Jewish owners (some of whom were warm and avuncular, while others treated you like a criminal). Storefronts were interspersed with apartment stoops that protruded onto the sidewalk, great for neighbors socializing in the evenings—save for the deadly iron borders strategically placed to discourage sitting. One could have been in any small town in America, with mom-and-pop grocery and stationery stores, shoe repair shops and dry cleaners, tire repair and hubcap stores, and, of course, funeral homes. On one corner of Amsterdam Avenue stood an old-time record shop, the kind that had faux 45s hung in the window and a wooden sign itself cut in the shape of a 45. Speakers were mounted above the doorway, blaring the latest hits onto the sidewalk. Gypsy cabs weaved through the traffic. The 101 bus barreled by, making local stops on its way to Fort Tyron Park and billowing out diesel smoke whenever it hit the gas. This, too, was my Harlem.

Our housekeeper, Mrs. Grandberry, served double duty as my nanny. She lived in a dank second-floor apartment near the Park Avenue Market, known locally as La Marqueta, down in Spanish Harlem. Every time she made it up those stairs, she "thanked the Lord," even as it took her breath away. She taught me to say grace and recite the Lord's Prayer—at noontime and bedtime. She gave me my first Bible and taught me to take nothing for granted. With her laborer husband long since dead, Nanny now cleaned and dusted, vacuumed and polished, and walked me to and from school every day through second grade. On the way home, she'd treat me to fifteen-cent popcorn and fried chicken drumsticks at the F. W. Woolworth's on Broadway and 145th Street. Next door was Copeland's, the upscale soul food establishment where Stevie Wonder, Harry Belafonte, and Sammy Davis Jr. had been regulars and my mom would stop in for takeout. Across the street was the West Indian barber, who gave me a classic buzz cut with the part down the side, at least until I began growing an Afro at age six. In Harlem, barbershops and beauty parlors were the hub of a thriving underground economy that predated the rise of the massive drug trades of the 1970s. Numbers runners made their rounds, memorizing or jotting down bets that stood to make a six-to-one return. Street hustlers stopped by regularly, selling their wares—anything from the latest dresses and handbags to steaks and shoes—all "off the back of a truck."

Harlem was the Dance Theater of Harlem, the Boys Choir of Harlem, and the AMAS Repertory Theatre—institutions that drew audiences from diverse racial and class backgrounds. It was the sophistication of the black middle class, exuded by women in my mother's circle like Rosetta LeNoire, who had played on Broadway in the 1930s, founded AMAS in 1968, and in 1975 produced the Broadway hit *Bubbling Brown Sugar: A Musical Journey Through Harlem*. These women were educated and cosmopolitan and shopped downtown at upscale department stores like Bonwit Teller, Bergdorf Goodman, and Saks Fifth Avenue.

In *Black Manhattan* (1930/1991, 169), Johnson told us that Harlem had "all the elements of a cosmopolitan center." Some thirty-five years later, this was still true. Doctors and lawyers lived down the street from our home and were a part of our lives. Two doors away was Dr. Dobson, my baby doctor (as well as my first boss—at age six, I earned a few nickels a day emptying the ashtrays in his office). The doctor's mother, a very proper elderly woman, lived with him and taught me to play Chopsticks on her baby grand piano. At the end of the block lived the Rawlings, a family of lawyers who handled our family business for decades. Dr. Morgan and his family lived around the corner on 147th Street toward St. Nick; other doctors had home offices up on 148th Street toward Amsterdam Avenue. In fact, growing up, I was surrounded by doctors—doctors and West Indians.

———

My childhood years were spent largely within the neighborhood. There were those who occupied far more modest jobs than did my social worker parents, and others who didn't seem to occupy any jobs at all and could be found on their stoops day or night, almost a permanent part of the cityscape. I attended summer camp at the neighborhood YMCA on 135th Street, just as my father had done in his youth. The kids at my neighborhood school, P.S. 186, represented the full spectrum of the area's class diversity. They came from dual-income households, single-working-mom households, and government-subsidized households. Some parents commuted to white- and pink-collar jobs downtown, while others worked at the neighborhood post office or grocery store. There were tough kids at the school, and in second grade the boys fought regularly. I still have a two-inch scar across my right kneecap from a fight with Tyrone, the class bully and my first friend. We all knew the class ranking and discussed it openly. But after I was mugged in the boys' bathroom in second grade, and with the impending New York City teachers' strike of 1968, my parents enrolled me in a private school downtown.

For the next ten years, I navigated two worlds. Many of my new downtown classmates were nouveau riche and lived in swank Manhattan neighborhoods—Sutton Place, Yorkville, and the Upper West Side. A few, like me, were middle class. Still fewer were black. For nearly all of them, 110th Street marked the boundary between light and darkness, rich and poor. For this short, slightly built kid, coming from Harlem gave me just the edge I needed to invoke fear in playground skirmishes. Some kids—as well as their parents—were taken aback when they learned that my family owned a brownstone in Harlem. "A brownstone in Harlem?" they'd ask, or, "You mean to say that your parents are still married?" This question always struck me as strange since most of my parents' friends were married and lived in homes at least as nice as our own. I was never questioned by my old classmates in Harlem about "acting white,"

a trope popularized by the Nigerian American scholar John Ogbu. (I did, however, get ribbed by them for listening to the Grateful Dead and the Rolling
Stones! Now that was acting white!)

———————

With two older brothers—seven and ten years my senior—I was exposed to
a variety of political viewpoints during the 1960s. In April 1969, a group of
students—black, Puerto Rican, and white—took over the South Campus and
Klapper Hall of the City University of New York, demanding more diversity
among the faculty and in the curriculum. My brother George, one of the key
leaders of the high school coalition, took me to the campus—just ten blocks
south of our home—at the height of the protests. As I took in the scene—students
in dashikis and Afros, drum circles, assorted smoke wafting in the air—I felt
like the entire campus had been turned into a giant fair. By the time the students agreed to vacate two weeks later, the administration had agreed to a controversial open enrollment plan and the university's president, Dr. Buell
Gallagher, had resigned. The impact of the protest was far-reaching. Thanks
to data from the U.S. Department of Labor and the award-winning research
of sociologists Paul Attewell and David Lavin (2007), we now know that some
70 percent of all disadvantaged women who were admitted to CUNY during
the early 1970s through its open enrollment plan graduated and boosted their
incomes while improving the educational success of their children.

———————

Harlem Heights has always held a certain allure. The land on which our home
was built (today Convent Avenue between 147th and 148th Streets) was once
the most coveted in Manhattan. Just five blocks south stood the original twelve-
room country estate of Alexander Hamilton. (The building has been moved
twice since that time.) Perched high on a hill, the site was chosen for its views
of the Hudson River to the west and the Harlem and East Rivers to the east
(Chernow 2004, 642–644). Less than half a block from our home, at the junc-
ture of Convent Avenue and 148th Street, stood the Pinehurst Mansion, the
country home of Dr. Samuel Bradhurst, heir of one of the oldest colonial families in New York State.

By the mid-1800s, Harlem Heights was losing its pastoral quality. New York's population had spiraled upward between 1820 and 1850, and already by the 1830s the city's reservoirs were insufficient and unsanitary. The Croton Aqueduct, completed in 1842, brought fresh water from upstate New York to Manhattan Island, but also cut through the Bradhurst estate by way of Tenth Avenue. In order to bury the large-diameter pipes, according to the New-York Historical Society, the land directly behind the mansion had to be elevated by more than ten feet, thus obstructing its magnificent views.

In the days before mass transportation, travel from midtown Manhattan to Harlem Heights was more than a two-hour coach ride. But in 1837, the New York and Harlem Railroad began running service from lower Manhattan to Harlem. And as New York expanded, parks were needed for leisure and recreation. In the late 1850s, the city purchased over 700 acres of rural, undeveloped land in the center of Manhattan to build a park that would rival the public spaces of European cities and fulfill the vision of a democratic urban space in which folks of all social ranks could commingle. By the time the project was completed in 1863, Central Park ran all the way to 110th Street, the southern-most boundary of today's Harlem.

A city park in Harlem was developed shortly afterward. Mount Morris Park was designed by the city's chief landscape gardener, Ignatz A. Pilat, and built on a wedge of Manhattan schist—the bedrock of the island. The neighborhood featured some of the grandest brownstones in Harlem as well as trees of all varieties—Osage orange, maple, oak, elm, and birch.

Improvements in urban transportation continued to displace horse-drawn vehicles on Manhattan Island. In 1879 the Eighth Avenue line, or the A train—later memorialized by Duke Ellington—opened stations at 135th, 145th, and 155th Streets in Harlem's Valley. Still, convenient access to Harlem Heights didn't come until 1904, when an IRT terminus opened a station at 145th and Broadway. The new service was promoted with the slogan "Fifteen Minutes to Harlem."

Long before its completion, the IRT project triggered mass speculation uptown. Architects designed dozens of French Provincial, Gothic, Italianate, and Classical Revival homes with a view to attracting well-to-do urbanites who could now commute to their downtown offices. Our own home, 411 Convent Avenue, was built in 1901 by the prominent New York architect Henri Fouchaux and was one of five Revival row houses that were constructed entirely of limestone. Speculators never intended for these bourgeois homes to house Negro families, but even the advent of the subway couldn't supply enough middle-class white folks to fill these grand spaces. Wealthy whites had built mansions on Fifth Avenue along the "Millionaires' Mile"—right up to Harlem's doorstep.

————

Scholarship on the American ghetto dates back to Max Weber (1978, 385), who argued that segregated spaces are marketlike creations that maintain social closure through spatial isolation of a "negatively typed" population (see also Haynes and Hernandez 2008). Urban historian Gilbert Osofsky noted that blacks have always lived in isolated neighborhoods in the worst sections of the city. "Despite the seeming transformations, however, the essential structure and nature of the Negro ghetto have remained remarkably durable since the demise of slavery in the North" (Osofsky 1968, 243).

Manhattan's black population had slowly been pushed northward for decades, beginning with their relocation from Prince Street (the old section of the city of New Amsterdam in today's Greenwich Village) to the Tenderloin District (the areas now known as Chelsea, the Garment District, and the then-red-light Times Square) and San Juan Hill (today the site of Lincoln Center). The development of Central Park in 1858 displaced hundreds of poor Irish immigrant farmers as well as the entire population of Seneca Village, the city's most stable Negro settlement at the time. The construction of the park was the largest public works project in the city's history, but it began just one year into a sharp economic downturn on Wall Street. Under the threat of mob violence by the Irish, not one black worker was employed in the massive public works project.

Physical violence was never far from the minds of black New Yorkers. It kept folks hemmed in to particular Negro jobs and physical spaces. Historians and sociologists have distinguished between two types of attacks against blacks: southern-style riots, in which white mobs attack and kill defenseless blacks, and northern-style riots, in which blacks fight back. Yet, Southern-style riots were not confined to the South. During the New York draft riots of 1863, eleven Negroes were lynched, untold numbers were killed, and a colored orphanage was burned to the ground. The weeklong siege of the city led to a sizable shift in racial space. Shortly after the riots, the more well-to-do Negroes moved to Brooklyn, a ferry ride away, and many blacks left the city altogether, moving to New Jersey or other states (Osofsky 1968; Bernstein 1990, 18; Harris 2003; PBS 2001). By 1865—within two years of the draft riots—New York's black population was the lowest since 1820, with just under 10,000 residents. Some forty years later, in 1910, when the Great White Hope, Jim Jeffries, was defeated in the boxing ring by Jack Johnson, thousands of black folks across the nation were attacked. The *New York Times* reported on July 5, 1910, that white mobs and marauding gangs of men attacked men, women, and children in Hell's Kitchen and San Juan Hill, and even in Harlem itself.

New York would not see a northern-style riot until pitched battles in the streets between blacks and whites hit the Tenderloin district in 1900 and, five years later, San Juan Hill, making Harlem even more attractive. And with the construction of (the original) Penn Station under way and the relocation of the garment industry from the Lower East Side to the Tenderloin, many Negroes were ousted from their tenements, and new loft construction prevented further residential expansion. But this was an era when Jack Johnson had inspired a "New Negro" attitude, and this New Negro fought back!

———

Pulitzer Prize–winning journalist Isabel Wilkerson has called the Great Migration—the migration of six million black Americans from the bowels of the Jim Crow South toward the promise and safety of the urban North and the uncharted West—"the biggest underreported story of the twentieth century" in an interview on NPR's *Fresh Air* (September 13, 2010). In her *New York Times* best seller, *The Warmth of Other Suns: The Epic Story of America's Great Migration*, Wilson remarks that "Perhaps it is not a question of whether the migrants brought good or ill to the cities they fled to . . . but a question of how they summoned the courage to leave in the first place or how they found the will to press beyond the forces against them and the faith in a country that had rejected them for so long" (Wilkerson 2010, 538). And while the continuous influx of migrants transformed cities, towns, and communities like Harlem across the country, it also gave rise to the "New Negro" and new institutions that transformed the experiences of the migrants themselves and made life bearable in the unforgiving promised land. Perhaps the single most important of these institutions was the National Urban League, founded on September 29, 1910. Labor relations was its focus, and "interracial cooperation for mutual advantage" its guiding principle. Its original mission was to train social workers, conduct research, and create job opportunities for black Americans through vocational guidance and policy advocacy. The progressives John D. Rockefeller Jr., Julius Rosenwald, and Alfred T. White provided the financial support, along with philanthropist and social activist Ruth Standish Baldwin. My grandfather, George Edmund Haynes, a black migrant from Pine Bluff, Arkansas, who was earning his doctorate in the new science of sociology at Columbia University, brought the vision. Together they stepped across the color line to challenge the status quo for Negro workers. This quintessentially American experiment in interracial cooperation resulted in a national organization that today boasts over one hundred local affiliates in thirty-six states and the District of Columbia and provides direct services and programs as well as research and advocacy to an estimated 2.1 million Americans.

In 1903 Haynes graduated as valedictorian from Fisk University, the preeminent Negro university and alma mater of W. E. B. Du Bois. Haynes met Du Bois when he was fifteen and still attending the preparatory high school at Fisk. Du Bois took an immediate interest in Haynes and became a mentor over the coming years. Under Du Bois's guidance and direction, Haynes took courses at the University of Chicago—then one of the more welcoming schools for blacks—in the summers of 1906 and 1907 and then went on to pursue graduate studies, first in sociology and economics at Yale University (studying with William Graham Sumner) and later in labor migration at Columbia University, where he studied under Albion Small (Wilson 2006). In 1912 Haynes became the first African American to earn a PhD from Columbia University. He was also the first prominent black labor economist, one of the first black urban sociologists in the country (Wilson 2006), and the first scholar to examine the Great Migration in sociological and economic terms and to predict that the black exodus would continue throughout the twentieth century (Haynes 1913). He understood the plight of the migrants firsthand and articulated a vision that would transform their determination into real jobs in the modern city. The very structures he created spurred the continued flow of migrants into New York, Chicago, and many other urban centers in the North and Midwest.

Black migrants were often met with discrimination in housing and exploitative working conditions, which led to new social problems that, in turn, heightened white angst, solidified social stigma, and fueled racial tensions. Many political and business leaders of the day focused on rural solutions, such as agricultural training to alleviate the labor problems of blacks, but Haynes understood that the movement of blacks away from the land was more than a temporary phenomenon and that economic empowerment in the industrial labor force was the key to their future success.

Kenneth Clark observed in *Dark Ghetto: Dilemmas of Social Power* that the ghetto was both spatial containment and its consequence, concentrated poverty for blacks, or "the problem of the slum" (Clark 1965, xxii). Indeed, the black ghetto has endured by embodying the historical process of racialization, a process that simultaneously links spatial isolation to racial stigmatization by manipulating housing markets along racial lines to aid in creating social closure; the ghettoization process solidifies race identity as well as the color line while handicapping blacks in the economic marketplace, reinforcing social stigma while concentrating poverty. Fifty years earlier, George Haynes (1913) observed that the makings of the urban ghetto had been established since the early days of the Republic: "But almost from the beginning, probably the environing white group had segregated the Negroes into separate neighborhoods. . . . In Manhattan, while the areas populated by Negroes have shifted somewhat from decade to decade, there have been distinctively Colored sections since 1800." These colored sections included San Juan Hill and Harlem—which already housed over 35,000 people within about eighteen city blocks. Philadelphia's Seventh Ward, Chicago's State Street, Washington's Northwest neighborhood, Baltimore's Drew Avenue, Atlanta's West End and Auburn Avenue, and Louisville's Chestnut Street and "Smoke Town" were cited by Haynes as additional examples of "segregation within the city" (Haynes 1913).

In 1904 the local real estate bubble burst in Harlem just as thousands of southern rural Negroes—especially from Virginia, the Carolinas, and Georgia—hit the city in search of work. Housing demand surged, and enterprising but shady middlemen offered their services to desperate white landlords, helping them rent out apartments to the new flood of colored tenants—often at inflated prices. According to National Urban League studies, black families paid upward of 45 percent of their wages for housing, and one scholar has referred to the period as a "slum boom." In Central Harlem, a single colored family on a block was sufficient to trigger a stampede, which in turn produced more housing stock for Negro tenants. This lucrative practice, known as blockbusting, was predicated on whites' desire for residential isolation from blacks and other racialized groups (Osofsky 1963). High rents and poor salaries led many folks to take in strangers as boarders, contributing to overcrowding and unsanitary conditions—the very makings of a ghetto.

Crossing into "white" territory could prove deadly, as folks sometimes learned, even in the city where money ruled. Philip A. Payton was perhaps the most well known and aggressive of the Negro brokers during this period. His earliest deals were confined to Harlem's Valley and met little resistance, but once he crossed Lenox Avenue—which served as an unofficial dividing line between white and black Harlem—some whites organized to purchase all the properties occupied by colored tenants in order to evict them (Osofsky 1971). Payton responded by forming the Afro-American Realty Company, an all-Negro corporation that acquired leases on white-owned properties and rented to blacks. What brought down Payton in the end, however, was not white resistance but overzealous speculation (Osofsky 1971, 103–104). Still, his activities provided a wedge for other entrepreneurs to integrate Harlem; in 1907 St. Philip's Episcopal Church—one of the first black churches in Harlem—purchased thirteen apartments on 135th Street and rented them to members of its congregation (Osofsky 1971; Watkins-Owens 1996).

While homes became vacant and prices fell sharply, the banks and lending institutions that took them over at first refused to sell or rent to Negroes. They held on to them until the outbreak of World War I, when demographic and economic forces compelled even the most resistant whites in Harlem to rent or sell to blacks. A house-to-house survey conducted by the National Urban League in 1914 estimated Harlem's Negro population at 49,555, almost five-sixths the size of Manhattan Island's Negro population. By 1915 the exodus of Irish, Italians, and Jews from Harlem was well under way.

The Harlem Renaissance has often been characterized by its jazz clubs and Prohibition speakeasies, its brothels and dance halls, and as a time when white dandies in top hats and canes came slumming for a thrill and maybe even a bit of authenticity. In 1927, when thousands flocked to theaters downtown to see Warner Brothers' new talking picture *The Jazz Singer*—the story of a Jew becoming American while pretending to be a Negro—America's social anxiety about racial difference could not have been clearer. The prevailing view had been that when downtown closed, uptown came to life. Black folks didn't sleep! Looking for a space to stretch the boundaries of contemporary sexual mores, young whites, especially those with cash to burn, dressed to the nines and flocked to Harlem's Valley for a walk on the wild side. During the Renaissance, they came to watch the whites-only burlesque shows at establishments like the Cotton Club or Connie's Inn or ventured over to Small's Paradise, where Charleston-dancing waiters carried Chinese food and bootleg liquor to an integrated clientele. It was not Claude McKay's classic novel *Home to Harlem* (1928/1987) or his celebration of Harlem's cultural richness in *Harlem: Negro Metropolis* (1940) that would shape popular conceptions, but rather books like Carl van Vechten's *Nigger Heaven* (1926/2000).

As America transitioned from the Gilded Age to the Progressive era, Negro lives were steeped in contradiction. On the one hand, the nation was being transformed through industrialization and capitalism; although some blacks were able to benefit from these changes, the solidification of the color line pushed many to the margins of society. And with this marginalization came an intense and unprecedented boom in cultural production. By 1922 Harlem was already amassing a cadre of notable artists. But still locked behind the veil, black writers lacked access to mainstream publishing houses, and visual artists worked in almost total obscurity, with little hope of sales or access to prominent art venues. White patronage was critical to many of the most successful New Negro poets and writers, sculptors, and landscape artists. Some individuals, like Zora Neale Hurston, had their personal patrons (whom she dubbed "Negrotarians"), but most Negro artists depended on organizational support.

Although outsiders marveled at Harlem's cultural products, culture was merely one dimension of a multidimensional community. The backbone of the community was its working people and the institutions they created: the men who worked as laborers, elevator operators, dockworkers, messengers, and porters, carrying, schlepping, digging, and serving while the women scrubbed, cleaned, and cooked—mostly in white homes. They created overlapping organizational networks that crisscrossed Harlem—from churches to fraternal and benevolent associations to burial societies to groups like the Eastern Stars and Masons to assorted Caribbean clubs and associations named after their home islands in Barbados, Antigua, Martinique, the Virgin Islands, the Bahamas, and Trinidad. Harlem had become a magnet for those seeking to make it. It always held its "voodoo charms," as the American essayist E.B. White quipped (White 1948, 46), but behind the smiles and laughter was a richer, darker Harlem. The institutions held its residents together; the music, the dancing, the laughter expressed their yearnings while masking the brutal lives they endured—the overcrowded and overpriced tenements they lived in and the underpaid work they performed. As Alain Locke (1936) eloquently wrote in the August 1936 issue of *Survey Graphic*: "It is easier to dally over black Bohemia or revel in the hardy survivals of Negro art and culture than to contemplate this dark Harlem of semi-starvation, mass exploitation and seething unrest." Harlem was always a tale of two cities.

Harlem's first race riot—that is, the first instigated by blacks—came in March 1935. It was touched off by a rumor that a young Negro boy who had stolen a ten-cent pocket knife at Kresge's Department Store on 125th Street was beaten by store detectives. Although the rumor was unfounded, Kresge's had a long history of discrimination in employment and inhospitable treatment of its black customers. It had already been the target of a local protest and had appeased residents by hiring a few Negro clerks, albeit placing them at a traditionally "Negro" job at the lunch counter. So when residents heard the rumors of the beating, the community exploded (Greenberg 1991).

———

For Osofsky (1963), the boundaries of the Harlem community have changed across the ages. The Harlem of 1920 ran north from 124th Street to 149th

Street and west from St. Nicholas Avenue to the Harlem River. But the Great Migration as well as immigration from the Caribbean expanded the area significantly, so that by 1930 Harlem proper stretched from 98th Street to 166th Street and from the Hudson River to the Harlem River, a very generous perimeter that included many areas that were less than 10 percent black and never even considered part of Harlem by locals.

In 2008 Andrew Beveridge, a sociologist and demographer at the Graduate School and University Center of the City University of New York, distinguished between Central Harlem—the area north of Central Park and east of St. Nicholas and Morningside Avenues—and Greater Harlem, which extends west of St. Nicholas Avenue (Hamilton Heights and Sugar Hill). As early as 1930, Central Harlem was 70 percent black, while Greater Harlem remained only 35 percent black. By 1950, the black population of Central Harlem had reached its peak—at 98 percent. Thirty years later, the number had dropped only slightly, to 94 percent, while Greater Harlem remained level at 58.8 percent black throughout the postwar period (Beveridge 2008, 361).

Even as Harlem has long sustained a diverse working- and middle-class community, its image as a hardened, drug- and crime-infested slum has stubbornly endured in the national consciousness. True, it has always had its pockets of extreme poverty, but the extreme poor remain marginalized even within Harlem. When I was growing up, I learned to steer clear of certain blocks, like Fifth Avenue near 126th Street, a known drug spot where some of the poorest residents lived. And public housing projects elicited the same fear among many Harlemites that Harlem elicited among most downtown New Yorkers. For us, the real slum was somewhere in Harlem, not embodied by Harlem. Even for those residents within the projects, particular apartments housed the real ghetto residents.

As working-class Harlemites continued to struggle in the 1970s—in the aftermath of de-industrialization, economic divestment, underemployment, and social isolation—the mainstream media projected a devastating image of a crumbling community laced with blocks of abandoned buildings and occupied by lazy welfare recipients and drug addicts. Harlem became synonymous with violence and destitute lives. Meanwhile, schools were underserved, under-staffed, and under-resourced, and infant mortality was double that of the city as a whole. A sign of the changing times in the Heights was the stealing of trash cans—the thirty-two-gallon tin cans common across the city—and their lids. Residents started chaining them to their stoops and spray-painting their addresses onto the lids and the sides of the cans. Heroin and later crack addicts took their place among the returning Vietnam vets, hustlers, and muggers. People on Convent Avenue began locking the outside doors to block access to their hallway vestibules, which had become popular hangouts for addicts. The double doors to our own home were padlocked to an anchor in the vestibule floor, bolted open by day. To further deter would-be muggers, my father installed three sets of locks on the front door. The original heavy ornamental brass handle was still in use as a slam lock. Three to four inches above was a medium-sized spring-bolt standard lock. The top lock—a Medeco deadbolt—was installed in the mid-1960s after a burglary attempt on our home.

As gun control legislation stalled in Congress, a code of violence began to spread in the streets of America's cities, and New York was always the leader of the pack. By the time I left high school, high-powered Mac 10s and Israeli-made Uzis were replacing the peashooters, the old .22-caliber pistol, common among an earlier generation. I escaped the fate of many of my neighborhood friends because my parents were able to scrape the resources together to send me to private school. By the time I began graduate school in 1988, Harlem had become the *New Jack City* of Hollywood's second wave of Blaxploitation films, a place where crackheads and crack dealers ruled the night. For too many young men like me, a code of violence shaped life on the street (Anderson 1999). Of course, for local residents, it was the reality of under- and unemployment and Harlem's cracked institutions that perpetuated the insanity. Race relations hit an all-time low in the city, and police and civilians declared open season on black folk. "Subway Vigilante" Bernie Goetz became a folk hero to at least some New Yorkers when he shot four young black men on the Seventh Avenue express train. And police brutality was epitomized with the murders of Eleanor Bumpurs and Michael Stewart. Spike Lee captured the decade with his 1989 classic satire *Do the Right Thing*.

Kenneth Clark (1965, xxii) stressed the role of power in the creation and maintenance of the "Dark Ghetto." As an "involved observer," he wanted to understand the psychological and human significance of ghetto confinement and its impact on black opportunity in the contemporary city. He argued that in order to change the conditions of ghetto residents, one needed to change the dynamics of power between them and those outside the confines of its "invisible wall." His concept of the ghetto as the absence of power parallels the scholarship of both Richard Sennett—who studied the role of the Jewish ghetto in Venice—and Michel Foucault, who examined the relationship between power and knowledge. The ghetto combines into a unified whole "the deployment of force and the establishment of truth"—that is, the ghetto stigmatizes while it also controls (Foucault 1977, 184; Sennett 1994). Indeed, surveillance and normalization are cornerstones of the maintenance of unequal power in the ghetto, while state institutions like schools, social services, and law enforcement serve the function of examiner. Sennett (1994) reminds us that the purpose of the ghetto is to quarantine the stigmatized body because it signifies moral difference and inferiority. While religion has remained at the heart of Jewish and North African moral difference in Europe, in America a combination of racial and class stigma has dominated the most extreme forms of social closure and spatial isolation.

Back in the late 1970s, when Oliver North was plotting cocaine deals in the L.A. 'hood, "health food" stores popped up across Harlem. They were actually undercover weed spots where one could buy dime, nickel, and even three-dollar trade bags of low-grade "Mexican" marijuana. Only a handful of legitimate items appeared on the shelves, and none were for sale. One of the more popular of these stores, on Amsterdam Avenue near 126th Street, was lined with bulletproof glass. To make a purchase, you'd walk up to the counter, reach through the Plexiglas maze, and drop the money; the attendant would eye you up and down, checking that you weren't a cop, and then reach behind the counter before passing a tiny sealed manila envelope through the compartment. The shops were open day and night, and when they did get raided, they were back in business within hours. Curiously, a squad car always seemed to be parked just down the block. No one from the community was surprised when the corruption in Harlem finally came to light years later. Officer Michael Walsh and some thirty rogue police officers from the 30th Precinct were brought down in 1994 for conducting illegal raids on drug dealers and stealing drugs, along with large sums of cash.

———

Just before I graduated from high school in 1978, I appeared in a TV commercial for the Coca-Cola Company that spoofed the "I Love New York" campaign that the city was running as a part of the city's effort to rebrand itself during the late 1970s and 1980s (Greenberg 2008). That chilly fall day, I drank more Coke on the deck of the Staten Island ferry than I care to remember. This was just a few years before the city began reinvesting in Harlem and one could still buy a Harlem brownstone for $25,000. During the 1980s and 1990s, new sidewalks were paved, lighting was installed, new water mains were laid, and sewers were dug. New businesses were drawn to Harlem by $300 million in development funds from the empowerment zone, with almost as much in tax breaks. In 1992 the Body Shop opened a branch on 125th Street; Ben and Jerry's, Starbucks, and Capezio's followed soon after. Within five years, both of my parents had passed away and I was forced to sell the home that had remained in our family for three generations. Although the property had appreciated from its low point in the 1980s, it required significant improvements and little did I know that in ten years' time its value would skyrocket!

In 2009 Harlem resident Fred Brathwaite, better known as the video jockey and documentary filmmaker Fab Five Freddy (and the new owner of our family home), acknowledged the many positive changes that have come to Harlem—fewer drugs, less crime, rising property values—while lamenting their high toll: "Yes, white people are jogging down the streets of Harlem, and pushing their baby carriages, and living happily and living comfortably. The problems are, poorer people of color, primarily black folks, can they move into Harlem right now? Chances are really slim, because the property values have gone up, the rents have gone up." Luxury doorman-attended buildings, with apartments that sell for a million dollars, have pulled in upper-middle-class New Yorkers both black and white, while pushing out poor and working-poor residents. On January 5, 2010, the *New York Times* ran an article titled "No Longer Majority Black, Harlem Is in Transition." While Central Harlem has grown considerably over the last decade, its black population has fallen to its lowest point since the heyday of the Renaissance (Beveridge 2008). As Howard Dodson, director of Harlem's Schomburg Center for Research in Black Culture, says, "Gentrification is about displacement." The poor of Harlem have little place to go.

As a folk ethnographer, I had observed the gentrification in Harlem during the mid-1980s as many apartment buildings turned into cooperatives, pushing poorer tenants into other urban spaces. By the time I completed my doctorate in sociology at the City University of New York Graduate Center in 1995, conflicts brought on by demographic change and class conflict were evident across the city and no less so in Harlem. On Friday, December 8, 1995, fifty-one-year-old Roland James Smith Jr., a former criminal with a thirty-year history of mental instability, broke through a line of protesters outside Freddy's Fashion Mart, a small discount clothing store on 125th Street, and set the store ablaze. The fire claimed eight employees, including Kareem Brunner, a black security guard, and a number of Latino and Guyanese immigrant workers (Kasinitz and Haynes 1996).

Freddy's was owned by an unpopular local merchant, the Syrian-born Jewish entrepreneur Fred Harari. Al Sharpton's National Action Network and Morris Powell of the 125th Street Vendors' Association had teamed up to protest the planned rent increase and subsequent eviction of the Record Shack, a long-standing black-owned business. Yet the actual owner of the building (and the party raising the rent) was the Black Pentecostal United House of Prayer for All People, which had been founded by "Sweet Daddy" Grace in the 1920s and is today one of the biggest landlords on 125th Street. While the event was heralded as a manifestation of local anti-Semitism and anger, little attention was paid to the fact that the murderer was a lone crazed individual and that the protesters did not represent broad community sentiment. In fact, the owner of the Record Shack, the South African–born Sikhulu Shange, had been sub-letting from Harari, a Syrian Jew. Both were recent immigrants.

The mix of new classes brought on by black and white gentrification into Harlem has led to race- and class-tinged proprietary tensions. In June 2007, an African drumming circle in Harlem's Marcus Garvey Park, formerly Mount Morris Park, was broken up by two police officers who were reportedly summoned to the scene when white upscale residents of a new luxury co-op across from the park complained about the noise. The drummers refused to leave, maintaining that they had been drumming there every week for the last thirty years. The controversy took to the streets of Harlem, the major city dailies, and even the national press and touched off a vociferous debate over whose claims to the space were more legitimate—the drummers or the gentrifiers.

Who indeed has a rightful claim to Harlem? And can it withstand its new-found popularity?

In 1960 one-half of all black households were living at the poverty level (as compared to 18 percent of white households); of these, nearly one in five was headed by a woman. Although the policies of both Democrats and Republicans over the next eighteen years helped lower poverty rates among both blacks and whites, the number of homes headed by women continued to rise, leading to a decline in real earnings and a rise in the number of poor black children in single-parent households. Social-scientific arguments have been embedded in tropes such as "the culture of poverty," which ties poverty to slavery and the black family. In 1965 Daniel Patrick Moynihan reported that, among blacks, out-of-wedlock birth rates had reached 25 percent, signaling a crisis in the black family. The crisis only escalated in the 1970s and 1980s as rates of out-of-wedlock births, black male unemployment, and incarceration for first-time drug offenders all rose. Moynihan's dire prognosis for the black family would prove prophetic, but his explanation—that the black family had been destroyed by slavery—was off the mark. Yet it was echoed by scholars such as Gilbert Osofsky (1963, 136), who believed that "slavery initially destroyed the entire concept of the family for American Negroes." The preoccupation with the crisis of the black family not only helped us ignore the many married and dual-wage-earning families like mine but perpetuated the myth of the dysfunctional black "matriarchal" family. Black poor folks themselves were touted as being the source of their own long-term poverty, when in fact the combination of racial segregation and joblessness—not slavery—was to blame.

Following the Moynihan report, social scientists like William Julius Wilson and Paul Jargowsky focused attention on urban poverty—defining the ghetto as a community with a poverty rate of at least 40 percent—and ignored the link between historically segregated urban neighborhoods and the growth of extreme poverty since the period of industrial decline in the 1980s and 1990s (Jargowsky and Bane 1991; Wilson 1987, 1991). Not only is the 40 percent threshold arbitrary, but it obscures the history of urban housing markets embedded within the state and private processes that handicapped blacks in the credit market while spatially concentrating them in particular neighborhoods (Gotham 2000; Wacquant 1997, 341; Wacquant 2002; Hernandez 2009; Haynes and Hernandez 2008; Rugh and Massey 2010).

Revived discussions of the ghetto provide an opportunity to reevaluate the concept, the discussions in urban research, and the conflation of ideas about race, culture, and poverty in colloquial and academic uses of the term. A key sociological problem with applying the term *ghetto* to Harlem or to any predominantly black community in this country is that it originated in Europe, where it denoted a compulsive Jewish area in Venice, and it has taken on an increasingly fuzzy meaning in modern sociological parlance. The ghetto has come to signify poverty, culture, and identity, while its causes remain institutional segregation and political, class, and social exclusion. Since the 1960s, despite the overwhelming evidence to the contrary, we have all too often inverted the cause (segregation) and the outcome (concentrated black poverty).

Assimilation and culture of poverty theorists, from Wirth to Moynihan, maintain that blacks have lived history in reverse as compared to foreign-born white ethnic groups, and that "ghetto conditions" have evolved not from decades of housing and employment segregation but from blacks' inability to escape poverty conditions as other Americans do, thus begging the question: Is there something wrong with black people or their culture? Do they have the right pluck or do they suffer from a "culture of poverty" that keeps them trapped in the ghetto? George Haynes addressed these questions back in 1913, predicting that better-off blacks would seek to move to other areas of the city, just as European immigrants had done before them. "But as Negroes developed in intelligence, in their standard of living and economic power, they desire better houses, better public facilities and other conveniences not usually obtainable in the sections allotted to their less fortunate black brothers. To obtain these advantages, they seek other neighborhoods just as the European immigrants who are crowded into segregated sections of our city seek better surroundings when they are economically able to secure them" (Haynes 1913, 109). Seventy years later, William Julius Wilson (1987) would similarly argue that the black middle class would seek better housing outside the ghetto.

Historically, racial segregation and poverty have been mutually constitutive and reinforcing processes that lead to the extraction of capital in all its forms from spaces we came to call ghettos after World War II. Rather than taking on the legacy of economic marginality imposed on the descendants of American slavery through racial ascription and spatial marginalization, liberal scholars have returned, again and again, to the notion that internal cultural mechanisms or cultural inadequacy explains their dilemma. Loïc Wacquant's (1997, 2001, 2002, 2008) institutional and state-focused framework challenges both the classic definition offered to us by Louis Wirth (1928, 4)—that the ghetto is merely a "form of accommodation between divergent population groups," that is, bounded areas of urban immigrant cultural transformation and assimilation—and Jargowsky and Bane (1991) and Wilson (1987), who argue that the real social problem is urban poverty. In the public imagination, the concept of the ghetto represents a nexus between urban poverty, black culture, and spatial marginalization. Of course, distinguishing the urban ghetto from what scholars have historically called the slum—disorganized areas of high crime—means disentangling historical segregation and racialization from its long-term consequences.

New York Times columnist Patricia Cohen made the front page on October 17, 2010, with her article "Culture of Poverty Makes a Comeback." The piece came on the heels of a special issue of the *Annals of the American Academy of Political and Social Science* titled "Reconsidering Culture and Poverty." In a sleight of hand, Cohen shifted the focus from an academic distinction between "culture and poverty" to a retrograde and sensationalist sound bite. Urban sociologist Stephen Steinberg (2011) calls this resurgence in mythmaking "a perverse obfuscation of American racial history." Still, social scientists, not wanting to miss out on the media spotlight, have danced around the issue, avoiding the rejection of the "culture of poverty" thesis outright while gently directing discussion back to the characteristics of neighborhoods and the structural mechanisms that reproduce poverty, while giving little attention to the centrality of race.

In 1927, at the height of the Harlem Renaissance, just before my grandfather bought his home in the Heights, Ira de Reid (1939/1969, 628) declared that Harlem was "neither slum nor ghetto," and he even challenged the notion that the segregated area constituted a single community. E. F. Frazier (1929, 420) simply avoided using the term *ghetto* altogether and struck a distinctly modern tone in arguing that "the spatial distribution of the Negro population is significant both because it forms the basis of group solidarity and class differentiation." As a descriptive term, *ghetto* both reflects and defines this class-race nexus. But analytically, "the ghetto" so resonates with epistemological, ontological, and moral dilemmas that perhaps it is time to take Karl Rasmussen (1968), Sharon Zukin (1998), and Mario Small (2008) seriously and return to discussions of the "spatial distribution of race" and its relationship to group solidarity and racial formation, class differentiation, and social closure, as Frazier and Weber once suggested. Harlem's duality is neither hell nor heaven, and its existence as a ghetto, and all that the word connotes, is in the end only a state of mind.

CONCLUSION

Although the all-white middle-class neighborhood may become a relic as we form more racially mixed communities, the residential concentration of the black poor seems likely to remain, whether in the city or the suburbs. Commercial and sentimental interest continue to coalesce around development and growth, especially in the real estate market, and to constrain choices for the black poor (Logan and Zhang 2011; Logan and Molotch 1987). In Harlem, efforts to alleviate extreme poverty will not alone eradicate the conditions that gave rise to and maintain segregation in the city. The North River sewage treatment plant endures, and however diverse, Harlem is likely to remain a trope—a symbolic boundary between civil society and the urban jungle—complete with its ill health (Downey 2005). Recent headlines heralding white middle-class gentrification in Harlem may lead us to conclude that the ghetto is disappearing. In fact, it has simply relocated. Osofsky (1963) observed long ago that race and poverty are equally to blame for the problems of the ghetto (at least in "northern cities").

Like New York City itself, Harlem is always changing: new buildings, new immigrants, new businesses, new people gentrifying old neighborhoods. In the "New Harlem" of today, we find an awkward blend of "culture, and the arts; global cuisine, and elegant accommodations," filtered through a history characterized by stark spatial marginalization, social and political exclusion, and economic marginality (Logan and Zhang 2010, 1077). Is Harlem a ghetto? At its foundation, the ghetto signifies the racialization of residential space, and it has varying consequences for community differentiation based on the institutional environment. Recent research suggests that many areas of global cities like New York are becoming more diverse while others are still in the process of becoming predominantly black, owing to a substantial exodus of white residents, and the few existing mixed-race areas reflect an influx of new minority groups in already white areas (Logan and Zhang 2010, 1090). We may already be entering a new and reinvigorated cosmopolitan Harlem where rich and poor share public space but still do not share schools, economic resources, or institutional power.

References

Anderson, Elijah. 1999. *Code of the Street: Decency, Violence, and the Moral Life of the Inner City.* New York: W. W. Norton.

———. 2004. "Being Here and Being There: Fieldwork Encounters and Ethnographic Discoveries." *Annals of the Academy of Political and Social Science* 595 (September): 14–31.

Attewell, Paul, and David Lavin. 2007. *Passing the Torch: Does Higher Education for the Disadvantaged Pay Off Across the Generations?* New York: Russell Sage Foundation Publications.

Bernstein, Iver. 1990. *The New York City Draft Riots: Their Significance for American Society and Politics in the Age of the Civil War.* New York: Oxford University Press.

Beveridge, Andrew A. 2008. "A Century of Harlem in New York City: Some Notes on Migration, Consolidation, Segregation, and Recent Developments." *City & Community* 7, no. 4 (December 2008): 358–365.

Chernow, Ron. 2004. *Alexander Hamilton.* New York: Penguin Press.

Clark, Kenneth B. 1965. *Dark Ghetto: Dilemmas of Social Power.* New York: Harper & Row.

Downey, Liam. 2005. "The Unintended Significance of Race: Environmental Racial Inequality in Detroit." *Social Forces* 83, no. 3 (March): 971–1007.

Foucault, Michel. 1977. *Discipline and Punish: The Birth of the Prison.* New York: Random House.

Frazier, E. Franklin. 1929. "The Negro Community: A Cultural Phenomenon." *Social Forces* 7, no. 3 (March): 415–420.

Greenberg, Cheryl. 1991. *"Or Does It Explode?" Black Harlem in the Great Depression.* New York: Oxford University Press.

Greenberg, Miriam. 2008. *Branding New York: How a City in Crisis Was Sold to the World.* New York: Routledge.

Gotham, Kevin Fox. 2000. "Racialization and the State: The Housing Act of 1934 and the Creation of the Federal Housing Administration." *Sociological Perspectives* 43, no. 2 (Summer): 291–317.

Harris, Leslie M. 2003. *In the Shadow of Slavery: African Americans in New York City, 1626–1863.* Chicago: University of Chicago Press.

Haynes, Bruce D., and Jesus Hernandez. 2008. "Place, Space, and Race: Monopolistic Group Closure and the Dark Side of Social Capital." In *Networked Urbanism: Social Capital in the City*, edited by Talja Blokland and Mike Savage. Farnham, U.K.: Ashgate Press.

Haynes, George Edmund. 1913. "Conditions Among Negroes in the Cities." *Annals of the American Academy of Political and Social Science* 49 ("The Negro's Progress in Fifty Years") (September): 105–119.

Hernandez, Jesus. 2009. "Redlining Revisited: Mortgage Lending Patterns in Sacramento, 1930–2004." *International Journal of Urban and Regional Research* 33, no. 2: 291–313.

Jargowsky, P. A., and M. J. Bane. 1991. "Ghetto Poverty in the United States, 1970–1980." In *The Urban Underclass*, edited by Christopher Jencks and Paul Peterson. Washington, D.C: Brookings Institution.

Johnson, James Weldon. 1991. *Black Manhattan.* Cambridge, Mass.: Da Capo Press. (Originally published in 1930 by Alfred A. Knopf.)

Kasinitz, Philip, and Bruce Haynes. 1996. "The Fire at Freddy's." *Common Quest* 1: 24–34.

Kasinitz, Philip, John H. Mollenkopf, and Mary C. Waters, eds. 2006. *Becoming New Yorkers: Ethnographies of the New Second Generation.* New York: Russell Sage Foundation.

Kasinitz, Philip, John H. Mollenkopf, Mary C. Waters, and Jennifer Holdaway. 2008. *Inheriting the City: The Children of Immigrants Come of Age.* New York: Russell Sage Foundation.

Locke, Alain. 1936. "Harlem: Dark Weather-Vane." *Survey Graphic* 25, no. 8 (August: 457–462, 493–495).

Logan, John, and John Molotch. 1987. *Urban Fortunes: The Political Economy of Place.* Berkeley and Los Angeles: University of California Press.

Logan, John, and Charles Zhang. 2011. "Global Neighborhoods: New Pathways to Diversity and Separation." *American Journal of Sociology* 115, no. 4 (January): 1069–1109.

Massey, Douglas S. 1990. "American Apartheid: Segregation and the Making of the Underclass." *American Journal of Sociology* 96, no. 2 (September): 329–357.

McKay, Claude. 1940. *Harlem: Negro Metropolis.* New York: E. P. Dutton.

———. 1987. *Home to Harlem.* Boston: Northeastern University Press. (Originally published in 1928.)

Moynihan, Daniel Patrick. 1965. *The Black Family: The Case for National Action.* Washington, D.C.: U.S. Department of Labor, Office of Policy Planning and Research (March).

New York City Landmarks Preservation Commission. 2001. *Hamilton Heights/Sugar Hill Northeast Historic District: Designation Report*, October 23.

Osofsky, Gilbert. 1971. *Harlem: The Making of a Ghetto: Negro New York, 1890–1930.* New York: Harper & Row. (Originally published 1963.)

———. 1968. "The Enduring Ghetto." *Journal of American History* 55, no. 2 (September): 243.

PBS. 2001. *New York, Episode 2: 1825–1865: Order and Disorder.* Released September 25.

Rasmussen, Karl R. 1968. "The Multi-Ordered Urban Area: A Ghetto." *Phylon* 29, no. 3: 282–290.

Reid, Ira de A. 1969. *The Negro Immigrant.* New York: Arno Press. (Originally published in 1939.)

Rugh, Jacob S., and Douglas Massey. 2010. "Racial Segregation and the American Foreclosure Crisis." *American Journal of Sociology* 75, no. 5 (October): 629–651.

Sennett, Richard. 1994. *Flesh and Stone: The Body and the City in Western Civilization.* New York: Random House.

Small, Mario. 2008. "Four Reasons to Abandon the Idea of 'the Ghetto.'" *City & Community* 7, no. 4 (December): 389–396.

Steinberg, Stephen. 2011. "Poor Reason: Culture Still Doesn't Explain Poverty." *Boston Review*, January 13.

Sze, Julie. 2007. *Noxious New York: The Racial Politics of Urban Health and Environmental Justice*. Cambridge, Mass.: MIT Press.

Van Vechten, Carl. 2000. *Nigger Heaven*. Champaign: University of Illinois Press. (Originally published in 1926.)

Wacquant, Loïc J. D. 1997. "Three Pernicious Premises in the Study of the American Ghetto." *International Journal of Urban and Regional Research* 21: 341–353.

———. 2002. "From Slavery to Mass Incarnation: Rethinking the Question of Race in the U.S." *New Left Review* 13 (January–February).

Watkins–Owens Irma. 1996. *Blood Relations: Caribbean Immigrants and the Harlem Community, 1900–1930*. Bloomington: Indiana University Press.

Weber, Max. 1978. *Economy and Society.* Berkeley: University of California Press.

Wilkerson, Isabel. 2010. *The Warmth of Other Suns: The Epic Story of America's Great Migration*. New York: Random House.

Wilson, Francille Rusan. 2006. *The Segregated Scholars: Black Social Scientists and the Creation of Black Labor Studies*. Charlottesville: University of Virginia Press.

Wilson, William Julius. 1987. *The Truly Disadvantaged: The Inner City, the Underclass, and Public Policy*. Chicago: University of Chicago Press.

———. 1991. "Studying Inner-City Social Dislocations: The Challenge of Public Agenda Research." *American Sociological Review* 56, no. 1: 1–14.

Wirth, Louis. 1927. *The American Journal of Sociology* 33 (no. 1, July), pp. 57–71.

———. 1928. *The Ghetto*. Chicago: University Press of Chicago.

Zukin, Sharon. 1998. "How 'Bad' Is It? Institutions and Intentions in the Study of the American Ghetto." *International Journal of Urban and Regional Research* 22, no. 3: 511–520.

CHAPTER 6

✦ ✦ ✦

The Spike Lee Effect:
Reimagining the Ghetto
for Cultural Consumption

Sharon Zukin

At the beginning of the second decade of the twenty-first century, a maker of upscale alcoholic beverages introduced a variation on its basic product that promoted—and was promoted by—a subtle new image of New York City's historic ghettos.[1] Bottles of Absolut Brooklyn vodka featured a colorful label designed in collaboration with the filmmaker Spike Lee, who grew up in one of the borough's African American neighborhoods, Fort Greene, and whose film *Do the Right Thing* (1989) centers on racial tensions in another, Bedford-Stuyvesant. The label shows a street scene typical of many blocks in these two areas (see Figure 6.1). At the center, a steep flight of steps—the stoop—leads up to the door of a stately brownstone house. Each step bears a nickname for, or slogan about, Brooklyn, from the old Dutch name "Breuckelen" on one step to the contemporary compliment "Brooklyn in Da House" on another. An advertisement for the vodka shows young people sitting on nearby stoops while a couple in their twenties and a man walking his dog stroll by. It's a visibly multiethnic group, sociable in a block-party way and definitely cool.

There is nothing that shouts "ghetto" on the vodka label. Nineteenth-century houses and cool people can be found in many gentrified neighborhoods. But if Fort Greene and Bed-Stuy are pictured as indistinguishable from the gentrified brownstone neighborhoods around them, the label represents a radically reimagined ghetto for cultural consumption. The new image reflects changes in population, investment, and cultural expression that have diluted and deflected old patterns of racial exclusion and social decay. At least in some areas of New York, the ghetto is losing its authentic character as a spatial intersection of race and poverty (Zukin 2010).

THE "DARK GHETTO"

As recently as the 1980s, experts predicted that gentrification would never reach majority–African American neighborhoods like Bed-Stuy and Harlem, the large area in upper Manhattan that has been the historic center of American black culture since the early twentieth century (Schaffer and Smith 1986). The psychologist Kenneth B. Clark (1965) had vividly depicted Harlem as the archetypal "dark ghetto" of the 1960s, where economic deprivation joined social disadvantage to create a bottomless spiral of despair. Living conditions in public housing projects as well as in private landlord-owned housing were often mean; public institutions like schools, the sanitation department, and the police did not respond to residents' needs. The high unemployment rates and low self-esteem of many Harlem youths, Clark wrote, led them to crime and drugs.

Increases in heroin traffic after the 1960s and the eventual spread of crack cocaine would only make these problems worse. Not surprisingly, whites—and many blacks—feared Harlem. Too much crime, too many blocks with dilapidated and abandoned buildings that had passed into the city government's hands after landlords defaulted on their taxes, a large concentration of public housing projects where tenants were poorer than ever and less likely to hold jobs or live in stable families (Bloom 2008): Harlem's dismal prospects seemed to range from terminal shabbiness to a stigmatized isolation from the rest of the city.

At the other end of the A train's line, a long subway ride away in Brooklyn, Bedford-Stuyvesant shared Harlem's stigmatization. Though their built environment was quite similar—a mix of stately brownstone townhouses and large churches dating from the 1880s surrounded by the red-brick towers of public housing projects constructed in the 1950s and 1960s and older tenements—their paths to the "dark ghetto" had differed.

FIGURE 6.1. Absolut Brooklyn Billboard

Source: Photograph by Sharon Zukin.

Harlem was built in the late 1800s and early 1900s for a white middle-class community, but too large a supply of new apartments, in an economic recession, left vacancies that real estate agents decided early on to market to blacks. The overcrowding in the areas of midtown Manhattan where African Americans then lived and the racism that prevented them from moving freely to other areas of the city made them receptive to advertisements for new homes in Harlem, and a small number of black realtors actively encouraged them to move uptown (Osofsky 1963). During the 1920s, Harlem became a majority-black community (Beveridge 2008), with black-owned businesses, black churches, and a black professional class. The area attracted so many artists, musicians, and writers that it gave its name to the wave of creative innovation associated with the Jazz Age: the Harlem Renaissance. Despite famous residents like the poet Langston Hughes and the musician Duke Ellington, however, most of Harlem's early black population worked in low-wage jobs, often as porters or domestic servants. Rents were higher than in comparable white neighborhoods, and "high rents and poor salaries necessarily led to congested and unsanitary conditions" (Osofsky 1963, 136).

Bedford-Stuyvesant, a district formed by joining the names of two adjacent neighborhoods in central Brooklyn, began to shift from white to black some-what later than Harlem, during the 1930s. Redlining by banks and government agencies made it difficult for ethnic and working-class whites to get a mortgage, and as they gradually moved to suburbs where it was easier to get a bank loan, they sold their old homes to blacks. "By the early 1940s," the historian Craig Wilder (2000, 195, 198) writes, the *New York Times* "was regularly referring to Bedford-Stuyvesant as . . . 'Brooklyn's Harlem,'" a label repeated with disgust by whites who protested the arrival of black newcomers. As in Harlem, because many new black residents could not afford to buy homes and were even less likely to get a mortgage loan than whites, one-family homes were subdivided into small rental apartments and single rooms.

In contrast to the Black Nationalist and black empowerment movements that gained support in Harlem during the Great Depression and prewar years, politics in Bed-Stuy centered on rising crime rates and declining public ser-vices, a situation that white residents and public officials openly racialized. "Let's be more frank about it," Mayor Fiorello LaGuardia said about a grand jury inquiry into conditions in Bedford-Stuyvesant in 1943. "This is the negro question we are talking about." Trouble is bound to arise, the mayor added, "when a neighborhood changes its complexion" (Wilder 2000, 196).

With migrants from the South streaming into both neighborhoods after World War II, their populations increased and became almost entirely black. Not only did African Americans and Caribbean Americans buy houses from white residents who moved out, they were actively recruited as "shock troops" of blockbusting by real estate agents who profited personally by buying low from white homeowners and selling high to blacks. Banks discriminated against areas where blacks lived, however, and that prevented new black home-owners from getting mortgages in the usual way (Wilder 2000, 201–204). They were forced to depend on high-interest loans from individual money lenders, credit agencies, and the real estate agents who sold them their homes—a sce-nario for a foreclosure crisis in black communities that was repeated through-out the 1950s and 1960s (on East New York, see Thabit 2003). Americans of African descent also "spilled over" into areas adjacent to their existing con-centrations, expanding the black Harlem community to the north and south and enlarging the area of black settlement in central Brooklyn from Fort Greene in the west to East New York on the border with Queens.

During the 1960s, community leaders in both Harlem and Bedford-Stuyvesant pressed the city government to ban racial discrimination in hiring by local stores, organized rent strikes against private landlords who would not make repairs, and demanded racial desegregation of public schools (Monti 1979). Lack of satisfaction on any of these fronts—while civil rights protests were erupting throughout the South—stirred more drastic action: riots in 1964 and a boycott of public schools for "community control" of education. (The public school boycott, which led to a lengthy, contentious teachers' strike in 1968, began with a militant movement for community control in Harlem, but it reached a more violent confrontation in Ocean Hill–Brownsville, a neigh-borhood in the Brooklyn ghetto; see Podair 2002.) Some residents, discouraged by landlords' continued disinvestment and apparent disinvestment by the city government as well, began to move out to newer areas in southwest Queens and nearby suburbs. White merchants, unable to get insurance on their stores and unlikely to get support from black community groups, began to shut down. This exodus left residents of Harlem and Bed-Stuy with sparse shopping op-portunities, few commercial entertainment venues, and increasing numbers of abandoned houses and vacant lots. Despite the blocks that remained in stable condition, the ghetto became a site and symbol of decay.

In these years, the *New York Times* routinely referred to Bedford-Stuyvesant as "the Negro and Puerto Rican ghetto in the heart of Brooklyn" (December 11, 1966). A headline used the g-word to herald the arrival of antipoverty funds: "Brooklyn Ghetto Given $7-Million; Federal Grant Will Be Used to Attract Industry to Bedford-Stuyvesant" (June 25, 1967). After a young Bed-Stuy man was killed by a cop, a community resident criticized "police behavior in the ghetto" (June 1, 1971). The same language, and the same conditions, applied to Harlem ("Lehman Scores Harlem 'Ghetto'; Senator Calls Civil Rights Problem a 'Crisis' as Acute in North as in South," *New York Times*, June 4, 1956).

During the 1970s, the "dark ghetto" trope shaped public consciousness, creating a monolithic image of black neighborhoods as decaying, dependent, and deprived. Whether whites' reaction was outrage at social injustice or fear that they would be attacked, they tended to see and describe the ghetto the same way. This image is especially vivid in the 1978 edition of the most authoritative guidebook to New York City's architecture, where the authors vented their concern about living conditions in Bedford-Stuyvesant in emotional terms. On the one hand, they praised the "great quality" and "magnificent townscape" of some of its brownstone blocks. On the other hand, they condemned the "considerable numbers of wooden tenements containing some of the *worst* slums in the country—fire traps and *vermin-infested* hovels that are a disgrace to the city and an insult to those whose bare subsistence incomes force residence there" (White and Willensky 1978, 443, emphasis in original).

Repeating the image years later in highly condensed form, a New York art critic (Schjeldahl 1994, 240) wrote that the painter Frank Stella named two of the all-black paintings he made in the late 1950s after buildings in "the depressed black Brooklyn neighborhood of Bedford-Stuyvesant." Still later, after one of these paintings was acquired by a German museum, an online catalog connected it to a "squalid New York housing project, Tomlinson Court Park in Brooklyn," although no public housing project by that name existed.[2] Alternatively, Sotheby's, which auctioned a small version of the painting for more than $1 million in May 2010, stated in its catalog description that the "dark subjects" of Stella's black paintings include "minority neighborhoods with tenement housing, such as Tomlinson Court Park in the Bedford-Stuyvesant area of Brooklyn" (Sotheby's 2010). By that time, whatever the specific form of the built environment, the trope of the dark ghetto had become a meme.

REGENERATION OR DESPAIR

Like many inner-city neighborhoods across the United States, Harlem and Bed-Stuy lost population in the 1970s and 1980s (Beveridge 2008; Rusk 1999). Upwardly mobile residents continued to move out, and rising incarceration rates, drug overdoses, and deaths from AIDS also took a toll. Moreover, the Rockefeller drug laws of 1973, which imposed severe prison terms on men and women convicted of selling small quantities of illegal drugs, had a disproportionate impact on blacks. (The mandatory minimum sentences were revised in 2009.) Public attention and federal programs had failed to make a dent in these neighborhoods' persistent poverty: Stores and houses remained vacant, shuttered, and—during the crack cocaine epidemic of the 1980s—pillaged by drug addicts and dealers. Though crime rates rose throughout the city, they were among the highest in Harlem and central Brooklyn. So were asthma rates, low birth weights, and children's risk of exposure to toxic levels of lead.

But actions that took place under the radar of outsiders planted the seeds of change. Bedford-Stuyvesant Restoration, a local development corporation begun by Senator Robert F. Kennedy with both corporate and government funding, renovated housing, set up health care centers, and ran job training programs. Though most parts of the neighborhood were even poorer in the 1990s than before, Restoration managed to maintain a certain degree of stability (Rusk 1999, 32–34). Residential stability was enhanced when then-mayor Edward Koch initiated a $5 billion citywide program for housing rehabilitation and ownership, which encouraged Restoration to shift its priorities from low- to middle- and moderate-income housing. Harlem's most influential local development corporation, the Abyssinian Development Corporation, partnered with the Homeworks Program too. But the new policy aroused severe criticism from other community organizations, for it threatened to leave the poorest New Yorkers in the lurch. It was also disliked because it concentrated most subsidies in the South Bronx, Harlem, and other areas of upper Manhattan, suggesting that the city government was "creating a new ghetto" (Mollenkopf

1992, 148). However, since by this time many African American New Yorkers had good public-sector jobs as teachers, police officers, social workers, and administrators (Waldinger 1996), the Koch administration's housing program laid the foundation for a middle-class and lower-middle-class group of residents to stay in the existing ghetto—in better housing.

Meanwhile, some families managed to buy or keep ownership of the stately houses that in other neighborhoods were beginning to attract white gentrifiers, banding together like the Brownstoners of Bedford Stuyvesant, Inc., a "civic organization" founded in 1978 "that would attract people from all walks of life who were willing to roll up their sleeves and become part of the vibrant network of residents who were waging a fierce battle for the survival of this community."[3] The New York City Landmarks Preservation Commission designated a small number of historic districts in these areas—St. Nicholas (1967), Mount Morris (1971), and Hamilton Heights/Sugar Hill (1974) in Harlem and Stuyvesant Heights (1971) in Bed-Stuy—but homeowners like the Brownstoners of Bedford Stuyvesant felt they were fighting an uphill battle: "to stop the f[l]ight by actively encouraging disillusioned residents and those who had already left to 'Come on Home to Bed-Stuy.'" They organized an annual house tour like the one in gentrified, mainly white Brooklyn Heights, "to reshape the media's concept of the community, and the way it reported on our daily lives." This house tour, the group's website declares, "sparked renewed pride in people who still lived here. It encouraged thousands of African Americans, young and not so young, to become part of a thriving and welcoming community." The cultural aspirations of group members give an early indication of how a "dark ghetto" might again become a socially diverse, though racially homogeneous, neighborhood.

Social class diversity grew with the arrival of upper-middle-class blacks who had college and postgraduate degrees and who began to buy big houses that needed updating either because they had remained in the same family for so long or because they had fallen into disrepair. These members of the "new black middle class" (Landry 1987) were attracted not just to the architectural beauty of the homes in Harlem and Bed-Stuy and to the areas' racial identity, but to the low sale prices of ghetto properties. Indeed, during the 1980s the Koch administration tried to auction off the enormous number of properties the city had acquired from tax foreclosures for only a few dollars apiece, though many willing home buyers were unable to take advantage of this extraordinary opportunity because banks refused to make loans for the extensive renovations that were required. Not even the community reinvestment acts passed by the federal government and New York State in the late 1970s forced banks to make enough loans available. Gradually, however, blacks in professional and high-wage positions began to buy houses in the ghetto and carry out renovations. Eric Sawyer, an investment consultant and AIDS activist, bought a Harlem brownstone for $26,000 in 1981. It was one of only three occupied buildings on the block. "I basically toughed out living here and watched the entire neighborhood come back to life," he recalled in 1998. Sawyer lived there through the crack epidemic and gang shootings, and eventually he invested in another brownstone nearby, "renting out floorthrough apartments in both to Columbia [University] students, artists, and . . . young professors" (Garb 1998).

During the next decade, while housing prices throughout New York City rose, buying a townhouse in Harlem or Bed-Stuy looked like a bargain compared to buying in neighborhoods that had already been gentrified. Justice Larry D. Martin of the New York State Supreme Court bought a three-story house on McDonough Street in the historic district of Stuyvesant Heights, near Bed-Stuy's southern edge, for $124,000 in 1989. The baseball player Jackie Robinson had briefly lived on this block in the 1950s, and the judge had grown up there. After buying the house, he restored the original architectural details and kept most of the old furnishings, all of which was respectfully, maybe even enviously, detailed by the *New York Times* (Whitaker 1997) a few years later: "Handmade moldings, featuring lacy spindles, frame doorways. Tongue-and-groove wainscoting panel walls. The master bedroom has a built-in armoire with drawers. Delicate banisters grace the staircases. . . . There are four fireplaces, and windows are often accentuated with stained glass. Many of the original brass light fixtures remain. There are even wooden door knobs."

But new upper-middle-class residents had to weigh the financial and architectural value of their homes against the still-prevailing conditions of poor services, high crime rates, and uncertainty about the ghetto's future (Hyra 2008; Taylor 2002; on Chicago, see Pattillo 2007). Daryl Bloodsaw, an advertising executive who had grown up in the South and who bought a four-family house in Harlem in 1998, described a "state of emergency" with drug dealers when he and his family moved in. Three years later, when Walter Biggs, an artist, and his wife, a fashion designer, renovated the house they bought in Harlem, they boarded up the parlor floor so that drug dealers would not set up shop there, and they found a gun in the backyard. But they also discovered a sweet satisfaction: "It's really unthinkable," Biggs said. "We couldn't afford an apartment in Lower Manhattan, but we can afford a town house in Harlem." For Bloodsaw, the satisfaction was living a historical and cultural dream. "When I walk these streets," he said, "and think that Langston Hughes lived here and Duke Ellington and all the others, it's wonderful. I can feel all of that history alive again" (Garb 2001).

The comparative advantages of homeownership in ghetto areas increased during the 1990s. Though few residents realized it at the time, crack cocaine addiction had reached a peak and would begin to decline. More aggressive policing, in the name of both "zero tolerance" and community improvement, decreased violent crime. With the establishment of a federal empowerment zone in Harlem in 1994, and after several years of political infighting, priorities finally shifted to new business development instead of the expected roster of social services. Whether or not the ghetto's elected officials, all Democrats, agreed with the free market policies of the new Republican mayor, Rudolph Giuliani, or the new Republican governor, George Pataki, they were forced to accept the substantial infusion of funds that the city and state provided for businesses through the Upper Manhattan Empowerment Zone (UMEZ). Both the money and the change of program sent a strong signal to chain stores and new retail entrepreneurs, which were in short supply in ghetto areas. Harlem was now poised to attract the kind of development that would draw more affluent residents, including whites, who felt priced out of homeownership in the gentrified neighborhoods of Manhattan and Brooklyn. "In the seventies you couldn't give these buildings away. Now we have loads of callers," said Willie Suggs, a well-known Harlem real estate agent (Garb 1998).

Yet the stigma of the "dark ghetto" was slow to wear away, maybe more so in central Brooklyn than upper Manhattan. "Whenever my colleagues ask me where I live, and by that I mean white colleagues and some black as well, when I say Bed-Stuy, there's a deafening silence," Judge Martin told the *Times* reporter. "I just chuckle to myself. If they only knew the beauty of the homes and the beauty of the people" (Whitaker 1997).

THE CULTURAL TURN

Within the next few years, both Bed-Stuy and Harlem emerged as desirable residential locations. Economics continued to play a major role as graduate students seeking inexpensive apartments and young professionals looking for good investments flocked to these areas. While many students were white or foreign, most young professionals were black, and couples with mixed-race backgrounds were especially interested in living in a majority-black neighborhood that promised spacious housing and racial tolerance. But cultural changes also had an effect on residential choices. New homeowners saw the beauty of the ghetto's brownstone houses, as Judge Martin said. They appreciated the creative history of past generations of jazz musicians, artists, and actors, a history that was used and abused by real estate developers to promote a "new Harlem Renaissance." In a less expected way, however, a new generation of black artists also drew interest to the ghetto, particularly in Fort Greene and Bedford-Stuyvesant. Spike Lee dramatized everyday life in these neighborhoods and used their brownstone blocks for location shoots for movies and music videos. He set up his company's offices in Fort Greene and lived there for years before moving to Manhattan. While Lee cultivated his image in pop culture as a vocal booster of central Brooklyn, so did rap musicians like Bed-Stuy's own Jay-Z and Biggie Smalls. Jay-Z grew up in Marcy Houses, a public housing project, but during his career he emerged as a record producer, music company executive, and financial investor. Not the ghetto of crime he rapped about but the place from which successful entrepreneurs come demanded respect.

Real estate articles in the media played up the ghetto's new culture of success. The *New York Times* reported that one of Bed-Stuy's new residents, a thirty-four-year-old portfolio manager at J. P. Morgan Chase and Columbia Business School graduate, had bought a home around the corner from where his father lived in the 1950s (Chamberlain 2004). Six other Columbia Business School graduates, the *Times* said, had also bought houses in Bed-Stuy during the previous four years. In a similar "racial profile," the *Times* described the extensive home renovations undertaken by a black couple in their thirties who bought a Civil War–era mansion on McDonough Street. They "were gentrifying [Bed-Stuy] from the inside," the article said. "Mrs. Bobb-Semple was raised in

Brooklyn, and her husband arrived from Guyana in the fifth grade. Her parents were longtime Bedford-Stuyvesant residents, and the couple had been live-in landlords in a nearby three-unit brownstone they bought for $155,000 in 1995" (Williams 2005). As a result of these investments—whether they are called a "return" to the ghetto or "gentrification"—the number of owner-occupied houses in the neighborhood increased more than six times between 1990 and 2000. Moreover, according to a study conducted by the Brooklyn Alliance, an organization connected to the Brooklyn Chamber of Commerce, the fastest-growing group of residents in Bedford-Stuyvesant was families earning more than $100,000 a year (Chamberlain 2004).

By 2005 *New York* magazine declared that the handsome brownstone blocks of Bedford-Stuyvesant were trembling on the brink of gentrification. On one street, "in addition to Graham [a filmmaker] and [his wife] Blu [an event producer], the roster includes two other mixed couples (one Dutch and Caribbean, one African-American and Puerto Rican); a law professor and a communications executive, both black Hispanics born in Panama; a single white male who works as a photographer; and a black female pediatrician" (Coplon 2005). Declining crime rates and increasing acceptance of ethnically diverse workplaces had helped whites feel more at ease in majority-black neighborhoods. But so did the historical cosmopolitanism of their neighbors in Bed-Stuy and Harlem, who for many years had been Caribbean Americans, African immigrants, and Latinos as well as American-born blacks. New highly educated migrants, especially in creative occupations, saw this cosmopolitanism as a cultural bonus that added to the financial, aesthetic, and experiential value of their new homes. No wonder that "Harlem [was] Staging Its Latest Renaissance," as a headline on a real estate article in the *New York Sun* declared (Stoler 2006). According to real estate developers, rising property values showed that Harlem was at last "starting to be perceived as part of Manhattan."

Yet shopping and services remained a problem. In Harlem the Upper Manhattan Empowerment Zone gradually reshaped the retail landscape, loaning money to new entrepreneurs—many of them members of the new black middle class—to open restaurants, cafés, clothing boutiques, cosmetics shops, and flower stores (Zukin et al. 2009). Between 2000 and 2006, though the number of stores was almost cut in half by demolitions for new development and construction of larger commercial spaces, the share of small, upscale boutiques rose from 2 to 10 percent, and that of old-style, inexpensive stores decreased from 82 to 74 percent. Because UMEZ also made loans available to chain stores, the chains' presence in Harlem rose from 7 to 16 percent. Though the number of upscale boutiques and even moderate-price chain stores was small, this was a huge change from 1995, when Harlem residents had to go downtown or drive to the suburbs to find any of those kinds of stores. The arrival of Starbucks may have been greeted with dismay in a hipster neighborhood, but for many Harlem residents the opportunity to buy a latte was a source of satisfaction.

Without the strong financial support of the state, retail stores in Bedford-Stuyvesant lagged behind. Commercial property owners on Harlem's main shopping artery, 125th Street, had established a public-private business improvement district (BID) as early as 1993, just before the empowerment zone was established; no BID was set up in Bed-Stuy until 2009. Throughout the 1990s, many stores on Fulton Street, Bed-Stuy's main shopping artery, remained empty while the sidewalks were crowded with street vendors and, as a visitor noted, the counter in a new Burger King restaurant was protected from would-be armed robbers by Plexiglas (Rusk 1999). Even today it is difficult to replace the overconcentration of nail salons and roti shops, as folks say, with the health food stores and wine bars that new residents want (BRIC Community Media 2010).

But beginning in the 1990s, the commercial redevelopment of Bed-Stuy benefited from the efforts of a very impressive business entrepreneur: Monique Greenwood, a professional with a publishing career and an MBA, who owns what may have been America's—and certainly New York's—first high-class bed-and-breakfast inn with a black cultural theme when it opened in 1995. Housed in an Italianate mansion built in the 1860s, Akwaaba Mansion features luxurious beds and Jacuzzi baths, "fourteen-foot ceilings," and "ornate fireplaces," along with "a blend of antiques and Afrocentric elegance."[4] Like most upper-middle-class newcomers, Greenwood and her husband bought the house from "a working-class African-American family who lived there for over 50 years after the parents and their eight young adult children pooled their money together to buy it as the family home." They decided to become innkeepers, and during the next few years Greenwood encouraged or persuaded other highly educated black people to become retail entrepreneurs in

her part of the neighborhood, the historic district of Stuyvesant Heights—
Akwaaba is, in fact, on McDonough Street, where Judge Martin lives. On these
few blocks, Greenwood bought several properties and oversaw the gradual
development of a retail node that would interest middle-class residents anywhere. The bookstore, café-bakery, children's clothing store, and florist were
often featured in lifestyle articles in the media, alongside accounts about similar
stores in other neighborhoods, including Harlem. According to Greenwood,
some merchants showed their devotion to the commercial uplift of the community by using equity in their nearby homes to borrow money to run their
businesses (Chamberlain 2004).

Yet commercial redevelopment took much longer than it might have in a
majority-white gentrifying neighborhood. Some of the early retail entrepreneurs failed (Chamberlain 2004), and conditions worsened during the economic recession that began in 2007. But lifestyle reports in the media continued
to cast Harlem and Bed-Stuy as districts for gracious living at moderate
prices—exactly what the cultural ideal of gentrification is all about. In an article
in the *New York Times* about Harlem's first sidewalk café, the headline read:
"A New Harlem Gentry in Search of Its Latte," and the reporter referred to a
universal signifier of good taste: the "pale mist curling from pale-hued scoops
of gelato in porcelain bowls" (Leland 2003). New boutiques and spas throughout central Harlem were promoted in mainstream media from the *Times* and
Vogue to *Black Enterprise* and *O* magazine.

Few clothing boutiques came to Bed-Stuy, but new restaurants and bakeries
received attention from the media. Peaches opened on Monique Greenwood's
stretch of Lewis Avenue in 2008; "at this pioneering Bed-Stuy restaurant,"
according to *Time Out New York*, "owners Craig Samuel and Ben Grossman
(both of the Smoke Joint) ably merge two trends—Greenmarket and upscale
Southern." Adding the magazine's stamp of approval for the restaurant's contribution to its urban surroundings, *TONY* said, "Peaches is a progressive addition to a still-emerging 'hood—guts like those play well in the South, and
in Brooklyn, too."[5]

The packaging of urban neighborhoods for cultural consumption took a
giant step forward when local blogs blossomed on the Web in the early 2000s
(Zukin 2010). Though Harlem, with its Manhattan location, gets the lion's share
of tourists, Bed-Stuy, like other Brooklyn neighborhoods, gets residents in cre-

ative occupations who generate buzz about the area in the blogosphere. Posts on Bed Stuy Blog, Bed-Stizzy, and other websites promote local businesses, call for volunteers for tennis camps and charity races, and reprint articles from mainstream media praising the area's rebirth. Bed-Stizzy lists the "creatives"— residents of Bed-Stuy who are actors, painters, writers, graphic artists, jewelry makers, and musicians. Like Yelp and other wikis, local blogs in Harlem and Bed-Stuy also review new restaurants and stores. When Tin City Drug & General Store opened on Lewis Avenue, Bed-Stuy Blog (2010) posted an ecstatic review that showed a desire for the amenities that would transform the ghetto into a neighborhood just as pleasant as any other: "It feels like a Main Street store in Anytown, USA," the post said. "Very country like. There's a mixture of organic, upscale and mainstream products on the shelves, so there's something there for everyone." This blogger bought "organic raw kombucha, Loacker hazelnut quadratini wafer cookies and a Gianduja (choco-hazelnut) milkshake!"— an esoteric combination in any store, let alone in Bed-Stuy.

Other bloggers openly talk about their ambivalence to gentrification. "I am baffled by what people think of my hood. On twitter you would think Bed Stuy is the equivalent of Beirut," wrote Lexie, a white woman in her midthirties married to a black man, who blogs on Living in the Stuy. "It is 2010," she noted on July 15, "and this [is] a public service announcement for all heads who want to know what Bed Stuy is really like.

"Bed Stuy has *CSAs* [community-supported agriculture groups], organic markets, outdoor flea markets, bike lanes, summer concerts in the park, block parties, block associations, summer camps, basketball tournaments and hundreds of other positive things. Why is this always left out of the conversation? Why is it so much easier to focus on the bad?"

A few months earlier, however, on January 21, 2010, Lexie had blogged about a disturbing spurt of crimes. "Cars have been getting broken into like it's Prospect Heights [a nearby neighborhood], people are getting jacked on the street supposedly at gunpoint early in the morning. The laundry mat got robbed 2 days ago and that's just what I heard or saw in the past few days." This news forced her to admit that "being part of gentrifying a neighborhood can be amazing and brutal at the same time." But what is a person who wants to live in a racially diverse neighborhood and does not have much money to do? She is caught between the ghetto's affordable rents and higher rates of crime, and being white, she is implicated as one of the shock troops of gentrification. "White people who are not well off are moving here because the blocks are beautiful, it's close to the train and you can rent a huge 2 bedroom brownstone [apartment] for like [$]1400–1500 a month. So is that even gentrification? Is it getting the best bang for your buck or is it an invasion?

"I think it's an invasion and we are part of it."[6]

A CHANGE OF CHARACTER

Gentrification has been a major issue in Harlem since the year 2000, when the Upper Manhattan Empowerment Zone began to lure chain stores to 125th Street and developers issued plans to build market-rate condos. By the time of public hearings on the rezoning of 125th Street, in 2008, some longtime residents were very angry. They resented the ongoing displacement of black merchants, some of whom had been doing business in Harlem for years, and they feared that rezoning the street for high-rises would lead to residential displacement (Ohrstrom 2008; Tucker 2008). While new social networks are emerging, the listservs that connect them sometimes betray the same suspicions. As Lexie of Bed-Stuy asks: Are new residents, especially homeowners, assuming that everyone in the neighborhood is just like them? Are they, the members of the new black middle class or whites with a little money, consuming the ghetto's cultural image but destroying its authenticity (Dominus 2010; Zukin 2010)?

That both Harlem and Bedford-Stuyvesant have been "whitening" in recent years is undeniable. Some of the evidence is anecdotal, as when my Brooklyn College student who lives in Bed-Stuy said, "I woke up one morning and there were white people jogging on my street." Or when a black woman in her twenties who lives in Bed-Stuy, interviewed on public access TV, said, "I've got people from France and Spain on my block now" (BRIC 2010). But these impressions are confirmed by census data. In 2000 the population of Community Board 3 in Bed-Stuy was only 1.4 percent white; six years later the number had risen to 16.9 percent (Coplon 2005).[7] In 2000 only 2 percent of residents in Community Board 10 in central Harlem were white; by 2006–2008, whites were 12.6 percent of the area's population.[8]

Though many longtime residents praise this racial diversity, it may make them feel a little uneasy, especially when the media contrast the uneven development of "intact" and "less so" brownstone blocks with new condos and luxury rental apartments "across the street from one of the local housing projects" (Vandam 2009). Even if they welcome better stores and services, it is reasonable for them to fear being perceived as second-class citizens in their own neighborhood.

It is difficult to know whether longtime residents have more to fear from the increase in white population or the increase in affluent, highly educated blacks. Homeowners have different economic interests from renters, regardless of race. A moral commitment to help others in the same ethnic or racial group, known as "racial uplift," may not extend to sending children to the same public schools or even to the charter schools that are springing up in majority-black and -Latino areas (on Chicago, see Pattillo 2007). The block parties that have been a tradition in the black neighborhoods of central Brooklyn are not held as often now, and whether it is because many old-timers have died or moved away or because of gentrification, there may be less social interaction among neighbors of different social classes. Moreover, it is uncertain how many longtime residents patronize some of the new retail stores. Though a bakery like Bread-Stuy is able to count on local supporters to stave off bankruptcy (Cardwell 2010), new retail entrepreneurs may be oriented toward customers who are as middle class as themselves. Consider the view of the Haitian-born lawyer who co-owns a new café in Bed-Stuy with a pastry maker from Fort Greene: "The people here are amazing," she said. "They have wonderful, rich lives. We have a Pulitzer Prize–winning writer, artists. The kids here are so gracious. I even live here, and I never expected this in a million years. *It feels like I imagine the Midwest to feel*" (Sheftell 2010, emphasis added).

With current residents, black and white, striving to maintain their place in a rapidly gentrifying city, the stakes of defining the ghetto's public image are high. Most local blogs and many newspaper articles assert pride in the neighborhood—the pride of survivors and of successors to an ethnically diverse, black-inflected history. "A Neighborhood Evolves, History Intact," says an article about black-owned retail stores and bakeries in Bed-Stuy that would appeal to cultural consumers of any race (Lee 2010). Both blacks and whites are careful to point out how *normal* life is, and how friendly people are, in the 'hood. "You don't have to be black to live in Bedford-Stuyvesant," a new resident who comes from Bulgaria told my student. Another of Bed-Stuy's new white residents, a theater director, and her boyfriend, an online news editor, take their baby daughter to the playground and the bookstore. "We were saying to a neighbor the other day it kind of feels like Sesame Street," they told a reporter from the *Times* (Vandam 2009). Among longtime black residents, however, there is sometimes an edge of defensiveness about the apparent new normalcy. They tend to take refuge in slogans of solidarity, like "Do or Die Bed-Stuy," the title of a hip-hop song of the 1980s that has become a motto of sorts for the neighborhood.

When my Brooklyn College student asked several men and women who live in her neighborhood whether Bedford-Stuyvesant is a ghetto, not a single person said yes. "A ghetto is just a state of mind," a sixty-year-old black man and longtime resident told her. "Bed-Stuy is not a ghetto, it's a neighborhood," a new Irish immigrant said. Though the vast majority of residents are still black, and many of them, especially in the public housing projects, are poor, the self-image of areas like Bed-Stuy and Harlem has greatly changed. Their new ethnic and social diversity is not unlike the picture on the vodka label, at least on the brownstone blocks. New residents take pride in the neighborhood for both its connection with Mos' Def and Biggie Smalls and its mainstream American feel. New stores provide the staffs of life, whether it is bean pie at Abu's Bakery on Fulton Street or focaccia at Settepani Café on Lenox Avenue. To some degree the ghetto has been relocated elsewhere—in poorer, still blacker Brooklyn neighborhoods; in older, inner suburbs; and in cities forsaken by globalization and outsourced production where a mainly African American population still faces abandoned housing, empty factories, and vacant lots.

Even in "gentrified" ghettos, problems worse than in most middle-class neighborhoods remain. As I write these words, Harlem and Bedford-Stuyvesant are challenged by gun-toting residents and quick-on-the-trigger police (Lee and Moynihan 2010), disproportionate numbers of mortgage foreclosures (Buckley 2010), and scandals surrounding political figures and community-based organizations (Barbaro 2010; Buettner 2010). I suspect that the future of these areas will not hold either a total racial transformation from black to white or an economic uplift of the entire existing population. But their present diversity, and the way residents see themselves as reshaping the city's ethnic mosaic, represents an enormous change of character. The question is whether the rise in the individual fortunes of some families and blocks will help the collective fortunes of those who are poor, undereducated, and unemployed. At the height of the protest movements of the 1960s, a lifestyle reporter for the *New York Times* wrote: "There are about three things that can be done with the walls inside a ghetto short of tearing them down: Escape from them, which is a lot easier said than done, endure them, or try to improve them" (Warren 1968). We will see whether today's "improvement" can tear down those walls.

Notes

1. Thanks to my Brooklyn College students, especially undergraduate Sandra Thomas and the master's seminar in urban research, for inspiration. They bear absolutely no responsibility for my interpretations.

2. See Virtual Museum of Modernism NRW's virtual catalog, available at: http://www.nrw -museum.de/virtuelles-museum-moderne-nrw. (accessed July 31, 2010).

3. See Brownstoners of Bedford Stuyvesant, Inc., website at: http://www.brownstonersof bedstuy.org (accessed August 9, 2010).

4. See Akwaaba Mansion website at: http://www.akwaaba.com/brooklyn (accessed August 10, 2010).

5. *Time Out New York*, "Restaurants: Peaches," available at: http://newyork.timeout.com/ restaurants/bedford-stuyvesant/22241/peaches#ixzz0wF1LnMv3 (accessed August 10, 2010).

6. See Living in the Stuy, "Live from Bedford Stuyvesant, the Livest One" (July 15, 2010) and "Rhymin' and Stealin' . . ." (January 21, 2010), http://www.himandherinthestuy.com (accessed July 16, 2010).

7. See also the New York City Department of City Planning website at: http://www.nyc.gov/ html/dcp/ (accessed July 31, 2010).

8. See New York City Department of City Planning, "Manhattan Community District 10" (http://www.nyc.gov/html/dcp/pdf/lucds/mn10profile.pdf, accessed August 11, 2010), and "Bronx Community Districts 1 & 2" (http://www.nyc.gov/html/dcp/pdf/census/puma_demo _06to08_acs.pdf#mn10, accessed August 11, 2010).

References

Barbaro, Michael. 2010. "For Rangel, a Birthday Party and a Display of Bravado." *New York Times*, August 12.

Bed-Stuy Blog. 2010. "Tin City Drug & General Store Grand Opening." July 26. Available at http://www.bedstuyblog.com/?s=Anytown+USA (accessed July 26, 2010).

Beveridge, Andrew. 2008. "An Affluent, White Harlem?" *Gotham Gazette*, August. Available at http://69.20.65.189/article/demographics/20080827/5/2620.

Bloom, Nicholas Dagen. 2008. *Public Housing That Worked: New York in the Twentieth Century*. Philadelphia: University of Pennsylvania Press.

BRIC Community Media. 2010. "Bed-Stuy Gateway: Neighborhood Beat: Bed-Stuy." Interview with Michael Rafferty. Posted June 30. Available at http://briccommunitymedia.word press.com/2010/06/30/bed-stuy-gateway-nb-bed-stuy/ (accessed July 31, 2010).

Buckley, Cara. 2010. "Rescued from Blight, Fall Back into Decay." *New York Times*, July 18.

Buettner, Russ. 2010. "Faltering Harlem Housing Deal Won City Cash." *New York Times*, August 12.

Cardwell, Diane. 2010. "Bedford-Stuyvesant Journal: Saving a Place to Bump into People." *New York Times*, February 12.

Chamberlain, Lisa. 2004. "Square Feet: Bedford-Stuyvesant; 'The Residential Is Hot, but the Commercial Is Not.'" *New York Times*, August 22.

Clark, Kenneth B. 1965. *Dark Ghetto: Dilemmas of Social Power*. New York: Harper & Row.

Coplon, Jeff. 2005. "The Tipping of Jefferson Avenue." *New York*, May 21. Available at: http://nymag.com/nymetro/realestate/neighborhoods/features/11775 (accessed August 9, 2010).

Dominus, Susan. 2010. "Big City; Via Listserv, Parents Clash in Harlem." *New York Times*, August 10.

Garb, Maggie. 1998. "If You're Thinking of Living In: West Central Harlem; Abandonment Down, Refurbishment Up." *New York Times*, June 21.

———. 2001. "If You're Thinking of Living In: West Harlem; Brownstones in Manhattan, at a Discount." *New York Times*, February 25.

Hyra, Derek S. 2008. *The New Urban Renewal: The Economic Transformation of Harlem and Bronzeville*. Chicago: University of Chicago Press.

Landry, Bart. 1987. *The New Black Middle Class*. Berkeley and Los Angeles: University of California Press.

Lee, Trymaine. 2010. "A Neighborhood Evolves, History Intact." *New York Times*, February 28.

Lee, Trymaine, and Colin Moynihan. 2010. "After 50 Shots in Harlem, One Dead and 6 Hurt." *New York Times*, August 8.

Leland, John. 2003. "A New Harlem Gentry in Search of Its Latte." *New York Times*, August 7.

Mollenkopf, John Hull. 1992. *A Phoenix in the Ashes: The Rise and Fall of the Koch Coalition in New York City Politics*. Princeton, N.J.: Princeton University Press.

Monti, Daniel J. 1979. "Patterns of Conflict Preceding the 1964 Riots: Harlem and Bedford-Stuyvesant." *Journal of Conflict Resolution* 23, no. 1: 41–69.

Ohrstrom, Lysandra. 2008. "*Today in 125th Street Rezoning News: 'Jim Crowism,' 'Harlem's Death Certificate,' 'White Supremacy,' Subsection 3 of Section 200*." *New York Observer*, April 1. Available at http://www.observer.com (accessed August 11, 2010).

Osofsky, Gilbert. 1963. *Harlem: The Making of a Ghetto*. New York: Harper & Row.

Pattillo, Mary. 2007. *Black on the Block*. Chicago: University of Chicago Press.

Podair, Jerald E. 2002. *The Strike That Changed New York: Blacks, Whites, and the Ocean Hill–Brownsville Crisis*. New Haven, Conn.: Yale University Press.

Rusk, David. 1999. *Inside Game/Outside Game: Winning Strategies for Saving Urban America*. Washington, D.C.: Brookings Institution Press.

Schaffer, Richard, and Neil Smith. 1986. "The Gentrification of Harlem?" *Annals of the Association of American Geographers* 76, no. 3: 347–365.

Schjeldahl, Peter. 1994. *Columns and Catalogues*. Great Barrington, Mass.: Geoffrey Young.

Sheftell, Jason. 2010. "High on Bed-Stuy: Furniture Stores, Cafés, Condos Bring New Life to an Old Brooklyn 'Hood." *New York Daily News*, July 30. Available at: http://www.nydaily news.com (accessed August 4, 2010).

Sotheby's. 2010. "Tomlinson Court Park" (first version, small). Contemporary art evening auction, sale N08636, lot 3. New York, May 12, 2010. Available at: http://www.sothebys.com/app/live/lot/LotDetail.jsp?lot_id=159596802 (accessed April 7, 2011).

Stoler, Michael. 2006. "Harlem Staging Its Latest Renaissance." *New York Sun*, September 14.

Taylor, Monique. 2002. *Harlem Between Heaven and Hell*. Minneapolis: University of Minnesota Press.

Thabit, Walter. 2003. *How East New York Became a Ghetto*. New York: New York University Press.

Tucker, Maria Luisa. 2008. "Harlem Residents Blast 125th Street Rezoning 'Sellout.'" *Village Voice*, May 1. Available at http://blogs.villagevoice.com (accessed August 11, 2010).

Vandam, Jeff. 2009. "Living In: Bedford-Stuyvesant, Brooklyn: History, with Hipper Retailing in Bed-Stuy." *New York Times*, August 21.

Waldinger, Roger. 1996. *Still the Promised City? African Americans and New Immigrants in Postindustrial New York*. Cambridge, Mass.: Harvard University Press.

Warren, Virginia Lee. 1968. "Decorators' Project: To Make the Homes in Ghettos Livable." *New York Times*, September 20.

Whitaker, Barbara. 1997. "Habitats: 536 McDonough Street, Bedford-Stuyvesant; Adding 1990s Function to Exquisite 1890s Details." *New York Times*, October 26.

White, Norval, and Elliot Willensky. 1978. *AIA Guide to New York City*. Rev. ed. New York: Collier.

Wilder, Craig. 2000. *A Covenant with Color: Race and Social Power in Brooklyn*. New York: Columbia University Press.

Williams, Stephen P. 2005. "Habitats: Bedford-Stuyvesant; A Home with Charm, and Challenges." *New York Times*, November 20.

Zukin, Sharon. 2010. *Naked City: The Death and Life of Authentic Urban Places*. New York: Oxford University Press.

Zukin, Sharon, et al. 2009. "New Retail Capital and Neighborhood Change: Boutiques and Gentrification in New York City." *City & Community* 8, no. 1: 47–64.

CHAPTER 7

✦ ✦ ✦

Places of Stigma:
Ghettos, Barrios, and Banlieues
Ernesto Castañeda

While concentrating on the Parisian periphery, this chapter implicitly compares different spaces of social stigma and exclusion: *ghettos, barrios,* and *banlieues.*[1] The ghetto was initially a state-designated space for a stigmatized group. It first appeared in Europe; the term was later applied in the United States to urban neighborhoods, especially the areas where African Americans lived after migrating from the South (Haynes and Hutchison 2008). The view of the ghetto as a place of insecurity needing strong policing became a top urban policy concern in the United States and later in Europe (Wacquant 2008). Immigrant enclaves on both sides of the Atlantic have also evoked this preoccupation with "dangerous" peoples and spaces.

I concur with Talja Blokland (2008, 377) that "the question is not 'which area is a ghetto' but instead 'how do mechanisms of border creation and maintaining create areas where residents consider themselves involuntarily segregated and what processes and mechanisms contribute to this understanding of social reality?'" The boundaries of concrete ghettos, banlieues, and immigrant enclaves shift over time. Studying their historical formation and dissolution as well as the actual views and practices of their inhabitants sheds light on the social processes and mechanisms that constitute them.

This chapter begins by briefly discussing the theoretical concept of the social boundary, which can be used to schematize the parallel processes that stigmatize space. Proceeding chronologically, it then looks briefly at the history of the ghetto and the banlieue to show how the current stigma of the Parisian banlieue draws on a long history of power relations inscribed in social space. The chapter turns next to ethno-surveys, participant observation, interviews, and secondary sources to describe how contemporary practices in and around the banlieue are in conflict with the political, journalistic, and sometimes socio-logical approaches used to frame them. It ends by making some general comparisons with the ideas of "the ghetto" and "el barrio." The processes that produce the mental maps of the ghetto, the banlieue, and the barrio are similar, even when their objective conditions differ.

Relational boundary-making mechanisms are the middle-range theory implied in the chapter. The argument and methodological approach is that from an analytical perspective it is impossible to understand banlieues, ghettos, and other stigmatized spaces without studying their relationship with what lies outside of them. One should not talk about the Parisian banlieue without talking about Paris, and one cannot talk seriously about Paris without taking into account its banlieue. Understanding the history and contemporary antagonistic relationship between places of stigma and their surroundings allows one to see that the same processes of framing and boundary-making are in place. Yet differences in the way these boundaries are produced and policed result in different social outcomes. Historical and ethnographical contextualization illuminates similarities and differences between the ghetto, the barrio, and the banlieue.

BOUNDARY-MAKING

Michèle Lamont and Virag Molnar (2002, 168) define *symbolic boundaries* as "conceptual distinctions made by social actors to categorize objects, people, practices, and even time and space." Categorization is a basic mental way of organizing the many stimuli that our brain is confronted with every day (Massey 2007; Simmel 1971; Zelizer and Tilly 2006). Social categories arise when there seems to be implicit agreement on how to categorize other people and determine their symbolic worth (Boltanski and Thévenot 2006). Group boundaries result from a process of relational identifications and feedback loops, since how group X defines itself in relation to group Y is likely to cause a response from group Y, and group Y's response, in turn, could affect group X's self-conception; the process repeats itself ad infinitum (Tilly 2005). Different mechanisms and boundary-work keep X different from Y (Massey 2007; Roy 1994; Thorne 1993; Tilly 1998, 2004). We see *social boundaries* when "a boundary displays both a categorical and a social or behavioral dimension . . . —how to relate to individuals classified as 'us' and 'them' under given circumstances" (Wimmer 2008, 975). Thus, the existence of social boundaries often affects life chances; for example, workers with an address in a stigmatized banlieue are less likely to be employed than those living in central Paris. Yet moral rationales are often provided to deny or justify unequal outcomes (Lamont 2000). "The act of giving credit or (especially) assigning blame draws us-them boundaries: We are the worthy people, they the unworthy" (Tilly 2008, 7). Once these beliefs are internalized, it is difficult to humanize "the other," and stigmatization appears "natural" (Bourdieu 1991, 1998).

As I show here in the case of Paris, when political and spatial configurations stress and underline differences, almost mirror-image moral and symbolic boundaries between groups form under what Georg Simmel (1964) called concentric social circles. The mental social circles and boundaries for natives in the ideal-typical nation-state would look something like this:

FIGURE 7.1. Imagined Concentric Circles of Identification

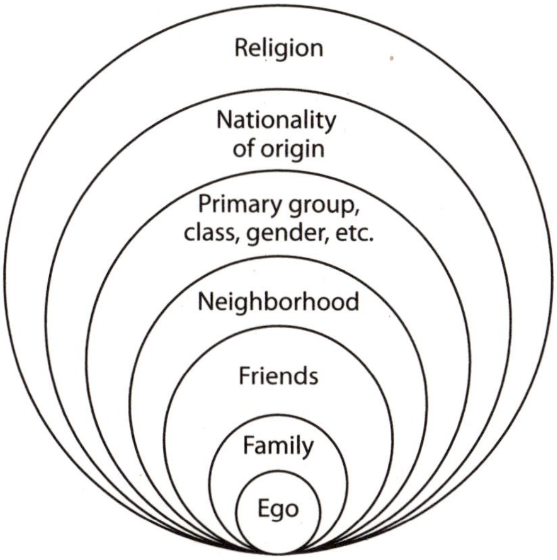

Religion

Nationality of origin

Primary group, class, gender, etc.

Neighborhood

Friends

Family

Ego

This is the picture assumed in liberal political theory. But in multicultural global cities, such as Paris and New York, different concentric circles overlap (especially at the neighborhood level) with those of immigrants or minorities with different religions, languages, or national origins (Sennett 2008). The challenge of a multicultural society is to go beyond these "primordial" groupings by minimizing spatial segregation and forming a civic community among cultural others—along the spirit of the motto *e pluribus unum* (of many, one)—resulting in an equal citizenship for all the residents of a city (Castañeda 2010).

THE GHETTO AND THE MYTH OF THE URBAN COMMUNITY

The word *ghetto* may come from the Venetian (local proto-Italian) word *gettare*, "to pour," used to name a foundry off of a Venetian island. In 1382, Jewish people were allowed to act as merchants in the medieval principality of Venice, but by 1516 they had to sleep within the confines of the island of the former foundry (Haynes and Hutchison 2008). In this fashion, the meaning of *ghetto* as a housing area concentrating a segregated and stigmatized group was born. Ironically, this coincides with the other meanings of *gettare*: to throw, to cast away.

Stigma was ascribed to space and marked in the body. When Jewish people went into Venice, the men had to wear a yellow circle and the women a yellow scarf, and they could not wear jewelry (Haynes and Hutchison 2008). This practice was adopted many years later throughout Europe. Nazism further reinforced the connection between ascribed characteristics and special treatment: Jews were marked physically (with yellow stars) and officially (with notes on identity cards and passports) and concentrated in living quarters and camps with known dire consequences. Ethnic spatial segregation does not always play the same role: The ultimate role of a concentration camp is extermination; a reservation's role is to keep social and spatial distance; and a ghetto can function as a prophylactic to maintain social boundaries while allowing for capital investment and labor exploitation (Sennett 1994; Wacquant 2010b).

At the birth of sociology in the United States, the Chicago School of Sociology assigned itself the task of conducting community studies that would map and designate "natural areas" within Chicago. These originally descriptive studies had a performative effect, since by partly describing the city of Chicago, these scholars also created neighborhood names and characteristics and went on to convince politicians, schoolteachers, social workers, and others to use these neighborhood labels and boundaries, even if many city residents would not have recognized them as characterizing "their neighborhood" (Venkatesh 2001).

Although the Chicago School left a legacy of great ethnographies and made many methodological and theoretical contributions, it also created a myth of transplanted rural villages in urban spaces. This myth led policymakers and social scientists to try to impose a certain order—grouping social groups into particular neighborhoods as if they were plants in a thick botanical garden. Through this process we see the romantic ideal of traditional rural communities being reproduced in the concepts of the ghetto, barrio, banlieue, and immigrant enclave alongside the desire to circumvent, round up, and fence in unknown "others," the poor, and the dangerous classes.

Major theorists of large social change, including modernization, industrialization, urbanization, and globalization (de Tocqueville, Durkheim, Simmel, Weber, Wirth, Thomas, Park, and so on), invariably contrast city urban life with the ideal-typical rural community. These theories posit city-dwellers as atomized, seemingly autonomous, and able to remake their identity without the social norms and integration provided by small communities. But this is not necessarily the case for rural and international migrants who arrive in their cities of destiny with customs and identities formed in a different cultural context (Castañeda 2010). Chain migration, social networks, homophily, cheap housing, and exclusion by others often combine to concentrate newcomers into ethnic enclaves (Tilly and Brown 1967; Wilson and Portes 1980), yet this does not signify that these newcomers lack a desire to assimilate structurally.

DEFINING THE BANLIEUE

The word *banlieue* refers to the areas surrounding a city; it is an update of the word *faubourg*, which used to mean "lying outside the city" but now commonly refers to areas in central Paris that were incorporated into the city centuries ago (Castañeda 2009a). There is a temptation to compare the French banlieues with the American "suburbs," but there are important differences. In the United States the word *suburb* usually carries a positive connotation and is associated with private property, middle-class ease, low-density population, and an overall high quality of life, even though suburbs originally emerged to provide afford-able housing for lower-middle-class white ethnics (Gans 1982; Katznelson 2005). Furthermore, the American suburbs have grown increasingly diverse in recent years (Fry 2009).

In contrast to the idyllic image of the homogeneous, peaceful, and affluent American suburbs, the contemporary immediate connotation of the banlieue and its inhabitants, the *banlieusards*, is one of overcrowded public housing, people of color, new immigrants (mainly from French former colonies), and crime (Wacquant 2010b). The banlieue is something closer to the stereotype of "the ghetto" in America, and although there are important differences, what both share today is the aggregate experience of exclusion from the labor mar-ket, categorical inequality, social boundaries, and housing policies and practices that result in residential segregation (Massey and Denton 1993).

Lately the word *banlieue* carries a negative connotation somewhat at odds with its complex history and social reality. The modern-day Parisian banlieues include some of the wealthiest areas of France, including La De-fense, Neuilly, and even Versailles and Fontainebleau. All of these places are, in the strict sense, banlieues, yet they are anything but shabby or humble; still, they are places of racial, class, and cultural homogeneity, featuring gated communities and wealthy enclaves (Frank 2004; Pinçon and Pinçon-Charlot 2007). Thus, it is important to keep in mind that not all French banlieues are the same (Wacquant 2008), given the differences between the western banlieues, which include areas like La Defense, Bois Colombes, and Neuilly (where French president Nicolas Sarkozy was mayor for many years), and the stigmatized and heavily populated *cités* (public housing projects), such as La Courneuve and Sarcelles. In this author's opinion, the latter are over-stigmatized in that they lack the objective poverty or lack of infrastructure that can be observed in American über-ghettos, Mexican *ciudades perdidas*, Brazilian *favelas,* and Argentinean *villas miseria,* not to mention the poverty in Haiti, rural Morocco, and sub-Saharan Africa, where some of their inhab-itants come from. Most people in the banlieues and the *cités* have a roof over their heads, food, health care, and provision of other basic necessities. Yet it is relative deprivation that matters, and some of the inhabitants of the banlieue—especially those living in the projects—feel a strong sense of physical and symbolic marginalization.

THE HISTORY OF THE BANLIEUE

The importance of the banlieue can be fully understood only in historical perspective and in relation to the city it surrounds. Like many medieval cities, Paris was a walled city for defensive purposes. As the city grew, new walls were constructed, eventually totaling six. A new wall was built in the years preceding the French Revolution, but this time mainly for taxation purposes. The wall demarcated Paris proper. Its doors included customs posts, and everyone entering or leaving with commercial goods had to pay a fee or tax called the *octroi*. These *murs d'octroi* were spatial and legal barriers to free trade and mobility for tax purposes, but they also created a real social boundary between those living inside (*intra-muros*) and those living outside (*extra-muros*), with economic consequences for trade and production (Fourcaut, Bellanger, and Flonneau 2007). Consequently, the cost of living was lower outside Paris than inside, resulting in an early division between the large percentage of the labor force that had settled in the banlieue and the consumers, visitors, financiers, and administrators who lived inside the city walls (Castañeda 2009a).[2]

During the Ancien Régime, the Parisian banlieue contained vast open areas where the nobility of Paris and Versailles went to spend time surrounded by nature. Later this taste was emulated by the *arrivistes* of the growing French bourgeoisie and by the petite bourgeoisie, who would go to the green banlieue on weekends as a sign of distinction, as depicted in the short stories of Guy de Maupassant and by Jean Renoir in his celebrated film *Une Partie de campagne* (1936). But as more people built houses in these idyllic lands, the banlieue was quickly transformed from forest into urban and suburban space. The remaining forests of Vincennes and the Bois de Boulogne are legally protected: Although technically located outside of the city limits, they are annexed to the city and under its jurisdiction.

After the French Revolution of 1789, the Constitutional Assembly decreed the limits of Paris to be a circle with a circumference determined by a radius of three leagues (*lieues*) around the center set at the Notre Dame Cathedral. In 1841 the politician Adolphe Thiers ordered the construction of a new set of walls and customs towers to be surrounded by a zone where it was forbidden to build. In 1860 the city was expanded by the Baron Haussmann, and crossing taxes continued to be levied. In this expansion, Paris officially engulfed *l'ancienne banlieue*, which included the communes of Batignolle, Belleville, Bercy, Passy, la Villette, and other neighboring areas. When the Paris octroi was instituted in these communes, many industries were forced to move out of the new city borders for fiscal reasons, and many workers followed (Harvey 2008). Some of the most developed and industrialized external communes decided to also charge octroi to raise funds for local infrastructure and public spending, while poorer banlieues, hoping tax incentives would attract industry and population, did not. The octroi of Paris and its surrounding metropolitan area was not abolished until 1943, during the German occupation, when it was replaced with a general sales tax (Fourcaut et al. 2007).

As the population density of Paris increased, the city looked to the banlieue to locate new cemeteries and public parks. In 1887 a large building went up in the exterior commune of Nanterre as a *dépôt de mendicité*—to house Parisian mental patients, the homeless, vagabonds, and aged people and to imprison "deviant" women. In 1897 this building was also turned into a hospital. To this day L'Hôpital de Nanterre offers shelter to the very poor of the region and to newly arrived immigrants who have neither a place to stay nor a supportive social network.

THE CONTINUOUS NEED FOR HOUSING

As elsewhere, French industrialization created a large rural-to-urban migration. The Paris region has always been a popular destination for both internal and international migrants. Female workers from the French provinces, Spain, Portugal, Yugoslavia, and Africa would live in servant apartments (*chambres de bonnes*) atop bourgeois buildings in western Paris, while the high cost of living and high occupancy rate in Paris forced the working class to move to the eastern part of the city and to the banlieues.

In 1914, following a public scandal about the *mal-lotis*—the people who, owing to overcrowded conditions, had built on open lots in the banlieue that lacked public services such as water, roads, electricity, and gas—the socialist politician Henri Sellier (1883–1943) pushed for the creation of *habitations à bon marché* (HBMs), or affordable housing. A number of HBMs were built around the city in the area where the Thiers wall had been laid. Between 1921 and 1939, the HBM administration built garden-cities (*cités-jardin*) inspired by the British urbanist Ebenezer Howard. In 1935 the architect and urbanist Maurice Rotival was the first person to use the term *grandes ensembles*—which corresponds to "the projects" in the United States—to refer to a set of large public housing buildings with shared common areas designed to house multiple families. Among the most infamous affordable housing projects was La Cité de la Muette in Drancy, built between 1931 and 1935, which was used as a Jewish internment camp during the German occupation, leading to the death of over 67,000 deportees.

The painter, architect, and urbanist Charles-Edouard Jeanneret, also called Le Corbusier (1887–1965), published influential books in which he presented detailed proposals for planned, rational, and utopian residential complexes formed by many large housing buildings (Le Corbusier 1923/1927, 1935/1967). His work influenced the construction of public housing and large public works in places like Brasilia, Brazil, Co-op City in New York, the Robert Taylor Homes in Chicago (Venkatesh 2002), and the cités built in banlieues throughout France that would house many thousands in areas that offered little employment.

At the end of World War II, the *îlots insalubres*—the slums in the construction-free zone around the Thiers walls—were replaced with modernist housing projects. After Algeria's independence in 1962 and the migration to France of *pied noirs* (white colonists), Jewish people formerly living in Algeria, and *harkis* (Muslims who had fought on the French side), the French state decided to house the new arrivals in projects in remote banlieues of Paris, Marseille, and Lyon, partly in the hope of hiding them from the public view of regular citizens.

To provide more formal housing for the new workers from Algeria, the Société Nationale de Construction de Logements pour les Travailleurs (SONACOTRA) was created in 1956. Yet, in 1964 there was a public scandal surrounding the conditions at the *bidonville* (shantytown on the outskirts of a city) of Champigny, a slum that housed more than 10,000 Portuguese immigrants in conditions of extreme poverty an hour away from the luxuries of Paris. Many Algerians lived in similar conditions in other *bidonvilles*. To appease public opinion the so-called Debré law was passed to improve the conditions of the migrant workers: It explicitly looked to prevent them from leaving France and thus hinder the successful reconstruction and growth of France from 1945 to 1973 during what came to be known as *Les Trente*

Glorieuses ("The Glorious Thirty"). Along with the Marshall Plan, foreign labor helped reconstruct France and make its economy grow after the war.

The rise of the welfare state, along with the increasing cost of living in Paris, led to the construction of *habitations à loyer modéré* (HLMs, subsidized public housing). Originally, the heavy concentration of French working-class families, many of them hailing from other regions of France and Europe, led to the appearance in certain banlieues of the "red banlieues," which often elected communist or socialist mayors and had a dense associational and cultural life (Stovall 1990; Wacquant 2010b). According to some hypotheses, this hegemony changed after the Communist Party failed to incorporate the large arrival of new immigrants into its local agenda and thus lacked their complete support (Fassin and Fassin 2006). French workers from Paris and the provinces lived there first, but eventually the population changed from working-class residents to relative majorities of immigrants from former colonies, even in the face of laws against the concentration of more than 15 percent of a given group in a given area; these laws were explicitly aimed at preventing the creation of ghettos, something disdained and deeply feared by the French. What many failed to see was that group concentration arose not only from processes of self-segregation but also from social networks, unemployment support, and solidarity acts that brought underrepresented groups together in order to survive strong labor market discrimination, spatial segregation, and social exclusion. Furthermore, discrimination and segregation did not necessarily result in concentration (Dangschat 2009); indeed, North African immigrants and their descendants (with the exception of a certain concentration in Barbès) are now dispersed throughout the Parisian metropolitan area. This trend does not mean, however, that they are structurally integrated into French mainstream society, and in fact it has only further discouraged collective identification and action.

Although the French government has opposed the creation of "ghettos," the political opposition from the richest quarters inside and outside Paris has pushed immigrants and workers out into certain distant and poor banlieues. This has resulted in an enduring inequality for many of the inhabitants of these areas, owing to lack of access to quality education and good jobs, and is the reason why many banlieue inhabitants live off of unemployment and other social benefits. To address these inequities, special education zones (*zones d'éducation prioritaire* [ZEP]) were created in 1981 to dedicate more educational funds to certain "sensitive areas." In this way the French government has been able to direct some resources to certain underprivileged groups by the territorialization of public policy (Doytcheva 2007).

BOUNDARIES OF DISTINCTION AND EXCLUSION

In 1954 the *boulevard périphérique*, an expressway around the city, was launched and built along HBMs in the zone formerly reserved for the Thiers wall. It further reinforced the boundary between Paris and the growing banlieue.

Many French banlieues still give testimony to their past as old provincial villages that have been engulfed by the growing metropolitan area and share many a common element, such as train stations, public squares, churches, city halls, stores, restaurants, and private houses and cités on their own peripheries, with regular buses that travel farther inside the banlieue and out to rural areas.

In *Paris et le désert français* ("Paris and the French Desert"), Jean-François Gravier (1947) blames Paris for devouring all the resources, talent, and wealth of the entire country and, one could add, the French colonies. According to Gravier, this centralization of power, influence, and resources will end in the symbolic desertification of the whole of France unless something is done to build industry in the provinces and decentralize public functions and priorities. Even Haussmann was concerned about a luxurious center surrounded by a proletariat ring of workers (Fourcaut et al. 2007). Thus, it is not only the poverty of the banlieue that is at issue, but the overconcentration of wealth in the western part of Paris and the continuous gentrification of the city. As many French thinkers have warned, twenty-first-century Paris risks becoming a city museum for the millions of tourists who visit every year, oblivious to the backstage that is the banlieue, which they "see" primarily through the train windows as they pass through it from the airport to their hotels. With the heavy gentrification of recent years, Paris, like New York, risks becoming the exclusive property of of its richest inhabitants, plus the young, the artists, and the immigrants who know how to share apartments and live frugally. This concentration of the very rich and poor in the city is a common characteristic of neoliberal global cities (Sassen 2001).

To this day there is a critical need in Paris for housing for students, single parents, artists, and the poor who cannot afford the city's rents but may not qualify for public housing. The housing crisis is especially acute for foreigners, who are categorically distrusted, and the *sans-papiers* (undocumented migrants), who cannot demand social welfare. Today many new citizens and people living in bad housing conditions (*les mal loges*) engage in social movements to demand what in modern France has come to be recognized as a basic human right: access to decent housing (Castañeda 2009b).

The residential concentration of the cités in the banlieues contrasts with the area of La Defense, a banlieue west of Paris, which in 2008 provided 150,000 jobs but housed only 20,000 residents (Price 2008). The project of La Defense was launched in 1958 with the goal of making Paris the financial capital of Europe and attracting multinational corporations. The plan succeeded in attracting transnational and French financial firms, but it failed to reproduce the busy and around-the-clock mixed-use public areas to be found in downtown Paris.

GHETTO DISCOURSE AND THE CASE
AGAINST (SINGLE) COMMUNITY STUDIES

Can a relevant distinction be made between voluntary and involuntary processes of spatial isolation and segregation? Right-wing politicians such as Le Pen and Sarkozy as well as pundits and many academics denounce the ghettoization of France and claim that poverty concentration and "neighborhood effects" have an impact on the integration of the youth living in the banlieues and especially in the cités or projects. Academics and politicians go there sporadically to point fingers—Fadela Amara, for instance, recently led a tour of the banlieues before presenting her anticipated but uneventful "Plan Banlieue"— but as demonstrated in the previous section through a review of the historical record, my claim is that the causation arrow goes the other way around: People live in ghettos because of initial discrimination and purposeful segregation by nonmigrants (Gans 2008) and because of compounded social network effects as information spreads about the availability of housing (Mahler 1995; Menjívar 2000), not because they refuse to "integrate."

Segregation in the Parisian metropolitan area may be due as much to the rich, who through the decades have gone to great lengths to make sure that they themselves are concentrated—for example, in the Parisian west—and spatially separated from immigrants and, even more, from the working-class French (Pinçon and Pinçon-Charlot 2004; Pinçon and Pinçon-Charlot 2007). In light of this possibility, the way to study the integration of immigrants and their descendants is not by looking closely at life in any one banlieue as a de facto segregated community but by looking at the larger unit of which it is a part: France.

Despite a long history of spatial boundary-making, the lived space and experiences of the *franciliens* (Parisians and the *banlieusards* who inhabit the Île-de-France, or Parisian metropolitan area) go beyond obsolete political and administrative boundaries. The banlieues are an integral part of Paris because much of the city's business, work, and daily life are conducted there, behind the scenes—without the backstage of the banlieue, the Parisian stage up front could not hold up. Thus, we cannot talk about the Parisian banlieue without talking about Paris, just as we cannot talk fully about Paris without taking its banlieue into account, and the same holds for other major francophone cities. That is why, against the common assumptions, I set out not just to study a French banlieue but also to study immigrants across the ecological system of the Parisian urban region, including Paris itself. My many visits to Paris and different banlieues have provided me with some opportunities to observe how united or divided the inhabitants of these areas are, and how they work as a social and urban system.

ETHNOGRAPHY OF THE CHAMPS-ÉLYSÉES

"The most beautiful street in the world!" gush many tourist-guides (Taylor 2005). The legendary Champs-Élysées arguably has some of the best marketing in the world, and with one of the world's most expensive rents for a shopping strip (Pinçon and Pinçon-Charlot 2009). Everyone knows about the Champs-Élysées. To foreigners the Champs-Élysées physically represents Paris, along with the Eiffel Tower, Notre Dame, and the Louvre. The thoroughfare goes from the Place de la Concorde to the Arc de Triomphe. Tourists, expats, and visitors have to pay homage to this street at least once; for the same reason, any self-respecting French Parisian avoids going to the Champs-Élysées (or at least denies it). Parisians shopping for luxury goods go to L'Avenue Montaigne, which is a few blocks south and much more expensive and exclusive stores (Pinçon and Pinçon-Charlot 2009). Although the Champs-Élysées does not equal Paris for most native Parisians, because of how trite and commercialized it has become, for most visitors and immigrants alike it does. A visitor with a few days to spend in Paris will stroll through the Place de la Concorde to the Arc de Triomphe and be amazed by its grandiosity. Interestingly, as Gordon Price rightly remarks, this public space is not very long, but given the contrast between its design-empty areas and the monumental constructions, as well as the area of La Defense further down, it makes Paris appear much bigger than it is: "Paris is an illusion!" (Price 2008, 13). Nevertheless, beautiful illusions are what attract not only tourists and romantics but also second-generation immigrants—or, as they would prefer to be called, first-generation French. Their parents rarely spent leisure time in the Champs-Élysées. They may have been too self-conscious, feeling out of place amid such luxury and modernity. But their children are legally French, and they want to belong. So, on the weekends and in the evenings, they get on the RER and Metro, undergo a routine security check for drugs (mostly for males) when they transfer trains at the Châtelet–Les Halles central hub Metro station (Goris, Jobard, and Lévy 2009), then get off at the Franklin D. Roosevelt stop and join their friends strolling the Champs-Élysées. This expedition into the center of the city shows the desire of the youth to integrate and connect with Parisian society, or at least their fantasized image of it. On the cover to one of his albums, French banlieue rapper Rohff appears as a giant dressed in a tracksuit using the Arc de Triomphe as a chair (see Figure 7.2). This may represent the desire of French citizens of color to be visible and respected in the French mainstream just as they are. Unfortunately, when groups of young men from North and sub-Saharan Africa walk in groups of ten, even if they are dressed up, freshly showered, and perfumed, the police, many locals, and tourists may take them to be potential criminals. Policemen always keep them under surveillance.

Furthermore, some first-generation immigrant Berbers may walk on Les Champs in traditional clothing as if in Marrakesh. Young women wearing veils are also seen as threatening: They pose a symbolic threat to the cult of *secularité* that the French elites hold dear (Bowen 2007). Topping it off are the Roma people ("Gypsies") and women from eastern Europe who may not necessarily be Muslim but who wear headscarves and kneel in silence, sometimes even in a form that could be misunderstood as praying to Mecca, and who often have signs in English about their suffering children that they use to ask money of tourists. So there may be some confusion for foreign and provincial French tourists, since what was supposedly a characteristically "French" area is full of "oriental" characters along with American, Latino, and European middle-class tourists. Casual outside observers like Christopher Caldwell (2009) may take mental pictures and draw a conclusion about Islam overtaking Europe.[3]

If members of the French elite are there, they are to be found indoors, protected by high prices, in restaurants like the Fouquet's and Maxim's, along with the middle class, who may be buying a couple of last-minute gifts in Sephora or Fnac. McDonald's or Starbucks outlets along the Champs-Élysées are de facto reserved for foreigners, immigrants, and the occasional French student on a budget looking for a place to study. Those who occupy this physical space may have shared a subway ride and a couple of feet of pavement, but their mental maps and worldviews place them in completely different symbolic universes. Thus, "symbolic segregation" exists at the symbolic heart of Paris. In this way, the Champs-Élysées is a microcosm of what happens in more extreme ways across the entire Parisian metropolitan area.

The immigrant youth and children of African parents may go to the Champs to show off their success, parking their brand-new luxury cars and motorcycles in the street while risking a ticket and police harassment for blocking traffic. Younger kids may come on Rollerblades or rented *velibs* (short for *vélo libre*, a public bicycle rental program). But it is forbidden (*interdit*) to ride bicycles on the sidewalks of the Champs, and by doing so they also risk police harassment. Thus, what in the eyes of these young people starts as an evening of fun in Paris, an opportunity to mix in, can easily turn into a game of cat-and-mouse with the police.

This game may turn out badly when these youths are denied entry into the exclusive nightclubs on the street, which happens even when, ironically, the doormen are of the same social origin (Dendoune 2007). I observed a verbal dispute between youth of immigrant origin and young tourists outside one such nightclub. In the blink of an eye, there were over twenty policemen on the scene, some wearing anti-riot gear. Minutes later, one "Arab" kid was brought to the ground and clubbed by a number of policemen. In a few seconds, blood started marking the pavement of the Champs-Élysées.[4]

Months later, immigrant youth and foreigners gathered in the cafés and restaurants around the Champs-Élysées to watch the end of the Eurocup soccer tournament. Spain won for the first time; many immigrants, especially Moroccans, wore their Spanish jerseys and celebrated as if their home team had won. Thousands of members of the Spanish community in Paris celebrated with big parties in the streets and were joined by Maghrebins and Latin Americans. That night I was out watching the game with a large group of Spanish and Latin American expats who worked for a transnational pharmaceutical company. As celebrations started, the police started to disperse the Spanish fans with a tone implying that a victory for Spain was not an event worth celebrating in Paris. This is the Paris known to the local, marginalized youth but unknown to many tourists.

PARIS ETHNOSURVEYS

While living in Paris as a visiting scholar at two prestigious universities (Sorbonne and Sciences Po) during the academic year 2007–2008, I conducted ethnosurveys of a purposive sample across the Parisian metropolitan area. Sixty-five respondents were Muslim, and to keep a control group I also conducted ethnosurveys among twenty-four immigrants who were not Muslim, but space limitations prevent me from discussing this other group in this chapter. From the Muslim North African sample, 75 percent were men and 25 percent women, with an average age of thirty-two and a median age of twenty-nine. (For more on the methodology and the other cases studied, see Castañeda [2010] and Castañeda [forthcoming].)

FIGURE 7.2. Map of Interviewees Residence in the Parisian Metropolitan Region

The people I interviewed included first-generation immigrants as well as citizens whose origins were in North Africa (Arabic or Berber) and most of whom were nominally Muslim. The results from my sample show medium levels of residential segregation (Wacquant 2008) but strikingly high levels of social distance from "mainstream" French society, especially among first- and second-generation males. A structural reason for their social invisibility and lack of sense of belonging was discrimination and the accompanying unemployment. Unemployment rates for people of Maghrebi origin, especially those who are phenotypically "Arab," are much higher than for other groups (Silberman, Alba, and Fournier 2007).

While in Paris, I spent a great deal of time with unemployed men who rarely left their apartments and who suffered high levels of depression, persecution anxiety, and reactive xenophobia. Although they spoke French, had residency papers, and had lived in France for a while, including some with high levels of education and skill, they were systematically denied long-term work contracts. For a few of these migrants the stress of their situation had made them vulnerable to mental illness (Grinberg and Grinberg 1989).

Many of my informants identified themselves as North African or Maghrebi, even when they had French papers. In one marginal but still representative case, a French citizen whose grandparents came from Algeria, but who had been to Algeria himself only once and whose Arab was very limited, told me that he identified as Algerian. When I asked him why this was so, he said, "Look at me, look at my camel face. Do I look French? When I am in the street, in the subway, people do not see a Frenchman but an Arab." He thus reported a racial description of the French as white. He was verbalizing a social boundary that existed inside and outside of the banlieue.

This individual no longer had formal employment by the time I met and interviewed him. He had worked in a factory until a job accident forced him to stop. He spent his evenings and nights hanging out in a bar next to some projects in a banlieue south of Paris.

When I asked him if he had friends different from himself, he first answered yes, saying that he had clients from all over Paris, but when I pushed him about the people he trusted and felt close to, he said that he preferred to stay by himself or with other Algerians. "About blacks," he said. "I respect them, but I prefer to keep my distance. I do not want any problems with them." He distrusted "whites" too, and he was worried about people he did not know who

would suddenly appear, walk around, and ask questions. If they were not sociologists like myself (I was accompanied that day by an Algerian man), they
must be policemen trying to pass as civilians. He said that his father, who
worked in construction and as a janitor in a public school, "worked so hard
when he came to France, and he sacrificed so much for me and my siblings."
To supplement his disability income and help his parents, this interviewee
sold drugs and engaged in other self-described "illegal activities."

My informants often responded that they preferred to stick to themselves
or be with close family members. They mistrusted strangers, including fellow
countrymen and coreligionists, who, they said, often used the socially expected
solidarity and charity between fellow Muslims to take advantage of them, so
they preferred not to make many friends. Their relative poverty and social
marginality prevented them from being able to satisfy those expectations of
generosity, aid, and reciprocity.[5] This common lack of resources combined
with the wide mistrust that French society has of ethnic communal life (Fassin
and Fassin 2006; Lacorne 2003) results in high fragmentation among young
immigrant Arab men in the Parisian metropolitan area, even among themselves.[6] In other words, many men are in the same structural position, undergoing the same feelings of exclusion, disempowerment, and desperation, but
they rarely talk about this with each other, even if they share the same spaces,
such as a coffee shop or a neighborhood.

As a whole, immigrant Arabs from North Africa lack representative organizations, legitimate spokespeople, and political representation within political parties and the government. The second and subsequent generations
are not much better off, but being more cognizant of their rights as French
citizens, they are more prone to anger and disorganized, semispontaneous
demonstrations, as in the riots of 2005 in reaction to the death of two young
French citizens of Maghrebi origin running away from the police (Schneider
2008). These riots were carried out mainly by disenfranchised second-generation French citizens. Indeed, most of my interviewees spoke against them,
since their neighborhoods and their possessions, cars, and businesses were
the targets of these riots, second only to buildings that represent the state:
schools, libraries, police stations, bus stops.

The riots showed a generalized discontent among youth in the banlieues,
who live in objectively positive conditions with all the basic services and are

not oversegregated in terms of ethnicity, race, or religion, but who are continuously harassed by police and thwarted by their limited prospects in the labor market.

SPATIAL SEGREGATION IN FRANCE

When people talk about immigration in France, the idea of the banlieue is often conjured. Scholars sometimes assume that studying immigration in France entails studying the banlieue. Many French citizens themselves like to compartmentalize the "problem of immigration" and relegate it to the banlieues. Since the riots of 2005, one often hears about "the crises of the banlieues." Deeper sociological analyses have demonstrated that the issue is more complex, that immigrant integration is not the exclusive problem of the banlieues, and that there is a lot of diversity within and among banlieues (Wacquant 2008, 2010b).

A common question in academic comparisons between urban exclusion in the United States and France is whether the concept of the ghetto can be applied in France. To answer this question, one should also listen to the voices of second-generation Africans who were born and raised in Paris or on its outskirts. In his memoir about growing up in France as a child of Algerian immigrants, journalist Nadir Dendoune (2007, 19) writes: "The projects are a glass cage. The frontiers are there; so inscribed in the asphalt, that you have the sense of an implicit message saying, 'you are not part of society.' Civilization stops here."[7] This quote reveals two components of his stigmatization: geography and a lack of the proper cultural capital (Bourdieu 1991).

In reaction to what many young French minorities see as blatant discrimination, some banlieues have produced a self-declared ghetto subculture with their own French rap deeply inspired by the popular countercultures originally created in the American black ghettos and then spread across social classes and countries by media and marketing (Daniels 2007; Pattillo 1999), yet expressing local concerns in *français*. Another related example of a growing counterculture is the *verlan*, or banlieue youth slang. For example, French people often use the word *Arab* in a derogatory sense and as a cultural putdown. They often fail to distinguish between citizens and noncitizens and between generations. Thus, in an example of reactionary identity (Portes and

Rumbaut 2001), second- and third-generation French Arabs in the 1980s called themselves *beurs*, a play on words based on inverting the syllables of *Arab*. This term is not that different from how the term *Chicano* is used in the United States. Words like *beur* mark, and reproduce, the symbolic boundaries between French of European descent and those of Arab descent, as well as the boundaries between Arabs, blacks, and Jews.

Thus it is that one can speak of *French ghettos*—in the original sense of the term combining ethnic stigma, spatial segregation, entrapment, and counterculture (see Chapter one, this volume). Loïc Wacquant (2008) argues that banlieues are structurally very different from black ghettos, partly because they lack their own subculture and informal cultural and political institutions. Yet the growing French rap industry, the banlieue-inspired movies and theater, and the particular language and clothing style of banlieue youth—as well as the growth of associations, movements like *Conseil Representatif des Associations Noirs* (CRAN) and the *Indigènes de la République,* and the car-burnings across banlieues—may contradict Wacquant's hypothesis. Furthermore, the relative lack of ethnic organizations and coordinated actions may have more to do with French republican laws and values than with a lack of discrimination against visible minorities (Castañeda, forthcoming). Whether or not the banlieues are ghettos, they surely are places of stigma.

Although there are differences in objective material conditions (Wacquant 2008) and the French government would argue against the existence of "real ghettos" in France, many French banlieue inhabitants embrace the term with its implication of segregation and lack of social integration and equality. This is most clearly seen in music: As in the United States, a certain ghetto pride and culture have emerged from the banlieue. This counterculture reflects a long history of differentiation between Paris proper and the "wild" and "uncivilized" rural areas outside of it that have always been economically and symbolically subordinated to it.

The daily experiences of the banlieusards sharply contrast with the stereotypes held by many Parisians. For example, the movie *La Haine* (1995), directed by Mathieu Kassovitz, presents a powerful metaphor, but also an exaggerated representation of life in the banlieues. It draws much-needed attention to the issue of police violence and broad discrimination, but it perpetuates the negative stereotype of the banlieue and underplays intergroup conflict. *L'Esquive*

(2003), directed by Adbellatif Kechiche, does a much better job of portraying the everyday reality of young banlieusards, whose lives are very different from those of their schoolteachers who try to teach them proper French and from those of the policemen who scare them away from public areas.

Although many of the young people living in the cités are unemployed and, because of many social and economic restraints, do not leave their neighborhoods every day, their main frame of reference is still the larger hegemonic concept of "French culture." They watch the same television channels as other French; they watch many American television series and movies and listen to music in English; and like their compatriots, they filter these non-French cultural experiences through a French lens, sometimes even by means of dubbing that tries to adapt the original content to the local context. In this way a very interesting and fecund French rap cultural scene has emerged, one obviously inspired by African American rappers but still distinctly French. As just one example, the banlieue rappers Rohff and Kéry James equate their situation in France to being unloved in their 2004 song *Mal aimé* (*Unloved*).[8] The lyrics, seemingly about a love affair gone sour, refer to the feeling of minorities in the banlieue: loneliness, mistrust, and a sense of betrayal of what school taught them France was all about.

In open-ended questions about how they would define their neighborhoods and neighbors, many interviewees used the word "ghetto" to describe the places they live in. Others used the equivalent of "immigrant enclave." As can be seen in Figure 7.3, many others pointed to the French or mixed character of the neighborhood. These findings point to both the diversity of Parisian and banlieue neighborhoods and the adoption of the term *ghetto* by some franciliens.

COMPARING FRANCE AND THE UNITED STATES

Wacquant coined the term *hyperghetto* to designate the ghetto after the neoliberal policymaking ideology and the accompanying de-industrialization of urban areas. He notes that compared with immigrant labor and cheap labor overseas, black labor has become unnecessary and relatively expensive. I would add that the rise of neoliberal thinking and its accompanying crisis has normalized certain levels of unemployment that are suffered mainly by North

FIGURE 7.3. How Interviewees Classify Their Neighborhoods

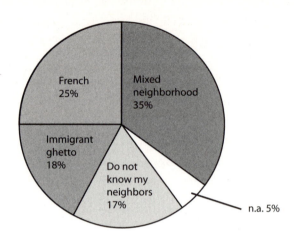

Africans in France and, in the United States, first by blacks, then by Latinos, and then by whites living in the Midwest and rural areas (Carr and Kefalas 2009). The economic crisis that started in 2007 further spread unemployment across different demographics, but these groups were especially affected.

Like socially mobile migrants in the barrios and banlieues, portions of the black middle classes have left the ghettos, and thus the poor and unemployed are overrepresented in these areas. Many have to rely on an underground off-the-books economy and drug-selling to make ends meet (Venkatesh 2006). The criminalization of these activities lands many people of color from poor neighborhoods in prison (Wacquant 2010a).

Unfortunately, fears, discourses, and remedies regarding ghettos have spread throughout the world. For example, French policymakers, terrified about the possible development of ghettos and immigrant enclaves, are quick to deny any similarity with places in French territory and quick to attack any ethnic mobilizations in the banlieues. France has reacted by emulating the policies of police departments in New York and Los Angeles. While they reject any structural similarity, they have acquired some of the same techniques to produce "law and order" through punitive action, as espoused by Sarkozy, first as a minister of the interior and later as president of France.

NORTH AMERICAN GHETTOS AND BARRIOS

In the United States, the practice of social segregation was historically related to the different social and legal rights of slaves and free individuals. Although there were both black and white slaves and indentured servants in the colonial years, after some decades a racial system had come into use as a way to categorize and reproduce inequality (Massey 2007; Tilly 1998). Despite the legality of slavery, in the South black and white quarters were often next to each other, showing the close interdependence and interaction between masters and slaves. As black Americans became emancipated from their slave condition, many migrated north in search of supposedly greater tolerance and work opportunities in industrializing urban areas. There they became concentrated in certain neighborhoods, not only because of social networks and affinity but also because of employer and public policies and the racism and exclusionary practices of northern whites who moved out of neighborhoods after a certain racial tipping point was reached (Massey and Denton 1993). Yet the ghettos of Harlem and the Bronx (areas where this author lived for years) are far more heterogeneous than the stereotype of them, as well as more heterogeneous than Chicago, a city that, with a large African American population, has often and wrongly stood as a representative city for all of the United States (Small 2008).

Puerto Rican migrants followed a pattern similar to blacks moving north. As citizens from a U.S. territory, they moved into the continental U.S. landmass in search of opportunities and often ended up in areas that bordered African American enclaves in cities like Chicago and New York.

The work of anthropologist Oscar Lewis (1966) on the poor *vecindades* of *El Barrio de Tepito* in Mexico City, extended later to working-class neighborhoods in Puerto Rico and New York, was important in documenting the daily lives of poor people in these neighborhoods. A misreading of what he termed "the culture of poverty" would contribute to a stereotype that blames the victim and questions the morality of the so-called "undeserving poor" (Katz 1996). The realities on which Lewis's "culture of poverty" was based only got worse following the large migration into central cities of blacks and Puerto Ricans and the loss of many jobs in urban areas due to offshoring and deindustrialization (Marwell 2007; Wilson 1997). The state provided subsides to white ethnics to build and inhabit suburban areas, but blacks and Latinos were left behind (Gans 1982; Katznelson 2005).

This resulted in ethnic and class concentrations in certain neighborhoods. Poverty became spatially concentrated in these neighborhoods, at first because of the struggles associated with first-generation migration and subsequent poverty, and then because of unemployment and lack of opportunities for social mobility. To this argument must be added the rise of neoliberal moral discourses and the socio-scientific literature and simplistic policies that criminalized and pathologized poverty and created symbolic boundaries between whites and blacks and between poor and successful blacks and Latinos (Lamont 2000). In the imaginations of the American public and policymakers, "the ghetto" became black and "el barrio" brown. In this view of these areas as dangerous, immoral, and undeserving places in need of drastic policy (and police) intervention, the effects of poverty were misunderstood as causes and justified what Wacquant (2008) calls a "malign neglect" that allowed these areas to fall into increasing disrepair. This response was answered by an increase in the language and action of "law and order," following the "broken windows" theories, and by an increase in the penalization of poverty, drug-dealing, and incarceration, mainly of minorities living in these neighborhoods.

New York has witnessed the arrival of many groups from Latin America and the Caribbean (Aranda 2008; Bourgois 2003; Dávila 2004; Fuentes 2007; Grasmuck and Pessar 1991; Jones-Correa 1998; Kasinitz, Mollenkopf, and Waters 2004; Kasinitz, Mollenkopf, Waters, and Holdaway 2008; Loveman and Muniz 2007; Marwell 2007). If we take a close look at the realities of Latino neighborhoods in the New York City metropolitan area, a more complex image of changing composition emerges—one that is relevant here because in many ways Latinos in New York City offer a closer comparison than African Americans to North Africans in Paris (Castañeda 2010; Wacquant 2008).

A neighborhood just north of the Upper East Side of Manhattan is known as Spanish Harlem, or El Barrio. This area has served as an arrival gate for multiple waves of significant numbers of immigrants (Bourgois 2003; Orsi 2002); the last such waves were Puerto Ricans in the 1940s and Mexicans in the last couple of decades (Smith 2006). Lexington and East 116th Streets may feel to a visitor like a small version of Chicago's Little Mexico, yet research by the author has shown that, despite the storefronts, the neighborhood is very heterogeneous and most Mexicans in New York have never lived in this area

(Castañeda 2010). Furthermore, although this place has offered a home and a sense of community to many ethnic groups, many socially mobile immigrants and their children have left the stigmatized East Harlem, even if they now remember it with nostalgia (Dávila 2004).

CONCLUSION

This chapter has shown that boundary-making processes and historical legacies are at play in the formation of banlieues, barrios, immigrant enclaves, and Jewish and African American ghettos. Most of these spatial boundaries disappear or dissipate over time. Place of residency matters because of its differential effect on life chances, yet scholarship and folk understandings tend to overstate spatial concentration—to a point of assuming that all members of a certain social group live in a particular neighborhood.

The built environment matters as well, because it displays social characteristics and embodies a particular cultural presence. The existence of a number of storefronts with foreign goods and symbols immediately marks a place as other, exotic, communal, ghettoized, premodern, or gentrified. The conclusions drawn from a superficial reading of streets and buildings are then applied to the inhabitants of that area. When this happens, spatial, symbolic, and social boundaries coincide and become anchored in place and reinforced in the public imagination.

Black Harlem, Spanish Harlem, and the Parisian banlieues are empirically more diverse in terms of social class and ethnicity than their popular representations would have us believe. Yet the mental maps, framing, and stereotypes—the *idées reçus* ("received ideas")—create social boundaries that pair stigmatized people with stigmatized places. In this sense, the ideal-type coming from the historical European Jewish ghetto is useful in describing contemporary inequalities, social boundaries, and limited mobility of labor across space. Unauthorized immigrants sell their labor, but they cannot move freely through space because of fear of deportation (Núñez and Heyman 2007); they may be as entrapped as Jews were in Venice. Banlieusards can legally move throughout France, yet some of them rarely do so.

For educated members of the second and later generations, the boundaries of "el barrio" and the banlieue may have been more permeable than for the inhabitants of the black ghetto after the great migration from the American

South, since, as with white ethnics, many middle-class Latinos and banlieue-dwellers who experienced social mobility moved out. Sometimes success means leaving the neighborhood where one was born. Yet in the American case, race trumped class mobility and blacks had a harder time moving far from the poor ghettos—Chicago's Hyde Park being the most common example (Pattillo 1999). Today, even as some blacks are better able to choose their neighborhood based only on income, urban ghettos, just like the barrio and some parts of the ban-lieue, continue to house the poorest members of a stigmatized group (poor in terms of economic, social, political, and symbolic capital). The residents of these areas suffer the scorn not only of the majority group but also of the mem-bers of their own group who have moved out, succeeded, assimilated, or "passed." They remain behind what is not only a symbolic boundary but a social boundary, since an undesirable address on a résumé often results in fewer em-ployment opportunities—and thus fewer opportunities for social mobility.

As social scientists, we reify and "ghettoize" neighborhoods if we study them in isolation. World systems theory reminds us that we cannot fully un-derstand the periphery without including its unequal relations with the core. The same applies to wealthy urban centers and stigmatized neighborhoods—they have to be understood relationally. The chic neighborhoods are so only in relation to stigmatized neighborhoods.

To conclude, despite somewhat enviable objective conditions for some of the "poor" population in the banlieue and in some public housing in New York City, relative deprivation is what matters the most for those who live in these areas. In the media and the popular mind, the banlieues now play an equivalent role to the U.S. ghetto. As in the United States, the French state has a very direct role in producing and limiting ethnic concentrations in public space—for ex-ample, through its colonial policies and the subsequent building of housing for migrant workers in particular areas of *metropole*. Long-lasting ethnic seg-regation is not voluntary but imposed from the outside. Objectively, material conditions in the American barrio and immigrant enclave tend to be very low (historical slums and present-day *colonias* in the Southwest being the most extreme examples), yet confinement to these areas tends to decrease over time, and with access to citizenship and work. Immigrant enclaves, including China-towns, tend to experience ethnic succession when their inhabitants are replaced by people from another country or region. In contrast, present-day banlieues have become problematic because, in the popular imagination, they house and contain immigrants and minorities. If the concept of the ghetto cannot be applied to France, it is only because France lacks the historical equivalent of an African American population. This does not mean, however, that contemporary social boundaries against stigmatized groups are not also inscribed in space, in minds, and in speech in the word *banlieue*. The term *ghetto* is a concept that classically represents stigmatization and spatial and social boundaries. But because of its long history and changing composition, it can sometimes create more polemic misunderstandings rather than provide clarity. Thus this chapter proposes the term *places of stigma* to designate the different spaces that result from the same categorical processes of creation and reproduction of social inequality (stigmatization, constraint, confinement, marginalization, underemployment) that become inscribed in flesh and stone.

Notes

1. Kevin Beck, Lesley Buck, and Natalie Schwarz helped in the preparation of the text. The NYLON research network, Gil Eyal, Emmanuelle Saada, Robert Smith, Craig Calhoun, Richard Sennett, Ray Hutchison, and Bruce Haynes provided feedback on earlier versions of this chapter. All errors remain my own.

2. To a large extent, this class segregation continues to this day and indeed has only been exacerbated by de-industrialization and the declining support for the welfare state.

3. These observations may be further biased when one observes the women covered head to toe who accompany oil millionaires from Saudi Arabia and the Emirates during the day but who stay home at night while the men, dressed in conservative religious clothing, go to bars, discos, and strip clubs and enjoy what they could not be seen consuming at home. This reality has little to do with the conclusions that a casual observer could draw from strolling down les Champs a couple of times.

4. I started filming this incident of unprovoked and unwarranted police brutality with my digital camera, until another bystander informed me that it was illegal to do so; I stopped filming before the police realized what I was doing and seized the camera. The footage of part of this incident is available on YouTube at: http://www.youtube.com/watch?v=mh8VXMPmkAU. Minutes later, ambulances arrived to take away the bleeding person, and everyone dispersed. I went next door to get a crêpe, and when I came back, the scene on the street was back to normal, as if nothing had happened, but I could still see the young man's blood on the pavement.

5. This is similar to the situation that Cecilia Menjívar (2000) documents among Salvadorans in San Francisco.

6. The second immigrant generation and subsequent generations tend to be more integrated into diverse social networks and to have more capital, depending on the social segment to which they have assimilated.

7. *"La cité est une cage de verre. Les frontières sont la. Tellement inscrites sur le bitume que tu as l'impression que c'est un message implicite: vous ne faites pas partie de la société. Ici, s'arrête la civilisation."*

8. Rohff was born on the African island of Comoros, a country that is 98 percent Muslim. Kéry James was born in the West Indies to Haitian parents. Both were former members of the influential Mafia K'1 Fry, a group of rappers from the banlieue of Val-de-Marne.

References

Aranda, Elizabeth M. 2008. "Class Backgrounds, Modes of Incorporation, and Puerto Ricans' Pathways into the Transnational Professional Workforce." *American Behavioral Scientist* 52: 426–456.

Blokland, Talja V. 2008. "From the Outside Looking In: A European Perspective on the Ghetto." *City & Community* 7, no. 4: 372–377.

Boltanski, Luc, and Laurent Thévenot. 2006. *On Justification: Economies of Worth*. Princeton, N.J.: Princeton University Press.

Blokland, Talja. 2008. "From the Outside Looking In: A 'European' Perspective on the Ghetto." *City & Community* 7, no. 4 (December): 372–377.

Bourdieu, Pierre. 1991. *Language and Symbolic Power*. Cambridge, Mass.: Harvard University Press.

———. 1998. *Practical Reason: On the Theory of Action*. Stanford, Calif.: Stanford University Press.

Bourgois, Philippe I. 2003. *In Search of Respect: Selling Crack in El Barrio*. Cambridge: Cambridge University Press.

Bowen, John R. 2007. *Why the French Don't Like Headscarves: Islam, the State, and Public Space*. Princeton, N.J.: Princeton University Press.

Caldwell, Christopher. 2009. *Reflections on the Revolution in Europe: Immigration, Islam, and the West*. New York: Doubleday.

Carr, Patrick J., and Maria Kefalas. 2009. *Hollowing Out the Middle: The Rural Brain Drain and What It Means for America*. Boston: Beacon Press.

Castañeda, Ernesto. 2009a. "Banlieue." In *Encyclopedia of Urban Studies*, edited by Ray Hutchison. Thousand Oaks, Calif.: Sage Publications.

———. 2009b. "The Great Sleep-In: Demonstrating for Public Housing in Paris." *Progressive Planning* 178: 31–33.

———. 2010. "The Political Voice of Migrants in a Comparative Perspective." PhD diss., Columbia University, Department of Sociology.

———. Forthcoming. "Exclusion and Everyday Citizenship in New York, Paris, and Barcelona: Immigrant Organizations and the Right to Inhabit the City." In *Remaking Urban Citizenship: Organizations, Institutions, and the Right to the City*, vol. 10, *Comparative Urban and Community Research*, edited by Michael Peter Smith and Michael McQuarrie. New Brunswick, N.J.: Transaction Publishers.

Dangschat, Jens S. 2009. "Space Matters—Marginalization and Its Places." *International Journal of Urban and Regional Research* 33, no. 3: 835–840.

Daniels, Cora. 2007. *Ghettonation: A Journey into the Land of Bling and the Home of the Shameless*. New York: Doubleday.

Dávila, Arlene M. 2004. *Barrio Dreams: Puerto Ricans, Latinos, and the Neoliberal City*. Berkeley and Los Angeles: University of California Press.

Dendoune, Nadir. 2007. *Lettre ouvert à un fils d'immigre: Cher Sarko (Open letter to the son of an immigrant: Dear Sarko)*. Paris: Danger Public.

Doytcheva, Milena. 2007. *Une Discrimination positive à la française: Ethnicité et territoire dans les politiques de la ville (Positive discrimination the French way: Ethnicity and territory in urban policy)*. Paris: La Découverte.

Fassin, Didier, and Eric Fassin. 2006. "De la question sociale à la question raciale? Représenter la société française" ("From the social question to the racial question: Representing the French society"). In *Cahiers Libres*. Paris: La Découverte.

Fourcaut, Annie, Emmanuel Bellanger, and Mathieu Flonneau. 2007. *Paris/Banlieues: Conflits et solidarités (Paris/Banlieues: Conflicts and solidarities)*. Paris: Creaphis.

Frank, Thomas. 2004. *What's the Matter with Kansas? How Conservatives Won the Heart of America*. New York: Metropolitan Books.

Fry, Richard. 2009. "The Rapid Growth and Changing Complexion of the Suburban Public Schools." Washington, D.C.: Pew Hispanic Center.

Fuentes, Norma. 2007. "The Immigrant Experiences of Dominican and Mexican Women in the 1990s: Crossing Boundaries or Temporary Work Spaces?" In *Crossing Borders and Constructing Boundaries: Immigration, Race, and Ethnicity*, edited by Caroline B. Brettell. New York: Lexington Books Press.

Gans, Herbert J. 1982. *The Levittowners: Ways of Life and Politics in a New Suburban Community*. New York: Columbia University Press.

———. 2008. "Involuntary Segregation and the Ghetto: Disconnecting Process and Place." *City & Community* 7, no. 4: 353–357.

Goris, Indira, Fabien Jobard, and René Lévy. 2009. "Profiling Minorities: A Study of Stop-and-Search Practices in Paris." New York: Open Society Institute.

Grasmuck, Sherri, and Patricia R. Pessar. 1991. *Between Two Islands: Dominican International Migration*. Berkeley and Los Angeles: University of California Press.

Gravier, Jean-François. 1947. *Paris et le désert français: Décentralisation, équipement, population (Paris and the French desert: Decentralization, equipment, and population)*. Paris: Le Portulan.

Grinberg, León, and Rebeca Grinberg. 1989. *Psychoanalytic Perspectives on Migration and Exile*. New Haven, Conn.: Yale University Press.

Harvey, David. 2008. "The Right to the City." *New Left Review* 53 (September-October).

Haynes, Bruce, and Ray Hutchison. 2008. "The Ghetto: Origins, History, Discourse." *City & Community* 7, no. 4 (December): 347–398.

Jones-Correa, Michael. 1998. *Between Two Nations: The Political Predicament of Latinos in New York City*. Ithaca, N.Y.: Cornell University Press.

Kasinitz, Philip, John H. Mollenkopf, and Mary C. Waters. 2004. *Becoming New Yorkers: Ethnographies of the New Second Generation*. New York: Russell Sage Foundation.

Kasinitz, Philip, John H. Mollenkopf, Mary C. Waters, and Jennifer Holdaway. 2008. *Inheriting the City: The Children of Immigrants Come of Age*. New York and Cambridge, Mass.: Russell Sage Foundation and Harvard University Press.

Katz, Michael B. 1996. *In the Shadow of the Poorhouse: A Social History of Welfare in America.* New York: Basic Books.

Katznelson, Ira. 2005. *When Affirmative Action Was White: An Untold History of Racial Inequality in Twentieth-Century America.* New York: W. W. Norton.

Lacorne, Denis. 2003. *La Crise de l'identité américaine: Du melting-pot au multiculturalisme* (*The crisis of American identity: From the melting pot to multiculturalism*). Paris: Gallimard.

Lamont, Michèle. 2000. *The Dignity of Working Men: Morality and the Boundaries of Race, Class, and Immigration.* New York and Cambridge, Mass.: Russell Sage Foundation and Harvard University Press.

Lamont, Michèle, and Virag Molnar. 2002. "The Study of Boundaries in the Social Sciences." *Annual Review of Sociology* 28 (August): 167–195.

Le Corbusier. 1927. *Towards a New Architecture.* New York: Payson & Clarke. (Originally published in French in 1923.)

———. 1967. *The Radiant City: Elements of a Doctrine of Urbanism to Be Used as the Basis of Our Machine-Age Civilization.* London: Faber. (Originally published in French in 1935.)

Lewis, Oscar. 1966. *La Vida: A Puerto Rican Family in the Culture of Poverty—San Juan and New York.* New York: Random House.

Loveman, Mara, and Jeronimo O. Muniz. 2007. "How Puerto Rico Became White: Boundary Dynamics and Intercensus Racial Reclassification." *American Sociological Review* 72, no. 6: 915–939.

Mahler, Sarah J. 1995. *American Dreaming: Immigrant Life on the Margins.* Princeton, N.J.: Princeton University Press.

Marwell, Nicole P. 2007. *Bargaining for Brooklyn: Community Organizations in the Entrepreneurial City.* Chicago: University of Chicago Press.

Massey, Douglas S. 2007. *Categorically Unequal: The American Stratification System.* New York: Russell Sage Foundation.

Massey, Douglas S., and Nancy A. Denton. 1993. *American Apartheid: Segregation and the Making of the Underclass.* Cambridge, Mass.: Harvard University Press.

Menjívar, Cecilia. 2000. *Fragmented Ties: Salvadoran Immigrant Networks in America.* Berkeley and Los Angeles: University of California Press.

Núñez, Guillermina Gina, and Josiah M. Heyman. 2007. "Entrapment Processes and Immigrant Communities in a Time of Heightened Border Vigilance." *Human Organization* 66, no. 4: 354–365.

Orsi, Robert Anthony. 2002. *The Madonna of 115th Street: Faith and Community in Italian Harlem, 1880–1950.* New Haven, Conn.: Yale University Press.

Pattillo, Mary E. 1999. *Black Picket Fences: Privilege and Peril Among the Black Middle Class.* Chicago: University of Chicago Press.

Pinçon, Michel, and Monique Pinçon-Charlot. 2004. *Sociologie de Paris* (*The Sociology of Paris*). Paris: Découverte.

———. 2007. *Les Ghettos du Gotha: Comment la bourgeoisie défend ses espaces* (*Ghettos of the Gotha: How the bourgeoisie defends its spaces*). Paris: Seuil.

———. 2009. *Paris: Quinze promenades sociologiques* (*Paris: Fifteen sociological walking tours*). Paris: Payot.

Portes, Alejandro, and Rubén G. Rumbaut. 2001. *Legacies: The Story of the Immigrant Second Generation.* Berkeley and Los Angeles: University of California Press.

Price, Gordon. 2008. "Périphérique." *Price Tags* 102 (April 7, 2008. Available at: http://www.price tags.ca/pricetags/pricetags102.pdf.

Roy, Beth. 1994. *Some Trouble with Cows: Making Sense of Social Conflict.* Berkeley and Los Angeles: University of California Press.

Sassen, Saskia. 2001. *The Global City: New York, London, Tokyo.* Princeton, N.J.: Princeton University Press.

Schneider, Cathy Lisa. 2008. "Police Power and Race Riots in Paris." *Politics and Society* 36, no. 1: 133–159.

Sennett, Richard. 1994. *Flesh and Stones: The Body and the City in Western Civilization.* New York: W. W. Norton.

———. 2008. "The Public Realm." Available at: http://www.richardsennett.com/site/SENN/Templates/General2.aspx?pageid=16.

Silberman, Roxane, Richard Alba, and Irène Fournier. 2007. "Segmented Assimilation in France? Discrimination in the Labor Market Against the Second Generation." *Ethnic and Racial Studies* 30, no. 1: 1–27.

Simmel, Georg. 1964. *Conflict and the Web of Group Affiliations.* New York: Free Press.

———. 1971. "The Metropolis and Mental Life." In *Georg Simmel on Individuality and Social Forms,* edited by Donald N. Levine. Chicago: University of Chicago Press.

Small, Mario Luis. 2008. "Four Reasons to Abandon the Idea of 'the Ghetto.'" *City & Community* 7, no. 4: 389–398.

Smith, Robert C. 2006. *Mexican New York: Transnational Lives of New Immigrants.* Berkeley and Los Angeles: University of California Press.

Stovall, Tyler Edward. 1990. *The Rise of the Paris Red Belt.* Berkeley and Los Angeles: University of California Press.

Taylor, Sally Adamson. 2005. *Culture Shock! France: A Survival Guide to Customs and Etiquette.* Tarrytown, N.Y.: Marshall Cavendish/Graphic Arts Center Publishing Co.

Thorne, Barrie. 1993. *Gender Play: Girls and Boys in School.* New Brunswick, N.J.: Rutgers University Press.

Tilly, Charles. 1998. *Durable Inequality.* Berkeley and Los Angeles: University of California Press.

———. 2004. "Social Boundary Mechanisms." *Philosophy of the Social Sciences* 34, no. 2: 211–236.

———. 2005. *Identities, Boundaries, and Social Ties.* Boulder, Colo.: Paradigm Publishers.

———. 2008. *Credit and Blame.* Princeton, N.J.: Princeton University Press.

Tilly, Charles, and Harold C. Brown. 1967. "On Uprooting, Kinship, and the Auspices of Migration." *International Journal of Comparative Sociology* 8 (September): 139–164.

Venkatesh, Sudhir Alladi. 2001. "Chicago's Pragmatic Planners: American Sociology and the Myth of Community." *Social Science History* 25, no. 2: 275–317.

———. 2002. *American Project: The Rise and Fall of a Modern Ghetto.* Cambridge, Mass.: Harvard University Press.

———. 2006. *Off the Books: The Underground Economy of the Urban Poor.* Cambridge, Mass.: Harvard University Press.

Wacquant, Loïc J. D. 2008. *Urban Outcasts: A Comparative Sociology of Advanced Marginality.* Cambridge: Polity Press.

———. 2010a. "Class, Race, and Hyperincarceration in Revanchist America." *Daedalus* 139, no. 3: 74–90.

————. 2010b. "Designing Urban Seclusion in the Twenty-First Century." *Perspecta: The Yale Architectural Journal* 43: 165–178.

Wilson, Kenneth L., and Alejandro Portes. 1980. "Immigrant Enclaves: An Analysis of the Labor Market Experiences of Cubans in Miami." *American Journal of Sociology* 86 (September): 295–319.

Wilson, William Julius. 1997. *When Work Disappears: The World of the New Urban Poor*. New York: Vintage Books.

Wimmer, Andreas. 2008. "The Making and Unmaking of Ethnic Boundaries." *American Journal of Sociology* 13, no. 4 (January): 970–1022.

Zelizer, Viviana A., and Charles Tilly. 2006. "Relations and Categories." In *The Psychology of Learning and Motivation*, vol. 47, *Categories in Use*, edited by Arthur Markman and Brian H. Ross. San Diego: Elsevier.

CHAPTER 8

✦ ✦ ✦

On the Absence of Ghettos in Latin American Cities
Alan Gilbert

The first ghetto was in Venice, and the term has evolved from the Venetian island where Jewish people were required to live. Later the term began to be used to describe any quarter of a city in which members of a minority group were forced to live.[1] Most ghettos have always contained racial or ethnic minorities, although in recent times the word has been applied to other kinds of outsider communities, such as those of hippies. Throughout its life, the term has always been used pejoratively; the people who live in ghettos are not like "us."

If the ghetto is defined as a spatially confined area containing a racial or ethnic minority, then there are very few ghettos in Latin American cities.[2] And if we adopt Loïc Wacquant's (2004, 2) more sophisticated requirement that the "four constituent elements of the ghetto" are "stigma, constraint, spatial confinement, and institutional encasement"—then there are rather few anywhere. Perhaps that is why, to my recollection, over forty years I have never heard the term *gueto* used by a Latin American.[3] Admittedly, my Spanish dictionary contains the word, along with its synonym, *judería* (ghetto or area of Jewish people), but that does not mean that it is in common usage. Of course, the fact that it is not used is neither a sign that Latin American cities are equal or homogenous nor that its people lack prejudices against minorities of most

191

kinds. What it signifies is that the structure of Latin American cities is very different from that of U.S. cities. Of course, Latin Americans may have ignored the term *ghetto* because they preferred to invent their own terms of abuse. Over time their preferred terms, like *marginados* and *favelados,* have often changed in meaning and the frequency with which they are used. The terms have also varied from country to country and even between cities within the same country.

This chapter explains why the term *ghetto* is rarely appropriate in a Latin American context. It also seeks to explain temporal shifts in the "topographic lexicon" for designating "those stigmatized neighborhoods situated at the very bottom of the hierarchical system of places that compose the metropolis" (Wacquant 2007, 1).

WHY THE WORD *GHETTO* IS
INAPPROPRIATE IN LATIN AMERICA

Latin American cities are very different from those of the United States and Europe.

First, the ethnic structure of Latin America is distinctive. Insofar as the word *ghetto* was originally applied to Jewish areas, few cities in Latin America have ghettos because there are so few Jewish people living there. Among a total population of some 457 million, at the very most 1 million are Jewish, and the great majority of them live in two countries, Argentina and Brazil (Farache 2002; Levinson, n.d.). While Jewish people constitute a distinct ethnic and religious minority, and in places an economically powerful one, their numbers are so small and their presence sufficiently benign that, at least over the last thirty years, they have rarely constituted any kind of threat. This was not always the case, particularly during the 1930s and 1940s when several dictatorial regimes held a distinctly favorable view of Nazi Germany. But in recent years, major violence has been directed against Jews only once, in the bombing of a Jewish community center in Buenos Aires in 1994, and that incident seemed to have been organized from the Middle East (BBC 2006). In any event, the Jewish population in the region "is aging and decreasing in size as a result of out-migration, a high intermarriage rate, and a rejection of Jewish values by some in the younger generations" (Levinson, n.d.).

Second, the term *ghetto* is rarely appropriate to describe concentrations of black people in Latin America. Again, this is sometimes because they are almost entirely absent—as, for example, in most cities of the Andes or in the south of the region (Figure 8.1). Elsewhere, as in many cities in Brazil and the Caribbean, black and mixed-race people are found in large numbers, but the term is inappropriate to describe their communities because they represent a majority of the local population.[4] Even in those Latin American cities that contain a variety of racial groups, the term is inappropriate because black people rarely live in isolation. In Brazil, even if the majority of black people live in the poorest areas, they live side by side with other racial groups (Bonilla 1961; Roberts and Wilson 2009, 149). As Janice Perlman (2004a, 128) puts it: "Rio's favelas have always been racially mixed. At the time of my original 1968 study the random sample showed 21 percent of *favelados* were black, 30 percent mulatto and 49 percent white; and these percentages are almost identical in

FIGURE 8.1. Black Population of Latin America

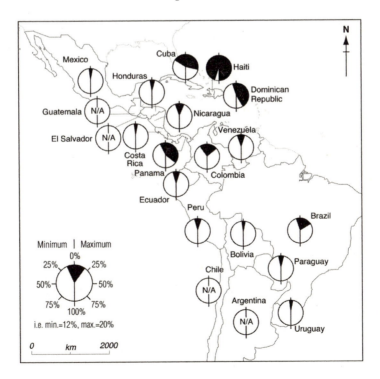

the current study." While the urban rich in Brazil live in almost exclusively white areas, poor settlements are multicolored.

Third, Wacquant (2004) argues that a key element in the construction of a ghetto is that residentially segregated ethnic groups must create a kind of subculture that both consolidates their feelings of separateness and differentiates them from those outside. This is what Afro-Americans have done in the United States. They have responded to various kinds of discrimination by absorbing and re-creating "an oppositional culture—that is, a set of behaviors, attitudes, and expectations that fundamentally conflict with those of the broader society" (Wilson 2010a). With trivial exceptions, this has never happened in Latin America because the poor do not try to cut themselves off from the rest of society. Indeed, the opposite is almost always the case. They have always wanted to be like their richer compatriots, however improbable that dream might be.

As such, I agree with Peter Marcuse and Ronald van Kempen (2000, 256–257) when they claim that the "excluded ghetto" is "primarily a phenomenon of the United States . . . [and] the pattern of 'racial' exclusion and segregation . . . is not at this time replicated elsewhere on any comparable scale." Latin American "slums" are unlike the contemporary black ghetto in the United States, the Jewish ghetto of the past, or the ghettos of the Burakumin in feudal Japan, all of which were highly segregated, ethnically distinct, stigmatized, and culturally homogenous (Wacquant 2008).[5] Nor are Latin American cities like those in many African and Asian countries where colonial regimes insisted that different ethnic groups live in separate areas (Abu-Lughod 1980; Betts et al. 1985; Grillo 2000; King 1976). And needless to say, they are wholly different from the cities of South Africa (Gilbert and Crankshaw 1999; Maylam 2001).

Fourth, unlike many cities in the United States, and increasingly many in other parts of the developed world, Latin America has not attracted many migrants from abroad.[6] Since 1914, it has been a region of massive emigration. As such, few contemporary Latin American cities are in any sense comparable to the increasingly multiethnic, multilingual societies to be found in London, New York, and Los Angeles. The only Latin American cities with large immigrant populations are those in relatively affluent countries with poor neighbors next door. Buenos Aires has large numbers of Bolivian and Paraguayan immigrants, many Colombians live in Caracas and other Venezuelan cities, and numerous

Bolivians and Peruvians are found in Santiago. But, while distinct ethnic differences between the natives and the immigrants are sometimes apparent, as in the case of Bolivian migration to Buenos Aires and Santiago, most of the immigrants speak the same language as the locals and merge relatively easily into the new environment.[7] This form of international migration is more akin to the movement of Irish people to the United States in the nineteenth century than to the later flows of Germans, Italians, and Hispanics.

More important in generating ethnically diverse cities in Latin America has been the movement of poor people from the countryside. In Mexico, Central America, and the northern Andes, many of the new arrivals did not speak Spanish as their first language. They were ethnically and linguistically different from most city-dwellers, even if they belonged to the same nation (Figure 8.2).

Fifth, even though income inequality in every Latin American country bar Cuba is greater than it is in virtually any other nation in the world bar South Africa, residential segregation is sometimes less extreme than in many

FIGURE 8.2. Indigenous Population of Latin America

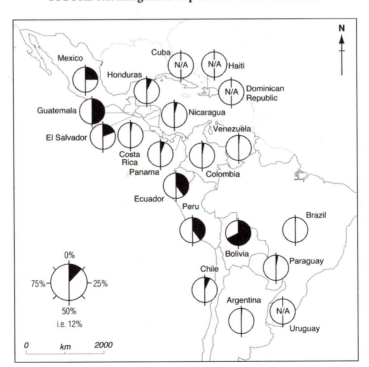

U.S. cities (de Ferranti et al. 2004). As Bryan Roberts and Robert Wilson (2009, 211) observe: "The Latin American cities [in this study] show levels of socio-economic segregation, as measured by the dissimilarity index, that are similar to or less than U.S. cities." Latin American neighborhoods tend to be more heterogeneous than those in the United States. And while there are no rich people in Latin America's poor neighborhoods, neither is everyone poor. "In Mexico, for example, . . . just 26 percent of residents of 'marginal' urban neighborhoods are below the poverty line, and only about 77 percent of eligible households live in such neighborhoods" (Fay, Cohan, and McEvoy 2005, 246). Many Latin American settlements are also mixed in term of tenure; the consolidated self-help settlements of Bogotá and Quito, for example, contain a mixture of both owners and tenants. In addition, many rich communities in Latin America have very poor neighbors. This is particularly true in cities with varied topography; many rich areas in Rio de Janeiro and Caracas, for example, have contiguous *favelas* or *barrios*. Nor are poor urban settlements in Latin America all the same.[8] In some the inhabitants feel safe while in neighboring areas the inhabitants feel threatened by drug gangs, criminals, or even the police. Some settlements have strong political affiliations with one party or political ideology, others with another. Some neighborhoods are united in a common cause, such as the need for land invaders to defend their flimsy settlement against removal, while other, much older settlements are much more diversified and highly consolidated and serviced and contain a mixture of owners and tenants with little in common.

Sixth, unlike the urban ghetto in the United States, and perhaps even some deprived areas of British and French cities, some people manage to escape poor Latin American neighborhoods. Insofar as there are many tenants in the consolidated self-help settlements, and tenants move frequently, there is constant flux. Although I would argue that many homeowners do get stuck in their homes because it is so difficult to sell their house, younger, tenant households tend to move about (Gilbert 1999). In Rio, Perlman (2004b, 192) observes, "we have robust evidence that the poor (even the black poor) are not consigned to 'bounded territories of urban relegation' [Wacquant 1997, 344]."

Finally, what is probably the critical difference between cities in the United States and Latin America is that in the latter the poor do not constitute a relatively small proportion of the population. Indeed, as Table 8.1 shows, the

TABLE 8.1. Poverty in Latin America by Country and Region, 2004–2007

		Percent of Population Below the Poverty Line			
Country	Year	Total Country	Metropolitan Areas	Other Urban	Rural Areas
Bolivia	2007	54.0	40.6	44.9	75.8
Chile	2006	13.7	10.4	16.0	12.3
Colombia	2005	46.8	33.8	48.6	50.5
Costa Rica	2007	18.6	16.2	23.9	19.6
El Salvador	2004	47.5	33.2	48.6	56.8
Honduras	2007	68.9	47.8	64.0	78.8
Nicaragua	2005	61.9	48.7	58.1	71.5
Paraguay	2007	60.5	53.1	58.3	68.0
Uruguay	2007	n.a.	18.9	17.4	12.6

Note: Complete data unavailable for Argentina, Brazil, Ecuador, Guatemala, Mexico, Panama, Peru, Dominican Republic, and Venezuela.
Source: United Nations Economic Commission for Latin America, 2008, Table 4.

poor in some Latin American countries constitute a majority of the urban population.[9] Related to this issue is the matter of "informal" housing. "Self-help" construction is rare in North American cities, but in many Latin American cities most people live in settlements that began informally and only gradually obtained proper services. If today "the term *ghetto* in the United States no longer refers to ethnic communities or even concentrations of urban minority residents" and "has, at least for some, become a pejorative expression that connotes déclassé or low class status," the term is inappropriate in Latin America because there are simply too many "low-class" people. To me, the word *ghetto* should always be reserved to describe a minority, and Latin America just has too many poor people to fit into ghettos! Louis Wirth's (1938) Chicago ghetto was an area where "the poorest and most backward" first-generation immigrants voluntarily settled and, over time, became assimilated to the mores of the larger society.[10] In Latin America, if the word *immigrant* is changed to *migrant*, then vast areas of most cities fit that definition. But surely it does not make sense to use the term *ghetto* to describe the situation of millions of people.

To summarize, the poor constitute a substantial proportion of the population in most Latin American cities and sometimes a majority. Those cities are also less racially segregated than their North American and South African counterparts, and the neighborhoods of poor "minorities" are not as isolated or as homogenous as U.S. ghettos. Pockets of extreme poverty generally merge into the general sprawl of self-help suburbia. Insofar as ghettos exist in Latin America, the term is best reserved for the neighborhoods of the rich: *barrios* that are racially distinctive, protected by private security guards, and in many ways closed off culturally from their neighbors outside. The affluent "gated communities" of some Latin American cities are arguably ghettos of extreme privilege, but surely a different term should be used to describe them.

THE CONSTANT URGE TO DEVELOP STEREOTYPES AND MODELS TO EXPLAIN POVERTY

People generally—and academics are clearly no exception—love to divide society into groups. For a whole series of differing reasons, we all simplify reality by devising stereotypical pictures of the people around us. Polar opposites are common elements in our descriptions—black and white, left and right—and our nation, our city, our team, our social class, and our children are not the same as, and are usually much better than, everyone else's.

Of course, we constantly modify our models as society changes and as our social understanding of society either improves or deteriorates. Newspaper headlines frequently create new targets for discrimination and prejudice, although sometimes they identify groups that need help. In Britain the bêtes noires were once West Indian immigrants, then East African Asians, then Pakistanis and Bangladeshis, and more recently Somalis and Poles. Today some powerful people have joined them: the bankers and most politicians!

The term *ghetto* seems to have gone through a similar transmogrification (Wacquant 2004; Wilson 2010b). Cora Daniels (2007) argues that *ghetto* has morphed from a noun denoting "overcrowded communities of filth, starvation, violence, and despair" to an adjective to describe an "impoverished" mind-set that embraces low expectations. Similarly, the term has been applied in the United States to describe other communities: William Partridge's *The Hippie*

Ghetto (1985), Kim England's "Suburban Pink Collar Ghettos" (1993), Charles and Grusky's *Occupational Ghettos* (2004), and Jessie O'Neill's *The Golden Ghetto: The Psychology of Affluence* (1997).

In this sense, Latin America is no different from anywhere else insofar as local descriptions of the poor, the migrant, or the slum-dweller have changed over time. Of course, Latin Americans nearly always use different words because most speak Portuguese or Spanish. But when they need to distinguish between good and evil, safe and dangerous, them and us, they tend to conjure up new terms, or reinterpret old ones, to describe new social phenomena and processes that regenerate age-old fears.

THE LATIN AMERICAN POOR

Over the last sixty years, Latin America has been transformed from a rural to an urban region. In 1950 two-fifths of the population lived in towns and cities; today it is 80 percent. And because the total population has increased greatly over that period, the number of city-dwellers has risen dramatically, from 67 million people in 1950 to 456 million in 2010 (UNDESA 2009a).

This urban revolution was first fueled by millions of people migrating from the countryside. Most of these urban arrivals were poor, and many were drawn from communities very different from those already living in the cities. Sometimes the migrants came from aboriginal societies where Aymara, Maya, Quechua, or some other indigenous language was spoken. Sometimes the migrants' first language was the same as that of the urban natives but they were racially distinctive, as with the movement of black people into the cities of Venezuela and southern Brazil.

These people were different from the urban elites, and alarmingly, they were arriving in large numbers. The urban population grew annually at over 4 percent during the 1950s and 1960s, with more dynamic cities expanding at an even faster rate (Table 8.2). In the absence of sufficient work in manufacturing and commerce, increasing numbers of itinerant traders, workers recycling waste materials, prostitutes, and criminals populated the streets. There was too little cheap accommodation to provide shelter for these people, so they proceeded to house themselves. Many obtained land by joining an organized invasion, and everywhere they proceeded to build their own dwellings.

TABLE 8.2. National and Urban Population Growth Rates in Latin America, 1950–2005

Year	Annual Urban Growth (Percent)	Annual National Growth (Percent)
1950–1955	4.4	2.7
1960–1965	4.4	2.8
1970–1975	3.8	2.4
1980–1985	3.0	2.1
1990–1995	2.4	1.7
2000–2005	1.9	1.3

Source: United Nations Department of Economic and Social Affairs, 2009b.

With the arrival of the bus, and hence a means of getting to work, self-help settlement in Latin America took off (Gilbert 1998).

"Respectable" society was naturally fearful and created new words to describe the emerging migrant neighborhoods. The deteriorating central areas, increasingly packed with recently arrived tenants, did not require new terms because existing words were still appropriate: *cortiços, vecindades, inquilinatos,* and *corralones.* But the phenomenon of the shantytown demanded a new terminology. Sometimes the new terms were purely descriptive, like the *tomas* (invasions) of Chile, or they were broadly sympathetic, such as the *villas miserias* (miserable towns) of Argentina. Sometimes they were more metaphorical, evocative forerunners of magical realism, as in the parachute settlements (*colonias paracaidistas*) of Mexico and the mushrooms (*callampas*) of Chile—imaginative ways of describing how self-help settlements seemed to appear overnight.[11]

But whether the terms were poetic or prosaic, every city invented new words and phrases to distinguish between the formal, planned city and what was perceived to be the unplanned, illegal, and unhygienic city. Venezuelans distinguished between the formal *urbanización* and the informal *rancho* or *barrio.* Peruvians spoke of the new *barriadas* and later, more euphemistically, of the *pueblos jóvenes* (young towns). In Chile, political rivalries led to distinctions being made between normal *poblaciones* and the socialist/Marxist *campamentos.* Colombians distinguished between places where the poor had invaded land (the *invasion*) and the illegal settlements where they had bought their plots (the *urbanización pirata*). A similar distinction was made in Brazil between *favelas* and *loteamentos*.

Without exception, these places were viewed negatively. Not only were they poor, but they were unsanitary, insecure, and, seemingly, politically dangerous. Bonilla (1961, 75) describes how, "as a group, the *favela* population is on the wrong side of every standard index of social disorganization, whether it be illiteracy, malnutrition, disease, job instability, irregular sexual unions, alcoholism, criminal violence, or almost any other on the familiar list." As more and more shantytowns, informal workers, and peasants appeared in the cities, academics began to invent new concepts to describe what Latin America was experiencing. Terms were needed to describe how modernization was failing to replicate the kind of urbanization that the First World was supposed to have experienced. The ghastly memories of the poverty and slums of nineteenth-century Manchester and New York were conveniently erased as journalists and academics compared Latin America's terrible reality with contemporary conditions in First World cities. Latin America's cities were suffering from some kind of chronic disease, including "over-urbanization," "parasitic growth," "tertiarization," "ruralization," "marginalization," "informalization," "subcultures of poverty," and many other symptoms of malaise (Gilbert 1998; Hoselitz 1957; Lewis 1959, 1966a, 1966b; Peattie 1974, 1975, 1987; Sovani 1964). Urbanization in Latin America was preceding industrialization—the reverse of what was supposed to have happened in northwest Europe and North America.

Ruralization, for example, described how urbanization in Latin America was failing to modernize the region (Leeds and Leeds 1970). Rather than being converted into true town-dwellers, the peasants migrating from the countryside were failing to adapt. Their vast numbers were actually ruralizing the cities. Whole books emerged with titles like *Peasants in Cities* (Mangin 1970) and *Cities of Peasants* (Roberts 1978).[12] *Over-urbanization* described something similar: The new urban world was not creating the prosperity found in the developed world (Sovani 1964).

Meanwhile, Oscar Lewis (1959, 1966a, 1966b) was transferring his studies of the inner city in New York to Puerto Rico and Mexico and developing the concept of the "culture of poverty." He studied the tenants living in the center of Mexico City, noting their deep poverty and their social position at the bottom of a class-stratified capitalist society. To adapt to their poverty and to cope with the implausibility of any kind of upward mobility, they had developed cultural defense mechanisms that they passed on to their children. This "culture" guaranteed that they would remain in poverty by reducing their faith in education, good family values, or the need to save money. These people, he believed, were "not psychologically geared to take full advantage of changing conditions or increased opportunities that may develop in their life time" (Lewis 1966b, xlv).

The growth of shantytowns was thought to be a sign that new arenas were developing where the "culture of poverty" would develop, and negative stereotypes of these areas emerged. As Licia Valladares (2007, 21) points out: "The term *favelado*, which initially meant inhabitant of a *favela*, linking a person to a *place*, ... ended up designating—pejoratively—anyone occupying a social *position* marked by poverty and illegality. The *favelado* now belonged not only to the world of the people, but also to that of social problems."

Gradually a new concept emerged—"marginality." The term was first invented by modernization theorists to describe Latin America's transitional stage: Even though the cities were modernizing, the hordes of new arrivals were temporarily marginalized by the lack of proper jobs and homes. However, modernization would eventually incorporate this marginal population into the city in the same way that Arthur Lewis's (1954) dualist theory argued that poor countries would industrialize because they had a comparative advantage over rich nations in the form of their cheaper labor forces.

However, another much more pessimistic interpretation of marginality was emerging from the left. Authors like Aníbal Quijano (1974) and José Nun (1969) argued that, given the nature of peripheral capitalism, the marginal population could never be absorbed. Manufacturing industry was too stunted and capital-intensive ever to employ the vast mass of urban migrants. The migrants did not even constitute an industrial reserve army, as described by Marx (1872), because there were simply too many to be any real use to capitalist enterprise. In dependent countries like Peru, modernization would never become an inclusive process and there would always be a surplus population.

A further development of the theory was perhaps even more disturbing. Brazilian sociologists working in CEBRAP (Centro Brasileiro de Análise e

Planejamento) argued that persistent marginality was a feature not only of slow-growing economies, like that of Peru (Oliveira 1972), but also of development in that most dynamic of Latin American cities, São Paulo. In the latter, informality was growing not because people were surplus to the needs of the formal sector but for the opposite reason: The very survival of capitalism in a dependent capitalist economy required a "marginal" population. In a reworking of Marx, they argued that informal work and self-help housing expanded because capital needed the sweated labor of the poor. Street traders cut the cost of distributing manufactured goods; outsourcing work to the favelas reduced production costs; recycled materials were cheaper than processing raw products; and informal housing allowed companies to pay lower wages. São Paulo showed that, rather than disappearing as economic growth accelerated, informal activity would continue to flourish. Modernization theory was fundamentally wrong: The example of Victorian cities in Britain being transformed into relatively healthy urban places by the 1960s and 1970s was not applicable to Latin America.

Meanwhile, a very different interpretation of urban life was emerging from academic research. Although they never discounted the unfairness of life in Latin America's cities, researchers were discovering a more positive side to migration. Those who came to the cities were positively selected: It was the most innovative and entrepreneurial who arrived in the city, while the old, the unskilled, and the conservative tended to stay at home. The people who came to the cities had skills that were helpful there: They could lay bricks, they drove buses, and they knew how to cook. They adjusted to the city by changing their dress, their customs, and even their language (Andrews and Phillips 1970; Doughty 1970; Lomnitz 1977; Roberts 1973). These people coped by helping one another and even their families back home through community associations. Moving to the city was a real challenge, but one to which most Latin Americans seemed to respond very well. There was little sign of "marginality," "irrationality," or a "culture of poverty" (Cornelius 1975; Mangin 1970; Perlman 1976; Portes 1972; Roberts 1973). Most migrants in the region stayed in the cities and in this respect were very different from the "circular" migrants typical of many parts of Africa, who tended to leave their families back home and planned to return there themselves. Latin American migrants came to the cities, bore children, and reared them in the new environment (Gilbert and

Gugler 1992). Gradually, migration ceased to be the principal cause of urban growth as more and more children were born in the cities.

The concept of "marginality" was soon demonized. Perlman (1976) argued that the term was both ambiguous and ideological. It was unclear who was included in the term. Did it mean that the "marginal" all lived in physically peripheral places? Or were they marginal because they did not adapt to the culture of the city? Or was it that they were politically apathetic, or that they did not contribute to the economy, or what? None of these stereotypes seemed to fit the poor in Rio de Janeiro, where

> favela residents were tightly integrated into society, albeit in an extremely perverse and asymmetrical manner. They worked in the least desirable jobs, under the worst conditions for the lowest pay; participated in the political life of their communities and city (to the extent permitted within the dictatorship) to little or no benefit; and contributed to the cultural and social life of the city without recognition. (Perlman 2004b, 189)

Meanwhile, studies of informal work showed how even the most apparently marginal activities, like rag-picking or collecting bottles, were directly linked to the formal economy (Birkbeck 1979; Bromley and Gerry 1979). This approach seemed to combine the perspectives of CEBRAP and the more positive demonstration of how poor migrants adjusted successfully to the city, although it was most certainly not modernization reincarnate because it forecast a less than rosy future. What it clearly demonstrated was that the poor formed an integral part of the economic and social life of the city.

A parallel argument was being developed with respect to housing. The shantytowns were not the "jerry-built, vertical islands of squalor" that housed "as many as a third of Rio's three million inhabitants" (Bonilla 1970, 73). Rather, as William Mangin (1967, 65) noted, writers about squatter settlements in Latin America "agree, sometimes to their own surprise, that it is difficult to describe squatter settlements as slums." Observers of the shantytowns discovered that self-help construction was an "architecture that worked" (Turner 1968a). These new sprawling settlements would, if properly supported by the state, develop into ordinary working-class suburbs. John Turner (1968b) even argued that self-help housing matched the needs of the urban poor much better than most government efforts to build social housing.

Life in the shantytowns had been reinterpreted: The new migrants were much like most other people. As Mangin (1970, 56) put it:

> The early stereotype held by most middle and upper class Peruvians of the *barriada* dweller as illiterate, non-productive, lawless, recent communistic Indian migrants is still held by many—but is giving way among young architects, politicians, academics, and anthropologists to an equally false picture. Perhaps as an antidote to the first, it paints them as happy, contented, literate, productive, adjusted, politically conservative—forever patriotic citizens. They are in fact about like the vast majority of Peruvians, moderately to desperately poor, cynical *and* trusting of politicians, bishops, outside agitators, and their own local leaders.

If reality in the shantytowns had been reinterpreted, remnants of Oscar Lewis's image of the inner city remained. Charles Stokes (1962, 190) differentiated between the "slums of hope" on the periphery and the rental "slums of despair" in the inner city. The most hopeful future for the latter was that the inhabitants would eventually move to the self-help suburbs of hope! Tenants would become owners (Turner 1968a, 1968b).

The general image of urbanization in Latin America slowly improved during the 1960s and 1970s. As more governments brought services to poor settlements, urban growth rates began to slow, and economic growth created more jobs, the doomsters' view of urban development was brought into question. Despite all of the problems, urbanization was working relatively well. Latin American migrants came to the city to better themselves, and a majority succeeded. They found some kind of employment and built homes. The shantytowns were not full of subversives. Few poor people had time for revolution— they were political conservatives working too hard to earn an income and to build their homes to bother with political activism. Community action programs launched after 1958 in an attempt to quicken the poor's integration into urban society and to prevent them from following the revolutionary Cuban path spread rapidly, and the U.S.-led Alliance for Progress was launched to accelerate economic growth, improve government policy, encourage land reform, and develop infrastructure.

Objective evidence certainly suggested that living in urban areas was helping to raise the quality of life, even that of the poor. Infrastructure provision was generally improving, and health and education facilities were expanding in most places. Infant mortality rates were falling fast and life expectancy increasing. Fertility rates were plummeting as educational opportunities increased, more women started to work, contraception became commonplace, and attitudes toward large families changed.[13] These shifts were most apparent in the cities, and the continued flow of people out of the countryside demonstrated that ordinary people recognized that life in the city was superior.[14] Where economic growth was occurring, genuine signs of development were visible. The quality of electricity, water, and education provision was gradually improving. And there were signs that modernization's argument that the informal sector would decline as societies became richer was correct. Table 8.3 shows that a smaller proportion of the workforce works in "informal-sector" jobs in cities in wealthier countries (for example, Argentina, Chile, and Mexico) than do those in poorer countries (for example, Bolivia, Ecuador, and Peru).

TABLE 8.3. "Formal" and "Informal" Employment in Selected Latin American Urban Areas, c. 2008

Country and Year	"Formal Sector"	"Informal Sector"
Argentina 2006*	63.7	36.3
Bolivia 2007	42.1	58.0
Brazil 2008	60.9	39.1
Chile 2006	71.9	28.2
Ecuador 2008	48.5	51.5
Mexico 2008	61.5	38.4
Paraguay 2008	49.8	50.2
Peru 2008	46.4	53.5
Venezuela 2008	53.6	46.3

* Buenos Aires

Note: "Formal" sector defined as employers, public-sector workers, professional and technical workers, and nonprofessional workers in establishments with more than five workers. "Informal sector" defined as nonprofessional workers in establishments with five or fewer employees, domestic servants, and nonprofessional own-account and unpaid family workers.

Source: United Nations Economic Commission for Latin America, 2009b, 255–257.

However, this more positive view of urbanization was not to survive very long. The onset of the Latin American debt crisis changed everyone's thinking. During the 1980s, most Latin American countries experienced negative per capita growth rates, and it was usually the cities that were hit hardest. Unemployment rose, and with it the number of informal workers. Urban poverty was increasing, both absolutely and relatively, and migrants began to stay at home (Table 8.4). The idea that the urban poor could improve their lives in a macro-environment of structural adjustment and neoliberalism now seemed implausible.

The debt crisis brought Latin America only one clear benefit. Before 1982, most countries were ruled by military dictatorships. They had come to power at various times after 1964, sometimes to confront the danger of guerrilla movements (Argentina and Uruguay), sometimes to overthrow a left-wing government (Chile), and sometimes to end a period of political chaos (Brazil and Peru). Everywhere the new military regimes had promised to bring order and progress. However, the lost decade of the 1980s showed that their promises had been empty, that their right-wing policies had failed, and that they had

TABLE 8.4. "Formal" and "Informal" Employment in Selected Latin American Urban Areas, c. 2008

| | Poor | | Indigent | |
Year	Millions of People	Percent of Total	Millions of People	Percent of Total
1970	41	25	NA	NA
1980	63	30	23	11
1990	122	41	45	15
1997	126	37	42	12
1999	134	37	43	12
2002	147	38	52	14
2006	127	31	35	9
2007	121	29	34	8
2008	118	28	36	8

Source: United Nations Economic Commission for Latin America, 2009b, 5–6.

too often abused basic human rights. Democracy now swept through the region, and by 1990 every military regime had gone.

The combination of military rule, economic crisis, and perceived economic interference from the International Monetary Fund (IMF) and the World Bank had spurred great academic interest in the political role of the poor. Developing their ideas from earlier ideas about the revolutionary potential of the poor, a series of left-of-center academics pointed to the wave of social movements and protest that was being unleashed throughout the region. The nature of community action and neighborhood activity had been transformed: The urban poor now wanted to change society rather than to integrate with it (Eckstein 1989; Escobar and Alvarez 1992; Foweraker 1995; Slater 1985). Different authors showed how the urban poor had contributed to the rise of democracy and were reacting against the evils of neoliberalism, structural adjustment, and privatization. The *caracazo* in Venezuela in 1989—when students and unions led protests against an IMF-type package and hundreds of people died (Gilbert 1998)—and more recent strikes and violence in Bolivia to fight privatization and large hikes in water prices (Assies 2003; Chávez 2005; Portes and Hoffman 2003) were seen as harbingers of the future. No longer would the poor be co-opted by patronage and clientelistic politics—they were now a force for real change.

Although many kinds of popular protest have broken out in Latin America in recent years, the experience is very patchy. Part of the variation lies in the fact that military rule had dismantled most of the organizations likely to support radical action. Growing unemployment and neoliberalism led to the decline of trade union membership in the few countries, such as Argentina and Brazil, where unions had once been powerful. But perhaps the most important deterrent to action was poverty and the lack of a sufficiently broad or deep social safety net: Desperate to supplement their incomes, people were generally too busy working to protest. As Mercedes González de la Rocha (2004, 192) puts it, the Mexican poor, "far from taking to the streets in protest, 'privatised' the economic crisis." They put their children and wives into the labor market and cut their budgets. The political consequence was that they protested little. As national economies recovered, the poor continued to work long hours, now motivated by the availability of cheaper consumer goods—urban radicalism was being undermined by consumerism (Paley 2001; Silva 2004).

In democratic Latin America the urban poor have generally "protested" in a more peaceful way by electing left-wing and/or populist leaders. Left-wing mayors have been victorious in numerous cities since 1990. In 2003 more than 200 million Latin Americans lived in municipalities governed by the left (Stolowicz 2004, 169). Many of the region's capital cities are now ruled by left-wing mayors, including Bogotá, Caracas, Lima, Mexico DF, and Montevideo. The votes of the urban poor have also contributed substantially to the election of national leaders of the ilk of Hugo Chávez, Lula, Fernando Correa, Fernando Lugo, Evo Morales, and the Kirchners.

One explanation of the shift toward the left in Latin America is that the "popular" classes have tired of neoliberal orthodoxy. As Cynthia Arnson and José Raúl Perales (2007, 6) argue:

The "rise of the left" would appear to owe much to core problems arising from the *quality* of democracy as experienced by the average citizen: the persistence of poverty and inequality; the growth of the informal sector (with the concomitant decline of labor unions); disenchantment with the institutions of democratic governance, especially political parties; the difficulty of establishing adequate mechanisms of participation, representation, and accountability; and dislocations related to the domestic efforts and foreign policy implications of globalization.

But not every country has moved to the left. Colombia has a right-wing government, the PAN has ruled Mexico since 2000, and in 2010 Chile voted for José Piñera. This reflects the fact that economic circumstances have often propelled Latin American electorates in very different directions. Some have accepted neoliberal policies wholeheartedly, while others have rejected them out of hand. Since 2000, some countries, notably Chile and Colombia, have done relatively well, while others, such as Argentina, Mexico, and Venezuela, have suffered wild fluctuations in their economic fortunes (UNECLA 2008, table 2.1.1.2).

In terms of poverty, Table 8.4 shows that since 1990 the incidence of urban poverty has generally fallen. However, it also shows that the numbers of poor people increased until the middle of the first decade of the millennium, when they began to fall again. Nevertheless, the urban poor were more numerous in 2007 than in 1990 as a result of a combination of continuing, albeit slowing, natural increase, cityward migration, and unconvincing economic growth rates. Within countries, of course, some cities have fared much better than others.

One result of this diverse experience is that academic discourse about the situation of the poor in Latin American cities is confused. There is doubt about the appropriate economic model that Latin America should follow. Those who have bought into the neoliberal belief that the only alternative is to compete more effectively in the world market cite Chile as an example of successful export expansion reducing poverty (Neilson et al. 2008). Others suggest that economic growth combined with a pro-poor government is the answer. Lula's Brazil is the exemplar here with its pro-poor policies like Bolsa Familia and its recent success in reducing income inequality (Hall 2006). Others reject neoliberalism out of hand and recommend a more left-wing approach. If no one actually recommends the Cuban economic model, Hugo Chávez's Bolivarian revolution is an example that has been followed with interest in Bolivia and Ecuador.

Meanwhile, some believe that the poor are worse off than they once were and that neoliberalism is at the root of the problem. González de la Rocha (2004, 193) denounces how, in Mexico, the "galloping consolidation of the neoliberal economic model has revealed new and alarming socioeconomic conditions for everyone and particularly for the poor" (my translation). The shortage of work now makes it impossible to put more household members into the labor force, increasing poverty inequality and social problems: "As local economic opportunities deteriorated," González de la Rocha (2004, 187) contends, "social problems proliferated. Drug addiction, violence, theft, and assault all increased with the austerity policies and peso devaluation of the 1990s." Susan Eckstein (2000, 185) argues that the Mexico City shantytown that she studied in the 1970s had become more a "slum of despair" than a "slum of hope." In Argentina, Javier Auyero (2000, 93) laments that, "as a consequence of the withering away of the wage-labor economy, the official indifference of the state, and the breakdown of the organizational fabric of these territories, shantytowns run the risk of becoming functionally severed from the larger society." According to this kind of interpretation, marginality is clearly back, even if the word is rarely used.

At the same time, there are some clear signs of improvement for the majority of urban dwellers. In many cities, life has arguably gotten better. Most of the poor now have access to light and piped water, and most homes have a television. Although the absolute numbers of urban people living in poverty may not have diminished, the great majority now live in better conditions than they once did. In Brazil, "the peripheries today have much better infrastructure and their residents have much greater access to consumption markets, the media and communication technologies, in spite of their poverty and of persistent unemployment rates" (Caldeira 2009, 851). And Perlman's (2004a, 124) comparison of life in the favelas of Rio in the 1960s and the 1990s shows that the *favelados'* "children and grandchildren—to varying degrees—have more education and higher incomes (if they are working) than they did. And many among this new generation have moved out of the original 'irregular' communities." Life is still extremely difficult and unfair, but most live longer, are better educated, and have access to basic services. And in some of the more dynamic economies, there are signs of urban mobility. In Chile, the evidence indicates that 54 percent of the poor in 1996 were not poor in 2001, while 48 percent of the poor in 2001 were not poor in 1996. Thus, the transient component of poverty amounts to 24 percent of the sample households that were poor in 1996 but not in 2001. The chronically poor consist of 10 percent of the population: households that were poor in both 1996 and 2001 (Neilson et al. 2008, 269).

Few are as positive about the poor as Hernando de Soto (1989, 2000), who clearly sees the problem very differently from most. To him, the urban poor are pioneers fighting against the damp hand of the mercantilist state. Give them property titles and reduce bureaucratic red tape and the pace of economic development will accelerate and the amount of poverty will fall. Those who are pushing micro-finance and property titling across the region would probably agree (Ferguson 2004; Fox 1995; IADB, n.d.), although fortunately there is now some opposition to those notions (Bateman 2010; Durand-Lasserve and Selod 2007; Gilbert 2002).

What is clear is that today virtually no academic in Latin America talks much about urban marginality.[15] As Caldeira (2009, 851) puts it: "The 'redundants' of Latin America became organizers of social movements in the 1980s and 1990s, articulators of NGOs from the 1990s on, and rappers, artists and writers in the 2000s, people who use notions of rights (rights to the city or human rights) to legitimate their public interventions and the reconstitution of their identities, despite poverty, violence, stigmatization and abuse." If the poor are voting and are clearly linked into the urban economy, they cannot be marginal. And in any case, governments everywhere in the region have changed their policies toward the poor. Slum upgrading programs are de rigueur; the Brazilians, Chileans, and Colombians have strong targeted support programs in place; participatory budgeting and decentralization are seen as ways to involve the poor actively in decision making; and in Venezuela community councils are intended to give people a direct voice in the decisions that affect their everyday lives.[16] Add to that the massive increase in NGO involvement in most urban areas and one can understand Roberts's (2004, 197) remark that "no one leaves the poor alone anymore."

The only way that "marginality" makes any sense in Latin American cities these days is in relation to crime. Perlman (2004a, 124) observes that today,

> even if *favelados* are no longer considered marginal, the *favelas*, as territories controlled by drug dealers, are seen as harboring "marginals," "the marginality" or "the movement" (i.e., drug dealers). As a result, the *favelados*, whose space has been occupied by drug traffickers (because it was unprotected and easier to hide in) are now associated with the dealers themselves. Inside the *favela* a distinction is made—we are "the workers," they are "the movement." But outside, a sense that the *favelas* are the source of the problem, rather than the home of its most obvious victims, has once again arisen.

At the same time, it is clear that most Latin American cities, like those in most of the world, have become more unequal (Gilbert 2007a). The well-educated have access to well-paid employment; those with little education have either no job or have work that provides a very low income. The poor are not excluded from the economy, as some branches of marginality theory once suggested, but are granted "a second-class citizenship in which disadvantage derives from the differentiation produced by the institutions of the state. In education, for example, all citizens receive a public education. The poor are not marginal to the educational system. However, the education that you get marks you for life, determining your occupational possibilities" (Roberts 2004, 196). In this sense, most cities across the world are very similar.

As inequality increases it accentuates social segregation. Latin American cities are highly segregated, and urban sprawl, speculative land-holding, ineffective urban planning, and limited taxation are not lessening that problem.

Every Latin American city has well-established rich areas and much more extensive areas allocated to the poor. The poor of Bogotá live mainly in the south and most of the rich live in an exclusive and environmentally more desirable area of the north (Amato 1970). In Santiago, most of the rich live in the northeast, while the settlements of the poor spread out across vast areas of the south and northwest. The high cost of land and housing—and, where necessary, of planning regulations and police controls—generally ensure that the poor live well away from the rich.

It is only in topographically variegated cities that the "normal" pattern of segregation is interrupted. In cities like Rio de Janeiro and Caracas, some informal settlements nestle against the neighborhoods of the rich. In Rio, one of the city's most exclusive *bairros*, São Conrado, occupies flat land next to the beach, while, across the road, one of the city's largest self-help areas, Rocinha, climbs up the hillside. The topography of Caracas has created similar aberrations: Although most of the rich live in the east of the city largely separated from the poor, the self-help settlement of Barrio Nuevo sits next to the Country Club.

More recently, a new form of spatial segregation has emerged with the growth of "fortified enclaves in rich neighbourhoods, which consist of walled condominiums, apartment buildings guarded by security towers, private policing, 'armed response,' and so on" (Sa 2007, 154). "Gated" communities house the very rich, and guards keep out everyone except employees and invited guests (Caldeira 2000; Enríquez Acosta 2007; Salcedo and Torres 2004; Souza e Silva 2007). Some of these communities are virtually autonomous, containing offices, supermarkets, and recreational facilities. In theory, their residents never need to leave them. These gated estates are safe from crime—fear of which is one of the key reasons why they are proliferating—and from the more unsavory aspects of urban life. In certain cities, these new gated communities occupy large areas. In Rio de Janeiro, the Barra de Tijuca is an exclusive area of shopping malls and gated communities that seems to contain no poor people at all. Marcuse and van Kempen (2000, 250) claim that walls and gates "prevent people from seeing, meeting and hearing each other; at the extremes, they insulate and they exclude." In Colombia, Gonzalo Sánchez (2001, 13) suggests that the growth of closed communities "can be considered a type of spatial apartheid, with impassable barriers for 'undesirables.'"

Of course, it is not only the rich who want to cut themselves off. Poor communities in Bogotá and Santiago sometimes build walls or erect fences around their settlements in an attempt to keep crime and violence at bay. And in cities such as Rio, the government has begun to construct walls around some favelas, either to prevent urban growth from destroying more of the Atlantic rain forest or to keep the criminals in (BBC 2007)! In this sense, Latin America has become like the rest of the world, where "walling and gating . . . [have] spread to virtually all sectors of society; today one finds public housing projects in the United States, middleclass suburbs, upper-middle class enclaves, retirement communities, with walls of various sorts around them, or with the equivalent measures designed to provide physical protection against social dangers" (Marcuse and van Kempen 2000, 254).

How real a threat gated communities represent in Latin America is debatable. Given that the cities have long been so clearly divided into rich and poor districts, it is difficult to believe that they could be much more residentially segregated than before. The old patio-style houses of the rich were always impenetrable except to the servants, and the high-rise apartments that proliferated as land prices rose and fear of crime increased have always been protected by guards at the main door. The children of well-off parents never attend ordinary schools and have long been transported to private institutions by fleets of buses. On the weekends the rich have swum, played tennis or golf, and eaten in private clubs. When sick, they have always gone to private clinics. Perhaps gated communities are even more effective in keeping out trespassers, but they do not keep out all of the poor, for the simple reason that many work inside the gates. For this reason, Rodrigo Salcedo and Alvaro Torres (2004) argue that the juxtaposition of gated communities and poor neighborhoods can be helpful to the poor because it creates new job opportunities for them close to their homes. It may also help improve the infrastructure and services of the area, and the inhabitants of the gated community, because they get to know the poor in their locality, may exclude them from their generally negative perceptions of poor people.

CONCLUSION

The obsession with the ghetto and with the underclass in the United States is a reaction both to fear and to a feeling of failure. The Great Society of the Johnson administration was meant to encourage upward mobility that would allow anyone who tried to succeed. If minority groups are failing to move out of poverty, it is an aberration that needs to be corrected, or at least explained. Continued use of terms like *the ghetto* is also a reaction to the fear generated by the violence, crime, and riots that are commonplace in such areas. Even if affluent whites can flee to distant low-tax suburbs to live in safety, protected by private security guards and the constitutionally justified ownership of a gun, many still feel threatened by the ever-present ghetto.

Their less affluent, although still well-heeled, neighbors in Latin America also feel threatened by poverty and the unfamiliar. Like their North American counterparts, they do not understand the poor and generally have a negative opinion of them. But there is a key difference: Since most people in North America are comparatively rich and so many people have a family history of parents or grandparents managing to make it out of the "slums," those who do not escape must blame themselves. If Asians and Latinos are following the earlier example of the Irish, Italians, Germans, and Poles in escaping poverty, why are so many African Americans not doing the same? The problem lies inside the ghetto rather than outside.

In Latin America, a lot of rich people share similar attitudes, but many others recognize that it is much harder to climb out of poverty in Latin America than in the north. Corruption, crime, poor schools and health facilities, and terrible levels of inequality make upward mobility difficult for the majority. Although there is little real social interaction between rich and poor in Latin American cities, at least the rich talk with their maids, gardeners, drivers, and security guards (Goldstein 2003). If in North America it makes a limited amount of sense to blame the ghetto minority for not getting on, in Latin America it defies any kind of logic to blame the majority for their continued poverty.

Of course, many continue to hope that Latin America will one day emulate the affluence of its northern neighbors. But in many countries there is strong suspicion about the efficacy of current macroeconomic policies. Perhaps this is why the left is making a comeback politically in Latin America. Although some may claim that this comeback amounts to populism more than real socialism, the fact that left-of-center governments currently rule in Argentina, Bolivia, Brazil, Ecuador, Paraguay, Uruguay, and Venezuela suggests that something has changed in Latin America. Behind that shift is a strong suspicion of neoliberalism and what it heralds for Latin America. Poverty will not be eliminated following the recipe laid down in Washington.

Even in countries that have more faith in the status quo—manifest in the fact that they elect governments to the right of center—all is not well. Colombians vote for the right because of their fear of violence and their desire for some degree of public order; inequality, corruption, and paramilitaries are acceptable when faced by greater dangers. Mexicans are likely to shift their allegiance back to the PRI given their disappointment with right-wing economic policies and in reaction to the rapidly rising rate of crime and violence. Chileans have just narrowly voted in a right-wing politician after twenty years of moderate left-wing governments that followed broadly neoliberal policies—a sign perhaps that progress has stalled.

This general confusion about the appropriate economic and social policy for Latin America complicates attitudes toward the urban poor. If economic growth is no longer guaranteed, then the urban poor's chances of improving their lives will decline. It is conceivable that this will motivate them to again pose a real or imagined threat to social stability. If the trend toward growing inequality in most countries, and particularly in the cities, is not addressed, then the danger of political protest may increase.

None of this is likely to encourage the use of the term *ghetto* in Latin America, because conditions there are just so different from those in North America. But new ways of thinking about the poor and their relationship to society and the economy at large will continue to be necessary. We are unlikely to return to any kind of belief in the "culture of poverty," "ruralization," or "over-urbanization," but no doubt some academic or—these days—journalist will produce an apocalyptic new interpretation of the situation of the poor. Who knows whether this will be the overly positive approach followed by those like Hernando de Soto or the excessively negative view of those like Mike Davis. Are the Latin American urban poor the equivalent of the pioneer settlers of the once-Wild West? Could life become impossible in the great slums "warehousing this century's surplus humanity . . . waiting to erupt" (Davis 2006, 201)?

What is not in doubt is that some new ideology or overgeneralized model will emerge to mislead us for the next few years. Of course we need models and theories to understand life. The trouble with most of the theories that have been generated over the years to explain life in Latin America is that they have rarely been terribly accurate. Latin American cities are so diverse and complicated that broad generalizations just do not fit. Unfortunately, in this world of tabloid journalism, and with the disease of information overload spreading rapidly, most authors are increasingly tempted by the banner headline. The ways in which disadvantaged locales are constructed and represented often act as euphemisms for problem people. The use of such euphemisms reminds us again of the ways in which U.S. liberals couch their embrace of conservative "blame the victim" discourses in a range of coy terms. But hidden not so far beneath the surface is a pathological view of working-class life. Call the poor anything dramatic enough and someone will pay attention. Maybe that is the cynical response of an aging academic who, despite many decades of careful research, doubts that our generalizations and models of the urban poor in Latin America have become much more accurate.

If ghettos do exist in Latin America, they are most certainly not like any in North America. The term might be appropriate in Latin America to the gated communities of the white, car-based, secure rich who are so well protected from the dangers beyond their walls. Alternatively, the term might describe the settlements controlled by drug gangs. But whether designating either as a ghetto actually helps in understanding them and their relationship with the rest of society is doubtful.[17] So perhaps the term should be junked along with most of the concepts that I have described in this chapter.

Notes

1. For a more detailed description of the origin of the term and the evolution of ghettos in Europe, see Wacquant (2004).

2. In this chapter, when I use the term *Latin American*, I am referring to those countries in the Americas where the majority speak Spanish or Portuguese.

3. Although Frank Bonilla (1961) does use the term.

4. Most black people in Colombia and Ecuador live in the coastal areas, and few live in the mountains. In Brazil the population of most cities in the northeast are predominantly black and mulatto, whereas those to the far south of the country have relatively small numbers of black people.

5. I use the term *slum* most reluctantly—see Gilbert (2007b).

6. In 1914 three-quarters of Argentines had been born in Europe. Uruguay and southern Brazil had also absorbed large numbers of immigrants.

7. Although it is conceivable that some immigrant communities are bunched together—as, for example, in Buenos Aires (Cravino 2006).

8. Teresa Caldeira (2009, 851) points out that "Brazilian urban peripheries have always been poor but heterogeneous," and she differentiates favelas from the impoverished urban peripheries. But, while I accept that there are differences, I do not buy her assertion that "what distinguishes the two are claims to ownership of house lots." If it is true that "the majority of the residents of the peripheries have bought the land where they built their houses and have claims to ownership" and that most favelas have been established through invasion, that does not mean that "residents of *favelas* do not have claims to the ownership of the land."

9. The extreme poverty line is based on a basket of foods as defined by the latest survey of expenditure and is defined at the income needed to buy that basket of goods. The poverty line is set at a level, usually twice as high, to cover other essential kinds of expenditure.

10. And was therefore erroneously described as a ghetto.

11. Licia Valladares (2006) claims that the origin of the word *favela* was also botanical, but the only support that I can find is the suggestion that the term may be a diminutive of *favo* (honeycomb) or *fava* (bean) in the *American Heritage Dictionary of the English Language* (4th edition).

12. Admittedly, these particular titles are more likely to be describing the fact that most urban migrants were born in the countryside than to be lamenting some kind of lost urban utopia. Perhaps the title of Van Luyn (2007)—*A Floating City of Peasants*—can be explained in the same way.

13. From 1950 until 1980, Latin America's population increased annually by 2.8 percent; currently the annual growth rate is around 1.2 percent. After 1960 most women in the region had fewer children. In 1970 the average Nicaraguan woman gave birth to 7.2 children during her lifetime; today the figure has fallen to 2.8 (UNDP 1997, table 22; UNECLA 2007, 31). Over the same period the gross fertility of Mexican women has fallen from 6.5 children to 2.2. The decline in fertility greatly helped to slow the pace of urban growth.

14. Of course, I recognize that some people—and in some countries large numbers of them— moved to the cities because they were forced to move by criminal or civil violence or as a result of "natural" disaster.

15. Although to some extent the term has become popular among some sociologists to explain poverty in First World cities; see, for example, Wacquant (1996, 1997).

16. On community councils, see Venezuela Notes (2008) and Ellner (n.d.).

17. Loïc Wacquant (2004, 5–6) notes that "the unchecked intensification of [the ghetto's] exclusionary thrust suggests that the ghetto might be most profitably studied not by analogy with urban slums, lower-class neighborhoods, and immigrant enclaves but alongside the reservation, the refugee camp, and the prison, as belonging to a broader class of institutions for the forced confinement of dispossessed and dishonored groups."

References

Abu-Lughod, Janet L. 1980. *Rabat: Urban Apartheid in Morocco*. Princeton, N.J.: Princeton University Press.

Amato, Peter W. 1970. "Elitism and Settlement Patterns in the Latin American City." *Journal of the American Institute of Planners* 36: 96–105.

Andrews, Frank M., and George W. Phillips. 1970. "The Squatters of Lima: Who They Are and What They Want." *Journal of Developing Areas* 4: 211–224.

Arnson, Cynthia, and José Raúl Perales, eds. 2007. *The "New Left" and Democratic Governance in Latin America*. Washington, D.C.: Woodrow Wilson International Center for Scholars.

Assies, Willem. 2003. "David Versus Goliath in Cochabamba: Water Rights, Neoliberalism, and the Revival of Social Protest in Bolivia." *Latin American Perspectives* 30: 14–36.

Auyero, Javier. 2000. "The Hyper-Shantytown: Neo-liberal Violence(s) in the Argentine Slum." *Ethnography* 1: 93–116.

Bateman, Milford. 2010. *Why Doesn't Microfinance Work? The Destructive Rise of Local Neoliberalism*. London: Zed Books.

BBC. 2006. "Iran Charged over Argentina Bomb." BBC, October 25. Available at http://news.bbc.co.uk/1/hi/6085768.stm.

———. 2007. "Rio Moves to Wall Off Its Slums." April 1, 2009. Available at http://news.bbc.co.uk/1/hi/world/americas/7975799.stm.

Betts, Raymond F., Robert Ross, and Gerard J. Telkamp, eds. 1985. *Colonial Cities: Essays on Urbanism in a Colonial Context*. Boston: M. Nijhoff.

Birkbeck, Chris. 1979. "Garbage, Industry, and the 'Vultures' of Cali, Colombia." In *Casual Work and Poverty in Third World Cities*, edited by Ray Bromley and Chris Gerry. New York: John Wiley & Sons.

Bonilla, Frank. 1961. *Rio's Favelas: The Rural Slum Within the City*. New York: American Universities Field Staff.

———. 1970. "Rio's Favelas: The Rural Slum Within the City." In *Peasants in Cities: Readings in the Anthropology of Urbanization*, edited by William Mangin. Boston: Houghton Mifflin.

Bromley, Ray, and Chris Gerry, eds. 1979. *Casual Work and Poverty in Third World Cities*. New York: John Wiley & Sons.

Caldeira, Teresa. 2000. *City of Walls: Crime, Segregation, and Citizenship in São Paulo*. Berkeley and Los Angeles: University of California Press.

———. 2009. "Marginality, Again?!" *International Journal of Urban and Regional Research* 33, no. 3: 848–853.

Charles, Maria, and David B. Grusky. 2004. *Occupational Ghettos: The Worldwide Segregation of Women and Men*. Stanford, Calif.: Stanford University Press.

Chávez, Franz. 2005. "Bolivian Water Rates Hard to Swallow." Available at TerrAmérica, http://www.tierramerica.net/2005/0312/iarticulo.shtml.

Cornelius, Wayne. 1975. *Politics and the Migrant Poor in Mexico*. Stanford, Calif.: Stanford University Press.

Cravino, María Cristina. 2006. *Las Villas de la ciudad: Mercado e informalidad urbana (The Villas of the city: The market and urban informality)*. Buenos Aires: Universidad Nacional de General Sarmiento.

Daniels, Cora. 2007. *Ghettonation: A Journey into the Land of Bling and the Home of the Shameless*. New York: Doubleday.

Davis, Mike. 2006. *Planet of Slums*. London: Verso.

De Ferranti, David, Guillermo E. Perry, Francisco H. G. Ferreira, and Michael Walton. 2004. *Inequality in Latin America: Breaking with History?* Washington, D.C.: World Bank.

Doughty, Paul L. 1970. "Behind the Back of the City: 'Provincial' Life in Lima, Peru." In *Peasants in Cities: Readings in the Anthropology of Urbanization*, edited by William Mangin. Boston: Houghton Mifflin.

Durand-Lasserve, Alain, and Harrand Selod. 2007. "The Formalization of Urban Land Tenure in Developing Countries." Paper prepared for the World Bank's 2007 Urban Research Symposium, May 14–16, Washington, D.C.

Eckstein, Susan, ed. 1989. *Power and Popular Protest: Latin American Social Movements.* Berkeley and Los Angeles: University of California Press.

———. 2000. "What Significance Hath Reform? The View from the Mexican Barrio." In *Social Development in Latin America: The Politics of Reform*, edited by Joseph S. Tulchin and Allison M. Garland. Boulder, Colo.: Lynne Rienner.

Ellner, Steve. n. d. "A New Model with Rough Edges: Venezuela's Community Councils." Available at North American Congress on Latin America, https://nacla.org/node/5750.

England, Kim. 1993. "Suburban Pink Collar Ghettos: The Spatial Entrapment of Women." *Annals of the Association of American Geographers* 83: 225–242.

Enríquez Acosta, Jesús Ángel. 2007. "Ciudad de muros: Socializacion y tipologia de la urbanizaciones cerradas en Tijuana" ("City of walls: Socialization and the typology of gated communities in Tijuana"). *Frontera Norte* 38: 127–156.

Escobar, Arturo, and Sonia E. Alvarez, eds. 1992. *The Making of Social Movements in Latin America: Identity, Strategy, and Democracy.* Boulder, Colo.: Westview Press.

Farache, Elias S. 2002. "Focus on Latin America's Jews." Available at http://www.hagshama .org.il.

Fay, Marianne, Lorena Cohan, and Karla McEvoy. 2005. "Public Social Safety Nets and the Urban Poor." In *The Urban Poor in Latin America*, edited by Marianne Fay. Washington, D.C.: World Bank.

Ferguson, Bruce. 2004. "Scaling Up Housing Microfinance: A Guide to Practice." *Housing Finance International* (September): 3–13.

Foweraker, Joe. 1995. *Theorizing Social Movements: Critical Studies on Latin America.* London: Pluto.

Fox, James. 1995. "Maximizing the Outreach of Microenterprise Finance: The Emerging Lessons of Successful Programs." *USAID Evaluation Highlights*, no. 49.

Gilbert, Alan G. 1998. *The Latin American City.* Rev. ed. New York: Monthly Review Press.

———. 1999. "A Home Is Forever? Residential Mobility and Home Ownership in Self-Help Settlements." *Environment and Planning A* 31: 1073–1091.

———. 2002. "On the Mystery of Capital and the Myths of Hernando de Soto: What Difference Does Legal Title Make?" *International Development Planning Review* 24: 1–20.

———. 2007a. "Inequality and Why It Matters." *Geography Compass* 1, no. 3: 422–447.

———. 2007b. "The Return of the Slum: Does Language Matter?" *International Journal of Urban and Regional Research* 31: 697–713.

Gilbert, Alan G., and Owen Crankshaw. 1999. "Comparing South African and Latin American Experience: Migration and Housing Mobility in Soweto." *Urban Studies* 36: 2375–2400.

Gilbert, Alan G., and Josef Gugler. 1992. *Cities, Poverty, and Development: Urbanization in the Third World.* Oxford: Oxford University Press.

Goldstein, Donna M. 2003. *Laughter Out of Place: Race, Class, Violence, and Sexuality in a Rio Shantytown.* Berkeley: University of California Press.

González de la Rocha, Mercedes. 2004. "De los 'Recursos de la Pobreza' a la 'Pobreza de Recursos' y a las 'Desventajas Acumuladas'" ("From the 'Resources of Poverty' to the 'Poverty of Resources' and 'Cumulative Disadvantages'"). *Latin American Research Review* 39: 192–195.

Grillo, Ralph D. 2000. "Plural Cities in Comparative Perspective." *Ethnic and Racial Studies* 23: 957–981.

Hall, Anthony. 2006. "From Fome Zero to Bolsa Família: Social Policies and Poverty Alleviation, Under Lula." *Journal of Latin American Studies* 38: 689–709.

Hoselitz, Bert F. 1957. "Generative and Parasitic Cities." *Economic Development and Cultural Change* 3: 278–294.

Inter-American Development Bank (IADB). n.d. *Microenterprise and the IDB: Credit Where It's Due.* Washington, D.C.: IADB.

King, Anthony D. 1976. *Colonial Urban Development: Culture, Social Power, and Environment.* London: Routledge & Kegan Paul.

Leeds, Anthony, and Elizabeth Leeds. 1970. "Brazil and the Myth of Urban Rurality: Urban Experience, Work, and Values in the 'Squatments' of Rio de Janeiro." In *City and Country in the Third World: Issues in the Modernization of Latin America*, edited by Arthur J. Field. Cambridge, Mass.: Schenkman Publishing.

Levinson, David. n.d. "Jews of South America" at Countries and Their Cultures. Available at http://www.everyculture.com/South-America/Jews-of-South-America.html (accessed April 9, 2010).

Lewis, Oscar. 1959. *Five Families: Mexican Case Studies in the Culture of Poverty.* New York: Basic Books.

———. 1966a. "The Culture of Poverty." *Scientific American* 215: 19–25.

———. 1966b. *La Vida: A Puerto Rican Family in the Culture of Poverty in San Juan and New York.* New York: Random House.

Lewis, W. Arthur. 1954. "Economic Development with Unlimited Supplies of Labor." *Manchester School* 22, no. 2: 139–191.

Lomnitz, Larissa. 1977. *Networks and Marginality: Life in a Mexican Shantytown.* San Francisco: Academic Press.

Mangin, William. 1967. "Latin American Squatter Settlements: A Problem and a Solution." *Latin American Research Review* 2: 65–98.

———, ed. 1970. *Peasants in Cities: Readings in the Anthropology of Urbanization.* Boston: Houghton Mifflin.

Marcuse, Peter, and Ronald van Kempen. 2000. "Conclusion: A Changed Spatial Order." In *Globalizing Cities: A New Spatial Order?* edited by Peter Marcuse and Ronald van Kempen. New York: Wiley-Blackwell.

Marx, Karl. 1872. *Das Kapital: Kritik der politischen Oekonomie* (*Capital: Critique of Political Economy*). Hamburg: Otto Meissner.

Maylam, Paul. 2001. *South Africa's Racial Past: The History and Historiography of Racism, Segregation, and Apartheid.* Aldershot, U.K.: Ashgate.

Neilson, Christopher, Dante Contreras, Ryan Cooper, and Jorge Hermann. 2008. "The Dynamics of Poverty in Chile." *Journal of Latin American Studies* 40: 251–273.

Nun, José. 1969. "Superpoblación relativa, ejercito industrial de reserva, y masa marginal" ("Relative overpopulation, the industrial reserve army, and the marginal mass"). *Revista Latinoamericana de Sociología* 5, no. 2: 178–236.

Oliveira, Francisco de. 1972. "A Economia Brasileira: Crítica á Razão Dualista" ("The Brazilian economy: Critique of dualist reasoning"). *Estudos CEBRAP* 2: 5–82.

O'Neill, Jessie. 1997. *The Golden Ghetto: The Psychology of Affluence*. Affluenza Project.

Paley, Julia. 2001. *Marketing Democracy: Power and Social Movements in Post-Dictatorship Chile.* Berkeley and Los Angeles: University of California Press.

Partridge, William. 1985. *The Hippie Ghetto: The Natural History of a Subculture.* Long Grove, Ill.: Waveland Press.

Peattie, Lisa. 1974. "The Concept of Marginality as Applied to Squatter Settlements." In *Latin American Urban Research*, vol. 4, edited by Wayne Cornelius et al. Thousand Oaks, Calif.: Sage Publications.

———. 1975. "'Tertiarization' and Urban Poverty in Latin America." In *Latin American Urban Research*, vol. 5, edited by Wayne Cornelius and Robert V. Kemper. Thousand Oaks, Calif.: Sage Publications.

———. 1987. "An Idea in Good Currency and How It Grew: The Informal Sector." *World Development* 15: 851–860.

Perlman, Janice E. 1976. *The Myth of Marginality*. Berkeley and Los Angeles: University of California Press.

———. 2004a. "Marginality: From Myth to Reality in the Favelas of Rio de Janeiro, 1969–2002." In *Urban Informality in an Era of Liberalization: A Transnational Perspective*, edited by Ananya Roy and Nezar AlSayyad. Lexington, Mass.: Lexington Books.

———. 2004b. "The Metamorphosis of Marginality in Rio de Janeiro." *Latin American Research Review* 39: 189–192.

Portes, Alejandro. 1972. "Rationality in the Slum: An Essay in Interpretive Sociology." *Comparative Studies in Society and History* 14: 268–286.

Portes, Alejandro, and Kelly Hoffman. 2003. "Latin American Class Structures: Their Composition and Change During the Neoliberal Era." *Latin American Research Review* 38: 41–82.

Quijano, Aníbal. 1974. "The Marginal Pole of the Economy and the Marginalized Labor Force." *Economy and Society* 3: 393–428.

Roberts, Bryan R. 1973. *Organizing Strangers: Poor Families in Guatemala City.* Austin: University of Texas Press.

———. 1978. *Cities of Peasants.* London: Arnold.

———. 2004. "From Marginality to Social Exclusion: From Laissez-Faire to Pervasive Engagement." *Latin American Research Review* 39: 195–197.

Roberts, Bryan R., and Robert H. Wilson, eds. 2009. *Urban Segregation and Governance in the Americas.* New York: Palgrave Macmillan.

Sa, Lucia. 2007. *Life in the Megalopolis: Mexico, São Paulo.* London: Routledge.

Salcedo, Rodrigo, and Alvaro Torres. 2004. "Gated Communities in Santiago: Wall or Frontier?" *International Journal of Urban and Regional Research* 28: 27–44.

Sánchez, Gonzalo. 2001. "Introduction: Problems of Violence, Prospects for Peace." In *Violence in Colombia 1990–2000: Waging War and Negotiating Peace*, edited by Charles W. Bergquist, Ricardo Peñaranda, and Gonzalo Sánchez G. Wilmington, Del.: Scholarly Resources Inc.

Silva, Patricio. 2004. "The New Political Order in Latin America: Towards Technocratic Democracies?" In *Latin America Transformed: Globalization and Modernity*, 2nd ed., edited by Robert N. Gwynne and Cristóbal Kay. London: Arnold.

Slater, David, ed. 1985. *New Social Movements and the State in Latin America*. Cinnaminson, N.J.: CEDLA/Foris Publications.

Soto, Hernando de. 1989. *The Other Path: The Invisible Revolution in the Third World*. New York: HarperCollins.

————. 2000. *The Mystery of Capital*. New York: Basic Books.

Souza e Silva, Maria Floresia Pessoa de. 2007. "Gated Communities: The New Ideal Way of Life in Natal, Brazil." *Housing Policy Debate* 18, no. 3: 557–576.

Sovani, N. V. 1964. "The Analysis of 'Over-urbanization." *Economic Development and Cultural Change* 12: 113–122.

Stokes, Charles J. 1962. "A Theory of Slums." *Land Economics* 48, no. 3: 187–197.

Stolowicz, Beatriz. 2004. "The Latin American Left: Between Governability and Change." In *The Left in the City: Participatory Local Governments in Latin America*, edited by Daniel Chavez and Benjamin Goldfrank. London: Latin America Bureau.

Turner, John F. C. 1968a. "The Squatter Settlement: An Architecture That Works." *Architectural Design* 38: 357–360.

————. 1968b. "Housing Priorities, Settlement Patterns, and Urban Developing in Modernizing Countries." *Journal of the American Institute of Planners* 34: 354–363.

United Nations Department of Economic and Social Affairs (UNDESA). 2009a. *Rethinking Poverty: Report on the World Social Situation 2010*. New York: UNDESA.

————. 2009b. *World Urbanization Prospects: The 2009 Revision Population Database*. Available at http://esa.un.org/unpd/wup/index.htm.

United Nations Development Program (UNDP). 1997. *Human Development Report 1997*. Oxford: Oxford University Press.

United Nations Economic Commission for Latin America (UNECLA). 2007. *Statistical Yearbook for Latin America and the Caribbean*. Santiago: UNECLA.

————. 2008. *Social Panorama of Latin America and the Caribbean, 2008*. Santiago: UNECLA.

————. 2009a. *Statistical Yearbook for Latin America and the Caribbean*. Santiago: UNECLA.

————. 2009b. *Social Panorama of Latin America and the Caribbean, 2009*. Santiago: UNECLA.

Valladares, Licia. 2006. *La Favela d'un siècle à l'autre (The Favela from one century to the next)*. Paris: Éditions de la Maison des Sciences de l'Homme.

————. 2007. "Social Science Representations of Favelas in Rio de Janeiro: A Historical Perspective." University of Lille I, LLILAS Visiting Resource Professor Papers. Available at http://lanic.utexas.edu/project/etext/llilas/vrp/valladares.pdf.

Van Luyn, Floris-Jan. 2007. *A Floating City of Peasants: The Great Migration in Contemporary China*. New York: New Press.

Venezuela Notes. 2008. "'Consejos Comunales' (Community Councils)—Participatory Democracy (or Direct Democracy) as Practiced by Campesinos in Venezuela." February 19. Available at http://venezuelanotes.blogspot.com/2008/02/consejos-comunales-community-councils.html.

Wacquant, Loïc. 1996. "The Rise of Advanced Marginality: Notes on Its Nature and Implications." *Acta Sociologica* 39: 121–140.

————. 1997. "Three Pernicious Premises in the Study of the American Ghetto." *International Journal of Urban and Regional Research* 20: 341–353.

————. 2004. "Ghetto." In *International Encyclopedia of the Social and Behavioral Sciences*, edited by Neil J. Smelser and Paul B. Baltes. Oxford: Pergamon.

———. 2007. *Urban Outcasts: A Comparative Sociology of Advanced Marginality.* Cambridge, UK: Polity Press.

———. 2008. "Ghetto, Banlieue, Favela, et Cetera: Tools for Rethinking Urban Marginality." In *Urban Outcasts: A Comparative Sociology of Advanced Marginality,* edited by Loïc Wacquant. Cambridge: Polity Press.

Wilson, David. 2010a. "Urban Underclass." In *Encyclopedia of Geography.* Available at Sage Reference Online.

———. 2010b. "Ghetto." In *Encyclopedia of Geography.* Available at Sage Reference Online.

Wirth, Louis. 1938. "Urbanism as a Way of Life." *American Journal of Sociology* 44, no. 1: 1–24.

CHAPTER 9

✦ ✦ ✦

Divided Cities:
Rethinking the Ghetto in
Light of the Brazilian Favela

*Brasilmar Ferreira Nunes
and Leticia Veloso*

This chapter offers a contribution to the discussion of marginalized urban spaces by addressing the following question: Is it possible to compare, conceptually, the Brazilian *favela* to the American ghetto, and what might we gain by making such a comparison?[1] More specifically, in what ways may such an inquiry illuminate the American ghetto? We begin our argument with a brief detour to some of the earliest studies on social exclusion in urban areas, and then we comment on how some of the most basic assumptions underlying those initial studies have been reconfigured in current scholarly arguments on the American ghetto. Finally, we turn to the Brazilian favela, which, in its specificity, may productively illuminate not only the problem of the ghetto but the wider issue of marginalized urban spaces.

In so doing, we suggest that the favela may provide a good way to think about the ghetto, both in terms of its historical development and its current predicament. Though they are, of course, very different phenomena, the fact that both are marginalized urban spaces with a long history in their respective societies allows for this comparative exercise. We also add to the discussion the problem of urban housing—central to discussions of the favela but often underemphasized in arguments about the ghetto—to suggest that this is a cru-cial dimension for understanding marginalized urban spaces.

To begin this discussion, it is useful to remember that already in the first Chicago School the microscopic study of the physical space of the city, tied to urban morphology and ecology, was treated as a means to gain more detailed and precise insights into broader processes, such as the nature of urbanization or the place of the city in the wider society. And even though these paradigms have been fastidiously criticized, some of their initial analytical assumptions might still be useful. For example, we may remember that Louis Wirth's (1980) study of the Jewish ghetto in Chicago was part of the broader research program referred to as the Chicago School of Urban Sociology, which sought to describe intra-urban mobility. Specifically, he assumed that a population would move from one area to another; according to the hypothesis, it would be from an older neighborhood (the ghetto) to a peripheral residential area (Lawndale).

One of the important points made by the Chicago School was that study-ing spatial mobility would reveal important tendencies in urban growth, thus turning mobility into a means for analyzing social, cultural, and psycho-sociological processes. Wirth (1980) himself was emphatic in this respect when he realized that, though he initially had set out to study a particular geographic area, what he really had to look into were the specificities of the people who inhabited that area. Importantly, Wirth took the ghetto as an object, treating it as (1) an institution, (2) an urban form, and (3) a social form. To do so, he basically started from the idea of Judaism, its history and future; it was this perspective that allowed him to consider the symbolic implications of ghet-toization rather than a sense of anti-Judaism in itself.

Wirth's work and that of others written under the guidance of Robert Park and Ernest Burgess (cf. Burgess 1979; Park, Burgess, and McKenzie 1925) con-solidated a notion of urban sociocultural processes in which segregated areas in general, and ghettos specifically, were more than mere accidental products of a particular process of urbanization: They were essential in determining the structure of urban space. In addition, at that time the ghetto was still read as a transient phenomenon that was marked by only temporary equilibrium and eventually would dissolve itself. By extension, residing in a ghetto was pri-marily thought to be just one step toward gradual assimilation.

Gradually, this mode of looking at the ghetto became a model for under-standing the stereotypical modes of urban occupation characteristic of American metropolises at the turn of the twentieth century. In this light, the ghetto as model became not only commonplace in the United States from the 1920s on but also, in the process, how residents described themselves and their place of residence. However, this mode of nomination of a concrete phenomenon, and even of a specific space, was reified by academics, so that a "concrete" phenomenon and habitual term in residents' self-description was turned into a theoretical concept serving as the basis for numerous urban sociology studies focused on marginalized spaces.

Even though the term itself may allow for different meanings, we suggest that this transposition of uses and meanings—from a space of dwelling for specific populations to an abstract sociological phenomenon—had concrete effects, positive and negative, on the study of urban marginalized spaces. Even so, we also suggest that the concept remains sociologically relevant to understanding not only those spaces most commonly associated with the term— marginalized and segregated areas on American soil—but also other urban areas that are equally marginalized and segregated and bear both similarities and differences vis-à-vis the ghetto.

To better consider the possibilities and limitations of the ghetto concept, it is useful to remember that the term was already present in medieval Rome, where it referred to that part of the *urb* inhabited by Jews. More than a century later, Richard Sennett (1996) shows, Christians were also isolating Jews. Then, in sixteenth-century Venice, the term *ghetto* referred to all those spaces where foreigners without official citizenship privileges lived; such enclosed spaces were meant to ensure that foreigners would remain there permanently (Sennett 1996). Interestingly, the ghetto at that time was not exclusive to the poor and dispossessed; it could also be home to wealthier persons, though isolation was still key.

Also noteworthy is another point mentioned by Sennett (1996): Venice ghetto residents, even with their imposed isolation and all the restrictions they lived under, were able to build new forms of community life and were thus able to achieve at least some level of self-determination. This, Sennett suggests, reflects a process whereby, from a space of segregation imposed by Christians upon Jews and foreigners, the ghetto could become a space of sociability where a particular culture sustained and reproduced itself. Significantly, this very same possibility was detected by Wirth in his research on the Chicago ghetto at the dawn of the twentieth century—even though, as we have noted, that ghetto continued to be seen, even by its own residents, as a "passageway" toward new areas and upward mobility.

In a sense, the term *ghetto* was transformed from a concept originally used to refer to a particular *space* into a sociological concept, and then it gradually came to refer mostly to those marginalized, impoverished, and segregated neighborhoods in U.S. cities—such as New York City; Detroit; Chicago; Pittsburgh; Washington, D.C.; and, somewhat later, Los Angeles and Philadelphia—that were inhabited by African Americans. But at the same time that the use of the term as a concept amplified itself, the ghetto as a concrete space inhabited by real persons underwent an even broader transformation—from the communitarian ghetto imagined and analyzed by Wirth to something more in the direction of the dilapidated and abandoned ghettos of the present.

Loïc Wacquant (2005, 2008a, 2008b), for example, has shown that, after a brief apogee in the 1950s and 1960s, ghettos in different American cities underwent rapid degradation, marked by the physical deterioration of not only buildings and empty spaces but also general living conditions, all combined with the exponential growth of crime and unemployment. One immediate result of such conditions has been that, most commonly, only those entirely bereft of the means to leave the ghetto would want to stay there; everyone else might be expected to leave as soon as feasible. In this light, ghetto residents are often seen as persons condemned to a form of internal exile, a process aggravated by the fact that tax-originated resources become all the more limited as wealthier residents choose to flee to the suburbs (Venkatesh 2000, 148–150).

It is thus that current academic work on the ghetto remains strongly focused on questions of degradation, loss, and the general demise of the former communitarian ghetto described by Wirth (1980). In trying to make sense of such new predicaments, the more recent literature has been rethinking most of the very first assumptions about the ghetto—some of which were already latent (or explicit) in works such as Wirth's. Assumptions such as that of the "gradual assimilation" of the ghetto into the wider society, or even of its presumed nature as a "disorganized" space, have been reconfigured in light of current transformations. In so doing, they open up interesting pathways for conceptualizing other marginalized urban spaces as well—such as the Brazilian favela.

RETHINKING SOME BASIC ASSUMPTIONS ABOUT THE GHETTO

One of the most prevalent assumptions about the ghetto since the 1920s has been that it is a provisory model of urban occupation, the space par excellence of recently arrived groups who bring with them their own culture and practices. Analytically, therefore, the next logical step would be to imagine that such differences are assimilated, allowing the ghetto to be gradually incorporated into the city. However, in recent years this assumption has been powerfully challenged, if not shattered by Anderson (1990, 1999); Venkatesh (2000, 2006, 2008); Wacquant (2001, 2005, 2008a, 2008b); Wilson (1987, 2009), and others. In these works, not only is the ghetto far from temporary, but the reasons for its reproduction are becoming stronger, through mechanisms even more perverse than the original ones. In this light, the ghetto could eventually come to be seen as an "eternal," insoluble space.

Another key assumption in ghetto studies, recurrent since the first Chicago School, has been that of the ghetto's presumed inherent "disorganization." According to this rather common viewpoint, ghettos are spaces where disorganization—materialized in high crime rates, so-called dysfunctional families, weak ties between community members, and so on—is not only inbred (that is, born from the very nature of ghetto life and the "peculiar" disorganized character of its residents) but actually intrinsic to all ghetto life. This point of view tends to regard such disorganization as *the* defining characteristic of what a ghetto is and how it functions.

Even though this assumption has already been fastidiously criticized in work that lays bare certain fundamental fallacies (Venkatesh 2000, 2006, 2008; Wacquant 2005, 2008a, 2008b; Wilson 1987, 2009), it is useful here to restate at least some of the more important points recently made against what we may call the "disorganization thesis." The first is that, as Sudhir Venkatesh (2000, 2008) has argued, the supposition of social disorganization hides precisely the minute and highly creative ways in which residents try to meet their most basic daily needs not only through a series of negotiations and disputes but also through cooperation and, hence, organization. He further argues that the ghetto cannot therefore be understood in terms of "disorganization" because what, to the eyes of outsiders, might *appear* as such merely reflects residents' responses to the many adversities they face every day and their attempts to satisfy some very basic human needs—such as food, clothing, and housing. In so doing, they respond with the resources they have at hand; it is these responses that, since they do not necessarily abide by mainstream criteria, are then interpreted as signs of "disorganization"—mainly because they include semilegal and illegal practices or forms of conduct deemed deviant by mainstream society.

Venkatesh (2000, 2008) goes one step further: Not only is the ghetto not disorganized, he argues, but it is in fact extremely organized—but according to principles that are specific to the space, being produced in reaction to a unique set of structural and strategic restrictions. And given that such restrictions have tended to affect these racialized inner-city enclaves more extremely than any other segment of the American population at any other period of time, residents' reactions to such effects can only be equally extreme as they make use of whatever means are available at any given moment, including illegality if and when needed (Venkatesh 2008). What this way of conceptualizing the ghetto suggests is that, if we look close enough, beyond internal differentiation and hierarchies, we can read the (postindustrial) ghetto as a community taking great pains to keep itself viable through often quite strong ties among its members, who, in turn, combine their meager resources to help one another out in the fight for survival (Venkatesh 2000).

The second argument against ghetto disorganization that is worth restating here has to do with the wider society's responsibility for the lives of the urban poor. For Wacquant, for example, what needs to be explained is not such assumed "disorganization," for what appears as "disorganization is a function of the ghetto's ever-more rapid demise in current times," a process he refers to as a "politics of concerted abandonment" of those neighborhoods by the state (Wacquant 2008a, 169). In other words, it is not that the ghetto *is* disorganized; rather, what looks like disorganization from the outside is in fact the result of a complex historical process whereby the state gradually removes itself from the ghetto, refusing to take responsibility for its residents. For Wacquant, ultimately, it is this politics of state disengagement, fueled by exacerbated neoliberalism, that causes the systematic destructuring (and hence the assumed "disorganization") of the ghetto and its gradual transformation into almost an "urban purgatory" (Wacquant 2008a). Increasingly, he says, what formerly may have been mere "disengagement" on the part of the state has been turning into a more active project of intentional disintegration that not only abandons the ghetto but criminalizes and penalizes it for its very existence—and the concept of the *hyperghetto* is meant to convey precisely this process, one whereby the ghetto gradually turns into, to borrow Wacquant's (2008a, 56) apt phrasing, a "deposit" for entire categories of persons seen to be of little or no political or economic use to society.

In short, Venkatesh (2000, 2006, 2008) and Wacquant (2001, 2005, 2008a, 2008b) turn both the "gradual assimilation" and the "internal disorganization" assumptions on their heads by showing that (1) the ghetto is becoming in- creasingly *less* assimilated, not more, into the wider cityscape; and (2) its pre- sumed internal "disorganization" is but the result of both residents' daily survival strategies *and* state abandonment. They are both pointing, as others have done before them (cf. Wilson 1987), to the idea that ghettos are what they are, and function as they do, not merely on account of their residents' behavior but, more importantly, as the result of societal and state abandonment, if not downright termination.

On the one hand, these insights help illuminate precisely the relational processes whereby outside influences affect life in the ghetto, thus showing just how socially embedded the ghetto is. On the other hand, focusing on the (negative) impacts of outside action on the ghetto can also lead to viewing it, and its residents, largely in terms of their victimization by the wider society, thus focusing more on the negative aspects of ghetto life than on any potential for change or betterment. To be sure, Venkatesh's ethnographic perspective in particular has been carefully portraying residents not as mere victims but as persons actively seeking to act upon their predicament—even though, at the end of the day, they may remain trapped in their subordinated position, con- tinuing to fall prey to state policies whose effects are mostly deleterious.

A similar point, we suggest, is implied in Wacquant's formulation of the "Janus-faced" nature of the ghetto: For those in a subordinated position (ghetto residents), the ghetto can also act as an instrument of integration and protec- tion in that it frees them from having to be in constant contact with those in power, stimulating internal collaboration (Wacquant 2008a, 82), yet for those in power (especially the state), the ghetto's reason for being is still the control and confinement of its residents. And with the so-called exacerbation of the hyperghetto, this bi-facial character seems on the verge of disappearing, be- cause the less room there is for the ghetto to act as a buffer against outside negative influences, the more it comes to function mainly as a weapon against residents (Wacquant 2008a).

INITIAL THOUGHTS ON THE BRAZILIAN FAVELA

Urbanization has been under way in Brazil since the 1930s, when industry began to turn into the main basis for the accumulation of capital in the national economy and industrialism became the key generating source of new social groups and classes (Leeds and Leeds 1978). Brazilian industrialization was different for two reasons: First, industrialization happened comparatively slower than in Europe or even the United States, and second, the multiplying effects of Brazil's industrial dynamics were relatively reduced, owing in great part to the need to continue importing most of the technology employed. Yet another characteristic set industrialization in Brazil apart: Even though Brazil, much like the United States, received massive waves of European immigrants in the final decades of the nineteenth century and the first decades of the twentieth century, a vast number of these immigrants moved initially to rural areas, and the cities grew mostly through internal migration—that is, Brazilians coming from the rural areas (Leeds and Leeds 1978). In addition, the country's continental dimensions, coupled with strong regional inequality in levels of development and the fact that most industry was located in a few large cities, led the population to move from depressed areas to those experiencing rapid growth.

However, movement was too fast and too vast, and because it became impossible for large numbers of the moving population to find employment in the formal sector, Brazil's enormous informal market expanded and the logics of social exclusion that are now key to Brazilian cities began to develop. Further, given the attraction for workers of urban activities (industry, commerce, services), an imbalance arose between the supply of workers and the demand for them, and that imbalance, in turn, has fed the expansion of informal work. Thus, the supply of labor power grows exponentially while the demand for it grows only arithmetically, and informal work leaves many people and families increasingly vulnerable.

This is one major reason why unemployment, peripheralization, "favelization," and so on, have remained central in the Brazilian metropolis, reflecting what some have called a "truncated modernity"—a "territory of deficits" that also reveals itself in the patterns of urban land occupation (Leeds and Leeds 1978; Nunes 2007). This notion of a "territory of deficits," or that of a "deficit territory," finds its utmost expression in the favelas, especially in Rio de Janeiro, but also in other large cities (Alvito and Zaluar 2005; Nunes 2007). In very general terms, favelas originally served as the spaces that rural migrants and former slaves went to while searching for a place in the urban-industrial economy that was then coming into being; having been denied a place in the formal economy, they stayed in the city and resorted to the informal market. In other words, the favela arose as a marginal space where economically and socially excluded individuals gathered—a function that has changed very little.

Though it might be tempting, for purposes of comparison with the American ghetto, to characterize the favela as an area populated mainly by blacks recently freed from slavery, the ethnic composition of favelas has actually always been more diversified as segregation, at least initially, was not purely ethnic but also economic. In this sense, the issue of racial stigma does not initially arise as strongly as in the American ghetto, given that neither race nor ethnicity is the main marker of difference for favela residents. The favela is first and foremost a place inhabited by the poor in the city—that is, it is the very space of a poverty that has proven itself, over the centuries, to be structural in Brazilian society. In this form of poverty, race and ethnicity are still important, but they are not the sole marker of exclusion, and probably not even the key one (Alvito and Zaluar 2005; Leeds and Leeds 1978). In fact, migrant families' initial reasons for settling in favelas have tended to be, for the most part, economic: Their low capacity for meeting the high costs of urban housing and their exclusion from formal work led them to occupy these areas that held little attraction for real estate capital.

Key to this dimension of the favela as a problem of housing are the economic dynamics of real estate in the cities, for housing is a huge business that operates under different logics depending on the market. Often, large real estate projects are offered a form of "surplus value" by the state through selective urban policies, while small enterprises, though they may also command large sums of money, do not have access to the same facilities. Favelas, in this light, obviously reflect a housing deficit that is not served by the formal housing market.

Besides such economic logics, another feature is important for under-standing favelas—namely, the state's inability to manage such spaces, mainly because favelas spread out, usually because of squatting, over areas that are ignored by public policies and real estate capital alike. Because many of these areas that are not prioritized in urban territorial politics would require special technologies to be adapted to the city, they are devalued in the expansion of the formal city.

Still, the focus only on what favelas *lack* is misleading: Given that these are areas where entire generations have lived and reproduced themselves parallel to the "formal" city, it is not too farfetched to assume that the very way of life in the favela has produced certain forms of sociability that are not unrelated to their physical constitution (Nunes 2007). In short, an intense process of cultural creation goes on in every favela through relations of neigh-borliness and cultural practices that, in turn, are strongly linked to place of dwelling (Alvito and Zaluar 2005). The most common example, of course, is the Brazilian *samba* itself, born and perfected in Rio's favelas in the early decades of the twentieth century (Leeds and Leeds 1978). From this less pes-simistic point of view, therefore, a favela is not just an area of deficit; it is also a subsidiary of a peculiar mode of life that would not have arisen or re-produced itself in quite the same manner outside of the favela. It is not too much to argue that the space of the favela helps produce a very specific mode of being and that it thereby acts directly upon identity forms and the socia-bilities of residents. This often translates into the unwillingness of residents to move out of the favela even when they have the economic means to do so (Nunes 2007).

FAVELAS: TERRITORIES OF DEFICIT
AND THE DEFICIT OF TERRITORY

In Brazil, favelas (the term comes from Rio) and their regional variations are the most common housing solution for poorer families and for those living and working in the informal sector. Since all urban dwelling obviously pre-supposes access to money—a token of the hegemony of the market in defining social interactions—those with low or uncertain incomes tend to be excluded from the formal, expensive housing market and are therefore led to seek alternative housing—the most common one being to live in a favela. This tendency is far from recent in Brazilian society, as Anthony Leeds and Elizabeth Leeds (1978, 187) have meticulously shown. In the 1880s, they say, there was already mention of such marginalized spaces and their characteristic form of housing (auto-construction)—though the term *favela* was yet to come into being. Then the phenomenon grew significantly, in both extent and volume, after the 1940s. By the 1950s, it was already deemed a very urgent problem, which also reflected the rapid growth of favelas and the relatively slow institutional response on the part of the government and planners.

Obviously, socio-territorial exclusion as a phenomenon appears in many different market societies. In fact, it is possible to draw direct comparisons between the Brazilian favela and other spaces that, at least in their physical form, are quite similar: *poblaciones* in Chile, *villas miserias* in Argentina, *cantegrils* in Uruguay, *ranchos* in Venezuela, *banlieues* in France, and, of course, the American ghetto. In all those cases, moreover, what tends to be emphasized in their respective societies—fueled by the media—are their negative aspects, such as crime, drugs, poverty, poor infrastructure, and so on. Yet these negative portrayals may also help to mask the particular sociabilities that take place in these spaces (Nunes 2007). Academic and media attention are generally drawn to such negative aspects, which are then treated as tokens or effects of global capitalism or neoliberal policies (cf. Wacquant 2008a, 2008b).

We wish to suggest, however, that especially in the Brazilian case (if not in most other contexts as well), we must be careful and avoid assigning too large a role to contemporary changes in capitalism or to the (equally recent) neoliberal model of policy making: The Brazilian favela has been structuring urban life for over a century and, as a dynamic socio-historical process, undergoing continuous changes. Further, conditions in all favelas, unlike in the American ghetto, have not been deteriorating at the same pace with the expansion of neoliberal capitalism. In fact, some favelas are becoming more consolidated and more integrated into the city, though to a limited extent (Alvito and Zaluar 2005).

It may even be argued that housing itself is not people's priority in the favelas; rather, the favela may address a combination of needs of the poor, including housing, proximity to place of work, access to public and other services, and logistical support by the state (transportation, water, sanitation, and so on). In other words, it may be fair to say that it is the location of housing, not its quality, that matters most. On the other hand, it is these very same factors that make the problem of housing so insoluble for the poor and that help explain why so many choose such precarious housing forms even when they might be able to afford something "better." The combination of affordable housing and being close to one's place of employment, then, is one important reason why so many migrants choose to live and stay in the favelas. After all, most migrants aspire to some form of social insertion, especially in the formal labor market—not to mention that it is work alone that will allow them access to the regular income they desire.

People's arrival in the larger cities is thus the result of their recognition of the employability potential of metropolitan areas, especially compared to smaller cities or rural areas. In this light, cities represent a positive expectation—but one that rarely materializes, for employment can be rare and difficult to come by, frustrating such expectations. On the other hand, the city, and perhaps even the favela, is a factor in itself, for it is seen to provide the very basis for social mobility through access to education, medical services, leisure, recreation, and so on. Corroborating this point, Leeds and Leeds (1978) argue that what is most present in favelas is the aspiration not so much to ascend to patterns above those held by the group, but to attain a full, comfortable life under existing conditions.

To emphasize this point, it may be useful to make an important analytical distinction between "housing needs" and the "demand for a home" (Oliveira, Givisiez, and Rios Neto 2009). The term "housing needs" is a social concept, that is, it is based on specific norms adopted in various countries as to what proper housing is and the related social needs that such housing will or will not meet. The "demand for a home" goes beyond social norms and needs (Oliveira, Givisiez, and Rios Neto 2009) and refers to the desires of actual persons for specific forms of dwelling, desires that they then seek (or intend) to fulfill.

In other words, families may express a *demand* for a new home, but that demand may not constitute a *need* from the social (and political-economic) point of view. Some families have access to housing through the formal market—they can either get credit or use their own savings to satisfy their demand for a new home—but a large proportion of the population who reside in less-than-adequate homes that are crowded or deficient in infrastructure lack the financial means to buy or rent their own home through the formal market. This fraction of the population represents a "housing need" from the social point of view, but it does not represent an actual economic need for housing in the same formal market (Oliveira, Givisiez, and Rios Neto 2009).

In general, favelas are the result of precisely such *need* for housing that does not constitute a *demand* for housing (in the formal market). After all, housing in favelas is mostly auto-constructed, there is no formal real estate market to speak of that caters to favelas, and urban public policies that might show that the state is addressing this problem are virtually nonexistent. This is not to say that favela homes are not also subjected to a market that functions according to supply and demand. However, the difference lies in the range of other dimensions this market incorporates—such as favors, informal personal credit, and barter without the use of actual money—thus constituting a very specific and separate market segment that operates along lines parallel to the formal market.

Still, cities—especially the metropolises—keep attracting migrants from other regions, as well as former residents of the outlying suburbs who wish to live closer to jobs and other attractive aspects of the city. Because of these inhabitants' housing needs and inability to operate in the formal market, however, increasingly it is those areas less targeted by real estate capital, such as hills, wetlands, and mangrove areas, that are being occupied. Through their proximity to the labor market and social infrastructure (schools, hospitals, shops, and other services), and even through the neighborhood relations that residents are able to build, such areas often compensate for—even economically—the precariousness of housing. A profound cleavage is thus established between those areas addressed by the formal market and urban planning, on the one hand, and on the other, those spaces that are deemed "unworthy" of attention by either capital or public policies and whose occupation is unplanned. The two different logics of urban territory in Brazil creates urban communities with extreme levels of economic, social, and cultural differentiation.

When looked at from the outside, favelas are usually seen as disorganized areas—with shacks, thin and tortuous pathways in place of streets, no infrastructure, difficult access, and so on—whose design lacks any rational logic (Alvito and Zaluar 2005). The spatial organization of a favela exposes economic inequality in a very immediate way, but it also, alternatively, serves to naturalize such inequality rather than foster projects aimed at overcoming it (Alvito and Zaluar 2005). As such, these areas are often perceived by the wider population as dirty and dangerous—a perception that has been exacerbated in Rio de Janeiro by the expansion of drug trafficking, and the crime it gives rise to, from inside the favelas. Such perceptions feed the ongoing stigmatization of the poor as the "dangerous classes," while the reverse is also true: Areas with "proper" dwellings are symbolically read as inhabited by "civilized" and educated persons.

The problem of popular or low-income housing in Brazil, then, is deeply ambiguous and contradictory. On the one hand, it is subjected to the neutralizing evaluations of bureaucrats and members of the elite, whose notions of what constitutes "proper housing" are very different from those espoused by the poor. On the other hand, the poor, much like everyone else, eventually produce their own notions of "adequate" housing based on a combination of their own economic means and their cultural values and taste. Urban policies are formulated, however, by people who do not belong to the poorer classes, and that produces an insoluble dilemma: The different housing patterns practiced by the poor—and the favelas where such patterns are manifested—are looked down on as nothing less than urban anomalies and are thus virtually ignored when priorities in urban planning are assessed.

A recent episode in Niterói, a city just across from Rio by Guanabara Bay, offers a poignant illustration of this very point. In early April 2010, after several days of severe rain, a favela on top of the Morro do Bumba (Bumba Hill)—whose houses had been mostly built on top of what had formerly been an enormous dump—literally collapsed in on itself, burying hundreds of homes and killing several dozen residents. It was later revealed that a study conducted several years earlier by the Universidade Federal Fluminense (the federal university located in Niterói) had uncovered fourteen favela areas where the risk of landslides was deemed "extreme"; the Morro do Bumba was one such area. Also, the study deemed the risk in three hundred other areas to be "imminent." According to local press reports, the study was presented to various government agencies as early as 2004, but no measures were taken.

Historically, attempts to solve the "favela problem" have tended to favor the removal of residents from entire areas (Alvito and Zaluar 2005; Jacques 2003, 2004; Leeds and Leeds 1978). In one (in)famous episode from the 1970s, for example, all residents were forcefully removed from what was then called the Favela da Catacumba, and their homes were torn down to make room for an inner-city park. Today this area is part of the upper-class neighborhood of Lagoa, which may be the only neighborhood in Rio with no favelas at all and which now has the highest human development index in the entire city. Most such wholesale removals of residents have failed. Such a policy fails from the point of view of residents because, when removed from their home favela, not only are their emotional ties to the community all but severed, but they are often placed in some outlying area that does not serve their immediate needs for jobs and transportation, and so they eventually move to another favela closer to the city center. Removal of favela residents is also a failure from the point of view of policymakers, not only because ultimately it is unfair to residents, but also because it is a pointless waste of resources, especially given the degree of geographic proximity, if not integration, of favelas to the cityscape.

What this points to is a process of territorial consolidation through which favelas, even though still stigmatized and symbolically distanced from the "formal" city, have become more and more physically integrated into it. In the same process, a new urban order seems to be at work, operating independently from the state and public policies (Nunes 2007). On the one hand, as we have tried to show, this new urban order arises partly because, subjectively and culturally, favelas function according to a logical principle based on *location* more than anything else. On the other hand, they remain subordinated to a double predicament. From one point of view, the state has been either absent or inefficient in designing and implementing adequate policies targeted at both urban planning and territorial organization. From another point of view, the stigmatization of favelas leads to the kind of repressive and controlling policies that have actually been implemented—such as the oft-attempted "removal" projects (Jacques 2003, 2004).

As such, the relationship between favela and the state is ambivalent at best, and highly negative at worst, for the state has mostly shown itself incapable of addressing the needs of this particular population. The state has neither been able to contain the expansion of favelas across the metropolitan area nor managed to offer the poor low-cost housing alternatives that attend to perhaps their most basic need—being integrated into, and reasonably close to, the labor market. The result of these policy failures has been not only the creation but the reproduction of these semi-clandestine areas inside the city. And at the same time that their very presence is becoming ever more consolidated—for it is undeniable now that favelas are part of the city, physically speaking (cf. Alvito and Zaluar 2005)—they remain largely outside the reach of adequate urban planning strategies (Jacques 2003, 2004). The consequences, as the Niterói episode so poignantly showed, are often dire.

To what extent, however, would it be possible to look at favelas as the Brazilian version of the ghetto? One feature they obviously share is that both are marginalized urban spaces par excellence, even if each is located within specific national and local configurations. By the same token, both are also marked by a distance between residents' views of themselves and those of the wider society. Both ghetto and favela appear to outsiders to be spaces defined by some intrinsic internal disorganization and the stigma attached to them—again, by the wider society. From the point of view of "insiders," living in a ghetto or favela may subject them to material lack and marginalization, but they refuse to let these conditions determine everything in their lives: In both spaces, residents are more focused on trying to make a world out of precarious circumstances, by whatever means are at hand. Thus, residents of both spaces have developed forms of living that ultimately result from the absence of institutional support and effective urban planning.

Another point of comparison resides in the uneasy relationship of both the ghetto and the favela to the state: Unable or unwilling to enact public policies that truly address the needs and viewpoints of residents, the state has tended either to completely disregard such spaces or to favor policies of containment, control, and repression. As Wacquant (2008b) suggests, the state's neglect and repressive policies have been somewhat more extreme in the American ghetto, as we pointed out earlier, but this is not to say that Brazilian policies have been any better, for omission can lead to results that are just as harmful. In a somewhat ambivalent manner, therefore, it is the very absence of an effective state that largely explains the internal dynamics of both spaces—as manifested, for example, in the quite explicit presence of drug-trafficking gangs and the accompanying violence.

Still, one important difference between the ghetto and the favela, we suggest, has to do with the *scale* of their development. Precarious as their living conditions are, it might be said that most if not all ghettos are minority phenomena, even in cities such as Chicago and Los Angeles. Yet this is hardly the case in a city such as Rio de Janeiro, where 1.2 million people now live in more than 1,000 favelas. Given that the Rio population is estimated to be around 6 million for the city itself and 12 million for the entire metropolitan area, it follows that between one-fifth and one-tenth of the population now reside in favelas. These figures make Rio a very peculiar example indeed of marginality and of what happens to whole cohorts of urbanites in the absence of adequate policies. In fact, favelas in Rio are so ubiquitous that to understand the history and place of favelas is to go to the heart of the history of the city.

CONCLUSION

Favelas and ghettos are socio-spatial phenomena that reflect deep-seated processes of social exclusion. Still, exclusion in itself, however instrumental in producing both ghettos and favelas, is insufficient to explain the present-day logics of these spaces or the relationship between marginality and the wider society. Perhaps the key point here is that, since urban planning policies have relegated both to a marginal position, ghettos and favelas ultimately resort, out of necessity, to creating their very own forms of urban living and even city-building and urbanization.

This is quite obvious in favelas, where auto-construction and auto-production have led to a peculiar identity molded not only by economic need but also through specific taste patterns and social relations. Such options, it would seem, are somewhat more limited in the ghetto, where auto-construction is not possible to the same degree. By extension, if it can be said that favelas reflect autochthonous modes of construction, occupation, and urbanization, what seems to be going on in the ghetto—and especially in the "hyperghetto"— is a more thorough process of deconstruction and demise. As Venkatesh (2006, 2008) has sharply noted, there are certainly strong ties among residents of the ghetto, and people seek to make their own worlds through them. But as Wacquant (2008b) suggests, such possibilities seem to be gradually diminishing in the face of state abandonment, criminalization, and penalization, which puts the ghetto at risk of becoming not a marginalized space per se but a true "nonspace" within the city. Both ghettos and favelas, however, remain spaces that almost thoroughly disrupt the logics of "legitimate" patterns of urban occupation, since they do not abide by the rationalism of urban and academic models.

Furthermore, it should be kept in mind that governmental actions targeted at cities have increasingly tended to follow the same global, homogenizing logics, through the imposition of common urban patterns on different social groups and societies. Global politics tends more and more often to play out in cities and, especially, metropolises, a shift that points to a tendency toward the homogenization of urban patterns and urban territorial occupation. Metropolises thus become spaces of extreme rationalization where tradition tends to give way to interested calculations, which in turn results in the homogenization of urban intervention projects. By the same token, the interest of financial agents in intervening in urban spaces points to the potential for the accumulation of capital in these spaces. This interest, however, is by definition ambivalent: While specific areas are selected for intervention, other important portions of city territories are not.

As a secondary result, alternative urban models eventually arise out of the void left by official policies. Hence, any given metropolis has certain "regular" spaces whose particularities are detached from the local culture as well as "spontaneous" spaces where improvisation, material lack, general precariousness, and often high doses of sociability are the rule. From this point of view, favelas might be seen as a crucial example of such invention, since their residents are truly responsible for the actual construction of their own space. Interestingly, the very opposite is true for residents of the formal city, who only very rarely can become involved in the production of urban space. Moreover, the territory of the favela is to some extent the result of spontaneous practices that, in turn, produce the individuals and social practices that inhabit the space. Through their multiple daily actions and their daily tactics of survival, then, favela residents give rise to a variety of informal configurations by which they seek to make up for the state's inaction.

In this sense, it is the very absence of the state that leads, in such territories of exclusion, to new urbanization patterns that may serve as alternatives to the homogenization of contemporary metropolises. In other words, in their exclusion from what is otherwise the homogenization of urban spaces, favelas may be suggesting ways to reverse such tendencies, mainly because they reflect a model of popular participation in the making of public space based on residents being the actual agents of its construction (Jacques 2004). From most studies of the American ghetto, it would seem that herein lies another crucial difference between a ghetto and a favela: In the ghetto the possibilities for such creativity in urban spatial intervention seem more limited than in the favela.

We would like to conclude by stating that by no means do we intend to imply a "positive" understanding of poverty, marginality, or urban exclusion; rather, we seek to reinsert such marginalized spaces—especially the favela—into the broader territorial context of which they are a part. We further suggest that the favela be considered part and parcel of the contemporary metropolis, but through a form of territorial production that reproduces itself on the fringes of schools of urbanism and urban planning, as well as of capital's rationalized actions. From this point of view, the favela can then begin to be considered as central in explaining contemporary urban logics.

Note

1. Both authors gratefully acknowledge the financial support of Fundação de Amparo à Pesquisa do Estado of Rio de Janeiro (FAPERJ).

References

Alvito, Marcos, and Alba Zaluar, eds. 2005. *Um Século de favela* (*A Century of Slums*). Rio de Janeiro: Editora FGV.

Anderson, Elijah. 1990. *Streetwise: Race, Class, and Change in an Urban Community*. Chicago: University of Chicago Press.

———. 1999. *Code of the Street: Decency, Violence, and the Moral Life of the Inner City*. New York: W. W. Norton.

Burgess, Ernest. 1979. "Croissance de la ville: Introduction à un projet de recherche" ("The Growth of the city: Introduction to a research project"). In *L´École de Chicago: Naissance de l´écologie urbaine* (*The Chicago School: The Rise of Urban Ecology*), edited by Yves Grafmeyer and Isaac Joseph. Paris: Aubier. (Originally published in English in 1925.)

Jacques, Paola Berenstein. 2003. *A Estética da Ginga: A Arquitetura das favelas através da obra de Hélio Oiticica* (*The Aesthetics of Ginga: Slum architecture through the work of Hélio Oiticica*). Rio de Janeiro: Casa da Palavra.

———. 2004. "A Espetacularização urbana contemporânea" ("Contemporary Urban Spectacularization"). *Cadernos do PPG-AU/FAUFBA* (special issue 2).

Leeds, Anthony, and Elizabeth Leeds. 1978. *A Sociologia do Brasil urbano* (*The Sociology of Urban Brazil*). Rio de Janeiro: Zahar.

Nunes, Brasilmar Ferreira. 2007. "Notas sobre sociedades metropolitanas na era global" ("Notes on metropolitan societies in the global era"). *Cadernos do PPG-AU/FAUBA* (special issue) 5, UFBA-FAU.

Oliveira, Elzira Lúcia, Gustavo Henrique Naves Givisiez, and Eduardo Luiz Gonçalves Rios Neto. 2009. *Demanda futura por moradia no Brasil, 2003–2023: Uma Abordagem demográfica* (*Future demand for housing in Brazil, 2003–2023: A Demographic Approach*). Brasília: CEDEPLAR, Ministério das Cidades.

Park, Robert, Ernest W. Burgess, and Roderick D. McKenzie. 1925. *The City.* Chicago: University of Chicago Press.

Sennett, Richard. 1996. *Flesh and Stone: The Body and the City in Western Civilization.* New York: W. W. Norton.

Venkatesh, Sudhir. 2000. *American Project: The Rise and Fall of a Modern Ghetto.* Cambridge, Mass.: Harvard University Press.

———. 2006. *Off the Books: The Underground Economy of the Urban Poor.* Cambridge, Mass.: Harvard University Press.

———. 2008. *Gang Leader for a Day.* London: Penguin.

Wacquant, Loïc. 2001. *As Prisões da miséria* (*The Prisons of Misery*). Rio de Janeiro: Jorge Zahar Editor.

———. 2005. *Os Condenados da cidade* (*The Wretched of the City*). Rio de Janeiro: Revan.

———. 2008a. *As Duas faces do gueto* (*The Two Sides of the Ghetto*). São Paulo: Boitempo.

———. 2008b. *Urban Outcasts: A Comparative Sociology of Advanced Marginality.* Cambridge: Polity Press.

Wilson, William Julius. 1987. *The Truly Disadvantaged: The Inner City, the Underclass, and Public Policy.* Chicago: University of Chicago Press.

———. 2009. *More Than Just Race: Being Black and Poor in the Inner City.* New York: W. W. Norton.

Wirth, Louis. 1980. *Le Ghetto.* Paris: Champ Urbain. (Originally published as *The Ghetto* by the University of Chicago Press in 1928.)

CHAPTER 10

✦ ✦ ✦

Demonstrations at Work:
Some Notes from Urban Africa
AbdouMaliq Simone

An unrelenting feature of urban life no matter where it takes place, impoverishment seems to be an inextricable aspect of all that cities promise and accomplish and a by-product of the city's capacity to create dense interchanges of materials and bodies, which the city puts to unanticipated uses that mark a space for aspirations, energies, and lives that cannot be productively used. At the same time, cities have always made a large proportion of their residents available to service the agendas of others, limiting the cost of their incorporation as labor and circumscribing their ability to use urbanization as a resource for a much broader range of projects and desires.

The political and economic relationships of cities cannot be separated from the particular and contingent forms through which cities have acted as mediators in the intersections of distinct imperial incursions, as incubators of accommodations among different kinds of actors and economic interests, or as concretizations of particular ways of using and adjusting to shifts in globalization (Chatterjee 2004; Prakash 2008; Roy 2008). For example, to invoke the notion of "postcolonial cities" does not explain much about what goes on within them, since highly differentiated practices, temporalities, and modes of subjectification must be included in the concept of colonialism in order to maintain it as a significant event. The ghetto is another such concept. Just because we can identify slums, *barrios*, *bidonvilles*, *favelas*, and *kampongs* across all major cities of the Global South gives us no indication of what they have been used for, when and how they arose, or what they "do" for the rest of the city and areas beyond. These kinds of generalizations make it difficult to identify viable courses of political action (Barnett 2006).

Cities have been places in which many different kinds of actors, both local and nonlocal—and including administrators, traders, proletariats, sojourners, missionaries, teachers, compradors, commerçants, bandits, academics, artisans, and domestics—worked out ways of relating to shifting forms of domination and autonomy and made the necessary realignments incurred by their own activities as a result. Therefore, there is no overarching model that accounts for the specific relational fields that exist within given cities—whether in terms of who constitutes a particular population (for example, "the poor"), the spatial profiles of where people reside, or what they do with given territories across the city (Bayart and Bertrand 2006; Leitner, Sheppard, and Sziarto 2008).

Yet such uncertainty has historically been experienced as a portent of danger. Dividing lines must be drawn as a way of constituting and anticipating particular vectors and agents of antagonism. Concentrations of poor and lower-middle-class residents in close proximity to factories, offices, and markets are socialized into making certain assumptions about themselves and their possibilities through the use of planning, service provision, and administration as control mechanisms. Control functions mainly through underfunding such districts, enforcing shifting expenditures of time, labor, and money that households have to make in order to maintain their residence, and specifying procedures through which residents have to make themselves accountable. What makes residents eligible for certain opportunities and services, on what conditions residents are entitled to use public and private spaces, and what constitutes infractions of acceptable demeanors become key considerations (Donald 1999; Joyce 2003).

Given the densities of the potential relationships spawned from the intricate ways in which city residents must be involved in each other's lives—in the workplace, on the trading floor, in neighborhood streets—solidarities, reciprocities, and collaborations are always being generated that exceed the frameworks through which these residents are to be included in the city. Economic transactions proliferate that circumvent dependence on formalized provision of goods and services, and they configure networks of interdependency and translation in which goods are exchanged according to locally specific valuation. As such, this density of concentration gives an apparently subjugated population dangerous leverage to act on the larger city in its own interests. When policymakers respond by deeming these districts to be beyond repair, as they so often do, the population has to be spread out, dispersed in the name of better living conditions (Duda 2008).

On the other hand, the opacity of boundaries that define specific populations and forms of economic activity can also make it unclear who is to be displaced. As metropolitan governance networks grow increasingly dependent on transactions that cannot be pinned down by any legal framework or standards of efficacy—but at the same time must usually cover up the fact that they do so—who will do the everyday work in the "trenches" to ensure that these myriad provisional deals and accommodations among key institutions are made? Those actors who constitute the prospective threat to projects of capital accumulation and social control may be precisely those who are turned to in order to keep projects together or at least demonstrate the wide range of possibilities for operating outside conventions and laws (Ruggiero and South 1997).

SKILLS AND RESISTANCE

For Vera da Silva Telles and Daniel Veloso Hirata (2007), residents in this situation are neither simply the subjugated nor the purveyors of skilled survival. Rather, they continuously navigate a world where no one set of assumptions or clearly delineated trajectory of efficacy and livelihood applies. Here residents must simultaneously avoid everyday violence and take into account all of those friends, family members, and neighbors who have not "made it"—who have not survived. This need to be incessantly cautious turns everyday transactions into an unrelenting scrutiny of what can be said to whom and how different worlds and alliances can be "ducked into." At the same time, residents have to do whatever it takes to not become poorer than the next person and to avoid becoming an object of charity or solely a beneficiary of the supports of others. Thus, whatever is constant in one's life as a platform of social supports must be experimented with and taken in unknown directions, but without "bringing down the house." What is important is the capacity to alternate continuously between acting in networks as if they are based on trust and cooperation and acting as if they are simply vectors of strategic manipulation where spaces are opened by immobilizing others (Grabher 2006).

In part, these issues concerning the social composition of cities have emerged in the political strategies and technical instruments that have predominated in efforts to organize the urban poor since 1976, after the first international gathering, the United Nations Conference on Human Settlements (Habitat 1), to consider urban settlement issues. Despite substantial rates of urbanization across the Global South and the exigencies entailed in accommodating a swelling population of former peasants, agricultural workers, artisans, and traders, a lack of political will and financial resources made it difficult to keep up with this urban growth. Policies gravitated instead toward sites and service schemes that provided basic demarcations of plots and skeletal services that would be "filled in" over time through the initiatives and resources of the poor themselves.

The idea was to establish a basic, identifiable platform on which residents could establish a secure foothold in the city. This security could then be progressively mobilized to affect the development of the settlement. Without having to worry about the basic right to be in the city, residents could get on with the business of using the city to build a livelihood and accumulate savings. By applying their own logics of spatial development, they also would "domesticate" the city in ways that would enable them to "recognize themselves" within it. In other words, they would build settlements that, by reflecting their practices, aspirations, and values, would constitute a particular capacity and set of rights materially inscribed within the built environment (Benjamin 2000, 2008; Boonyabancha 2001, 2009; Khosla et al. 2002; Mitlin 2002, 2008; Sharma 2000).

Although such policies have been contested all along, implicitly they defer difficult challenges about rights, inclusion, and responsibilities to a future time. Everyone can then argue that development is under way, that a trajectory of progressive inclusion in urban life has been charted. This policy logic has been reinforced by pointing to all of the failed projects undertaken by states to comprehensively house and service low-income residents. Observers attribute this failure, in part, to low-income residents not being fully prepared to deal with urban life and having behaviors of habitation that are out of synch with the expectations embodied in these public housing projects. Thus, there has been little political distance between supporting the capacities of residents to build the city in ways that reflect different aspirations and collective arrangements, on the one hand, and concluding that the poor fundamentally lack the capacity to come to grips with urban life. Exclusion is reframed as lack of competence, which is addressed with various capacity-building programs centered on teaching the poor how to save and govern themselves (Appadurai 2002).

Faced with relentless hostility from institutions of municipal power, resident associations and political mobilizations of the poor coupled the demands for citizenship rights with discourses that valorized the capacities of the poor to manage their own lives and settlements. In order not to internalize the violence directed toward them—as manifested through forced removals and the harassment of livelihood activities—urban social movements emphasized the unyielding capacities of low-income residents to make the city their own regardless of efforts to exclude them. Thus, when residents looked upon the dense, underserviced, and insalubrious urban environment, they would also recognize their specific abilities to be part of urban life, to concretize their rights to the city.

These efforts by thousands of local associations—made visible to a larger international audience through the efforts of organizations such as Habitat International, Shack/Slumdwellers International, and the Asian Coalition on Housing Rights, to name a few—helped generate a broader interest by researchers, architects, and artists in various city-making practices "from below." Urban literature in recent years has been replete with examples of the efficacies of slums or the productivity of urban frisson. This proliferation of interest once again raises the question about representation and the politics of a subaltern urbanism. Here there are a wide range of claims, from more modest ethnographic examinations of the toiling poor just managing to keep their heads above water to claims that the subaltern shows us what all cities "really are"—essentially destabilized, fluid assemblages of bodies, materials, and affect on a field of constant improvisation.

All of this long-term detailing of urban life—its descriptions of people, neighborhoods, and conditions—has been fraught with ethical dilemmas. It is almost impossible to explore the sociality of the "slum" without the obligation to recognize the essential vulnerability of those who live within it. But what is the recognition of vulnerability? What is the relationship between the purported sense of weakness or precariousness that exists in the present and the elaboration of the events and conditions that are probably forthcoming as a result of such weakness? Development discourses have long raised the issue that what is important is not what takes place now—not the characteristics of conditions in the present—but what is likely to happen in the future as a result of those conditions. What is it, then, that is recognized as vulnerability? In other words, how do the limitations of the present turn into the inevitability of some future disaster? How is all that is practiced or accomplished now in the present subsumed under this inevitability?

Lack of sanitation, for example, will mean shortened lives, household conflicts, and depreciation of livelihood. Although it is certainly possible to enumerate all kinds of causal effects, it is this positing of an original state of vulnerability from which causal chains then "take off." But who recognizes vulnerability? Who determines that a place is unlivable? When residents across a city look at themselves, who sees vulnerability, and under what conditions? What is important is not so much the truth value of such attributed status, but the extent to which the recognition facilitates or forecloses an engagement with the "vulnerable" in ways that exceed their anticipated trajectory—a trajectory that takes them "away" from us. For as Radhakrishnan (2008, 82) points out, "In our recognition of vulnerability, we as humans admit the unrepresentability of death and dying within human discourse and, at the same time, create a normative framework governed and informed by the very phenomenon that we cannot represent." Given this, what obligations and latitude exist to engage the vulnerable as "ordinary" urban citizens in ways that do not exaggerate commonalities as a means of also dismissing them from our lives?

Whereas cities embody a critical inability to hold together stable relationships among such elements, it is another thing to insist that this notion of the city is "proved" by its most vulnerable inhabitants—thus equating vulnerability and the exigencies of constant compensation and adjustment with some "essence" of urbanity. The actions of the poor certainly can point to how the city is not all that it is "cracked up" to be. Still, these fissures in the normative—that is, the constituent gaps that enable urban governance and urban norms to consolidate themselves—do not become visible and usable by unveiling a prior and more "real" version of the city. Rather, they become instrumental through the active disruption of municipal power and capitalist relations. It is in the fight of the poor to overcome the very conditions that supposedly embody the fractal character of urban life that its potentialities are concretized.

We know many things from studies of cities in the Global South, yet what do they mean, and for whom? What does all of this subaltern capacity mean in the long run? Must it mean anything in particular? Can all of this "skilled action" exist simply as what it appears to be—skilled action—without having to be mobilized for an instrumentality outside of its own surface applications? Since cities seem so resistant to being swayed by any particular evidence of their functioning, does it really matter what claims are made on behalf of and through a subaltern urbanism? Does the need to address the provision of urban rights, citizenship, and services and to remake the structural conditions that link urban growth to dispossession mandate against demonstrations of efficacy and vitality on the part of poor in ways other than their political actions? Are there ways of representing, or at least pointing to, the practices of city-making that are cognizant of the city as a fundamental aspect of global capitalist relations, yet that recognize the city as a viable arena of experimentation that continuously hones the aspirations and concomitant practices for different ways of living? In the following section, I take up some of these questions with reference to contemporary urban central Africa, and Kinshasa in particular.

SHELTERS AND STAND-INS, HEDGES AND VALUES: THE OSCILLATING ECONOMIES OF AFRICAN URBAN LIFE

Across much of today's urban Africa, most residents seem to tend to their own waiting games—waiting either for something to drastically change or simply for time to run out. There are few opportunities and resources to construct narratives of any discernible progression, and inordinate effort may be expended to maintain a provisional sense of sameness—of holding on, putting food on the table, keeping a roof over one's head, and minimizing the intrusions of others. Although there may be large measures of circulation, mobility, resilience, and innovation in the ways in which residents navigate volatile spaces and livelihoods, these rarely constitute a platform for the conviction that things are getting better.

At the same time, many urban residents—rich and poor alike—obsessively adhere to the trappings of modernity, playing the game by the book. Regardless of whether school fees take up half of a household's income, kids are properly dressed in spotless school uniforms and ready at the school door exactly on time every morning. It matters little that all of the evidence points to the fact that this education will have minimal impact on what happens later. A woman civil servant in a municipal agency is at her desk every morning on time, brings her own lunch to eat at her desk, and completes the day's paperwork after twelve hours even though there is no guarantee that she will receive a paycheck at the end of the month.

Still, cities continue to spill over their bounds, often across places barely accessible by two-wheeled vehicles, pushing back hinterlands. Although most residents at these new peripheries seldom venture very far into the interiors of older urban sediments, they are convinced that proximity to the city exists and that it constitutes a basis to at least service forthcoming expansions. However, without solid links to the histories that have socialized workable structures of urban authority or to the traditions of the often volatile, depleted regions they came from, these nascent residents will sometimes "live on each other" (as they say in Douala's Brazzaville district). They insert themselves in whatever stands out in the particular details of each other's existence, such as bodily and social practices or ways of getting and doing things. As a result, even the simplest activities—eating, loving, talking—may have too many unanticipated implications, and so it is important to "let the wind take you places"—that is, to not be overly concerned about holding one's ground or being known as one thing.

In some central African cities, such as Douala and Kinshasa, notions of economy manifest in the practice of interweaving discrete people and things with others in relations that often are unfamiliar and make little sense. Things that do not readily belong are assembled into provisional bundles, not only to create new forms of consumption but also, more importantly, to keep the discreteness of things intact, as a shelter against the easy parasitism. Economy, then, is reassemblage of valuation or keeping the value of things open to new uses and sites (Callon 2008). Thus, to grasp the fierce ambivalence of many clearly impoverished urban districts requires an appreciation for the oscillations of value as bodies, lives, built environments, and materials continuously enjoin and break from associations that enable the temporary shelters and opportunities where the civil and uncivil, the benevolent and the manipulative, propel each other somewhere else, momentarily away from homogenized misery or individual advantage. No one can go it alone; it is not clear with whom one should or could go; and one must go somewhere or else be swallowed by "more powerful mouths," which are always plentiful.

Urban living has been associated not only with the individuation of selves from an encompassing social context but also with individuation of persons from associated webs of things, infrastructure, and territory. The body and self stand out because they step out of a meshed world, and then things take on a support role at the service of personhood—creating an environment for it that maintains proximity to virtuous inputs while keeping the deleterious at bay (Sloterdijk 2008). Personhood requires a particular spacing-out, a field of attention that allows culpability and capacity that is claimed and attributed, as well as a narrative line through which objectives are set and to which subsequent action is directed.

But one of the aspects that makes slum life normatively intolerable is the intense proximity of lives, as well as organic and inorganic matter in various states of composition that seem to make it impossible to account for, let alone imagine, a line of progression. This is the case despite the plenitude of available stories about the rise and fall of built environments, social projects, and individual lives. In contrast to the routinized middle-class orderliness that creates the veneer of an endless, stable present, the slum shows its daily wear-and-tear, but in ways and in response to events too numerous and variegated to provide a discernible account. The highly visible acts of responsiveness—the impacts that events have on each other—become the arena of daily interventions. Since there are no "strong narratives" that steer these interventions in a readily identifiable direction, some residents depend on "stepping into the middle of things" to see what kinds of advantageous scenarios can be put together. This is why African urban markets are full of people, the majority of whom are neither buying nor selling anything in particular. Rather, they are present in the market simply to take their chances, to act as if there are deals about to be made, or simply to be the person called upon to be the extra hand or the stranger nobody knows ready to stand in at a moment's notice.

BLOOD ECONOMIES

Kasa-Vubu, a centrally located district in Kinshasa, is named after one of Congo's most prominent political leaders. It had been developed as a combined commercial-residential area just on the other side of the southern limits of the former colonial enclave. Its advantageous location enabled it to develop a cosmopolitan edge, reflected in the varied backgrounds of its traders and residents. The commercial area has been redeveloped several times, but each such effort seems to invite more overuse and overcrowding. The surrounding residential areas have some of the highest density levels in the city and are places of rough conditions and rough characters.

For a crew of guys I know in Kasa-Vubu, it is hard to tell when the work really begins or even what it is. The most intense activity seems to occur in the late afternoon in the intersection of various satisfactions and apprehensions. Some are relieved to have made more than they anticipated and can look forward to treating their friends to a beer. Others have barely sold or made anything and are reluctant to return home. There are those who will hide from creditors and those who will under-count the day's receipts. And some will bundle what they have left with the surplus of others and try quickly to pass off the package deal to those who roam the markets at this hour looking for last-minute bargains.

Cedric, Lumanu, Makoto, Bazana, and Armando are the titular heads of the "Bloods" in the quarter of Kasa-Vubu just south of Kinshasa's central market area. With their red bandanas, they have styled themselves around the American gang and indeed are well informed about its history, personalities, and organizational structure. The K-V crew intends not so much to be a "branch" of a global organization as to appropriate certain "themes" and ways of operating in order to instantiate themselves into the local economy. With the exception of Makoto, all are university graduates, and their grooming and eyewear convey the look of young professionals rather than thugs. They all occupy a parcel left to Armando when his family unexpectedly departed for Europe without informing him; he recruited his present "associates" to help him hold on to the parcel in the face of competing and aggressive claims from kin.

The crew spreads across Marché Gambela at the start of the trading day. They canvass the initial expectations—for a market is a field of affective textures, from indifference to driven urgency, and these forces compel an array of discursive tactics and deals. With the decaying infrastructure of the market and the various cloggings of the transport routes in which it is embedded, the trading day must also circumvent incessant delays from dealing with gridlocked traffic, waiting for deliveries, setting aside goods for pickups that are slow in coming, coping with sporadic supplies of electricity, and getting into unanticipated arguments that are not resolved quickly. Given that marketing entails getting what one has access to out into the largest conceivable world of consumers willing to pay a good price, trading is concerned with opening up vistas of sight and perspective. Marketing is not just about what traders can actually see but also about what they can anticipate, what they imagine to be taking place beyond their immediate field of vision. To a large extent, this is what the Bloods do: At the outset of the day, they try to get a sense of what the market, in all its various individuated and grouped sensibilities, anticipates, how the market "feels" about how it is situated in the larger context of events.

As hopes, anxieties, exigencies, and indifference swirl around in the market, each trader interferes with the capacities of others. Whether crowding in or stepping away, the traders shape the spaces of transaction, for it makes little sense in an overcrowded arena of small transactions to simply wait for customers. Traders have to circulate, to round up possible sales, to make certain products, services, and prices readily available to those whose intention was only to acquire a specific good and not others, to try to convince them of certain associations between discrepant items. Although some traders stay still in the recesses of this mobility, as a means of offering discretion and limited visibility, Gambela is a stage for showing cards by those who mostly do not hold them. Nevertheless, they are convinced that, once the cards trade hands, they know enough about where they are to make them appear almost immediately.

For the Bloods, it is important to assess how the traders they deal with think about their location at the start of the day: Is this the day they have to pay off the big Lebanese creditors? Is this the day wives will collect from their *tontine*? Is this the day groups of buyers will come in from the distant suburbs beyond the airport? Traders in the market are rarely alone—they belong somewhere—and in Gambela the company includes the West Africans, who have been in the market for generations, and traders affiliated with Chinese, Lebanese, or Indian wholesalers or brokers, who can mobilize credit and connections to facilitate supply and advantageous prices. There are those who walk in various uniforms, which, in the market, tend to obscure rather than clarify representation, as many try to invoke an authority from somewhere. There are traders linked to big politicians and others with ties to churches or to the growers and brokers whose provinces supply the bulk of specific goods.

As traders try to put together an expansive vantage point—that is, a plane along which they can envision a ramifying series of events and people to articulate what they have access to—the actions of others in the market become fundamentally ambiguous, for they can both block and facilitate, both elucidate and dissimulate.

In a city of intense scarcity and constantly shifting possessions, where there are a limited number of games and resources to work with, success is often a matter of slowing others down to allow one time to get to some piece of information, some money, some customer, before others have a chance. This means throwing up detours and deviations. At the same time, straight paths, while often enabling speed, have their own limitations. When people are forced into deviations and onto circular paths, they may pay attention to scenes and people they otherwise would not have thought twice about, and in these encounters they may discover unforeseen possibilities. Here, regardless of the spatialization entailed, a straight path means little to someone who is unable or unwilling to move fast, and the circuitous path means little to those who are too impatient to take in the view. All of these factors are the "materials" that the Bloods work with.

But at the beginning of the day, they simply try to "take it all in"—to get a sense of the intensity of aspirations, the willingness of certain traders to assume various ways of seeing and figuring, and the way the market is "coming together," how the transports, goods, stalls, affects, and openings are interacting. They spend no more than an hour at this, and then they go back to sleep, as if to make any dreams they may have an important modality for designing what they will attempt later.

The crew returns to Gambela in the late afternoon just as things are both winding down and thus speeding up. It is a time when those who are trying to unload, to make some money, are most desperate, and this feeling intersects with the accruing patience of those who feel that they have done as well as possible, that it is important to sit tight and not make any mistakes, that it is not the time to go out on a limb. It is also a time when the market is at its messiest, and not simply because it has been "worked" all day, although the mess is certainly a sign of that work. It is also messy because traders have been holding goods for others, bundles may have been proposed but are not going anywhere, and things now have to be disentangled and returned to their proper places, but just as they are on their way back, something else may intervene to convince the traders of other possible last-minute destinations. This is one facet of what the Bloods do. They wait until the last minute and try to force through different kinds of "alliances" between these goods on "their way back." Given what they observed in the morning—the various assessments of location, moods and expectations, and opening prices and bottom lines—it is time to reassess these sentiments, expectations, and assessments now that the trading day is almost at a close.

Additionally, no matter how much a trader has made at the end of the day, the reality remains that he or she owes something to someone—creditors, family members, fellow traders, patrons. These others may not need to be paid that day, but at least in the abstract something must be set aside. What the Bloods do is to "suggest" (and sometimes compel) that this extra something be put into "play"—for example, to help fund a last-minute purchase; to cover an urgent debt in return for a favorable volume of a certain good or service; to join in a collective purchase of a service, such as protection; to expedite a delivery; to circumvent a tax or duty; or to help fund someone who is traveling and has a good jump on a favorable price for some bulk purchase. Because the Bloods have nothing easily discernible to buy or sell themselves, they put all of their efforts toward reading the potential willingness of traders to take actions they would not readily consider and toward getting a sense of how traders think they are connected, not only to each other but to wider scenarios. For example, since relations between Lebanese wholesalers and Gambela retailers can be characterized by the latter's docility in the face of manipulation and sometimes extortionary merchandising, the Bloods will identify ways to try to "go back door." They might arrange for a theft to occur at a warehouse, or see that a wholesaler's kid goes missing for a few days, or capture a competitor's wife in a compromising position, or spread rumors about certain big merchants holding back on payoffs to their guys in the government. Although reluctant to use violence, they find it necessary to maintain a reputation for violence as a kind of guarantor of authority in the market that cannot rely simply on threat or extortion.

For at the end of the day the task is to work with the loose ends and concretize potential futures from what is left over, not because this is the only way to concretize potential futures but because the task of working with leftovers reconfigures relations within the market and beyond. Cajoling, seducing, steering, sometimes forcefully bringing different actors to each other's attention, the Bloods "suggest" ways of packaging leftover food, recently arrived bundles of clothes, and "diverted" electronics that did not quite find their way to the expected pickup into a nearby waiting van that could quickly arrive at a mega-prayer meeting in Matete and park near the bevy of food-sellers hoping to catch the pre- and post-meeting multitudes. As everyone rushes from the market and into the crowded thoroughfares and minivans and buses, a Blood or two makes sure that certain vehicles are able to jump the queue, as long as their drivers are willing to make room on their rooftops for a few bags of cement and deliver it for free to a group of construction workers willing to do a few hours of underpaid overtime at a trader's little satellite shop in the suburbs in return for a connection he has with the ministry handling a big project in Gombé.

The end of the day also requires the management of impressions. The appearance of success is critical. Traders often mask their desperation and insist on certain prices until the end. But this adamancy can also be thrown into the mix: It can hedge those who want to get rid of something for almost any price because they need something for the dinner table that night. The work of the Bloods is to bring together all these divergent expectations and levels of desperation or patience, as well as those who think long and those who think short, those who see far and wide and those who see only the immediate area around their stall. The "today I will do for you if you will do this tomorrow" is founded on these differences. There will be those who can wait to be paid a month, two months down the line because they see the fluctuations in the supply chain and know that they can afford to have someone hold something now—a good, a price, a service—because its value will be markedly different later on. There are those who know that in a few weeks a client or potential customer will probably need a certain quantity of an item just when supply is constrained, and thus they are willing to acquire now and hold on. Then there are those who are willing to take a chance on an item or class of goods that they would not have considered before, but can now easily acquire, and simply put it into play as an instrument to affect the price of something they really want.

The Bloods' work is the choreography of these intersections and exchanges. What counts first and foremost is extricating a good or service from the use and value that is anticipated for it at the beginning of the day, seeing later on the extent to which this "hold"—the association between the good and its framing—has been maintained, and deciding whether there is now flexibility to dislodge the equations that link trader, good, price, and use and set other connections in motion. Again, there are goods that are left over, those that arrive late or never come, those that come in the wrong quantities or are delivered to the wrong hands. There is spillage and scarcity; things that circulated during the day may have assumed advantageous locations and bundles but are now on their way back to their "proper" owners. In the first instance, the Bloods attempt to link these materials—food, wire, cement, cloth, hardware, pharmaceuticals—regardless of their designated uses. They are simply things making a last-minute appearance (or disappearance) in the market, and the objective is to interrupt the flows normally suggested by their marketing to carve out transactions that may have little to do with the actual or potential number of customers for a particular type of commodity, either now or tomorrow.

Of course, all these materials in circulation belong to someone; they have actual or potential value to someone, and they are someone's property and set of possibilities. Things are not easily dissociable from what they represent. Once held and then exchanged, it is not always clear under what conditions they can be replenished. In a city where the institutions of mediation are weak, claims to authority are suspect, and predictable trajectories of input and output are usually provisional, there may seem to be little room for maneuver. Such conditions may emphasize the need for steadfastness, trust, and stringent codes of reliability. These characteristics are certainly on display in the market. At the same time, in a city where individuals try to embed themselves in the lives of others and where performing consistently in any endeavor is fraught with unforeseen contingencies, since people are weakly anchored in ongoing institutional roles, keeping goods and services within strict parameters of specific uses is difficult and often not in people's best interests. Things have to be converted into unexpected uses and values in order to keep them moving and use that movement to maximize a person's exposure to a wider playing field.

This is precisely what the Bloods trade on: They use the circulation of objects, infused as they are with various intensities of expectation and guile, as a way to piece together relationships that promise, if never guarantee, a widening of the field of vision. The "promise" is that traders can have access to contacts and experiences that might not otherwise be available to them, and the first step is to disinvest from the particular sentiments and calculations with which they have approached the things that pass through their hands. Such opportunities ensue only if they can let go of the particular meaning that these things have and let them exert their "own forcefulness." At the same time, things are imbued with meaning, and this disjunction is not something to be reconciled or negotiated. Instead, it produces volatility—a moment when things could go in many different directions. It is this volatility that the Bloods attempt to both provoke and steer.

The Bloods can do the work they do—trying to put things into play, trying to use them as instruments to bring different scenarios and actors into an unanticipated proximity—only because they do not care about what these things mean. Although they may be bearers of intensities of expectation, disappointment, need, and imagination, these sentiments are important to the Bloods only because they signal a difference from other sentiments and uses, and that difference then opens up an opportunity for a deal.

As I skim the surface here of complex microeconomics, what I am trying to illustrate is the importance of broadening the usual notions of livelihood. Livelihood as a domain and problem has been too often reduced to considerations of employment, business, or discernible production activities. It is taken to refer to the amassing and deployment of material resources and money, usually as these activities are applied to the effective management of households. But livelihood can also refer to a field of maneuverability, to the act of creating spaces where living can be exercised and deployed. Life seeks to perpetuate itself and maintain stability by producing conditions that bring its critical details into view and minimize the uncertainties incumbent in the stretching of its capacities. The increasing complexities and aggrandizements necessary to secure life can undermine its largely improvised efficacy.

The market operations described here, performed repeatedly as much as possible, also act as ways of taking things apart—and some of these things are long-established relationships and organizations that persist but increasingly with varied "half-lives." If what the Bloods attempt to do is to circumvent the effects of actors and things on the market according to particular redundant arrangements, the "stuff" of the market is also catapulted, or returned, to a different phase of existence—not necessarily transformed but rendered in a form that makes it available to different calculation and sometimes simply to the "highest bidder." This practice constitutes a particular limitation on the productivity of experimentation, for it comes to devalue certain hard-won accomplishments of consistency. It could problematically signal that all that has been accomplished—through negotiations and practice over the years—can be simply superseded by an "experimental moment" and that the problems of legitimacy and available resources in the larger society authorize experimentation for its own sake.

In Kasa-Vubu, the Bloods have no job, official position, or discernible future. In the time I spent with them, I was not even able to determine how in the end they get paid. They have money, but not large amounts. They exert some kind of authority, but it is not clear exactly what. Sometimes what they do works; more often they are laughed at or met with complete indifference. They are a highly visible presence in the quarter, but only for short spurts of time. They never socialize locally and are apprehensive about being too exposed. Some are wanted for crimes and make a big deal about avoiding the police, but at other times they could not seem to care less. Clearly a particular kind of force field is being "played" here—the ebbs and flows of intersecting ambitions, constraints, claims, losses, hopes, calculations, tactics, impressions, and manipulations. Kinshasa is a city full of tricks and deceptions, as well as grinding boredom and limited options. How speech, dress, words, gestures, timing, speculation, reading, and intuition are deployed becomes a critical aspect of livelihood—that is, making a "hood" for life, a place, a cover, and a performance that interweaves various instantiations and expressions of living in order to move life somewhere else, if only for the time being. In many ways, the Bloods in Kasa-Vubu would not appear out of place in the marginalized urban spaces of U.S. cities or elsewhere.

DEMONSTRATING URBAN CAPACITIES, LIMITATIONS, AND POTENTIALS

At the heart of urban modernity has been the attempt to circumvent demonstration—to bring to a close the need to make visible how things work, how things are put together. For demonstrations can be contested and offset by other kinds of demonstrations. So the built environment is used as a language of summation that brings to a close what can be remembered and what can be said about what the nation is—its eventuality and composition.

But cities clearly have always been places of experimentation through the application of different ways of being urban, and new exceptions to the predominant constellations of urban form and economy are always coming to the fore. These exceptions require particular intellectual tools and technologies of navigation and habitation. What are these tools and technologies, particularly as they assume specific modes of visibility? In other words, the very process of their construction and deployment constellates and cuts across so many different sectors and walks of life that they become increasing "invisible." This may entail the relationship between dissimulation and the empirical, speculation and survival, degradation and potentiality, or the confluence and interdependencies of divergent social groups and cognitions. To return to the example of Kinshasa detailed earlier, the simultaneity of the incongruities that point to the apparent absence of effective regulation and clear market rules is also a demonstration of potentials that are difficult for conventional analysis to apprehend.

The postcolonial conundrum, then, is how to reconcile the need to demonstrate difference where the difference that would be most clearly demonstrable lies in the relatively invisible piecing together of aspects of city life—people, things, spaces—that are not conventionally thought to be associable. The convergence of actors, things, speech, and spaces that are not easily seen as having a basis to associate is something that always must be demonstrated. In other words, to use Latour's language, it must be made a matter of concern, a matter that not only opens up new discussions and explorations but mobilizes attention and publicity, assembles an audience, and generates a willingness to remain engaged and take seriously that which is demonstrated as a matter of reality (Callon 2004; Latour 2004). A demonstration does not remain within its own terms, although, as a demonstration, it is has to be more than a proposal; it must also be an indication of something that really exists. This is not simply to reiterate a matter of accepted fact but to open up a space where new connections among disparate elements and events can be debated and recognized.

If cities embody different possibilities of both inclusion and exclusion, of life and death, of power for and power against, then there is no one way to address the political challenges of urban life. This means that the demonstrations of intersections among different districts, actors, economies, and ways of life cannot simply reiterate evidence that cosmopolitan urbanity, more efficient urban governance, and the rectifying of fundamental inequalities are needed. These demonstrations must open up new questions about the unacknowledged relationships and forces acting on the city that in the long run signal something different being enacted in relationship to the cosmopolitan, to governance, and to inequality.

References

Appadurai, Arjun. 2002. "Deep Democracy: Urban Governmentality and the Horizon of Politics." *Public Culture* 14: 21–47.

Barnett, Clive. 2006. "Reaching Out: The Demands of Citizenship in a Globalizing World." In *A Demanding World*, edited by Clive Barnett, Jennifer Robinson, and Gillian Rose. Milton Keynes, U.K.: The Open University.

Bayart, Jean-François, and Romain Bertrand. 2006. "De quel 'legs colonial' parle-t-on?" ("Which 'colonial legacy' do we speak about ?"). *Espirit* (December): 134–160.

Benjamin, Solomon. 2000. "Governance, Economic Settings, and Poverty in Bangalore." *Environment and Urbanization* 12: 35–56.

———. 2008. "Occupancy Urbanism: Radicalizing Politics and Economy Beyond Policy and Programs." *International Journal of Urban and Regional Research* 32: 719–729.

Boonyabancha, Somsook. 2001. "Savings and Loans: Drawing Lessons from Some Experiences in Asia." *Environment and Urbanization* 17: 9–21.

———. 2009. "Land for Housing the Poor—by the Poor: Experiences from the Baan Mankong Network Slum Upgrading Project in Thailand." *Environment and Urbanization* 21: 309–322.

Callon, Michel. 2004. "Europe Wrestling with Technology." *Economy and Society* 33: 121–134.

———. 2008. "Economic Markets and the Rise of Interactive *Agencements*." In *Living in a Material World: Economic Sociology Meets Science and Technology Studies*, edited by Trevor Pinch and Richard Swedberg. Cambridge, Mass.: MIT Press.

Chatterjee, Partha. 2004. *The Politics of the Governed: Popular Politics in Most of the World*. New York: Columbia University Press.

Donald, James. 1999. *Imagining the Modern City*. Minneapolis: University of Minnesota Press.

Duda, John. 2008. "Naturalizing Urban Counter-Insurgency." *Critical Planning Review* (Spring): 61–76.

Grabher, Gernot. 2006. "Trading Routes, Bypasses, and Risky Intersections: Mapping the Travels of 'Networks' Between Economic Sociology and Economic Geography." *Progress in Human Geography* 30: 1–27.

Joyce, Patrick. 2003. *The Rule of Freedom: Liberalism and the Modern City*. London: Verso.

Khosla, Romi, Sikandar Hasan, Jane Samuels, and Budhi Mulyawan. 2002. "Removing Unfreedoms: Citizens as Agents of Change." Brussels: United Nations Habitat Program Liaison Office.

Latour, Bruno. 2004. "Why Has Critique Run Out of Steam? From Matters of Fact to Matters of Concern." *Critical Inquiry* 30: 25–248.

Leitner, Helga, Eric Sheppard, and Kristin Sziarto. 2008. "The Spatialities of Contentious Politics." *Transactions of the Institute of British Geographers* 33: 157–172.

Mitlin, Diana. 2002. "Addressing Urban Poverty Through Strengthening Assets." *Habitat International* 27: 393–406.

———. 2008. "With and Beyond the State—Coproduction as a Route to Political Influence, Power, and Transformation for Grassroots Organizations." *Environment and Urbanization* 20: 339–360.

Prakash, Gyan. 2008. "Introduction." In *The Spaces of the Modern City: Imaginaries, Politics, and Everyday Life*, edited by Gyan Prakash and Kevin M. Kruse. Princeton, N.J.: Princeton University Press.

Radhakrishnan, R. 2008. "Grievable Life, Accountable Theory." *Boundary* 2, no. 35: 67–84.

Roy, Ananya. 2008. "The Twenty-First-Century Metropolis: New Geographies of Theory." *Regional Studies* 43, no. 6 (July): 819–830, available at: http://rsa.informaworld.com/10.1080/00343400701809665.

Ruggiero, Vincenzo, and H. Nigel South. 1997. "The Late City as a Bazaar: Drug Markets, Illegal Enterprise, and the Barricades." *British Journal of Sociology* 48: 54–70.

Sharma, Kalpana. 2000. *Governing Our Cities: Will People Power Work?* London: Panos Institute.

Sloterdijk, Peter. 2008. "Foam City: About Urban Spatial Multitudes." Translated by Antonio Petrov. In *New Geographies* 0, edited by Neylan Turan. Cambridge, Mass.: Harvard University Graduate School of Design, pp. 136–143.

Telles, Vera da Silva, and Daniel Veloso Hirata. 2007. "The City and Urban Practices: In the Uncertain Frontiers Between the Illegal, the Informal, and the Illicit." *Estudos Avançados* 21: 173–191.

CHAPTER 11

✦ ✦ ✦

From Refuge the Ghetto Is Born: Contemporary Figures of Heterotopias
Michel Agier

In this chapter, I propose to de-center the way we look at the central question that has been asked—that of the ghetto—and change the way we think about it. On the one hand, I will not talk about ghettos in their most established and recognized forms; the American ghetto or the French "ghettoized" suburbs, for example, will be brought up only by way of comparison in the analysis. I will change our perspective by turning toward spaces set apart and separated, precarious places to which populations with uncertain futures are relegated. More generally, we will turn toward spaces I call *heterotopian*, according to the concept launched by Foucault; we usually find these spaces "somewhere else"—such as in southern countries, particularly in Africa, the Middle East, or Latin America—but they are also found nearby, for example, in the encampments of foreigners in Europe. I have studied these places in my fieldwork investigations and am striving to construct an integrated description of them.

In anchoring my reflection on these spaces that are set apart, I will not speak about ghettos themselves, since ghettos are already part of a visible—albeit marginal—urban structure; rather, I will speak of the original process of urban formation that takes root in camps, informal encampments, and all sorts of off-places that have a role as places of refuge. The empirical starting point of my reflection is therefore *refuge*, which is, first of all, a shelter created in a hostile context (war, violence, xenophobic or racist rejection) and whose permanence, under certain conditions, brings about the ghetto. It is *contemporary* logic about the ghetto that is the object of my reflection here. I am describing and analyzing this logic of a place in the making—*in process*—as *urban* logic, before considering the aspects of identity and, most of all, politics that contribute to the sedimentation and fixation of the ghetto.

The possible descriptions of this contemporary and urban logic of the ghetto in process are uncertain, as is the future of the places themselves. The specter of the place's disappearance combines with the technical precariousness of its facilities to determine the occupants' daily lives and make the atmosphere of the refuge one full of anxiety and paranoia, which give rise to a permanent tension in the occupants as they face the surrounding risks of violence, destruction, and expulsion. However, while acknowledging these characteristics of uncertainty, I will try to convey from my personal experience in refugee camps and self-settled migrant camps the conviction that I formed there: Reusing and updating the old phrase (dating from 1831) credited to the historian Jules Michelet, "the city begins with asylum"—and reciprocally, but without seeing any rigid determinism in it, "from asylum the city is born"—I set forth here the hypothesis that the ghetto begins with refuge. Thus, from the viewpoint of the empirical anchoring of my analysis, this hypothesis implies that *from refuge the ghetto is born.* For its part, *asylum* (as much as we can say that it still exists today, for example, in public immigration policies conceived as institutional hospitality resources) would be what gets refugees out of the refuge and makes the refuge itself disappear (by abandonment or transformation) by eliminating what made it necessary, whether hostility, war, or xenophobia.[1] *Hospitality* favors sharing the city as common space, whereas refuge is a shelter that one creates for oneself in the absence of hospitality. Later, in the conclusion, we will see how refuge, asylum (whose double-sidedness as an immigration policy and as a confining institution is considered in this chapter), and *confinement*—of which prison is the paragon—make up the three principal figures of heterotopia today.

I proceed according to an inductive method. Starting from a statement of fact that is indisputable in both its specific materiality and its globalization— the multiplicity and variety of the forms of encampments worldwide—I consider the transformation of these refuges (the variable of the duration is essential here) and the birth of new ghettos. This analysis illuminates a logic that is both urban and political—that is to say, I look at the ghetto from the point of view of its relationship to the city and its distance from the state, and not from an aprioristic ethnic or religious point of view.

LIVING IN REFUGE

A first observation concerns the existence today of the relatively stable and vast network of camps, waiting zones, detention centers, and encampments found along the routes of refugees, migrants, and asylum seekers. I would like to clarify this observation by drawing a quick picture of the types of encampments found around the world today.[2]

In 2008 the United Nations High Commissioner for Refugees (UNHCR) ran more than 300 refugee camps in the world. Dozens had more than 25,000 inhabitants, and some had up to 100,000. About 6 million statutory refugees (recognized as such by the UNHCR) were held in these camps, close to half of which were in Africa and a third in Asia. One and a half million people lived in the 60 Palestinian refugee camps in Middle Eastern countries run by the United Nations Relief and Works Agency for Palestine Refugees in the Near East (UNRWA), the UN agency created for Palestinians after the 1948 exodus. Lastly, camps for internally displaced persons (IDPs)—people who have fled their region but remain in their country—are the most numerous as well as the most informal. Their number is constantly fluctuating, and they are difficult to keep track of because they often come into being as self-settled camps. There are an estimated 600 such camps in the world: In the region of Darfur in Sudan alone, there were 65 camps where close to 2 million displaced persons were living in 2008. In that same year, the camp in Gereida, known for being the largest camp for displaced persons in the world, sheltered 120,000 people. In 2008–2009, aside from Sudan, four other countries—Uganda, the Democratic Republic of the Congo, Afghanistan, and Iraq—were the main countries with a high concentration of internally displaced persons in dozens if not hundreds of camps. In total, there are now over 1,000 camps in the world where at least 12 million refugees or displaced people live.[3] This figure does not include the numerous self-settled encampments, which are the most ephemeral and least visible among all of these facilities; nor does it include the 250 detainment or detention centers and waiting zones in Europe where several tens of thousands of individuals are held each year in endlessly fluctuating numbers. It is important to note that in December 2008 the European Union (EU) authorized the extension of the length of detainment to eighteen months (instead of the policy of thirty or sixty days that had been in force up until then, depending on the country). This is a radical change: It not only implies but ratifies the logistical strategy of building more centers and waiting zones, as well as taking advantage of guarantees of humanitarian aid.

Among all of the camps created today, the informal, self-settled encampment occupies a separate place. It is first a hideout on a dangerous journey, a place of refuge set up on an emergency basis in a hostile environment lacking hospitality or a refugee policy. The self-settled encampment is also often the first stop on a long exile route that can include several more stops, depending on the migratory journey. For example, if an army here, a militia there, or the police elsewhere have not yet chased off the undesirables, it is once they have established themselves in self-settled camps that humanitarian interventions usually arrive. In Africa, in particular, if the people on the move remain close to a national border without crossing it, the informal encampment may progressively be transformed into a camp for internally displaced persons by humanitarian organizations with sanitary facilities, infrastructures, or medical care. Or if a border has been crossed, the camp's occupants may be rounded up and driven by truck to an older existing camp farther away that has already been set up by the UNHCR. Later in the chapter, I return to the urban transformations of the refugee camps that settled in for the long run and have remained in place for several decades. First, however, I look at the evolution of one encampment in particular: The one that remains informal, possibly illegal, and yet tolerated.

Specifically, I examine the encampments established along the route of Afghan migrants in Europe, whether in the Greek town of Patras near its harbor or in the forest near Calais in the north of France. Places of survival, of hiding, of urban invasion—that is to say, places of refuge in the true sense of the word—become part of different forms of settlements even if they are only tolerated for several years before being destroyed and evacuated by the police. This was the case for the camp in Patras, which was created in late 1996: After having sheltered up to two thousand occupants—Iraqi Kurds first, then

Afghans (Pashtuns and Hazara)—it was destroyed in July 2009 by police bull-dozers and the fires that broke out at the same time. This was also the fate a few months later of the more than sixty barracks and shacks at an Afghan refugee camp in Calais. Called "the jungle" by its occupants, a term reused pejoratively by the press, this camp was destroyed in September 2009 by the French police. It had been set up at the end of 2002 after the evacuation and dismantling of the Sangatte refugee camp, which had existed for three years.[4]

It was in a national and European context of a "war on migrants" (Blanchard and Wender 2007) that these refuges were created. They remained in place for many years because of a power struggle between national and local authorities, on the one hand, and organizations working to protect foreigners' rights and humanitarian agencies working in them, on the other. They also endured, in part, because of the insistence, resistance, and even resiliency of their occupants, who fixed them up and settled into the urban cityscape. The idea of tolerance corresponds to this unstable product of the power struggles over the existence of these places—unwelcome, and thus not met with hospitality, the occupants are merely tolerated.[5] In Patras, over the twelve-year period from 1996 to 2009, more than one hundred shacks were constructed (and frequently rebuilt after partial destruction by the neighborhood or the police). The occupants also took over a building under construction that had been abandoned and stood vacant. This space was anchored on a vacant lot surrounded by the buildings and residences of the middle-class inhabitants of Patras. It was also located a mere twenty meters or so from the entrance to the harbor in Patras (where cargo ships leave for Italy).

Over time, after the first emergency tents and plastic tarps go up, what emerges from these precarious places are portions of cities made out of canvas and cardboard, scrap metal and plastic. Planks of wood and wire mesh stolen near the docks are used to build frames for shacks. Warehouse pallets are put on the ground to serve as insulated flooring, while the "walls" are insulated with salvaged Styrofoam boards that have been reassembled. The rest of these "walls" are made from plastic sheeting and cardboard. Bits of scavenged carpet become rugs for the floors and patchworks of material and blankets make curtains.

In the self-settled camp in Patras that lasted for twelve years, a certain "model" habitat developed: In one day a "house" (consisting of a single room of about twelve square meters) could be built by a group of workers who seemed to have been there for as long as the camp itself. (In reality, the turnover of people was very high. People generally stayed for only a couple of months, although the obstacles to travel forced a small number of migrants to remain for more than a year or two.) The shelters were often destroyed, however, and had to be rebuilt quickly: A dozen stakes became fifty-centimeter-high piles, a floor made of salvaged boards was put down, and walls were made out of cardboard covered with plastic sheeting (Agier and Prestianni 2011).

This "architecture" resembles that of refugee camps that have remained in place for several years. In these refugee camps, large tin cans are unrolled and assembled into shutters for windows, rice or bulgur sacks are transformed into curtains for doors, and branches are used to make frames for individual huts, which little by little replace the big collective tents from the first months. We return to this subject later.

In the clandestine camps in the forests of Bel Younech and Gourougou in northern Morocco, a few kilometers from the border crossing into the Spanish enclaves of Ceuta and Mililla in Moroccan territory, the occupants call their camps "the ghetto." Other such self-settled camps appeared in Liberia and Sierra Leone during the Mano River War (1989–2004). For example, Liberian exiles gathered in a self-settled camp near the village of Buedu in Sierra Leone, about fifteen kilometers from the Liberian border, before there was any UNHCR acknowledgment or control. A large number of Liberian refugees had arrived in the region in 2001, after fighting had broken out again in Liberia. More than thirty-five thousand Liberians arrived in the district of Buedu alone from towns and villages located just on the other side of the border. Even though they arrived from nearby places belonging to allied lineages, their arrival overextended the village's available residential possibilities and, to a large extent, its food supplies. The inhabitants thus asked their refugee "relatives" to settle in an empty space on the outskirts of Buedu. This turned into a self-settled camp in 2001. After two years, it had up to four thousand occupants when the UNHCR completely evacuated it by force, arguing that the camp was too close to the border and that all of the refugees had to be relocated to UNHCR camps in the center of the country (a set of seven camps between the cities of Bo and Kenma).

The Buedu camp had been strictly organized, with a camp chairman and a secretary who kept very detailed records of the arrivals and departures of the Liberians, the makeup of their families, and so on. Two years later, the secretary and the former chairman, who refused a further displacement to the UNHCR camps, had kept the record of the camp's inhabitants and still remembered them.[6] A similar type of social organization was observed by Smaïn Laacher (2007, 92–147) in the self-described "ghettos" in northern Morocco. Even though turnover is high in all of these places, the establishment of certain hierarchical responsibilities ensures their continuity and internal organization. Even if these encampments take on names like "jungle" or "ghetto," it should be noted that they sometimes take on other kinds of names. For instance, at the end of the war in Sierra Leone a group of Liberian migrants who were not recognized as statutory "refugees" by the UNHCR named their neighborhood in the town of Kailahun "Kula camp": The neighborhood was transformed into a settlement or encampment for the last waves of migrants, displaced persons, and "returnees."[7]

These are the "city planners" who appear in the refuges, shelters, and hideouts in the heart of Europe or in Africa. What they do is similar to what we call "self-building districts" in the outlying areas of towns in Africa, Asia, or Latin America: The practices and knowledge learned and experimented with in precarious social situations are comparable. With the available natural resources (dried mud, water, wood from the forest) or residual matter from manufactured products (boards, plastic sheeting, canvas bags, sheets of metal packaging, Styrofoam), a camp architecture is developed, just as favelas or slums have an architecture. In this world constructed from scraps and waste (for a good analysis, see Bauman 2004), a new technical and social framework arises in the margins and in the shadows—because life in such a place is most of all about being invisible, or at least as discreet as possible. The place finds itself cornered, even confined, in these marginal areas, stigmatized by the prejudice and stigma associated with the physical border between a fantasized interior and exterior, between "us" and "them" (Douglas 1971).

The transformation of precarious settlements takes place over time. This is particularly clear in the case of *favelas*—mentioned here briefly because favelas are spaces that were created by migrants seeking to establish a place in the margins of a city and thus anchor themselves in the city. Through local conflicts and new intra-urban displacements and returns, stability emerged on the thresholds of the city when the fragile shelters set up in the *bush* (the meaning of the word *favela*) on the outer limit of the urban perimeter were transformed on the spot. The shelters were turned into shacks just as the housing became denser and the layout of the place (streets, stairs, a tangle of lodgings) more complex. Finally, things are built with permanent materials, and multistory houses and buildings emerge.[8] Moreover, after the architectural evolution and the urban evolution, the political struggle of the *favelados* allowed a third evolution to take place and to consolidate the first two: an administrative and political consolidation when the human world residing in the favela was acknowledged. Then the favela finally gained the status of a district, official access to the city's network and grid (water, electricity, sewers, garbage collection, transportation), and municipal political recognition, including even the deliverance of urban title deeds to the residents.[9]

Each transformation of a precarious shelter into a town district (favela-bairro) is obviously much more complex than is conveyed in this brief summary; usually the process is spread out over several decades. However, it was observed as a strong urban trend in numerous Latin American countries between 1940 and 2000. At first the urban "invasions" of migrants from 1940 to 1960 were followed by their violent expulsion from the "legal" *intra-muros* city, which was itself increasing in population and extending geographically toward the exterior outskirts. These violent expulsions often expressed social rejection of the poor and undesirable migrants and political determination to keep them at a distance. The failure of these urban cleanup strategies combined in the 1990s with their political and economic costs to bring on a policy change: From then on, progressive and on-site transformations of these precarious urban zones were negotiated.

These different observations of the urban logic of encampments and favelas as self-settled and transformed places of refuge show the need for a decentering, not only a geographical one (from north to south) or an analytical one (from a built ghetto to the building of a ghetto), but also an epistemological one. It is about putting "the structure" back in its place: that of a rational construction striving to put meaning and order in a world that runs its course chaotically, or to be more specific, in the chaos of the world (in a completely undramatized sense). Structural anthropology certainly gives us the pleasant intellectual exercise of discovering the "underlying structures" in myths or social relations that, at first glance, seem disorderly (Lévi-Strauss 1958/2003);

the description of order thus produces its "reality." But when the very reality of this social order is challenged by the vitality of these spaces of disorder and spaces in the margins, not only does "the order" come into question, but so does the very reality defined by the thought of this order.[10] There is thus a transparency between, on the one hand, the theory of the relationships between order and disorder, between structure and anti-structure, and on the other hand, the politics of order and of the margins.

Thus confronted with its unplanned and even unthinkable social nature and vitality, the structural analysis takes up another role, a political one: that of an instrument of control when it has to do with founding a sovereign power and the encompassing knowledge that accompanies and legitimizes it. In this scenario, which associates structure and function, it is always necessary to flush out and expose the inevitable intrusion of "disorder" into an intellectually prestructured whole in order to firmly reestablish order—through endless programs, projects, and master plans, drawing borders and limits while the wastefulness of this policy to establish order is haphazardly confined to the margins. Then the "disorder" in the margins is exposed as a piling up of rubbish, with its repulsive stain. This *radically "other" space* and its inhabitants are then rejected as the foreigners' world that must be evacuated and removed. Thus, the most widespread images of "the jungle" in Calais in the French press a couple of days before the settlement was razed by the police in September 2009 showed heaps of garbage and dirty people in a subhuman state.

Conversely, a de-centering allows us to imagine the transformation within the disorder. When we observe the logic of human survival amid the chaos of the facilities in modern places of refuge in the form of self-organized camps, we can describe a contemporary logic of urbanization of the margins within the space of refuge that moves toward the form of the urban ghetto.

TRANSFORMING THE CAMP AND FOUNDING THE GHETTO

If we can establish a direct analytical relation between the self-settled camp— whose essential purpose is to serve as a place of refuge in a context that, owing either to hostility or to saturation, excludes the "refugees," pushing them toward the margins that at the same time it creates—and an urban evolution that takes on the form of a ghetto, this relation can also take a detour. It often includes the establishment of a plan of control and humanitarian assistance in the margins—what I call a humanitarian government of the undesirables.

To better understand this detour I examine the refugee camps in sub-Saharan Africa from the perspective of urban ethnology. My inquiry has no normative or evolutionist content. I am not examining the camps with any predefined goals for them—for example, to function as an organization of space with normative architectural forms and institutional structures. I am looking to give an account of the social creations, cultural changes, and possibly new political forms that appear when people gather together for an indefinite time in a given space, no matter what it is or whether it can be considered "a relatively permanent and dense settlement of heterogeneous individuals," according to Louis Wirth's (1938/1984, 260) definition of a city. I am also interested in understanding the transformations of space that this type of situation implies. A five-year-old camp is no longer a row of tents. It can look like a huge slum, or it can resemble an ethnographic museum where everyone tries with the resources found in the camp to reconstruct their native habitat as best as possible. The result is sometimes a colorful landscape, a hybrid formation, the blue and white UNHCR tarps covering fragile structures of branches or dried mud, canvas sacks stamped with "European Union" or "USA" used as curtains for the doors to the huts.

In northeast Kenya, around the village of Dadaab, more than 170,000 people live in a humanitarian zone formed by three nearby camps.[11] The camps, which have been in place since 1991, shelter mostly Somali refugees but also Sudanese and Ethiopians. Although the camps' total population is greater than that of the administrative district they are located in, the camps do not appear on the map of Kenya because, as spaces conceded to the UNHCR by Kenya, they are not under the country's control. Therefore, officially they do not exist, and it can be said that everything in the camps reflects this image of apparent nonexistence and lack of recognition. The lives of the refugees in the camps are lives of waiting—up to twenty years for the occupants who have been there the longest. Nongovernmental organizations (NGOs) are responsible for their food supplies, their sanitary security, and their bits of social activity. Theoretically the refugees do not even have the right to work or to move about the country. Their presence in the humanitarian space is considered a transitional stop before returning "home," a return that is largely uncertain. Whether they have gotten used to living in a corner of the camp or whether they move about the country illegally (secretly paying the police who control their passes), the refugees in Dadaab seem to have integrated the camp's space into their present living environments as the prospects of returning home decrease from year to year.

The UNHCR organized the camps' space according to a preestablished regimen. The agency built fences from prickly shrubs and barbed wire to enclose the camps and close off the "blocks" on the inside. (About 300 to 500 refugees occupy each block.) The refugees were grouped according to where they came from, by their ethnic group, or even by their clan; most were sorted by ethnic or national origin. In the beginning they all received the same plastic tarps from the HCR, a mattress, and some kitchen utensils, and they found wood around the camp to build huts using the UNHCR tarps. They salvaged tin cans donated by the United Nations World Food Program (WFP): By unfolding and assembling the tin cans, they could make gates, windows, and tables.

The fences sometimes erected between the different blocks are responses to past or potential ethnic conflicts. Certain ethnic minorities within the camp—for example, the Sudanese, the Ugandans, and some Ethiopians—tend to close their spaces off from the Somali majority. This insularity expresses fear, rejection, withdrawal, or self-defense. For example, one block is made up of Christian Sudanese from urban areas in the south, mostly young men who fled their region when they were still children or teenagers. Having traveled from one camp to another for almost ten years, they created their own space by closing off their block with high hedges and barbed wire. In this space, they re-created a micro-urban space, with everything built out of dried mud. There is a main street with a Catholic church at one end and a Protestant church for several evangelical religions at the other end. Rows of housing line the two sides of the main road; there is an area for the latrines and even a volleyball court. All of this creates an image of a miniature city neighborhood. "Equatoria Gate" is written on the entrance gate; Equatoria is the name of the Sudanese district they came from. Every night young men take turns patrolling the block's perimeter. They fear in particular their direct neighbors, who are Bantu Somalis; especially when children go from one block to the other, conflicts sometimes arise between the Christian Sudanese and this group of outcaste Somalis (who are recognized as a minority by the camp administration).

Although certain spaces are closed off and protected, inhabitants can go to other places that are more open and mixed. This can be seen in the growing number of coffee shops and video stores located away from the residential areas, along the roads and markets near the camp entrance. Here interethnic meetings take place, to the dismay of the elders from certain superior Somali clans. Other important changes include work for international organizations or in association with them. People employed by NGOs as "volunteer community workers" and those who are considered the most vulnerable in the population (widows, handicapped people, or those from the lowest castes) receive credits to undertake projects called "revenue-generating activities." All of these people, along with those who are appointed leaders of a sector,[12] create a category of refugees who may compete with or challenge the power of the ethnic elders and the values on which their power is based.

Attempts to symbolically appropriate spaces are also reflected in the names that the inhabitants have given to completely anonymous and insignificant places. In one of the three camps, for example, two little dirt alleys, each fifty meters long, are lined with stalls where certain refugees have set up micro-retail businesses selling portions of WFP food rations, vegetables (rations do not include tomatoes and onions, which are grown in plots in the blocks), and basic necessities. The refugees call this place "the town," or *magalo* in the Somali language. Leaving this "town," a stretch of sand leads toward the zones where the refugees' huts are; at least a kilometer long, this very wide lane is called "the highway."

Observation of the camps shows an emerging space that is completely unknown to researchers, as well as to new occupants upon their arrival. In a certain way, an urban ethnography of humanitarian sites can go further than is possible with a philosophy of the camps, in that it is a critical philosophy with no *subject*. Thus, Giorgio Agamben's (1997) analyses, in an exemplary manner, came to the conclusion that the camp had led to "the end of the city." However, for Agamben, policy is completely merged with the exercise of biopower (a savant technology of power acting over global "populations," in Foucaldian conception) in the spaces of exception, and the question of political subjects remains unexplored (Rancière 1995, 2000). It is precisely this critique and theoretical question that forms the foundation of the urban ethnography of the camps. They give us a glimpse of the city and policy at work in the heart of exceptional and extraterritorial spaces, which is what humanitarian sites are. The investigation of social changes, the undertaking of initiatives, and the voicing of opinions on the appropriations and transformations of a space that was initially empty—all of this reveals a transformation at work in the camps that is both urban and political and whose analysis will guide our attempts to understand the ghetto-form.

I end this survey of the camps with one last example: The Palestinian camp is the model on the horizon for research on present-day camps, and in particular all the camps that have existed for several decades in Africa and Asia.

In Lebanon, Syria, Jordan, and the Palestinian Territories themselves (Gaza and the West Bank), refugee camps have existed for more than fifty years. They offer the most convincing examples from an urban logic point of view of the slow but inevitable transition from the precarious and temporary encampment (tents in a sandy desert at the end of the 1940s while waiting for the promised return to lost lands) to today's political and urban ghetto. Throughout modern Palestinian history—from the 1948 exodus to the stabilizing of the camps during the 1950s and 1960s, the hard-line politics of the 1980s and 2000s, and the sixty or so camps and their 1.5 million inhabitants in 2010—the housing became denser and denser and was progressively built as permanent structures. As an informal economy developed, the housing was completely transformed: The basic twelve-square-meter unit built under the aegis of the UNRWA in the 1950s became structures with more and more stories piled up, since the strict and definitive perimeter prevented any horizontal expansion. Today the camps have even become a place of marginal urban polarity. In addition to the initial 1.5 million occupants (the Palestinian refugees) and their descendants, other exiles—Iraqis and Africans with no refugee status—have come to the camps in the last couple of years seeking asylum. Thus, for example, in the Chatila camp in Beirut, fewer than half of the residents today come from the original Palestinian families, and the camp has the city's highest population density.

These camps were not initially planned to last any longer than the others were. Over time, they gradually became places with a strong local identity and a hard-core political Palestinian identity. Maintaining the camps in a political and legal "place-out-of-place" has fueled the justification felt by Palestinians that returning to their land is the only solution for recognition. The camps pay a heavy tribute to the Palestinian cause. At the same time, however, the inhabitants reorganized their lives a long time ago in the interior of these spaces. A gap is continually widening between the theoretical "camp" as a spatial exception and legal and political waiting zone, on the one hand, and the continually changing urban and social realities of the Palestinian camps, on the other.[13] The camps are changing: They have been experiencing over the years an urbanization process that is similar—in its social organization, economic, and material aspects—to that seen in other urban outskirts in the world. The distinction between city-dwellers and refugees is being completely blurred by the confrontation with an urban integration that is as real as that observed in numerous urban invasions and in the Latin American favelas. All that remains unchanged is the legal status of refugees, who remain noncitizens and city-dwellers without a city. It is at this moment of being unbearably maintained apart that the ghetto becomes political and a question of identity.

CONTEMPORARY FIGURES OF HETEROTOPIAS

A specific reflection and conceptualization provides a generic description of the spaces produced by this worldwide, multiform exclusion: "Heterotopian" spaces are those "other" places, according to Foucault (1984, 752), "that are outside of all places even though it is possible to indicate their location." The fact that they can be located allows us to observe them, to spend time in them and to understand, through ethnographic investigation, their inner experience. Then, describing them according to the de-centering approach mentioned earlier, we can grasp the transformative power that emanates from them. These "off-places"—which I call *hors-lieux* in French (Agier 2008)—form first as places "outside," locations on the edges or limits of the normal order of things. This characteristic confinement gives them a certain *extraterritoriality*.[14] This extraterritoriality takes shape for refugees and displaced persons in the experience of a double locality exclusion: They are excluded from the native places that they lost through displacement, and they are excluded from the space of the "local population" where the camps or other transit zones are located. Another notion from Foucault, that of being "confined outside," is also related to heterotopia. Speaking about the "boat people" from Vietnam—the boats full of refugees from Vietnam drifting on the seas at the beginning of the 1980s—

Michel Foucault declared in a militant speech that "refugees are the first to be confined outside." And a couple of years earlier, he had said: "The ship is the heterotopia par excellence."[15] It is possible to make an inventory of "pieces of floating space" (Foucault 2009, 35). The small Nauru and Christmas Islands in the Pacific should be included in this inventory. These islands are used by the Australian government as vast detainment centers for Afghan and Sri Lankan exiles.[16] They are thus prevented from entering Australian territory in order to request asylum. Boats, islands, harbor waiting zones, detainment centers, and refugee camps—the fact that all of these off-places make up real "pieces of space" indicates the possibility of a lasting and confined settlement that is kept apart.

A certain *exception* is associated with this extraterritoriality. From the point of view of the sovereign power that creates the heterotopia, the fiction of the outside is a pure mirage with no distinctive thought or identity. Its real space is occupied by the "inside" of another state. To put it another way, those confined outside are people who are "cast out inside" within the state-space. The extraterritoriality of *outcasts* is thus defined by this constant tension between an inaccessible inside, in regard to the categories of national citizens, and the experience outside as a form of assisted and constrained living. It is through this tension or double constraint that the heterotopia builds its artifact—boat, island, or camp—into a place of confinement and a place to live that seems to be in the middle of a void but is actually always on the border of a social or national order. No matter who the actual administrators are (humanitarian, administrative, or community organization), the spaces put into heterotopia have the shared trait of removing, delaying, or suspending any recognition of political equality between the occupants of these other spaces and ordinary citizens. There is indeed a treatment of exception associated with these spaces that is permitted by the fiction of extraterritoriality. The exception can be declared in order to confine a "crisis" or a "deviation"—for example, such declarations are the basis of psychiatric clinics, prisons, and retirement homes (Foucault 1984, 756). Yet, by settling them and grouping them collectively, these other spaces turn their occupants into lasting pariahs.

Thus, an *exclusion* from the social structure is associated with legal and political exception and with extraterritoriality in regard to the organization of space and borders. Lives thus excluded carry risks, and it must be acknowledged that those who live in these spaces are not surprised by the police harassment they experience on a daily basis. We should hear the occupants' use of terms like *ghetto* or *jungle* or *outlaw town* as a form of objectification and self-assertiveness. These terms give a specific and accepted meaning (if not precisely "positive" in the sense that they would be desirable) to the places they occupy and live in. The first spaces used as places of refuge are abandoned buildings, vacant lots, forests (or fragments of forests in urban settings), and docks. The state of abandonment of these places confirms and intensifies the absence of territorial citizenship among those living there: Neither their country of national origin nor the one they are exiled in guarantees them the local exercise of citizenship in these marginal spaces. The occupants are excluded socially; however, their social exclusion does not prevent them from being occasionally and unofficially used as a workforce in the margins in certain sectors, such as in shop work, housework, construction work, and farm work.

Contemporary heterotopias are recognizable by the fact that they combine these traits of extraterritoriality, exception, and exclusion. If the situations I observed during my research in camps, informal encampments, and urban invasions fit into these heterotopias, I believe it is possible to synthesize and give shared meaning to these different spaces that are apart and in the margins, in a continuous analytical sequence, through three figures that provide the model of thought and action in today's heterotopia: imprisonment, asylum, and refuge. These figures are closely related, not only because all three represent a form of confinement for their occupants, but also because they are affected by the ambivalence that links them: Imprisonment can be found to a certain extent in asylum, and likewise asylum offers, in part, refuge. Each figure is present and incarnated in different forms of the other two spaces, and all three become, at different rates, *spaces for others*. These heterotopias evolve toward the two poles represented by the form of prison at one extreme and the urban ghetto at the other. See Figure 11.1 for a representation of these forms and figures.

The first model in this landscape is imprisonment, an extreme and, at the same time, ambivalent pole when it comes to the aims and practices of confining undesirables. In general, prison is a place of punishment and banishment, but contemporary prisons have also become spaces for managing undesirable populations. The length of imprisonment is increasing, especially the time before and after the actual penal sentence, just as the size of the prison population

FIGURE 11.1. Contemporary Principles, Figures, and Forms of Heterotopia

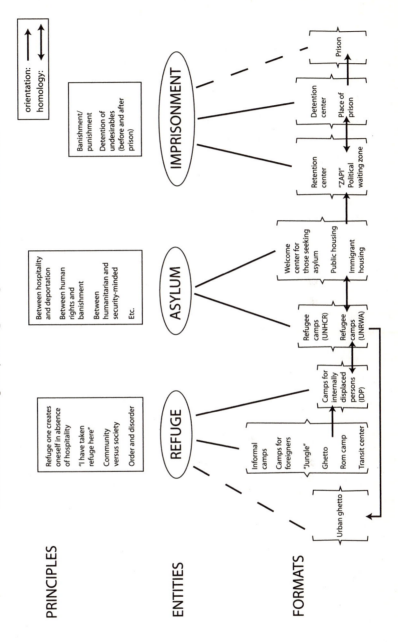

has increased in the last couple of years to such an extent that prison now appears to be one of the ways of confining undesirables—particularly in France
and the United States, two countries that imprison foreigners and social outcasts.[17] Moreover, in the context of the European—and in particular the
French—policy of detaining and expelling undesirable foreigners, prison has
become the setting for this detainment of foreigners with no papers when
there is no more room in the detention centers (Beaulieu-Garnier 2010).
Waiting zones and administrative detainment centers in France (or detention
centers in most of the other European countries), even if they are not part
of the penal network, are in fact places of administrative confinement under
police control.

The second model, asylum, is symbolically strong yet just as ambivalent.
Asylum is the welcoming portal giving access to a shared world, but it is also
a place of confinement itself where undesirable persons (the insane, the elderly,
foreigners) are set apart. The asylum we provide has the same name as the asylum that confines. Thus, the walled asylum is the implementation of an extraterritorial fiction—a re-creation of a place-out-of-place within the shared
world and even within cities. This is what unites the worlds of welcome centers
for asylum-seekers in France (Kobelinsky 2010) and UNHCR refugee camps
in Africa and Asia. It is also what explains the similar sense of uneasiness felt
by the social workers working in these centers and the humanitarian workers
in refugee camps. The welcome centers in France and similar spaces (housing
shelters, migrant homes, and so on) and the camps for refugees and internally
displaced people on other continents (Africa, Asia, South America) are located
in the intersection between two conflicting topographies: the topography
of the foreigner as an undesirable person and the topography of hospitality.
The material and social forms of this ambivalent principle of asylum create
places of tension, conflict, and unease because the actors—those who are
housed or confined there and those who work or volunteer there—are maintained in a suspended temporality and uncertainty in regard to the common
rules of their existence.

Lastly, the figure of refuge is used to justify the existence and management
of refugee camps, which, as we have seen, are largely concerned with providing asylum for banished people who are kept apart, in regard to territoriality
and law, from the society of nation-states. Refuge is also the essence of self-

organized IDP camps: the places of refuge established by internally displaced persons who have left their own residences without crossing a national border. These encampments usually witness, in a second phase, the arrival of humanitarian organizations or UN agencies, either to provide aid or to regroup the residents or move them toward other camps. Finally, informal migrant camps ("jungles," "ghettos," and so on) can be likened to the older figures of self-settlements on the margins of cities that were generally tolerated, such as camps of foreigners, Roma gypsy camps in Europe, or, going even further back in history, the caravanserai in Africa and the Orient.

Thus, it is possible to look far away from the criminalization of undesirable foreigners found in the political news today around the globe and compare self-settled off-places and other historic forms of self-settlement. In modern terminology, as in the past, we find the making of "the ghetto" as a hideout and a rest area by the side of the road, a camp in the forest, a space granted in the outer margins of the city to the merchants, migrants, and travelers who stay there without completely giving up the possibility of leaving (Simmel 1908/1984).

THE GHETTO: GLOBALIZATION'S PLACE OF BANISHMENT

After following the line from the refugee camp and other camps to the possibility of the ghetto, and after sketching the heterotopian situations that give meaning to the relations between the different forms of off-places today, I conclude by examining the political and urban qualities of the ghetto.

As soon as we accept the non-essentialist definition of the making of the ghetto, it is possible to position the ghetto analytically among the forms of socialization (including urban) in heterotopian figures—as I have done in this chapter. With such an analysis, as well as an analysis of social conditions, race relations, and sociological contexts of spaces of relegation, Loïc Wacquant (2008), for example, has come to the conclusion that a ghetto exists for African Americans, but not in the multiethnic case in France. This point is indisputable from the point of view of the effects of context and the rhetoric of relegation to the margins. Moreover, Wacquant's distinction casts an important light on the public controversies (whether about urban policy, schools, nationality, or religion) that regularly break out over the question of the working-class suburbs in France and the off-putting ghetto imagery that the elites use in regard to them. For all that, the anthropology of "city making" that I defend here cannot avoid exploring the increasing number of situations where, as we have seen in the case of the camps, social and cultural activity develop within the very limits of the places of confinement. It is an urban process whose moral quality—I'm referring to Robert E. Park's (1926/1984) "moral regions" (ethnic, racial, religious, and so on)—is constructed in relation to this urban confinement in order to justify it, consolidate it, and adapt to it. To put it differently, the apparently radical and initial otherness that is lodged there and that seems to give it distinct or inner meaning is in reality the result of the relation of conflict, rejection, and resistance between the central power and the margins it has instituted. If there is always an *urban* ghetto, it sets itself up in a political relationship. I would like to clarify this essential point, which questions any a priori vision of identity (racial, ethnic, or religious) in the ghetto-form.

When we wonder what a camp can become, there is no more enlightening way to approach this inquiry than by looking at what the camps established decades ago in the Middle East, Asia, and Africa have become. No longer completely camps, they are now a kind of ghetto, or a portion of the city: Their world, which was empty at the beginning, has been transformed and has been filled up from the interior. The initial bare space has been populated, and social, cultural, and political relations have developed within a limited if not totally closed off space. Likewise in the general history of urban ghettos, the development of an "other" life inside a relative and lasting confinement leads to identity politics, no matter what the foundation (ethnic, racial, national, religious, and so on). In the camp, a *place* is formed, and the camp itself becomes the environment where an identity strategy is born, not the contrary, as is often implied. Of course, national and ethnic groups may have existed before the camp, but it is within the camp's space that they are transformed and come up against one another or even mix together; it is there that ethnopolitical forces may come into being with new contours of identity and multiple forms of expression.[18]

Moreover, territorial and social consolidation of camps has numerous consequences for the occupants, beyond the most visible political interpretations. From this point of view, a forced displacement—closing a camp and sending its occupants away—can be just as violent as the displacement that led to the refugees' arrival at the camp. In other words, when the idea of the "anthropological place" enters the originally empty world of the off-place, then the ghetto is the urban form that accompanies it.[19] We can then wonder if a ghetto is not better than a camp insofar as the ghetto would be the camp that developed a social and cultural life in the very space of its confinement.

The black American ghetto and the French so-called ghettoized suburbs, as well as the Palestinian refugee camps, become places that we want to leave as soon as social mobility makes it possible, even if they have become places of identity or have a social, cultural, and even possibly political anchoring. To come back to the example of the Palestinian refugee camps, it is important to underscore that to be a refugee living in a camp in the Palestinian Territories—for example, in the Balata camp (25,000 inhabitants) in the city of Naplouse (300,000 inhabitants)—is to live in a city as an inferior on a daily basis. Refugee status is the inferior status in urban Palestine. There is indeed an urban form that emerges from the history of Palestinian refugees. It is the "ghettoization" of the camps (in the sense of a relative spatial, social, legal, cultural, and political confinement) that drives the refugees to leave the camps to seek social betterment or to transform themselves by developing an informal economy, but also to "localize" in the camps their identity as victims of the Naqba (the 1948 exodus) and therefore, as Palestinians, as incarnations of the wait and the absence of the "return" (Sanbar 2004).

Before exploring the otherness of the ghetto, it is useful to evoke what an Afghan migrant and leader in the Patras camp called the "outlaw city" in reference to that camp. The material and social forms of these facilities are defined as "unauthorized or unofficial" only when they are represented in relation to a state and only the state can define the distances necessary to the limits of common order. Spaces of banishment (*ban-lieu*[20]) are kept apart and on the boundaries of the city, as well as on the boundaries of the state, and are located at a distance and in the margins decided by the state itself.[21] The state localizes its own margins, its outside and its outer border, and in this outside it contains and confines any idea of otherness defined by dissection or separation, by distance, and by opposition to the city and to the state. It is within this environment that an urban as well as political evolution then becomes apparent and that the term *ghetto* comes to designate this space set apart at this moment in the process, as if it had always been there and as if it was obvious that it would be endowed with inner, natural, and essentialist meaning. The state, in its role as police, will forcefully point out the dangers of essentialism in a place that it produced, including its limits and its motives. The relation between these other spaces and the state takes on the appearance of a relation of exteriority or conflict (for example, in the French republican rhetoric of the state against "communitarianism"). Furthermore, it is always a policy of rejection and separation (incarnated by the state's violence when it defines its limits and its space of banishment) that produces the real essence of the ghetto as a political and territorial separation.

Born from refuge, every ghetto is transformed according to a dynamic that is ambivalent and contradictory, especially in relations of power: In this context, the relation to "the exterior" is always present, even omnipresent, and represented by the relation to the state's public authorities, its police, its administration, its violence, and its law and order.

It is possible that at a given moment in the world different states of this urban form in the margins exist. The internal structure of the ghetto has broken down in the United States, according to Wacquant (2008, 57–76), owing to institutional processes that chained the ghetto's history to the rest of American society, which then brought on the "hyperghetto" as a "territory of abandonment," the fruit of the growing de-proletarianization process and social alienation. I wonder if today, everywhere in the world, another history has not already taken over from local and national histories that are no longer only local or national. Certainly, the hyperghetto is locally an internal transformation of the ghetto—related, in this regard, to American social and ethnic history—but it also participates in a worldwide evolution toward the harsh fragmentation of the world and the creation, as globalization progresses, of a vast space of relegation, a generalized *ban-lieu*, a place of banishment that finds something like its limit in the hyperghetto. In the context of world history, the ghetto in its traditional form has been outstripped and redefined by an excluding globalization. Bauman (2004) explores this broader phenomenon, and in particular its use of the worldwide image of the hyperghetto to describe the extraterritoriality of the supernumeraries as "human waste" on a planetary scale. A variety of limited spaces or spaces in the limits—the intermediary spaces of transit or transition—make it possible to characterize the extent to which this place of banishment (*ban-lieu*) is socialized or urbanized in the process of globalization.

Therefore, a change of scale is necessary. In the camps and the transit zones, the "communitarian ghetto," just like the legal status of "refugee," has become a desirable possibility because it is forbidden or extremely difficult to achieve. In the meantime, their facilities are erected and perceived as spaces of rejection: It is the world of "illegal and clandestine aliens" and "nonsuit immigrants" (or "closed files," in the UNHCR term for those who no longer have the right to anything). Engin Isin and Kim Rygiel (2007, 177–209) present an inventory of a group of "abject spaces" on borders, in zones, and in camps—they lodge, in an extraterritoriality, occupants who have nothing, who are indefinite individuals worthy of the greatest scorn because they are "neither subjects nor objects, but abject." Wacquant (2009a), on his side, is developing a global way of describing spaces of "seclusion" that partly intersects with my concept of the global *ban-lieu*. Wacquant's project and mine share at least two main positions: (1) I agree totally with the necessity of a global vision of the socio-spatial fragmentation of the world, although, since I think (with, for example, Lussault 2009) that today's struggles take the form of struggles of "place," I would not put in the same category *gated communities* and *refugee camps*, which are more like two symbols of a social confrontation of places on global scale; and (2) we both defend the de-essentialization of the ghetto. Further, it seems unnecessary to treat the "ethnic cluster" apart from the ghetto and as a counterpoint to it, for the concept of the refuge as the birth in conflict of the ghetto can also be applied to other confinements—such as "ethnic clusters." Ethnic clusters can also be analyzed in the framework of an anti-culturalist anthropology.

On the world scale even more than on the local scale, the problem is essentially anti-culturalist: It is a matter of understanding the formation of the new spaces that are erected at the social and national boundaries, in limbo, and in the margins. Then we may see that the globalization of the place of banishment necessarily leads to questions about the *fiction of extraterritoriality* that creates the meaning of these off-places. The fiction of extraterritoriality takes on what Didier Lapeyronnie (2008, 189) calls, in regard to the urban ghetto in France, the "two narratives of the ghetto." Moving to a global scale, these two narratives are closely linked in the same tension that characterizes the relation of the ghetto to its state. One narrative relates the stigmatized rhetoric of rejection of everything defined as "ghettoized": These are the governmental speeches of a political, identity, cultural, or, especially in Europe, ethno-national nature that legitimize the proliferation of walls, fences, camps, and closed-off areas by endlessly inventing new forms of foreignness.

On the other hand, another globalization of the ghetto is achieved by the spreading of the word itself. The word *ghetto* has become a rallying symbol: From the self-designation used by rap groups in the interethnic working-class suburbs of France to the urban street gangs in Abidjan and the self-settled African migrant camps in the forests of Morocco near the Spanish border, *ghetto* is the distinctive personal name of an immediate response to being cast aside, of survival that is organized on the spot.

Notes

1. Later in the chapter, I return to the ambivalence of asylum, on the one hand, as a policy of hospitality as described here and, on the other hand, as a place and institution of confinement.

2. A detailed analysis of these encampments, as well as monographs on several refugee camps and an analysis of the worldwide humanitarian network, can be found in Agier (2010).

3. See UNHCR (2007); Amnesty International (2008); Agier (2010).

4. The migrants' experience of the permanence of the Sangatte camp was the subject of an investigation by Smaïn Laacher (2002), who, among others, played an important role in disclosing the phenomenon of camps of foreigners in Europe to the world of charitable organizations as well as to social science researchers. Among the works that publicized the Sangatte camp at this time, the text and photographs of Jacqueline Salmon (2002) should be mentioned. Numerous demonstrations led by activists and intellectuals followed the public controversy around the Sangatte "camp" (in official terms it was a Red Cross "humanitarian emergency reception and housing center") and its violent closure in late 2002 by Nicolas Sarkozy, then the minister of the interior of the French government. This action underscored the government's determination to evacuate, expel, and in general render invisible exiles and potential asylum seekers and immigrant workers. During this same sequence of political events at the beginning of 2003, MIGREUROP, a network of agencies that watch migration, borders, and camps in Europe (http://www.migreurop.org/), and the scientific network TERRA (Works, Studies, and Research on Refugees and Asylum, http://www.reseau-terra.eu/) were created.

5. The term *tolerated* is the official designation for the symbolic "no-man's-land" status of the Chechen exiles in Poland, who are neither integrated nor expelled, just tolerated and held in detainment centers.

6. This case and other similar ones are described and analyzed in Agier (2010).

7. The "returnees" were refugees who had settled in Guinea during the war and were repatriated in Sierra Leone by the UNHCR, often collectively and against their will.

8. For an architectural study of the habitat of the favelas, see Drummond (1981); for a historical synthesis of the favelas and their representations in Brazil, see Valladares (2006).

9. Our knowledge about this terrain is frequently updated by the studies of the political and social dynamics of favelas that are conducted regularly. On political forms in the favela in Recife, see Vidal (1998). Christophe Brochier (2009) addresses the relationship between schools and the *favelados*. On the relationship between the *favelados* in Rio and violence, see the edited collection of works in Machado da Silva (2008).

10. For a critical analysis of "the reality of the constructed reality" through knowledge and power and its distance from the "world" as it runs its course (what I call here the chaos of the world), see Boltanski (2011).

11. My field investigations of these camps date from 2000 and were the subject of Agier (2002).

12. A "sector" is a group of several blocks or clusters. There are about ten per camp, and the administration appoints two representatives for each sector, a man and a woman.

13. On the urbanity of the Palestinian camps, see Doraï (2006), Bulle (2007) and Seren (2004).

14. Zygmunt Bauman (2002) explores an increasing extraterritoriality on a planetary scale. A discussion of the meaning of places in the context of displacement and refuge can be found in Malkki (1995).

15. See "Heterotopias," radio broadcasts on France Culture, December 7–21, 1966, reprinted in Foucault (2009, 36).

16. The center on Christmas Island opened in late 2007 and has 1,400 spots.

17. Recent research shows a rise in the use of "prison for poor people" in the United States and prison for undesirables in France; there is more and more talk in these two countries of "confining" and setting people apart outside of the penal framework strictly speaking (Wacquant 2009b; Combessie 2009).

18. Liberation movements of all different kinds have been born in camps—for example, the Palestine Liberation Organization (PLO) or the Rwandan Patriotic Front (RPF) for the Tutsi resistance in Rwanda.

19. For Marc Augé (1992), the "anthropological place" is characterized by the fact that a given space is the referent and the medium of a memory, an identity, and a group of relations.

20. *Translator's note:* The author uses the term *ban-lieu*: *lieu* means "place" and *ban* is from the word *banir* ("banish"). The term for *suburb* in French is *la banlieue,* and that is where ghetto-forms are observed in France. So the author is emphasizing the link between the origin of the word and what it has come to represent in France today.

21. For Wacquant (2008), the relation to the state must be taken into account in order to understand how the ghetto can be defined. On the *ban-lieu,* or place of banishment, see Agamben (1997). For the relationship between the anthropology of the urban margins and the anthropology of the margins of the state, see Das and Pool (2004) and Agier (2009).

References

Agamben, Giorgio. 1997. *Homo sacer: Le Pouvoir souverain et la vie nue (Homo sacer: Sovereign power and bare life).* "L'Ordre philosophique" Collection. Paris: Seuil.

Agier, Michel. 2002. "Between War and City: Towards an Urban Anthropology of Refugee Camps." *Ethnography* 3, no. 3: 317–366.

————. 2008. "Quel temps aujourd'hui en ces lieux incertains?" ("What's the time today in these uncertain places?"). *L'Homme* 185–186 (L'anthropologue et le contemporain: Autour de Marc Augé [Anthropology and the contemporaneous world: Around Marc Augé]): 105–120.

————. 2009. *Esquisses d'une anthropologie de la ville: Lieux, situations, mouvements* (*Sketches of an anthropology of the city: Places, situations, movements*). Louvain-la-Neuve: Academia Bruylant.

————. 2010. *Managing the Undesirables: Refugee Camps and Humanitarian Government.* Cambridge: Polity Press.

Agier, Michel, and Sara Prestianni. 2011. *"Je me suis réfugié là!" Bords de routes en exil* (*"I took refuge there!" Roadsides in exile*). Paris: Éditions Donner Lieu.

Amnesty International. 2008. *Soudan: Les Déplacés du Darfour: La Génération de la colère* (*Sudan: Displaced in Darfur: The Generation of anger*). Paris: Amnesty International.

Augé, Marc. 1992. *Non-lieux: Introduction à une anthropologie de la surmodernité* (*Non-places: Introduction to an anthropology of supermodernity*). Paris: Seuil.

Bauman, Zygmunt. 2002. *Society Under Siege.* Cambridge: Polity Press.

Beaulieu-Garnier, Emilie. 2010. "Étrangers derrière les barreaux: La Prison dans le dispositif de mise à l'écart des étrangers indésirables en France" ("Foreigners behind bars: Prison in the disposition of undesirable foreigners in France"). Master's thesis (directed by M. Agier), École des Hautes Études en Sciences Sociales, Paris (June).

————. 2004. *Wasted Lives: Modernity and Its Outcasts.* Cambridge: Polity Press.

Blanchard, Emmanuel, and Anne-Sophie Wender, eds. 2007. *Guerre aux migrants: Le Livre noir de Ceuta et Melilla* (*War on migrants: The Black book of Ceuta and Melilla*). Paris: Syllepse/Migreurop.

Boltanski, Luc. 2011. *On Critique: A Sociology of Emancipation.* Translated by Gregory Elliott. Cambridge: Polity Press. (Originally published in French as *De la critique* in 2009 by Gallimard).

Brochier, Christophe. 2009. *Les Collégiens des favelas: Vie de quartier et quotidien scolaire à Rio de Janeiro* (Students from favelas: Neighborhood life and scholarly life in Rio de Janeiro). "Travaux et Mémoires" ("Works and Memories") Collection, no. 82. Paris: Éditions de l'IHEAL.

Bulle, Sylvaine. 2007. "Domestiquer son environnement: Une Approche pragmatiste d'un territoire confiné: Le Camp de réfugiés de Shu'faat à Jérusalem" ("Harnessing its environment: A Pragmatic approach to a confined area: The Refugee camp at Shu'faat in Jerusalem"). *Asylon(s)* 2. Available at http://terra.rezo.net/article672.html.

Combessie, Philippe. 2009. *Sociologie de la prison* (*The Sociology of the prison*). Paris: La Découverte.

Das, Veena, and Deborah Poole, eds. 2004. *Anthropology in the Margins of the State.* Santa Fe, N.M.: School of Advanced Research Press.

Doraï, Kamel. 2006. *Les Réfugiés palestiniens du Liban: Une Géographie de l'exil* (*Palestinian refugees in Lebanon: A Geography of exile*). Paris: CNRS Éditions.

Douglas, Mary. 1971. *De la souillure: Essai sur les notions de pollution et de tabou* (*Purity and danger: An Essay on the concepts of pollution and taboo*). Paris: La Découverte.

Drummond, Didier. 1981. *Architectes des favelas* (*Architects in the favelas*). Paris: Dunod.

Foucault, Michel. 1984. "Des espaces autres" ("Other spaces"). In *Dits et écrits* (*Talks and writings*), vol. 4. Paris: Gallimard.

———. 2009. *Le Corps utopique: Les Hétérotopies* (*The Utopian body: The Heterotopias*). Introduction by Daniel Defert. Paris: Nouvelles Éditions Lignes.

Isin, Engin, and Kim Rygiel. 2007. "Of Other Global Cities: Frontiers, Zones, Camps." In *Cities of the South: Citizenship and Exclusion in the Twenty-First Century*, edited by Barbara Drieskens, Franck Mermier, and Heiko Wimmen. Beirut: Saqi Books.

Kobelinsky, Carolina. 2010. *L'Accueil des demandeurs d'asile: Une Ethnographie de l'attente* (*The Reception of asylum seekers: An Ethnography of waiting*). Paris: Éditions du Cygne.

Laacher, Smaïn. 2002. *Après Sangatte: Nouvelles immigrations, nouvelles questions* (*After Sangatte: New immigration, new questions*). Paris: La Dispute/Snédit.

———. 2007. *Le Peuple des clandestins* (*Illegal people*). Paris: Calmann-Lévy.

Lapeyronnie, Didier. 2008. *Le Ghetto urbain* (*The Urban ghetto*). Paris: Éditions Robert Laffont.

Lévi-Strauss, Claude. 2003. *Anthropologie structurale* (*Structural anthropology*). Paris: Pocket. (Originally published in 1958.)

Lussault, Michel. 2009. *De la lutte des classes à la lutte des places*. Paris: Grasset.

Machado da Silva, Luis Antonio, ed. 2008. *Vida sob cerco: Violência e rotina nas favelas do Rio de Janeiro* (*Life under siege: Violence and routine in the favelas of Rio de Janeiro*). Rio de Janeiro: Editora Nova Fronteira.

Malkki, Liisa. 1995. "Refugees and Exile: From 'Refugee Studies' to the National Order of Things." *Annual Reviews of Anthropology* 24: 495–523.

Park, Robert Ezra. 1984. "La Communauté urbaine: Un Modèle spatial et un ordre moral" ("Urban community: A Model and a moral space"). In *L'École de Chicago: Naissance de l'écologie urbaine* (*The Chicago School: The Rise of urban ecology*), edited by Yves Grafmeyer and Isaac Joseph. Paris: Aubier. (Originally published in 1908.)

Rancière, Jacques. 1995. *La Mésentente: Politique et philosophie* (*The Disagreement: Politics and philosophy*). Paris: Galilée.

———. 2000. "Biopolitique ou politique?" ("Biopolitics or politics?"). *Multitudes* 1: 88–93.

Salmon, Jacqueline. 2002. *Sangatte, le hangar* (*Sangatte, the hangar*). Paris: Trans Photographic Press.

Sanbar, Elias. 2004. *Figures du Palestinien: Identité des origines, identité de devenir* (*Figures of the Palestinian: Identity of origin, identity of becoming*). Paris: Gallimard.

Seren, Hélène, ed. 2004. *L'Urbanisation des camps de réfugiés dans la bande de Gaza et en Cisjordanie* (*The Urbanization of refugee camps in the Gaza Strip and the West Bank*). Project 93 research report. Paris: GEMDEV, Programme de Recherche Urbaine pour le Développement (PRUD); Ramallah: Palestinian Diaspora and Refugee Center (SHAML).

Simmel, Georg, 1984. "Digressions sur l'étranger" ("Digressions on the stranger"). In *L'École de Chicago: Naissance de l'écologie urbaine* (*The Chicago School: The Rise of urban ecology*), edited by Yves Grafmeyer and Isaac Joseph. Paris: Aubier. (Originally published in 1924.)

United Nations High Commissioner for Refugees (UNHCR). 2007. *La Cartographie des camps de réfugiés à l'appui de la gestion et de la planification* (*Mapping of the refugee camps to support management and planning*). Geneva: High Commissioner for Refugees, Operational Services Division.

Valladares, Licia. 2006. *La Favela d'un siècle à l'autre (The Favela one century to the next)*. Paris: Éditions de la Maison des Sciences de l'Homme.

Vidal, Dominique. 1998. *La Politique au quartier: Rapports sociaux et citoyenneté à Recife (Politics in the neighborhood: Social relationships and citizenship in Recife)*. "Brasilia" Collection. Paris: Éditions de la Maison des Sciences de l'Homme.

Wacquant, Loïc. 2008. *Urban Outcasts: A Comparative Sociology of Advanced Marginality*. Cambridge: Polity Press.

———. 2009a. "Designing Urban Seclusion in the Twenty-First Century." Roth-Symonds Lecture. Reprinted in *Perspecta: The Yale Architectural Journal* (September 2010) 43: 165–178.

———. 2009b. *Punishing the Poor*. Durham, N.C.: Duke University Press.

Wirth, Louis. 1984. "Le Phénomène urbain comme mode de vie" ("The Urban phenomenon as a lifestyle"). In *L'École de Chicago: Naissance de l'écologie urbaine (The Chicago School: The Rise of urban ecology)*, edited by Yves Grafmeyer and Isaac Joseph. Paris: Aubier. (Originally published in 1938.)

CHAPTER 12

✦ ✦ ✦

Where Is the Chicago Ghetto?
Ray Hutchison

If the Black Ghetto does eventually disappear (by a process of thinning out and expanded opportunity) will a Bronzeville still remain, as a separate but well-ordered Negro community of people who prefer to maintain their own sub-culture within the larger urban setting?

—Drake and Cayton, *Black Metropolis*, 1945

The ghetto has long served as an important concept in American social science, although it is likely that most persons would more immediately connect it with inner-city black neighborhoods than with older areas of Jewish settlement. But ghetto refers first to the Venetian Ghetto, and the word ghetto is derived from the Italian *verg gettare* (to caste), used to describe the island where Jews were confined in early modern Venice (Davis and Ravid 2001). References to the term *ghetto* have become commonplace: Louis Wirth and *The Ghetto*, one of the well-known studies from the Chicago School of Urban Sociology; Kenneth Clark's *Dark Ghetto*, describing the pathological consequences of lives confined to the inner city; Ulf Hannertz's ethnographical study of the inner city in *Soulside: Inquiries into Ghetto Culture and Community*; the various histories of African-American city communities (Gilbert Osofksy's *Harlem: The Making of a Ghetto*, Allan Spear's *Black Chicago: The Making of a Negro Ghetto*, Arnold Hirsch's *The Making of the Second Ghetto*); and more recently the well-known studies by W. J. Wilson and Loïc Wacquant that refer to living conditions and life opportunities in the black ghetto.

Because much of this research refers directly or indirectly to the Chicago ghetto, and because both the earlier research of the Chicago School and the more recent research of Wilson, Wacquant, and others holds a central place in urban sociology, my starting question may seem unusual. Where is the Chicago ghetto? It must be the "Black Belt," shown in Ernest Burgess's diagram of the growth of the city, which is reprinted in every urban geography, urban sociology, and urban studies textbook. It must be Bronzeville, described by St. Clair Drake and Horace Cayton in *Black Metropolis*. Perhaps it is Woodlawn, the community that features prominently in William Julius Wilson's *When Work Disappears* and Loïc Wacquant's *Urban Outcasts*. Or maybe it is the Robert Taylor Homes, the housing projects described by Sudhuir Venkatesh in *American Project*?

But the ghetto is none of the above. By the time W. J. Wilson began the Urban Poverty and Family Life project, many of the neighborhoods described in *Black Metropolis* had lost half or more of their population, and residential areas had dispersed across other areas of the South Side. Loïc Wacquant's photographs, reproduced in *Body and Soul* (2004), and in the more recent article on the cover of *Social Psychology Quarterly* (2010), shows 63rd Street in the 1980s, many years after the last major stores had disappeared. The housing projects described by Sudhuir Venkatesh in *American Project* (2002), which played such a prominent role in *Gang Leader for a Day* (2008), no longer exist. Although there remain areas of concentrated poverty within the city of Chicago, other areas are distant from the original Black Belt areas described by Wilson. Many are located in suburban areas and other communities in the Chicago metropolitan region that are not discussed in recent research.

These observations raise a number of important questions for research in the various urban disciplines and for urban studies more generally. Because much of our understanding of the black ghetto has been built upon the Chicago experience, what does it mean if the ghetto described in earlier studies no longer exists? What if ghetto residents have been dispersed from earlier areas of concentration to other areas of the city? And if the ghetto has moved from the inner city to the suburbs, does this mean the earlier research is no longer useful? Although this chapter addresses these and other questions with specific reference to "the Chicago ghetto," it should be clear that there is a broader purpose here, asking researchers to consider more critically the revealed image of the classic ghetto and to move forward with new studies of the changing conditions of everyday life in marginalized urban neighborhoods in the emerging revanchist city of the twenty-first century.

ORIGINS OF THE CHICAGO GHETTO

Our common understanding of the American ghetto is rooted in the work of the Chicago School and later generations of scholars from the University of Chicago, although the connection between this research and more recent discussions of the black ghetto is often confused.

For Louis Wirth, the ghetto referred to the Halsted Street Ghetto, the first area of settlement for Jewish immigrants in the 1880s. But he did not use the term to refer to other areas of Jewish settlement, nor did he use it to describe other areas of the city. For Robert Park, racial colonies like Chinatown might be compared to the ghetto but were different in significant ways, and both Park and Wirth cautioned that the social processes resulting in the segregation of racial colonies appeared to be different from those affecting other ethnic groups. In Ernest Burgess's mapping of the growth of the city, the area of black settlement on the south side of the city was labeled the Black Belt. Other well-known Chicago School studies—*The Gold Coast and the Slum*, *The Gang*, and the like—more generally made reference to the Black Belt, not to a black ghetto. In Drake and Cayton's (1945) *Black Metropolis*, although there is an extended discussion of the process of ghettoization that produced the black ghetto, the African-American community was referred to as Bronzeville. It is worthwhile to follow the presentation of the ghetto in the classic work of the Chicago School more closely.

Louis Wirth's study of *The Ghetto*, published in 1928, focuses on the original area of Jewish settlement in the Maxwell Street Ghetto and describes the movement of the community out of this area to the Lawndale neighborhood to the west and the beginning of the move to the north side neighborhoods and suburbs. By the time Wirth had completed his research, there was little left of the original immigrant community, and African Americans had begun to move into parts of the Maxwell Street neighborhood. Wirth suggests that the pattern of assimilation described for the Jewish community should apply for other ethnic and racial communities but also notes the growing isolation of the black community and says that this "may be creating ghettos of non-white groups where assimilation is blocked."

The most important early study of the black population in Chicago is Charles S. Johnson's study of the Chicago race riots and the relegation of the black population to segregated neighborhoods on the South Side. In the summer of 1919 Chicago was convulsed in a two-week race riot that resulted in the deaths of more than forty individuals, most of them African Americans. The Chicago Commission on Race Relations, established later that year to study the causes of the riots and suggest ways to improve race relations, included six African-American and six white members drawn from social philanthropy and leadership positions in the respective communities. Charles Johnson, Robert Park's prized graduate student at the University of Chicago and a researcher at the Chicago Urban League, was named associate executive director (along with Graham Taylor). The resulting 672-page book, *The Negro in Chicago* (Johnson 1921) included a detailed history of the race riot (in Chapter 1) and outbreaks in other areas of the state (Chapter 2), but more importantly, documented the migration of African Americans from the South (Chapter 3) and the history of the African-American community and the development of community institutions during the first several decades of its time in the city (Chapters 4 to 8) before returning to questions about public opinion in race relations (Chapter 9) and a summary and recommendations (Chapter 10). Johnson's work provides the background for much later research, including Spear's *Black Chicago* (1967) and Massey and Denton's *American Apartheid* (1993).

The Negro in Chicago includes a series of maps showing the black population in the city in 1910 and in 1920, using data from the U.S. Census. These mappings have been adapted to better show the areas of settlement described in later research (removing the areas south of 103rd Street on the South Side). The first set of maps shows the Distribution of Negro Population mapped for each census tract in the city (Figure 12.1); the second set of maps shows the Proportion of Negroes to Total Population for each census tract in the city (Figure 12.2).

Between 1910 and 1920 the black population more than doubled, from 44,103 to 109,594 persons. As Johnson notes, "The outstanding fact concerning these data for 1910 and 1920 is that the large increase in the Negro population did not bring into existence any new large colonies but resulted

FIGURE 12.1. Distribution of Negro Population, 1910–1920

Source: Adapted from Johnson, *The Negro in Chicago*, 1921.

FIGURE 12.2 Proportion of Negroes to Total Population, 1910–1920

Source: Adapted from Johnson, *The Negro in Chicago*, 1921.

in the expansion and increased density of areas in which groups of Negroes already lived in 1910." He goes on to discuss the emergence of the South Side community:

> While the principal colony of Chicago's Negro population is situated in a central part of the South Side, Negroes are to be found in several other parts of the city in proportions to total population ranging from less than 1 percent to more than 95 percent. In some of these neighborhoods whites and Negroes have adjusted to one another; in others they have not. . . . The most striking example of "adjusted neighborhoods" is the district known as the "Black Belt." Because 90 per cent of the Negroes of Chicago live within this area, it is usually assumed that the district is 90 per cent Negro. This, however, is not the case. The area between Twelfth and 39th streets, Wentworth Avenue and Lake Michigan, includes the oldest and densest Negro population of any section of its size in Chicago. However, the actual numbers of whites and Negros living there are 42,797 and 54,906 respectively. In this area the Negro population has increased gradually and without disturbance for many years. [108–109]

The census mappings clearly articulate the areas described here, where the doubling of the black population during the decade resulted in a sizeable expansion of residential settlement to a broader area on the South Side. But the visual information adds important detail to Johnson's description: there is a second area of black concentration on the west side of the city, and the extent of the mixed areas on the South Side is much larger than later mappings of the Black Belt might lead one to think.

Ernest Burgess presents us with one of the iconic images in urban sociology and beyond; as noted earlier, the diagram (see Figure 12.3), has been reprinted in virtually every textbook in urban geography, urban sociology, and more.

The concentric zones are described by Burgess in his essay, "The Growth of the City" (1925), in the following terms:

> This chart represents an ideal construction of the tendencies of any town or city to expand radially from its central business district—on the map "The Loop" (I). Encircling the downtown area there is normally an area in tran-

FIGURE 12.3. Burgess's Concentric Zone Model, Showing Black Belt

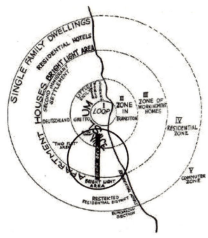

Source: Adapted from Burgess, 1925.

sition, which is being invaded by business and light manufacture (II). A third area (III) is inhabited by the workers in industries who have escaped from the area of deterioration (II) but who desire to live within easy access of their work. Beyond this zone is the "residential area" (IV) of high-class apartment buildings or of exclusive "restricted" districts of single family dwellings. Still farther, out beyond the city limits, is the commuters' zone—suburban areas, or satellite cities—within a thirty- to sixty-minute ride of the central business district.

Burgess is clear that the purpose of the map (or chart) is to show the process of neighborhood succession, a central concept for the Chicago School:

This chart brings out clearly the main fact of expansion, namely, the tendency of each inner zone to extend its area by the invasion of the next outer zone. This aspect of expansion may be called *succession*, a process which has been studied in detail in plant ecology. If this chart is applied to Chicago, all four of these zones were in its early history included in the circumference of the inner zone, the present business district. The present boundaries of the area of deterioration were not many years ago those of the zone now inhabited by independent wage-earners, and within the memories of thousands of Chicagoans contained the residences of the "best families." It hardly needs to be added that neither Chicago nor any other city fits perfectly into this ideal scheme.

Often overlooked in the discussion of Burgess's concentric zones is the placement of particular areas and sectors within and overlapping the concentric zones. These are the "moral areas" and research locales—the mosaic of social worlds—that would figure prominently in the Chicago School studies. It is clear that the ghetto—the immigrant colony of ethnic Jews—is different from the Black Belt—the area of settlement for African Americans:

> In the expansion of the city a process of distribution takes place which sifts and sorts and relocates individuals and groups by residence and occupation. The resulting differentiation of the cosmopolitan American city into areas is typically all from one pattern, with only interesting minor modifications. Within the central business district or on an adjoining street is the "main stem" of "hobohemia," the teeming Rialto of the homeless migratory man of the Middle West. In the zone of deterioration encircling the central business section are always to be found the so-called "slums" and "bad lands," with their submerged regions of poverty, degradation, and disease, and their underworlds of crime and vice. Within a deteriorating area are rooming-house districts, the purgatory of "lost souls." Near by is the Latin Quarter, where creative and rebellious spirits reside. The slums are also crowded to overflowing with immigrant colonies—the Ghetto, Little Sicily, Greektown, Chinatown—fascinatingly combining Old World heritages and American adaptations. Wedging out from here is the Black Belt, with its free and disorderly life.

Davarian Baldwin (2007) critiques Burgess's mapping of the Black Belt and the attendant description of vice and disorder in a chapter titled "Mapping the Black Metropolis: A Cultural Geography of the Stroll." Comparing Burgess's diagram with a mapping of cultural institutions that appeared in *Half Century Magazine* in 1922 and Duke Ellington's descriptions of the South Side, Baldwin notes: "Such divergent mappings of the same place and the inclusion of different figures and institutions under the same banner of respect and dignity are significant. They reveal the larger spatial transformations, class conflicts, and ideological struggles that took place in both the physical and conceptual space of the emerging black metropolis" (22).

Central to community life in *Black Metropolis* was the commercial entertainment and business district stretching along State Street from 26th to 39th Streets, popularly known as *The Stroll*. Langston Hughes (1940, 33) described this area in 1918: "South State Street was in all its glory then, a teeming negro street with crowded theaters, restaurants, and cabarets. And excitement from noon to noon. Midnight was like day." The *Chicago Whip*, a black newspaper, described the area as the "Bohemia of the Coloured Folk." River Walk Jazz (September 10, 2010) noted that "as the black population in Chicago grew, the epicenter of nightlife, known as The Stroll, moved south to the Royal Gardens ballroom on 31st and Cottage Grove, then on down to 35th Street—home of the top 'black and tan' cabarets—the Dreamland, the Sunset, and the De Luxe Cafe."

Burgess's chart includes the commercial district known as The Stroll in the area labeled as the Black Belt. Baldwin laments that the description of this area is limited to a "free and disorderly life" (Baldwin, 2007, 25). Burgess includes a district labeled "Bright Light Area" at the bottom of the Black Belt to indicate the well-known areas of entertainment within it. It certainly is interesting to think of the later interpretation and impact of Burgess's mapping if we were to simply replace the Black Belt with The Stroll. What Burgess did include in his original version of the chart, which is on display in the Sociology Department at the University of Chicago, is not The Stroll, but an area labeled *Cabarets*. This area was studied extensively by Walter Reckless (1934) in *Vice in Chicago*—but surely inclusion of this "natural area" would be disconcerting to Baldwin, because it is actually referring to the "red light" district of the city, which included a disproportionate number of establishments with black sex workers (see Blair 1999; Mumford 1997). Burgess's work-in-progress is different from the more common published version in other ways as well, particularly with respect to the portrayal of African-American communities in the city.

There are many changes in the draft of what Burgess referred to as his "chart" of ecological zones and the growth of the city. We can tell from various erasures that the concentric *zones* were originally labeled *areas* and that a number of subareas have been crossed off (such as *Pilsen* and *California* on the southwest side, originally areas of settlement for Eastern European

FIGURE 12.4. Burgess's Concentric Zone Model Showing Two Black Belts

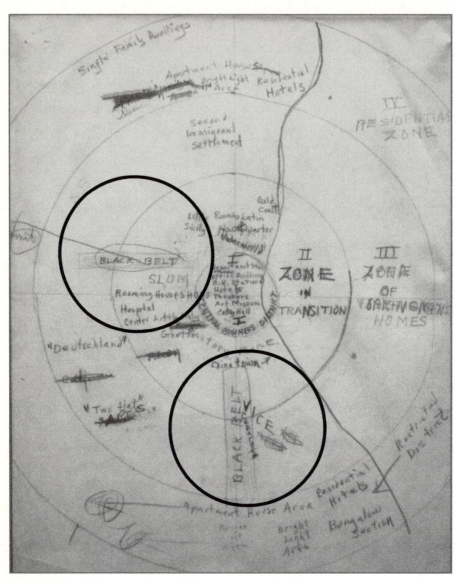

Source: Photograph by Ray Hutchison.

immigrants, now the core of the Mexican community). Few of the notations for the diverse west side of the city survived to the final version—gone are the notations for *Little Italy, Hobo, Hospital Center*, and *Rooming Houses*. And one of the more obvious differences from the final version is that Burgess originally mapped *two* distinct Black Belts in the city—one along the west side, that would not make it into the final, and the second, on the south (see Figure 12.4). This revision creates problems for later descriptions of the black community that have focused almost exclusively on the South Side. Adjacent to the South Side Black Belt, Burgess labeled the *Cabaret area*, and yet another area has been crossed out. This is the *Art Area*, corresponding to the emerging entertainment district along 35th Street—the "Bohemia of the Negro" and the center for the New Negro in Chicago (Baldwin 2007). Davarian Baldwin is correct to draw attention to the fact that The Stroll and other important areas of African-American life are not included in Burgess's final chart. Even more significant, these areas were included in the early version of the chart but then dropped from the published version, for reasons we are not likely to discover. (Unfortunately, there is no further information in the Burgess papers or Park papers in the Regenstein Collection at the University of Chicago that could shed light on the chart's development.)

E. Franklin Frazier's study *The Negro Family in Chicago* (1932) presents information on the Black Belt that delineates "ecological zones" indicating the "best areas," "mixed areas," and "worst areas" within the African-American community (Figure 12.5). As Pattillo (2003) notes, Frazier identified seven zones in the South Side of the 1920s, using measures such as percentage of southern-born heads of households, rates of illiteracy, percentage of white-collar workers, and proportion of mulattos, to determine the social class composition of each zone. The social class composition of the districts improved as one moved south from 12th Street. And although Burgess shows a very narrow Black Belt in his chart of the growth of the city (see again Figure 12.3), Frazier includes a significantly larger area in his mapping of the South Side, corresponding to the broader expanse of African-American neighborhoods shown in Johnson's earlier mappings of the 1910 and 1920 census data.

St. Clair Drake and Horace Cayton's *Black Metropolis* is recognized as a classic study of African-American life in the urban north; it also represents

FIGURE 12.5. Ecological Areas Within the Negro Community, 1920

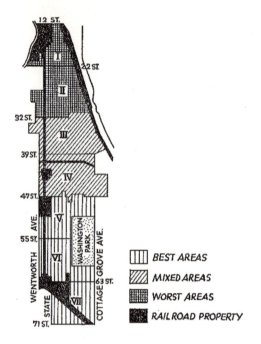

Source: Adapted from Frazier, *The Negro Family in Chicago,* 1932.

one of the most significant if overlooked works in urban sociology at mid-century. The research was directed by W. Lloyd Warner, intended as part of a series of studies of race relations comparable to the Yankee City Series, after Warner moved to Chicago. (St. Clair Drake had recently worked as a member of the research team that produced *Deep South: A Social Anthropological Study of Caste and Race,* also directed by Warner; see Wallach 2009.) *Black Metropolis* begins with a history of the African-American community in Chicago, following the general contour provided by Johnson two decades earlier, with an update of the expansion of the community in the 1920s (the decade Drake and Cayton describe as the most successful for the African-American community) as well as the effects of the Great Depression. This period is described in several recent books, including Davarian Baldwin's *Chicago's New Negroes* (2007) and Adam Green's *Selling the Race* (2007), which highlight the growing racial consciousness of the New Negro that would result in the American

Negro Conference held in Chicago in 1940. Drake and Cayton present both a history and contemporary narrative of Bronzeville, as the South Side community had come to be known and which had now expanded from 39th Street to 47th Street. The name has some significance, corresponding to references to famed boxer Joe Lewis (the Bronze Bomber) and screen star and singer Lena Horne (the Bronze Nightingale) as cultural icons of the period.

Drake and Cayton (1945) provide an extensive discussion of the internal structure of the community, documenting the culture and everyday life of various groups; this includes a 40-page chapter on the upper class titled "Style of Living," a 60-page chapter on "The Middle Class Way of Life," and two chapters (130 pages total) on the lower class titled "Sex and Family" and "The World of the Lower Class." They also present an analysis of "The Black Ghetto" in their chapter of the same name, which includes information from the then-recent report of the Mayor's Commission on Race Relations, including health and living conditions, and introduces the term *ghettoization* (taken from the report) to describe worsening conditions in the black community.

The differences among social class groups in Bronzeville are represented in physical space as well, as the mapping from the Drake and Cayton research papers demonstrates (Figure 12.6). Their diagram updates Frazier's mapping of ecological areas in the black community. On the South Side, the "worst areas" have become concentrated between 22nd and 31st Streets and in a growing area at the west edge of Bronzeville (the expansion of the Federal Street Slum), while two districts, also indicated as "worst areas," are shown on the west side in the older Halstead Street ghetto. (As noted earlier, the movement of African Americans into the Jewish ghetto had been mentioned in research predating Wirth's study of *The Ghetto*.) "Mixed areas" are the districts between 31st and 47th Streets. The "best areas" are the districts south of 47th Street. Although Drake and Cayton's mapping of Bronzeville shows a strong correspondence to the ecological areas identified by Frazier some twenty years before, there has been an expansion of the "worst areas," particularly on the west side of the city.

The extensive literature on Chicago's ethnic and racial communities includes a number of important historical studies on the growth of the African-American community as well as housing and social reform; chief among these are Allan Spear's *Black Chicago: The Making of a Negro Ghetto, 1890–1920*

FIGURE 12.6. Ecological Areas Within the Negro Community, 1940

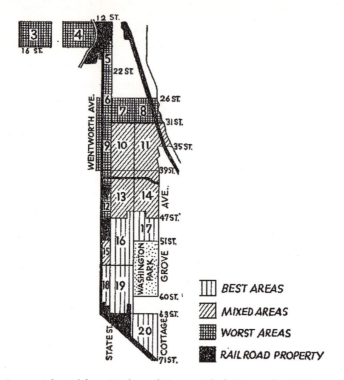

Source: Adapted from Drake and Cayton, *Black Metropolis*, 1945.

(1967); Thomas Philpott's *The Slum and the Ghetto: Neighborhood and Middle-Class Reform, 1880–1930* (1978); and Arnold Hirsch's *Making the Second Ghetto: Race and Housing in Chicago, 1940–1960* (1998). Spear (1967) follows Gilbert Osofky's (1963) study of Harlem as the first generation of ghetto studies (Hirsch 2003) that looked at the development of black ghettos in American cities. As the preceding summary of work by Johnson, Frazier, Drake and Cayton, and others indicates, Spear had excellent source material to draw from. Both Johnson (1921) and Drake and Cayton (1945) provide detailed histories of the origin of the African-American community, the race riots, and the later segregation of those in the Black Belt and elsewhere. To this earlier history Spear adds information about the "Negro elite" and the formation of what he calls "the institutional ghetto":

The rise of the new middle-class leadership was closely inter-related with the development of Chicago's black ghetto. White hostility and population growth combined to create the physical ghetto on the South Side. The response of Negro leadership, on the other hand, created the institutional ghetto. Between 1900 and 1915, Chicago's Negro leaders built a complex of community organizations, institutions, and enterprises that made the South Side not simply an area of Negro concentration but a city within a city. Chicago's tightening color bar encouraged the development of a new economic and political leadership with its primary loyalty to a segregated Negro community. By meeting discrimination with self-help rather than militant protest, the leadership converted the dream of an integrated city into the vision of a "black metropolis." [91]

Spear rejects any comparison to other immigrant and ethnic communities:

The persistence of the Chicago Negro ghetto, then, has been not merely the result of a continued immigration from the South, but the product of a special historical experience. From its inception, the Negro ghetto was unique among the city's ethnic enclaves. It grew in response to an implacable white hostility that has not basically changed. . . . No physical wall has encircled the Black Belt. But an almost equally impervious wall of hostility and discrimination has isolated Negroes from the mainstream of Chicago life. [229]

Thomas Philpott (1978) extended the now-common history to study the impact of middle-class reformers on both (ethnic) slum and (black) ghetto during the same period covered by Spear. His discussion includes important materials that have not always been included in later studies, particularly the work of settlement houses and the early efforts at housing reform that produced the Marshall Field Garden Apartments (1929) and the Rosenwald Gardens (1929). The Rosenwald Fund (established from profits of Sears and Roebuck, headquartered in Chicago) contributed millions of dollars to support Negro schools, clinics, boy's clubs, and other institutions in the black community for many years. Julius Rosenwald viewed the Michigan Boulevard Garden Apartments, as they were formally called, as a business model that would demonstrate the profitability of better housing for blacks, thereby attracting additional (white) capital into building up the Black Belt. The Chicago *Defender* hailed the project as a first step toward wiping out black belts and slums in general—even though the project was segregated—and *The Rosenwald* would become the most prestigious address in the Black Belt (Philpott 1978, 263–267).

Much of Philpott's description is of the South Side Black Belt—just as Burgess's final diagram deleted the west side Black Belt, most of the later research on Chicago's African American community focuses on the South Side neighborhoods. In a chapter titled "The Outlines of the Ghetto," Philpott describes the impact of the movement of thousands of African Americans from the South during the period known as the Great Migration (Grossman 1989) on the African-American community and includes a diagram showing the extent of black enclaves for 1900 (Map 5) and 1910 (Map 6) within political wards. The data that Philpott uses to detail the historical growth of the black population is taken from Duncan and Duncan (1957); the maps are from Burgess and Newcomb (1931):

> Sociologists at the University of Chicago (in exclusive Hyde Park, opposite the Black Belt) constructed a map based on the 1930 census to show the spatial distribution of the city's major ethnic groups. Robert Park, Ernest Burgess, and Louis Wirth, the pillars of the Chicago school of sociology, believed and taught their students to believe that all ethnic neighborhoods were—or had once been—ghettos, like the Black Belt. They viewed Negros as just another ethnic group, whose segregation was largely voluntary and would prove to be only temporary. They subjected Chicago's social life to "blinding scrutiny," but they never saw the difference between the ethnic enclave and the black ghetto. [139–141]

Although the percent of "ghettoized" population ranged from 2.9 for Irish to 61.0 for Polish, the figure was 92.7 for African Americans (Burgess and Newcomb 1931). Philpott concludes (1978, 142), "The Negro ghetto, it turns out, was Chicago's only real ghetto." Although the Chicago School sociologists did not generally use the term to describe the African-American community's area of residence (as noted above), by the time of the second-generation studies of Chicago's African-American history it had become commonplace to assert that they had in fact done so.

Philpott makes clear that much of the social reform and housing programs in the prewar period had the consequence, if not the express purpose, of maintaining segregation of the African-American community. The overlap of business interests, social reform, and segregation are clearly shown in his description of the various Rosenwald projects, and the broader program of the Metropolitan Housing Association during this period was designed to build up the Black Belt so as "to effect a sensible concentration of the negro population" (257).

Hirsch's (1998) *Making of the Second Ghetto* follows Philpott's work in the postwar decades as the city continued a policy of segregating the black community on the south and west sides through the construction of vast stretches of public housing. These developments would create the ghetto landscape more familiar to visitors to the city in the last decades of the century, with the massive Robert Taylor homes (twenty-eight 16-story buildings, completed in 1962) rising over the southern expressway, Cabrini-Green (1958–1962, twenty-eight 20-story buildings) towering above the gentrifying near northside neighborhoods, and the Henry Horner homes (sixteen buildings, 7 to 16 stories, built in 1957, made famous by Alex Kotlowitz's *There Are No Children Here* and featured in a *New York Times* opinion piece titled "What It's Like to Be in Hell," Walinsky 1987) looming near the newly built United Center on the west side. The focus on housing and housing policies is crucial for understanding the changes that would take place in the African-American community in the post–World War II period, because by the end of the century the ghetto would come to be identified with public housing.

For many readers, the Chicago ghetto may best be known from William J. Wilson's studies, beginning in the mid-1980s, designed to address claims made by Charles Murray (1984) that increased poverty and other social problems in the inner city were endemic to black culture and had been worsened by government programs. Wilson's research looked at the association between structural changes in the economy, increasing joblessness, and "ghetto-related behavior and attitudes," including children born out of wedlock, drug use, crime and gang violence, and hopelessness. The extensive research agenda involved surveys of Chicago's inner-city poor, using three surveys conducted between 1987 and 1993. In *The Truly Disadvantaged*, Wilson (1990) wrote of the link between growing joblessness and the concentration of urban poverty in the inner city. In *When Work Disappears* (1997) Wilson went further to describe how inner-city neighborhoods, caught in a downward spiral wrought by vast economic transformations in the new global economy, coupled with the withdrawal of funding and support for programs to aid the inner city, might produce the "ghetto-related behavior and attitudes" mentioned a few sentences back. These are of course the behaviors and outcomes associated with the iconic ghetto. But unlike those who blamed a "culture of poverty" among inner-city residents, Wilson emphasized that structural changes to reverse declining employment would reduce these problems.

Data for both Wilson (1997) and Wacquant's (2007) autopsy of the Chicago ghetto come from a series of studies completed by the Center for the Study of Urban Inequality in the late 1980s and through the 1990s. The first part of the research involved the Urban Poverty and Family Life Study (UPFLS), which included a survey of 2,490 inner-city residents; an open-ended survey (the Social Opportunity Survey) of respondents selected from the main survey; and ethnographic field research involving intensive case studies and participant observation in poor neighborhoods that had concentrations of either black, Mexican, Puerto Rican, or white residents. The main UPFLS study employed a stratified probability sample of African-American, non-Hispanic Mexican, and Puerto Rican parents ages eighteen to forty-four who lived in poor neighborhoods, defined as census tracts in which at least 20 percent of families had incomes below the federal poverty line in the 1980 census. The Social Opportunity Survey included a smaller group of 167 respondents from the larger survey who lived in the poorest census tract. These data sources (and others) are used to describe the world of the new urban poor. (There is further information concerning the methodology of the study in the appendix of the *When Work Disappears*.)

Wilson focuses on the ways in which everyday life in "poverty tracts" and "ghetto poverty tracts" was affected by economic and political change in the last decades of the twentieth century. Much of the book focuses on the Douglas, Grand Boulevard, Washington Park, and Woodlawn neighborhoods on the city's South Side, areas that have been decimated since World War II, all having lost more than half of their population and an even larger proportion of businesses. The increase in joblessness combined with the exodus of higher-income families have caused declining levels of social organization in communities like Bronzeville. By "social organization" I mean the extent to which the residents are able to maintain effective social control and realize their common values.

The outmigration of higher-income families and increasing and prolonged joblessness make it considerably more difficult to sustain basic neighborhood institutions. Stores, banks, credit institutions, restaurants, and professional services lose regular and potential patrons. Churches experience dwindling numbers of parishioners and shrinking resources; recreational facilities, block clubs, community groups, and other information organizations suffer too. As these organizations decline, the means of formal and informal social control becomes weaker. Crime and street violence increase as a result, leading to further neighborhood deterioration (li).

Wilson's methodological approach has been critiqued by many persons for making poverty and ghetto one and the same, although others have used similar definitions of concentrated poverty to define ghetto neighborhoods (Jargowsky 1997). Interestingly, Wilson does not engage the ghetto as a sociological concept in the way that Weaver (1948) or even Drake and Cayton (1945) did—instead, we are introduced to "the ghetto" in the introduction and to "ghetto poverty tracks" in the first chapter. The ghetto is simply there, and it is defined as "census tracts in which at least 40 percent of residents had family incomes below the federal poverty line." While Drake and Cayton spoke of ghettoization to refer to the poverty and living conditions that affected "all citizens of the Black Metropolis" (as they might write), Wilson's methodology narrows the reference to include only those areas of concentrated poverty. Wilson does not provide us with a map showing the specific census tracts that figure in the Urban Poverty and Family Life Study, but he does include a map showing the community areas in Chicago's Black Belt that is reproduced, in part, in Figure 12.7 (Wilson 1997, 13).

Wilson describes his mapping of community areas in Chicago's Black Belt as including communities that represent the historic Black Belt—but this mapping shows areas that are very different from the Black Belt in Burgess (that is to be expected, as Burgess's diagram includes only a portion of the area mapped by Frazier). It is different from that shown in the Drake and Cayton Research Papers as well, in part because the community areas mapped in Figure 12.7 are the larger community areas defined by the City of Chicago, while Drake and Cayton (following Frazier and Johnson) mapped census tracts in the city.

Sometimes overlooked in the more general discussion of the Chicago ghetto—and in the review symposiums devoted to Wilson's *When Work Disappears* and Wacquant's *Urban Outcasts*—are the ethnographic studies

FIGURE 12.7. Community Areas in Chicago's Black Belt

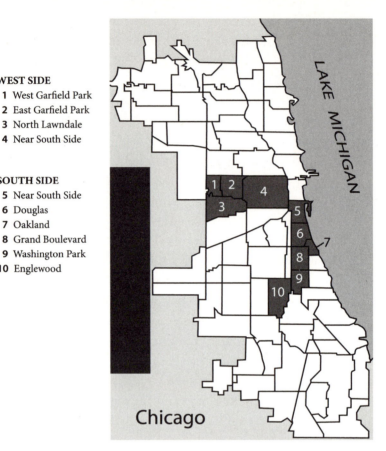

WEST SIDE
1 West Garfield Park
2 East Garfield Park
3 North Lawndale
4 Near South Side

SOUTH SIDE
5 Near South Side
6 Douglas
7 Oakland
8 Grand Boulevard
9 Washington Park
10 Englewood

Source: Adapted from Wilson, *When Work Disappears,* 1997.

produced by students from the University of Chicago within the general area that Wilson has identified as the historic Black Belt. These include Elijah Anderson's *A Place on the Corner* (1976), located along 47th Street; Mary Pattillo's *Black on the Block* (2007), about the black middle class in the North Kenwood-Oakland neighborhood; Mitch Duneier's *Slim's Table* (1994), which is set in Hyde Park, but is about African-American men from the surrounding ghetto neighborhoods; Sudhir Venkatesh's *American Project* (2002), situated in the Robert Taylor homes; and Loïc Wacquant's *Body and Soul* (2004) based on his experiences in the late 1980s at the Woodlawn Boys Club and a professional

FIGURE 12.8. Ethnographic Studies in Chicago's Black Belt

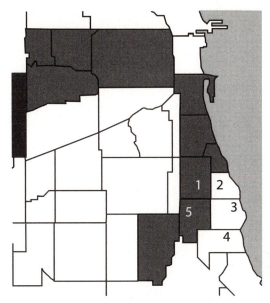

1 Elijah Anderson, *A Place on the Corner*
2 Mary Pattillo, *Black on the Block*
3 Mitch Duneier, *Slim's Table*
4 Sudhir Venkatesh, *American Project*
5 Loïc Wacquant, *Body and Soul*

Source: Adapted from Wilson, *When Work Disappears,* 1997.

boxing gym on 63rd Street in the Woodlawn neighborhood. Three of these studies (Pattillo, Venkatesh, and Wacquant) are associated with the ethnographic studies that Wilson describes as part of the larger family and urban poverty project. The approximate location of each of these studies is shown in Figure 12.8. Not surprisingly, the locations cluster around the Hyde Park (University of Chicago) neighborhood. It is important to note that to date we have no similar ethnographic research of communities on the west side of the city, or of other African-American communities on the South Side.

In a review symposium on Wilson's work, Mary Pattillo (2003) asks, "What is a ghetto? Where is the ghetto? Who lives in the ghetto?" She notes that "while William Julius Wilson and I both write about 'ghettos,' the places and people we study are not the same. Wilson's 'ghettos' are places of concentrated poverty with high rates of joblessness. My definition includes such places and adds working- and middle-class black neighborhoods as well. I argue that my usage of the term as *the entirety of the spatially segregated and contiguous black community* is more historically faithful and analytically powerful" (1046).

Pattillo's comments on the definition that Wilson brought to the Chicago ghetto highlight a concern raised by other scholars—that the area encompassed by the ghetto, as described in *When Work Disappears*, is not inclusive of the diverse African-American communities across the city (and, increasingly, the suburbs as well). She goes on to explain that although Wilson's research has focused on communities where residents have "weak attachments to the labour force, strong attachments to the welfare system, and behaviours that differentiate them from the mainstream world," she studies black nurses, public employees, receptionists, and others who "live in neighborhoods populated mostly by people like themselves, but that also house a non-trivial minority of neighbors who are unemployed, or on drugs, or in and out of jail. These generally lower-middle-class African Americans live in close proximity to the poorer areas that Wilson describes (and they even have family and friends in these places), and I call the places I study ghettos" (Pattillo 2003, 1046–1047).

In addition to the problems posed by lower-income individuals in their neighborhood, the persons that Pattillo (and others) have studied face many of the same problems as people who live in the ghetto—lack of access to quality education, limited employment opportunities, increasing threats to personal security, and the like. She asks if the boundaries of the ghetto should not be expanded to include a larger area made up of *the entirety of the spatially segregated and contiguous black community.*

Wilson's response to Pattillo raises a number of critical questions about how one defines the ghetto, which connects directly with our core question: "I have no objection to Mary Pattillo's use of an atheoretical definition of 'ghetto' to describe the unique experiences of many middle- and upper-income blacks. But her conception of the ghetto is not an adequate substitute for the theoretically derived empirical definition that I employ in *The Truly Disadvantaged* and *When Work Disappears*" (2003, 1106–1107).

Wilson argues that the definition used for the Urban Poverty and Family Life project was based on identification of census tracts that include poverty rates of 40 percent because this level would allow for an empirical test of theoretical arguments about "concentration effects" and "social isolation." He notes that these measures are "consistent with and driven by" his theoretical assumptions and that "the use of census tracts as a proxy for neighborhood allows for an empirical test of the theory not just in the neighborhoods of a given city, but in a comparison of neighborhoods in different cities" (2003, 1107). Moreover, Wilson asserts that the use of Pattillo's definition of the ghetto would mean that he would be unable to talk about the impact of concentrated poverty, concentration effects, and social isolation, and unable to articulate the consequences of these transformations on ghetto neighborhoods.

Wilson's response—that the Urban Poverty and Family Life project employed a theoretical definition of the ghetto, while Pattillo's definition is atheoretical—does not at face value make sense. We do not have documentation from other studies that a neighborhood differs significantly when the level of poverty comprises just 35 percent of households below the poverty line rather than 40 percent. Although Wilson wants to argue that his approach is superior to Pattillo's, and does so by suggesting that he has applied a theoretical argument to determine the extent of the ghetto, there is little to indicate that this is in fact a theoretical definition sufficient for establishing the boundaries of the contemporary urban ghetto, or that other definitions may not be equally valuable. And neither definition reflects the original use of ghetto to describe the legal physical segregation impressed upon Jews in early modern Venice (Davis and Ravid, 2001).

Wilson's response may be somewhat contradictory, but there are other problems in making use of Pattillo's call for a more expansive definition of the ghetto, one that would in effect define nearly all African American neighborhoods as ghettos. This problem becomes apparent if one looks at the location of black neighborhoods not for the historic boundaries of the black ghetto— as Wilson has done—but for the Chicago metropolitan area as a whole. The final set of mappings in Figure 12.9 shows the location of the black population in the Chicago metropolitan region in 1980, at the time of the Wilson research, and then in 2010, the most recent data available. These mappings were produced by the Map USA program designed by John Logan at Brown University; the darker census tracts show areas with 30 percent or more black, non-Hispanic population. The black population has expanded far beyond the boundaries of areas shown by Wilson. Even in 1980, the year Wilson uses to locate the census tracts for his research, the community extends past the historic

FIGURE 12.9. African-American Population in Chicago Metropolitan Region, 1980 *(top)* and 2010 *(bottom)*.

Source: Mappings by Ray Hutchison, from Brown University, MapUSA system. Used with permission of John R. Logan, Brown University. www.s4.brown.edu/mapusa.

Black Belt to the west and especially to the south. Mary Pattillo offered the following observation about the extent of the African-American community in 1990:

> The *worst* sections of today's black ghetto in Chicago encompass the *entirety* of the black community of the 1930s, plus a bit more. That is, Washington Park, Grand Boulevard and Douglas, in addition to some new neighbourhoods like North Kenwood, are now the poorest parts of the ghetto, with high rates of joblessness, crime, and family dissolution. Wilson narrowly focuses on this 'worst' section of the contemporary Black Belt, referring to it only as the 'ghetto'. Yet at the southern end of today's ghetto, the two small census tracts that had been the homestead of the early black middle class have been replaced by a band of contiguous community areas nearly seven miles long and seven miles wide, with a total population of more than a quarter million. Over 95 percent of the residents in this area are black, over 60 percent work in white-collar jobs, and the median family income in 1990 was above $30,000 (the Chicago median was $30,707).

In 2010 we are presented with an even larger area of black settlement. On the west side of the city, African-American neighborhoods have expanded to the boundaries of Marquette Park (the area contested by white demonstrations against Martin Luther King in the 1960s) and in some areas approach the city limits itself. On the far South Side, African-American neighborhoods have grown to encompass nearly all of the city neighborhoods and beyond, enveloping many of the inner suburbs (some of these areas have black populations dating to the 1800s, and at least one—the town of Robbins—began as a black suburb). There are other older areas of black settlement as well, notably the town of Chicago Heights on the far south side, that have provided core areas for later expansion. Many of these are communities that Harold Rose (1977) described as suburban ghettos some thirty-five years ago.

Also notable in the mapping for both 1980 and 2010 is the extensive development of black areas in the industrial towns in northern Indiana. These areas have a long history of black settlement going back to the very beginning of industrial development in Gary, Hammond, and the surrounding area. In the 1960s the town of Gary gained national attention for the election of

Richard Hatcher, one of the first black mayors in a northern city, and by the end of the century most areas of the city were solidly black. From this second urban core within the metropolitan area, the black community has spread into areas of second settlement in northwestern Indiana, solidifying the vast expanse of black neighborhoods across the southern region. In many respects these neighborhoods look like Woodlawn and other areas inside Chicago, with all of the attendant problems of vacant lots and abandoned buildings, declining urban infrastructure, abandonment by the (black) middle class, and increasing threats to personal security. Most persons would have difficulty distinguishing these neighborhoods from other areas of inner-city Chicago. When confronted with this vast expanse of territory, one must ask what is to be gained by referring to such a large area of the metropolitan region as a ghetto?

There are obvious and important differences from the time of the research reported by Wilson (1997) and again in Wacquant's *Urban Outcasts* (2007). Comparing maps for the entire 1980–2010 period shows that much of the expansion of black areas occurred in the 1990 to 2000 decade. The black population has moved further south and into the suburban areas of the city, moved further west from Englewood into Marquette Park, and grown in the northern Indiana cities of Gary and Hammond. Substantial population loss in many of the South Side neighborhoods and the demolition of housing projects in the former Black Belt areas of the South Side have further dispersed the black population. This results in a very different urban landscape from that described in earlier articles, and may signify important change in the nature of the Chicago ghetto.

WHERE IS THE CHICAGO GHETTO?

In this concluding section, I consider several scenarios that might answer our initial question.

The ghetto no longer exists. The definition of the Chicago ghetto is contested, as is the definition of ghetto more generally. For Burgess, the ghetto was represented by the Black Belt(s), shown in his model (chart) for the growth of the city (Figures 12.3 and 12.4). If we follow Wilson and consider the ghetto as areas of extreme poverty—a definition which in the first instance would connect with the Black Belt, the area of the original Federal Street Slum—then the ghetto no longer exists, because the slum has long since disappeared (replaced by public housing projects in the post–World War II era; see the following paragraphs). If we define the ghetto in a broader sense, as Drake and Cayton did in *Black Metropolis,* then we need to ask a different question. There is little of the Bronzeville area remaining (the City of Chicago has recently designated this as a historic district) and the visitor would have a difficult time squaring the existing urban landscape with the teeming community shown in photographs of the 1940s. If Bronzeville represents the ghetto, and if Bronzeville has disappeared, then the ghetto no longer exists.

The ghetto no longer exists. By the end of the 1900s, many would equate the ghetto with the housing projects of the post–World War II era. This is how many within the community identified these areas, as captured by the title of Venkatesh's study of the Robert Taylor Homes (*American Project: The Rise and Fall of a Modern Ghetto*). Over the last decade, high-rise public housing structures (as well as many other housing projects) have been demolished. In a very literal sense, these areas no longer exist, having been replaced by public parks, soccer fields, and even new condominium developments for middle- and upper-income groups. If the public housing projects represent the ghetto, and if the public housing projects have disappeared, then the ghetto no longer exists.

The ghetto has expanded. Pattillo has argued that we should extend the definition of the ghetto to include all areas of contiguous black settlement. This definition creates a number of problems above and beyond Wilson's objection that the ghetto should be reserved for those areas of high poverty concentration. As shown in Figure 12.9, if we were to expand the ghetto to include all contiguous areas of black settlement, we would have to consider all of the South Side of Chicago, much of the south suburban region, and many older communities and suburbs in northwest Indiana as well. But the expansive South Side contains many middle-class neighborhoods similar to those described in other studies of African-American suburbs (Lacy 2007), including high-status suburbs such as Homewood, Flossmor, and Olympic Fields. There are other areas that might well correspond to Wacquant's definition of the *hyperghetto,* most would conform to Marcuse's definition of the *soft ghetto,* but at some point we need to consider what is gained by referring to these areas as ghetto territory—in effect, we have then surrendered the social sciences to popular culture—all neighborhoods that are black are ghetto. To the degree that ghetto refers to all marginalized and stigmatized urban space, this may not be the direction that we want to take.

We should abandon the ghetto. In his article titled *Four Reasons to Abandon the Idea of "The Ghetto"* Mario Small discusses the various definitions that have been used for the ghetto in contemporary research. Some researchers employ a *weak conception* of the ghetto, referring back to the definition given by Weaver (1948): "a set of neighborhoods that are exclusively inhabited by members of one group, within which virtually all members of that group live." Wilson, as we have seen, uses ghetto to refer to neighborhoods with high concentrations of poverty. Small notes:

For other scholars, however, *the ghetto* is not merely a neighborhood that happens to cross a demographic threshold; instead, it is an institution (Wacquant, 1997, 343; see Marcuse, 2002, for a discussion). This *strong conception* of the *ghetto* varies from scholar to scholar, but advocates tend to support one or more of the following ideas: the *ghetto* is a particular *type* of neighborhood; it exhibits a cohesive set of characteristics, such as deteriorating housing, crime, depopulation, and social isolation, that recur from city to city; it is directly or indirectly perpetuated by either dominant society or, specifically, the state; and it constitutes a form of involuntary segregation (Small 2008, 389).

Small argues that we should abandon the use of the " hard definition" of the ghetto for four reasons: "the unacknowledged heterogeneity of poor black neighborhoods, the failure of most poor black neighborhoods to exhibit the characteristics of popular archetypes, the inadequacy of sole-entity conceptions of the state deployed in strong conceptions of the *ghetto*, and the failure of the idea of 'involuntary segregation' to capture the complexity of contemporary black urban residential patterns" (Small 2008, 389). He demonstrates that poor black neighborhoods simply do not conform to the image of the ghetto presented in much research; for example, they tend to be more dense than other neighborhoods, they do not show lower organizational density than other neighborhoods, and organizational density varies widely across poor black neighborhoods. He concludes, "Neither population nor organizational density helps distinguish poor black neighborhoods as 'types' from other neighborhoods— and both characteristics vary widely across poor black neighborhoods" (392).

AbdouMaliq Simone (2010) cautions that we cannot understand cities in the South if we look at them with models constructed through the Western sociological lens. In a chapter titled 'Reclaiming Black Urbanism,' he writes:

At the heart of city life is the capacity for its different people, spaces, activities and things to interact in ways that exceed any attempt to subsume them into cemented trajectories of social, symbolic, or semiotic relationship, and thus regulate them. Despite the many sociological studies that divide the rich from the poor, the core from the periphery, the residential from the commercial, or even the night from the day, these divides are never fixed in city life. They are, at most, a temporary snapshot of what exists at a given moment. . . . This logic of spatial organization can operate at multiple scales and becomes the vehicle to draw connections amongst various histories and modalities of territorial division. Importantly, it enables us to connect late colonialization in Africa and Asia, particularly, to the remaking of cities in the Western metropolis.

There are many ways to experience the Chicago ghetto. One may start with Loïc Wacquant on 63rd Street, just a block or two from the new law school buildings at the University of Chicago—the area is described by Wacquant (2007, 53) as a "lunar landscape"—and head west along 63rd and 67th Streets from Woodlawn to the borders of Marquette Park, a distance of some five miles. The urban landscape is unflinching: block after block, mile after mile of vacant lots, city blocks that once had a mix of single-family homes, two-flats, apartment buildings, and mixed commercial structures, now reduced to just one or two buildings per block. One may start at the same spot in Woodlawn and travel the same distance south and encounter a similar urban landscape. But too much of urban sociology and urban studies is about the city; continue further and you will encounter the same landscape in the inner suburbs. Turn to the east and you will discover similar areas in Gary. For some reason, *ghetto* does not seem to be such a useful concept, and even *hyperghetto* fails to capture the depth and extent of despair and lost opportunity. As Simone has realized, the usual social science models and methods no longer apply.

To make sense of this new urban landscape, I have come to think of these areas of Chicago (and one can encounter similar areas in St. Louis, Detroit, and other cities) as part of an emerging Fourth World. I use *Fourth World* to refer to those persons, groups, and places left behind in the process of globalization and the resulting changes in urban and regional systems—including urban and nonurban spaces in both developed countries and the developing world. The term has an interesting history, emerging from an earlier discourse that highlighted the social exclusion of indigenous and minority populations, then highlighting increased poverty and social exclusion in Third World nations, and now finding its place within urban studies with new and significant meanings (Hutchison 2009).

Manuel Castells (2000) offered important revisions to Wallerstein's schema of a stable core, semiperiphery, and peripheral countries. Wealth accumulation based on networks and flows of information has replaced manufacturing and trade. Within the new international division of labor there is an emerging Fourth World that Castells describes as "the poorest of the poor," where increasing inequality and social exclusion have produced conditions of life characterized by polarization, poverty, and misery throughout the world. In the new "network society," areas that do not have access to or control of significant economic or political interests are excluded from opportunities that would allow them to engage with the emerging informational economy. The exclusion of both people and territory from participation in the network society means that entire countries, regions, cities and neighborhoods are left behind, denied the social rights of citizens for participation in the major economic, occupational, and social opportunities that might enable them to pursue an acceptable standard of living within their society. One's position relative to the world system and thus one's opportunity to participate fully as a citizen of that system no longer depends upon residence within a specific nation state, but instead is defined by the position that the region and urban area occupies within the world system.

In the 1980s we spoke of deindustrialization and wondered about the impact of the new global economy on urban communities (the theme of Wilson's research in *When Work Disappears*). Now we think in terms of globalization and have begun to realize that one consequence of the global transformation has been the emergence of a Fourth World within developed nations, whether this be the banlieues of the French city; the inner-city ghettos of the American city; or, with the collapse of the global manufacturing economy, entire regions that evolved within the Fordist mode of production (such as Detroit and other cities that developed around the concentration of automobile manufacturing).

In his discussion of cities in the South, Simone (2010, 8–10) notes:

> In cities there are two senses of time in operation. In other words a city is
> full of memories about what has taken place in the past, and those memories

also include a certain amount of imagination—of hopes and dreams that the city could have been a certain kind of place, but that never seemed to reach fruition.

We can extend this notion to other forms of "double time." For example, in some cities that were strongly marked by a colonial history, the time of the "postcolonial" finds many of their inhabitants believing that it is impossible to make a life in the city in which they live. Conditions are too uncertain and fluid, or they are certain that they have no prospects to make a life within them.

At the same time, but in a different time, there is the persistence of colonialism, but now as something which comes to characterize the conditions in most any city. For example, the spatial segmentation and highly particularized interests and ways of doing thing things that seemingly cannot be integrated, and which once characterized life in the colonial city, are true of cities everywhere.

Certainly one would want to caution against applying a discussion of cities in the south to Chicago—but the case may be compelling. Does our post-industrial world, our new global economy, correspond in some way to the postcolonial? Do the marginalized urban spaces of the contemporary city correspond in some way to the postcolonial condition? Do our cities include that same amount of imagination, of hopes and dreams that the city could have been a certain kind of place, but that never was realized? When traveling through the new Fourth World of Chicago, it may be worthwhile to remember that the persons who occupy this new urban landscape are the children and grandchildren of those came to the city from the Deep South with hopes and dreams and aspirations for a new and better life. Many of these hopes and dreams were realized. Many were not.

There is yet another answer to our beginning question. It would seem that the ghetto is nowhere—with respect to those areas identified in the urban landscape of the iconic ghetto of the late twentieth century—and everywhere at the same time. Academic scholarship has compared favelas in Brazil and neighborhoods in the United Kingdom and shantytowns in Africa to "the American ghetto" and too often has labeled these marginalized urban spaces as ghetto-like or perhaps even real ghettos when in fact they have independent origins rooted in earlier colonial regimes and systems of economic discrimination. Popular culture has created yet another version of the American ghetto and exported the sights, sounds, and physical culture to the corners of the earth—the ghetto is everywhere even as we try to dismantle the systems of urban apartheid that created the American ghetto and subjected generations of African Americans to conditions rivaling those of urban slums in many developing nations. Dismantling the folk concept of the ghetto may prove even more difficult.

References

Anderson, Elijah. 1976. *A Place on the Corner.* Chicago: University of Chicago Press.

Baldwin, Davarian L. 2007. *Chicago's New Negroes: Modernity, The Great Migration, and Black Urban Life.* Chapel Hill: University of North Carolina Press.

Blair, Cynthia M. 1999. *Vicious Commerce: African American Women's Sex Work and the Transformation of Urban Space in Chicago, 1850–1915.* Cambridge, Mass.: Harvard University Press.

Burgess, Ernest W. 1925. "The Growth of the City: An Introduction to a Research Report." In Ernest W. Burgess, Robert E. Park, and Roderick McKenzie (eds.), *The City.* Chicago: University of Chicago Press.

Burgess, Ernest W., and Charles Newcomb. (eds.). 1931. *Census Data of the City of Chicago.* Chicago: University of Chicago Press.

Castells, Manuel. 2000. "The Rise of the Fourth World" (pp. 348–354). In David Held and Anthony McGraw (eds.), *The Global Transformations Reader: An Introduction to the Globalization Debate.* Cambridge: Polity Press.

Clark, Kenneth. 1967. *Dark Ghetto: Dilemmas of Social Power.* New York: Harper & Row.

Davis, Robert C., and Benjamin Ravid, eds. 2001. *The Jews of Early Modern Venice.* Baltimore: Johns Hopkins University Press.

Drake, St. Clair, and Horace Cayton. 1945. *Black Metropolis.* Chicago: University of Chicago Press.

Duncan, Otis Dudley, and Beverly Duncan. 1957. *The Negro Population of Chicago: A Study of Residential Succession.* Chicago: University of Chicago Press.

Duneier, Mitchell. 1994. *Slim's Table: Race, Respectability, and Masculinity.* Chicago: University of Chicago Press.

Frazier, E. Franklin. 1932. *The Negro Family in Chicago.* Chicago: University of Chicago Press.

Green, Adam. 2007. *Selling the Race: Culture, Community, and Black Chicago, 1940–1955.* Chicago: University of Chicago Press.

Hannertz, Ulf. 1969. *Soulside: Inquiries into Ghetto Culture and Community.* Chicago: University of Chicago Press.

Hirsch, Arnold R. 1998. *Making the Second Ghetto: Race and Housing in Chicago 1940–1960.* Chicago: University of Chicago Press.

———. 2003. "Second Thoughts on the Second Ghetto." *Journal of Urban History,* 29, no. 3 (March): 298–309.

Hughes, Langston. 1940. *Big Sea: An Autobiography.* New York: Knopf.

Hutchison, Ray. 2009. "Fourth World." In *The Encyclopedia of Urban Studies.* Thousand Oaks, CA: Sage Publications.

Jargowsky, Paul A. 1997. *Poverty and Place: Ghettos, Barrios, and the American City.* New York: Russell Sage Foundation.

Johnson, Charles S. 1921. *The Negro in Chicago.* Chicago: University of Chicago Press.

Kotlowitz, Alex. 1991. *There Are No Children Here: The Story of Two Boys Growing Up in the Other America.* New York: Knopf Doubleday.

Lacy, Karyn R. 2007. *Blue-Chip Black: Race, Class, and Status in the New Black Middle Class.* Berkeley: University of California Press.

Massey, Douglas, and Nancy Denton. 1993. *American Apartheid: Segregation and the Making of the Underclass.* Cambridge, Mass.: Harvard University Press

Mumford, Kevin J. 1997. *Interzones: Black/White Sex Districts in Chicago and New York in the Early Twentieth Century.* New York: Columbia University Press.

Murray, Charles. 1984. *Losing Ground: American Social Policy, 1950–1980.* New York: Basic Books.

Osofsky, Gilbert. 1963. *Harlem: The Making of a Ghetto, Negro New York 1890–1930.* Chicago: Ivan R. Dee Publisher.

Pattillo, Mary. 1999. *Black Picket Fences: Privilege and Peril Among the Black Middle Class.* Chicago: University of Chicago Press.

———. 2003. "Extending the Boundaries and Definition of the Ghetto." *Ethnic and Racial Studies,* 26, no. 6 (November): 1046–1057.

———. 2007. *Black on the Block: The Politics of Race, Class, and Status in the New Black Middle Class.* Berkeley: University of California Press.

Philpott, Thomas Lee. 1978. *The Slum and the Ghetto: Neighborhood Deterioration and Middle-Class Reform, Chicago, 1880–1930.* New York: Oxford University Press.

Reckless, Walter. 1934. *Vice in Chicago.* Chicago: University of Chicago Press.

Simone, AbdouMaliq. 2010. *City Life from Jakarka to Dakur: Movements at the Crossroads.* London: Routledge.

Small, Mario Luis. 2008. "Four Reasons to Abandon the Idea of 'The Ghetto.'" *City & Community:* 389–396.

Spear, Allan H. 1967. *Black Chicago: The Making of a Negro Ghetto, 1890–1920.* Chicago: University of Chicago Press.

Venkatesh, Sudhir. 2002. *American Project: The Rise and Fall of a Modern Ghetto.* Cambridge, Mass.: Harvard University Press.

Wacquant, Loïc. 2007. *Urban Outcasts: A Comparative Sociology of Advanced Marginality.* Cambridge, UK: Polity Press.

———. 2004. *Body and Soul: Notebooks of an Apprentice Boxer.* New York: Oxford University Press.

———. 2010. "Urban Desolation and Symbolic Denigration in the Hyperghetto." *Social Psychology Quarterly,* 73, no. 3 (November): 1–5.

Walinsky, Adam. 1987. "What It's Like to Be in Hell." *New York Times.* December 4. http://www.nytimes.com/1987/12/04/opinion/what-it-s-like-to-be-in-hell.html

Wallach, Jennifer Jensen. 2009. "New Introduction." In *Deep South: A Social Anthropological Study of Caste and Race.* Columbia: University of South Carolina Press.

Weaver, Robert C. 1948. *The Negro Ghetto*. New York: Russell & Russell.

Wilson, William Julius. 1990. *The Truly Disadvantaged: The Inner City, the Underclass, and Public Policy*. Chicago: University of Chicago Press.

———. 1997. *When Work Disappears: The World of the New Urban Poor*. New York: Vintage Books.

———. 2003. "Race, Class and Urban Poverty: A Rejoinder." *Ethnic and Racial Studies,* 26, no. 6 (November): 1096–1111.

Wirth, Louis. 1928. *The Ghetto*. Chicago: University of Chicago Press.

ABOUT THE CONTRIBUTORS

Michel Agier is an ethnologist and anthropologist. He is a reasearch director at the Institute of Research for Development (IRD) and a member of the Center for African Studies at L'École des Hautes Études en Sciences Sociales (Paris). He has conducted anthropological research in cities of Africa and Latin America, with a focus on the dynamics of social change and urban cultural movements, mostly in marginal areas, while also studying social groups in precarious and marginalized situations. His current studies focus on how groups reconstruct their identities after having been forced into in exodus because of wars, and in particular, living in refugee camps. On these subjects he has published *L'invention de la ville: banlieues, townships, invasions et favelas* (Paris, 1994); *Aux bords du monde, les réfugiés* (Paris 2002; published in English as *On the Margins of the World: The Refugee Experience Today*); and more recently, *Gérer les indésirables: Des camps de réfugiés au gouvernement humanitaire* (Flammarion, 2008; published in English as *Managing the Undesirables*).

Elijah Anderson is the William K. Lanman Jr. Professor of Sociology at Yale University and one of the leading urban ethnographers in the United States. His publications include *Code of the Street: Decency, Violence, and the Moral Life of the Inner City* (1999), winner of the Komarovsky Award from the Eastern Sociological Society, and *Streetwise: Race, Class, and Change in an Urban Community* (1990), winner of the Robert E. Park Award from the American Sociological Association for the best published book in the area of urban sociology. His classic sociological work, *A Place on the Corner* (1978) was published in a second edition in 2003. Anderson's most recent ethnographic work, *The Cosmopolitan Canopy: Race and Civility in Everyday Life*, was published by W. W. Norton in March 2011.

Ernesto Castañeda received his doctorate in sociology from Columbia University in New York. He is assistant professor of sociology in the Department of Sociology and Anthropology at the University of Texas at El Paso, located on the U.S./Mexico border. He has been a visiting scholar at the Sorbonne and the Institute of Political Studies/Sciences

Po in Paris. He has conducted ethnographic fieldwork in New York City, Paris, Barcelona, and in many cities and communities in Algeria, Mexico, and Morocco. His dissertation takes a transnational perspective, comparing Latino and Muslim immigrants in the U.S. and Europe and analyzing the relation between the contexts of reception, including the avenues available for political voice, and the political inclusion of immigrants and minorities. His research is forthcoming in "International Migration," and a number of edited volumes.

Alan Gilbert is professor emeritus at University College London. He holds a first-class honors degree in social sciences from Birmingham University and a doctorate from the London School of Economics. The University of London recently awarded him a doctorate in literature and he has been elected to the Academy of Learned Societies for the Social Sciences. Dr. Gilbert has published extensively on housing, poverty, employment, and urban problems in developing countries, particularly in Latin America. He has authored or co-authored ten books, edited four others, and written more than 150 academic articles on these topics. He has acted as an adviser to several international institutions including the Inter-American Development Bank, UN-HABITAT, United Nations University, UNESCO and United Nations Population Fund, the Woodrow Wilson Center, and the World Bank.

Bruce D. Haynes is associate professor of sociology at the University of California, Davis, and an authority on race, ethnicity, and urban communities. His recent publications include *Red Lines, Black Spaces: The Politics of Race and Space in a Black Middle-Class Suburb* (2005). This work draws upon historical documents, unpublished census records, in-depth interviews, and participant observation, and shows that a combination of systematic factors led to the racialization of an otherwise typical suburban community. His research interest includes suburbanization, the black middle class, racialization and racial formation, and community organization. He is currently writing a book about black Jews in America.

Ray Hutchison received his MA and PhD in sociology from the University of Chicago and is chair of Urban and Regional Studies at the University of Wisconsin-Green Bay. He is coauthor (with Mark Gottdiener) of *The New Urban Sociology* (2010) and editor of *The Encyclopedia of Urban Studies,* a two-volume encyclopedia from Sage Publications (2009). With Bruce Haynes, he is the editor of the *Ghetto Symposium,* published in *City & Community* in 2008. Dr. Hutchison is also series editor of *Research in Urban Sociology* (Emerald Press) and author of more than thirty chapters, articles, and monographs on street gangs and gang graffiti, race and ethnic relations, and urban recreation. In 2008 Dr. Hutchison received the International Award of Merit from the Del Bianco Foundation in Florence, Italy, for his work with students and faculty in the international programs sponsored by the foundation.

Christina Jackson is a doctoral candidate in sociology at the University of California-Santa Barbara. In fall 2011, Jackson started as a Frederick Douglass Teaching Scholar at Bloomsburg University where she teaches and continues to work on her dissertation. Jackson earned her BA in sociology at Temple University and her MA in sociology from University of California-Santa Barbara.

Nikki Jones is an associate professor of sociology at the University of California-Santa Barbara. She is the recipient of the New Scholar Award from the American Society of Criminology's Division on Women and Crime (2010) and Division on People of Color and Crime (2009). She is also a William T. Grant Scholar (2007–2012). Jones has published three books, including the sole-authored *Between Good and Ghetto: African American Girls and Inner City Violence* (2010); *Fighting for Girls: New Perspectives on Gender and Violence,* with Meda Chesney-Lind (2010); and *Sociologists Backstage: Answers to 10 Questions About What They Do,* with Sarah Fenstermaker (2011). Her writing also appears in peer-reviewed journals in sociology, gender studies, and criminology. Jones earned her PhD in sociology and criminology at the University of Pennsylvania.

Peter Marcuse, an urban planner and lawyer, is professor emeritus of urban planning at Columbia University in New York. Born in Berlin, Germany, he has lived and practiced civil rights and labor law in Waterbury, Connecticut. His fields of research include city planning, housing, homelessness, the use of public space, the right to the city, social justice in the city, globalization, urban history, the relation between cultural activities and urban development, and most recently, solutions to the mortgage foreclosure crisis. Before Germany reunited, he taught in both West and East Germany; he has also taught in Australia, the Union of South Africa, Canada, Austria, and Brazil and has published widely. His most recent books, with Ronald van Kempen, include *Globalizing Cities: A New Spatial Order?* (1999), *Of States and Cities: The Partitioning of Urban Space* (2002), and with multiple co-editors, *Searching for the Just City* (2009).

Brasilmar Ferreira Nunes received his MA in urban and regional planning from the Federal University of Rio de Janeiro and his PhD in sociology from the Université de Picardie, France. He has a postdoctorate from the Centre de Sociologie Européenne at the École des Hautes Études en Sciences Sociales (2001). He authored two books on Brasília, one on the construction of the everyday (2000) and one on Brasília's embodied fantasy (2004). Dr. Nunes also organized two other volumes and published more than thirty journal articles and several book chapters on urban planning, housing, urban space and heterogeneity, youth, and sociability. He is currently full professor at Universidade Federal Fluminense, where he also chairs its MA program in sociology, and holds a Scientist of Our State fellowship from FAPERJ, Rio de Janeiro.

AbdouMaliq Simone is an urbanist with particular interest in emerging forms of social and economic intersection across diverse trajectories of change for cities in the Global South. Simone is presently professor of sociology at Goldsmiths College, University of

London, and visiting professor of urban studies at the African Centre for Cities, University of Cape Town. His work attempts to generate new theoretical understandings based on a wide range of urban practices generated by cities in Africa, the Middle East, and Southeast Asia, as well as efforts to integrate these understandings in concrete policy and governance frameworks. His publications include *In Whose Image: Political Islam and Urban Practices in Sudan* (1994), *For the City Yet to Come: Urban Change in Four African Cities* (2004), and *City Life from Jakarta to Dakar: Movements at the Crossroads* (2009).

Leticia Veloso received her MA and PhD in anthropology from the University of Chicago and did postdoctoral work in sociology at IUPERJ in Rio de Janeiro. She organized a volume on consumption and sociability (2009) and is currently finishing a monograph on children, violence, and rights in urban space. Dr. Veloso has published in English, Portuguese, and Spanish. She is the author of several articles and chapters on children and youth, poverty, urban violence, urban imaginaries and sociability in Rio, citizenship, and consumption. She is a professor at Universidade Federal Fluminense, where she teaches in its MA in sociology and MA and PhD programs in sociology and law. She holds a "Young Scientist of Our State" fellowship from FAPERJ, Rio de Janeiro.

Loïc Wacquant is professor of sociology at the University of California, Berkeley, and researcher at the Centre Européen de Sociologie et de Science Politique, Paris. A MacArthur Foundation Fellow and recipient of the 2008 Lewis Coser Award of the American Sociological Association, his research spans urban relegation, ethnoracial domination, penalization, embodiment, and social theory and the political of reason. His books have been translated in some dozen languages and include *Urban Outcasts: A Comparative Sociology of Advanced Marginality* (2008), *Punishing the Poor: The Neoliberal Government of Social Insecurity* (2009), *Prisons of Poverty* (2009), and *Deadly Symbiosis: Race and the Rise of the Penal State* (forthcoming).

Sharon Zukin is professor of sociology at Brooklyn College and the Graduate Center of the City University of New York. She has a PhD from Columbia University and specializes in modern urban life, urban culture, and real estate, with a focus on New York City. She is the author of *Naked City: The Death and Life of Authentic Urban Places* (2010), *The Cultures of Cities* (1996), *Loft Living: Culture and Capital in Urban Change* (1999), and other books and articles on urban themes. Professor Zukin received the Robert and Helen Lynd Award for career achievement in urban sociology from the Community and Urban Sociology Section of the American Sociological Association, and the C. Wright Mills Award from the Society for the Study of Social Problems for *Landscapes of Power: From Disneyland to Detroit* (1991).

INDEX

Abandoned ghetto defined, 35

Absolut Brooklyn vodka labels, 137–138, 139 (fig.), 154

Across 110th Street (film), 111

Afghans
in detainment centers, 279
in refugee camps, 268–269

Africa. *See* Cities of Africa; *specific places*

African-American middle class
gentrification and, 144, 145
ghetto evolution and, 34
leaving ghettos, 131, 180
white out-migration and, 23

Against the Wall: Poor, Young, Black and Male (Anderson), 101

Agamben, Giorgio, 276

Agnew, Spiro, 47

Amara, Fadela, 170

American Project (Venkatesh), 294, 312, 313 (fig.)

Anderson, Elijah, 85–86, 101, 311, 313 (fig.)

Annals of the American Academy of Political and Social Science, 132

Anti-ghettos
banlieues as, 16–18, 18–19 (fig.)
ethnic diversity and, 18, 18 (fig.)
examples of, 18
upward mobility and, 17–18, 18 (fig.)

Anti-immigrant policies
Calais, France encampments, 268, 269
effects of, 54
in Europe, 53–54, 268–270, 285
Patras, Greece encampments, 268–270, 285
See also Banlieues; Detainment/detention centers

Arnson, Cynthia, 209

Asylum as heterotopia, 280, 281 (fig.), 282

Auyero, Javier, 210

Bachelard, Gaston, 1

Baldwin, Davarian, 300–301, 303, 304–305

Baldwin, Ruth Standish, 120

Banlieue
as anti-ghetto, 16–18, 18–19 (fig.)
concentration of groups/laws and, 168
definitions/descriptions, 16–17 (fig.), 164
development of, 170–171, 175, 178
diversity and, 183, 283–284
HBMs/administration, 166–167, 169
history/changing boundaries of, 165–168
housing needs/housing projects and, 166–167
inequalities/education zones, 168–169

Lapeyronnie on, 16–17 (fig.), 287–888
relationship with Paris and, 171
relative deprivation and, 164
riots (2005), 176–177
spatial segregation with, 177–179, 183–184
subjective orientation and, 16–17 (fig.)
unemployment and, 175, 179–180
U.S. suburb vs., 163–164

Barrio, El (Spanish Harlem), 111–112, 113–114, 182–183

Barrios
of poor, 181–182, 183–184, 196, 200
of rich, 198

Becker, Howard, 104–105

Bedford-Stuyvesant (New York City)
blogs on, 150–152
description/image, 138, 140–143
Do the Right Thing and, 126, 137
gentrification and poor, 138, 143–148, 149–155
history, 140–142
redlining, 140
stores/services and, 141–142, 149–150

Bedford-Stuyvesant Restoration, 143–144

Belafonte, Harry, 114

Berlusconi government (Italy), 20 (fig.)

Beurs, 177–178
Beveridge, Andrew, 125
Biggie Smalls, 147
Biggs, Walter, 146
Black Belt (Chicago), 299
   (fig.), 302 (fig.) 299-303
*Black Chicago; The Making of
   a Negro Ghetto, 1890–
   1920* (Spear), 293, 296,
   305–306
Black Manhattan (Johnson),
   112, 114
Black Metropolis (Drake and
   Cayton), 293, 294, 295,
   301, 303–304, 306
   (fig.), 311, 312 (fig.),
   313 (fig.), 318
Black Panthers/murder of
   leaders, 47, 48
Black Picket Fences (Pattillo),
   311, 313 (fig.)
Blockbusting, 122, 141
Blokland, Talja, 159
Bloods. *See* Kinshasa
Bloodsaw, Daryl, 145–146
Body and Soul (Wacquant),
   294, 312, 313 (fig.)
Bonner, Luc, 17 (fig.)
Boundaries. *See* Social
   boundaries
Bradhurst, Samuel/home,
   116, 117
Brathwaite, Fred (Fab Five
   Freddy), 128
Brazil
   CEBRAP, 202–203, 204
   immigrants and, 232
   industrialization/urbaniza
      tion of, 232
Bronzeville, Chicago, 13, 14,
   21, 293, 294, 295, 304–
   305, 318–319
Brunner, Kareem, 129
*Bubbling Brown Sugar: A
   Musical Journey
   Through Harlem*
   (Broadway hit), 114
Bumpurs, Eleanor, 126
Burakumin, Japan, 2, 8–9, 194
Burgess, Ernest
   Chicago Black
      Belt/mapping, 20–21,

294, 295, 298–301, 299
   (fig.), 302 (fig.), 303,
   308, 311, 318
concentric zones of, 298–
   301, 299 (fig.), 302
   (fig.), 303
ghetto concept, 226
Bush, George H. W.
   administration, 49, 52
Bush, George W.
   administration, 49, 52

Calais, France, encampments,
   268-269
Caldwell, Christopher, 173
Carrion, Adolfo, Jr., 51
Carter administration, 49
"Caste cities," 10
Castells, Manuel, 322
Cayton, Horace, 8, 293, 294,
   295, 303–305, 306, 311,
   318–319
CEBRAP and Brazilian
   sociologists, 202–203,
   204
Central Park, 117, 118
Chávez, Hugo, 209, 210
Chicago
   African-American
      population
      (1980/2010), 316 (fig.)
   American Negro
      Conference (1940),
      304–305
   "Black Belt(s)," 294, 295,
      298, 299 (fig.), 300, 301,
      302 (fig.), 303, 307–
      308, 309, 311, 312 (fig.),
      315, 317, 318
   Bronzeville, 13, 14, 21, 293,
      294, 295, 304–305,
      318–319
   communities in Black
      Belt, 311, 312 (fig.)
   concentric zones of
      Burgess, 298–300, 299
      (fig.), 301, 302 (fig.),
      303
   critiques of Burgess's
      mapping, 300–301, 303
   "ecological" areas, 304
      (fig.), 306 (fig.)

Fourth World areas, 321–
   322, 323
housing projects, 294,
   307–308, 309, 312, 319
   maintaining segregation
      in, 309
Negro population
   distribution/proportio
   n (1910–1920), 296,
   297 (fig.), 298
poverty statistics, 50–51
race riots (1919), 296
Stroll, The, 300, 301, 303
Chicago ghettos
   abandoning idea of, 319–
      320
   ethnic neighborhoods vs.,
      20–22
   Jewish ghetto, 226, 293,
      295, 300, 305
   joblessness and, 309–311,
      314, 322
   as "no longer existing,"
      318–319
   origins, 295–296, 297 (fig.),
      298–301, 299 (fig.), 302
      (fig.), 303–315, 304
      (fig.), 306 (fig.), 312
      (fig.), 313 (fig.), 316
      (fig.), 317–318
   question on where ghetto
      is, 318–324
   research overview, 293–
      295
Chicago school of urban
   sociology
   Chicago ghetto and, 226,
      293, 294, 295, 299–300,
      308
   ghetto concept, 3–4, 9,
      226–227, 229, 293, 294,
      295, 308
   maps, 304 (fig.), 305, 306
      (fig.)
   "natural areas" 3–4, 9,
      162–163, 299–300, 299
      (fig.), 301, 302 (fig.),
      303
   See also specific individuals
Chicago Whip, The, 301
Chicago's New Negroes
   (Baldwin), 304–305

"*Chicano*" term, 178
Cities
  blaming the poor and, 248–249
  definition/description, 245–246
  efforts to organize the poor and, 248–249
  livelihood notion/experimentation and, 254–261, 262–263
  networks of interactions, 246–247
  profit vs. human use, 34
  residents' skills/resistance and, 247–251
  vulnerability of the poor and, 249–251
Cities of Africa
  dependence on others, 252–253
  modern activities and, 251–252
  survival and, 251
Civil Rights Act of 1968 (United States), 48
Civil rights movement (United States)
  about, 4, 5, 23, 46, 47, 141
  legislation and, 48, 85, 87
  marketization of the ghetto and, 46
  riots and, 68, 141
Clark, Kenneth, 4, 8, 121, 126–127, 138, 293
Clinton administration, 49
Clustering defined, 41
Coca-Cola Company TV commercial, 128
Cockburn, Alex, 46–47
Cohen, Patricia, 132
Communitarian ghetto, 228, 286, 287
Concentric Zones. *See* Burgess
"Cosmopolitan canopies," 112
Cosmopolitan Canopy, The (Anderson), 85–86
Culture and Civility in San Francisco (Becker and Horowitz), 104–105

"Culture of poverty" term/blame, 130–132, 181, 201–202, 203, 216, 310

Daniels, Cora, 198
Darfur, Sudan camps, 267
Dark Ghetto: Dilemmas of Social Power (Clark), 4, 121, 126, 138, 293
Davis, Sammy, Jr., 114
De Reid, Ira, 132
De-spatialization of the ghetto
  definitions/description, 33, 35, 36, 38, 41
  in ghetto development, 52–53, 54
  militancy of residents and, 37
  as new, 38
  population/pattern changes, 55
  spatial boundaries and, 55
  Third World and, 37–38
Debré law (France), 167
Definitions, about, 41–42
Dendoune, Nadir, 177
Denton, Nancy, 44
Detainment/detention centers
  in Australian, 279
  in France, 282
  as ghettos, 24–25
  as heterotopias, 267–268, 279, 281 (fig.), 282
  length of detainment, 268
  statistics on, 268
Dilution of the ghetto
  definition, description 33, 36, 41
  shift to weak ghetto, 54-59
  urban renewal and, 33
  See also Gentrification
Discursive redlining
  description, 92–93
Fillmore neighborhoods and, 85–86, 92–99, 103, 104, 105–107
  newcomers to neighborhood and, 85–86, 92–96

official redlining vs., 86
  See also Redlining
Dispersed ghetto
  definition, 35
  See also De-spatialization of the ghetto
Do the Right Thing (film), 126, 137
Dodson, Howard, 128
Douala, Cameroon, 252–253
  economy, 252-253
  expansion, 253
Drake, Clair, 8, 293, 294, 295, 303–305, 306, 311, 318–319
Du Bois, W. E. B., 8, 120
Duneier, Mitch, 311–312, 313 (fig.)

Economic crisis and ghettos/poor, 55, 58, 71
Ellington, Duke, 117, 146, 300
Employment programs use of poverty, 56
Empowerment zone programs
  description, 49–50, 59
  effects, 50, 57, 59
  Harlem and, 128, 146, 148–149, 152
  Upper Manhattan Empowerment Zone (UMEZ), 146, 148–149, 152
Enclave defined, 40, 45
Ethnic homogeneity
  as property of the ghetto, 18, 18 (fig.)
Ethnosurveys, 174–177, 179, 180 (fig.)
European Union (EU), 268
European "war on migrants", 269
Exclusion defined, 36

Fair Employment Practices Commission (United States), 87
Favelas
  as *bairro* (district), 272
  creativity/existing conditions and, 234, 236, 241, 242–243

Favelas (continued)
 description, 14, 164, 196,
  201, 232–233
 etymology, 271–272
 future possibilities, 37
 ghetto (U.S.) comparison,
  225–226, 233, 235,
  240–242
 history, 235, 272
housing alternatives/
  self-construction,
  234–235, 237, 241,
  242–243
 housing shortages and,
  233
 "housing needs" vs.
  "demand for a home,"
  236–237, 238
 image of, 201, 235, 237–
  238, 239, 240
 informal market and, 232,
  236, 237
 integration of, 204
 landslides and, 238
 linking person to place,
  202
 location priority, 235–236,
  239
 population statistics, 241
 as racially/ethnically
  mixed, 193–194, 233
 real estate economic
  dynamics, 233
 removal of residents/
  effects, 238–239
 samba, 234
 state relationship, 234, 237,
  238–240, 242
Fillmore District (San
  Francisco)
 bed-and-breakfast owner
  on, 83–85
 before World War II, 86–
  87
 blacks and the war
  effort/work, 87–88
 combating poverty
  concentration/effects,
  107
 condo sales/discursive
  redlining, 96–99
 crime/violence, 90, 91

discursive
  redlining/effects, 85–
  86, 92–99, 103, 104,
  105–107
 as ghetto after World War
  II, 88–90
 highway dividing
  neighborhood, 89
 image of young black
  men/effects, 99–103,
  105, 106
 newcomers/warnings and,
  91–99, 103, 104
 outsiders/media image of,
  84–86, 92–96, 99–103
 public housing projects
  and, 89, 93–94, 95, 100,
  104
 redlining in, 84
 "renewal" and, 90–91
 slum removal and, 84, 89
 targeted policing
  strategies, 100–101, 106
 vegetable gardens and, 84
Fillmore Center (San
  Francisco)
 about, 91
 online
  conversation/discursiv
  e redlining on, 93–96
Folk concept of ghetto, 1, 324
Foucault, Michel, 127, 265,
  278–279
Fouchaux, Henri, 117
Fourth World
 description, 321-322
 in Chicago, 323
France
 Calais encampments, 268,
  269
 centralization of
  power/resources, 169
 ethnography of Champs-
  Élysées, Paris, 171–174
 Paris housing needs, 170
 use of "Arab" term, 177–
  178
 See also Banlieue
Frazier, E. Franklin., 8, 132–
  133, 303, 304 (fig.), 305,
  306, 311
Fresh Air, NPR, 119

Gang Leader for a Day
  (Venkatesh), 294
"Gated communities," 15, 38,
  60, 164, 198, 213, 214,
  217, 287
 See also Segregated
  (voluntary)
  communities
Gates, Henry Louis, Jr., 45–46
Gay ghetto, 23
Gaza
 as spatial ghetto, 42
 See also Palestinian
  refugee camps
Gentrification
 class differences and, 56
 definition/description, 36
 displacement/eviction of
  ghetto with, 33, 36, 56,
  57
 Harlem/effects, 128–130,
  133–134, 138, 145–147,
  148, 152, 154–155
 locations of, 37, 56–57
 replacement with, 56
 social/economic changes
  and, 56–57
 soft segregation with, 57
 when/where occurs, 37
 See also Weak ghetto
Gereida camp, Darfur, 267
Ghetto, The (Wirth), 3–4, 9,
  293
Ghetto
 addressing power
  relationships and, 105–
  106, 107, 126–127, 184,
  284–286
 adolescent girls behavior
  in, 103–104
 America before Civil War
  and, 45
 assimilation vs.
  dissimilation, 21–22
 assumption of assimilation,
  226, 227–229
 causation, 106, 130–132,
  180, 181, 323–324
 causes of poverty and, 106,
  130–132, 140
 changes overview (since
  1995), 37

closure and control, 5–10
concept and definitions,
    39, 44, 130, 133–134,
    159, 178, 179–180, 185,
    191, 194, 231, 231–232,
    283–284, 287, 319, 321
conceptual confusion, 2, 3,
    14–15
culture/identity and, 7,
    10–11, 11 (fig.), 12
current patterns of
    control, 47–52
de-spatialization, 52–53, 54
degradation, 50–53, 182,
    228, 230, 231, 240, 241,
    286
describing other
    community types, 5,
    23, 198–199, 227
dilution of and shift to
    weak ghetto, 54–59
drug trade, 74-76
employment, 68-69, 70-71
formal economy, 68-69,
    70-71
and ethnic
    neighborhoods, 21-22,
    22-23
etymology, 6, 162, 293
Europe's ethnoracial
    division and, 5
exploitation of a group,
    43–44
functions of, 7, 39, 162
future of, 34, 35, 38–39
as globalization's place of
    banishment, 283–288
hard ghetto, 35, 39-40, 41,
    45
history and, 227
hyperghetto, 19 (fig.), 23–
    24, 179, 230–232, 241,
    286, 319
iconic ghetto, 67–68,
    69–73, 74–77, 80–81
iconic ghetto, burden of
    image for blacks, 67–68,
    80–81
iconic ghetto, economy of,
    69–72, 74–77
immigrants, competition
    with, 70, 73, 78

informal economy, 74–77
institutional parallelism, 7,
    8, 15–16
late nineteenth century/
    Progressive era, 3
living conditions and life
    chances, 1, 15, 161, 183,
    184, 293, 309–311, 322
marketization and, 33–34,
    41, 59–60
neutralization of the
    ghetto, 36, 37,
organization and, 229–231
outsiders/media image of,
    67, 68, 80–81
poverty assumption, 12–14
properties overview, 18
Giuliani Rudolph/
    administration (New
    York City), 53, 56, 146
Goetz, Bernie, 126
González de la Rocha,
    Mercedes, 208
Gravier, Jean-François, 169
Great Migration, 3, 86, 119–
    121, 125, 141, 181, 308
Greenwood, Monique, 149–
    150
Grossman, Ben, 150
Gulags (Russia) as ghettos, 24
"Gypsies" (Roma people), 19–
    20 (fig.), 172–173, 283

Haine, La (film), 178
Hamilton, Alexander/home,
    116
Hampton, Fred, 47, 49
Harari, Fred, 129
Hard ghetto
    definitions/description,
    35, 39–40
    disappearance of, 35
    as spatialized method of
    social control, 40
Hard ghettoization defined,
    41
Harlem, New York City
    in 1960s, 111–115
    1964 riots, 113
    1970s–1980s, 125–128, 143
    African drumming circle
    and, 129–130

boundary changes, 124–
    125
disappearance of hard
    ghetto, 60
drugs/crime and, 114,
    125–126, 127, 138, 143,
    145–146
empowerment zone
    programs and, 128,
    146, 148–149, 152
Freddy's Fashion Mart fire,
    129
gentrification/poor
    people, 128–130, 133–
    134, 138, 145–147, 148,
    152, 154–155
"ghetto" term and, 132–133
guns and, 126
"health food stores," 127
health problems and, 112
history overview, 117–118,
    140, 141–142
homeownership push and,
    58
housing (early 1900s),
    121–122
image, 125–126, 138, 142
living conditions, 60
neighborhoods of, 111–112
North River sewage
    treatment plant and,
    112, 133
police brutality/corruption,
    126, 127
race riot (1935), 124
shift to weak ghetto, 42
stores/services and, 141–
    142, 148–149
tourism/effects, 58, 150
Harlem Renaissance, 13, 45–
    46, 123–124, 132–133,
    140, 147
Harvey, David, 37, 38
Hatcher, Richard, 317
Haussmann, Baron, 165, 169
Haynes, George Edmund,
    120–121, 131, 132
Heterotopias
    asylum as, 280, 281 (fig.),
    282
    as "confined outside," 278–
    279

Heterotopias *(continued)*
definition/description,
265, 266, 279–280, 281
(fig.)
extraterritoriality of, 276–
277, 278–280, 282, 286,
287
imprisonment as, 280, 281
(fig.), 282
refuge as, 280, 281 (fig.),
282–283
types of, 266, 280, 281
(fig.)
use as workforce, 280
Vietnam "boat people"
and, 278–279
See also specific types
Hippler, Arthur, 88
Hirata, Daniel Veloso, 247
Hirsch, Arnold, 306, 309
Home to Harlem (McKay),
123
Homeownership
effects on "weak ghetto"
residents, 58
subprime mortgage
market/vulnerable
people, 58
Hoover, Herbert,
Commission on Home
Ownership, 58
Horne, Lena, 305
Horowitz, Irving Louis, 104–
105
Housing
blockbusting, 122, 141
discrimination tests
results, 60
Low-Income Housing Tax
Credit (LIHTC), 50
vouchers/effects, 50
See also Ghettos; Harlem,
Homeownership;
Redlining
Howard, Ebenezer, 166–167
HUD (Department of
Housing and Urban
Development), 84
Hughes, Langston, 11 (fig.),
140, 146, 301
Hurston, Zora Neale, 123
Hutton, Bobby, 47

Hyperghetto, 19 (fig.), 23–24,
179, 230–232, 241, 286,
319

"I Love New York" campaign,
28
Iconic ghetto, 67-68, 69-
73,74-77, 80-81
Identification and social
boundaries, 160–162,
161 (fig.)
IDP camps. *See* Internally
displaced persons
(IDPs) camps
Immigrant enclaves
ethnic succession with,
184
image, 159
Inner-city adolescent girls
relational isolation, 103,
104
situational avoidance,
103–104
"Inner city" as "ghetto," 57
Internally displaced persons
(IDPs) camps
countries with most, 267
Darfur, Sudan camps, 267
definition/description, 267
self-settled encampments
transformation to, 268
International Monetary Fund
(IMF), 208
Iraqi Kurds, 268–269

James, Kéry, 179
Jargowsky, Paul, 130, 132
Jay-Z, 147
Jazz Singer, The (film), 123
Jeanneret, Charles-Edouard
(Le Corbusier), 167
Jeffries, Jim (Great White
Hope), 119
Jewish ghettos
Chicago, 226, 293, 295,
300, 305
closure and control, 6–7
culture/identity and, 7, 10
distinctive garb and, 6, 162
Frankfurt's ghetto, 10, 13
as hard ghettos, 39, 40
history, 6–7, 227

Nazis and, 24, 40, 162
oppression in, 44
in Venice, 6, 14, 127, 131,
162, 183, 191, 227, 293,
315
Johnson, Charles S., 296, 297
(fig.), 298
Johnson, Jack, 119
Johnson, James Weldon, 13,
112
Johnson, Lyndon, 4, 48, 214–
215

Kassovitz, Mathieu, 178
Kechiche, Adbellatif, 178–179
Kennedy, Robert F., 143
Kerner Commission, 4, 48,
52–53
Kinshasa, Congo
Bloods background, 254
Bloods "work" at market,
254–261
economy, 252–253
Kasa-Vubu description,
253–254
market
interactions/activities,
254–261
King, Martin Luther, 47
King, Rodney, 47, 48, 53, 68
Koch, Edward, 143, 144–145
Koreans in Japan
as ghetto/ethnic cluster
hybrid, 22–23
as "Kimchee Towns," 22

Laacher, Smaïn, 271
LaGuardia, Fiorello, 140–141
Lamont, Michèle, 160
Lapeyronnie, Didier, 16–17
(fig.), 287–888
Latin America
absence of ghettos,
191–192, 194–196,
196–197, 198–199,
200–201
black populations and,
193, 193 (fig.)
debt crisis/effects, 207–208
drug trade/violence and,
196, 211, 212, 213–214,
215, 217

education, 205–206, 211,
  212, 214
gated communities of the
  rich, 198, 213, 217
ghetto definition and,
  191–192, 199, 200–201
governance/politics, 207–
  209, 215–216
growth rates, 200 (table),
  204, 206
heterogeneous
  populations, 193, 195–
  196
immigration/emigration
  and, 194–195
indigenous populations of,
  195 (fig.)
inequality increase, 212–
  213, 216
informal economy, 199,
  201, 203, 204, 206, 206
  (table), 207, 209
"marginality" concept and,
  202–203, 204, 210,
  211–212
neoliberalism and, 207,
  208, 209, 210, 215–216
positive view of
  urbanization, 203–
  204
poverty, 196-197, 197
  (table), 207 (table),
  209–210
protests/revolution and,
  205–206, 208–209
quality of life
  improvements, 205–
  206, 210–212
rich barrios, 198
self-help settlements, 196,
  197, 198, 199–200, 203,
  204–205, 213
"ruralization," 201
urbanization/effects, 195,
  199–204
villas miserias, Argentina,
  14, 164, 200, 235
See also favelas
Law of the Ghetto, The
  (Bronner), 17 (fig.)
Lee, Spike, 126, 137, 139 (fig.),
  147

Leeds, Anthony/Elizabeth,
  235, 236
LeNoir, Rosetta, 114
L'Esquive (film), 178–179
Lewis, Arthur, 202
Lewis, Joe, 305
Lewis, Oscar, 181, 201–202,
  205
Liberian refugees/camps
  Buedu camp, Sierra Leone,
    270–271
  Kailahun "Kula camp," 271
  Mano River War (1989–
    2004) and, 270
  social organization, 270–
    271
  UNHCR and, 270–271
Life chances and place of
  residency, 1, 15, 161,
  183, 184
Locke, Alain, 124
Low-Income Housing Tax
  Credit (LIHTC), 50

Making the Second Ghetto
  (Hirsch), 306, 309
Malcolm X, 47
Mangin, William, 204, 205
Marcuse, Peter, 194, 213, 319
Market ghetto, 40
  See also Weak ghetto
Marketization (of the social
  control function of
  space)
  definitions/description,
    33–34, 41
  from formal to informal
    policies, 34
Martin, Larry D., 145, 146,
  147
Marx/Marxism, 200–201,
  202, 203
Massey, Douglas, 44
Maupassant, Guy de, 165
Mayer, Margit, 54
McKay, Claude, 123
Michelet, Jules, 266
Migrant ghettos of Western
  Europe
  racism and, 44
  See also specific types
Molnar, Virag, 160

Moynihan, Daniel
  Patrick/report, 130, 131
Murray, Charles, 309

National Urban League, 59,
  120, 122
Negro Family in Chicago, The
  (Frazier), 303, 304 (fig.)
Negro in Chicago, The
  (Johnson), 296, 297
  (fig.), 305–306
"New Negro," 119–120, 123,
  303, 304–305
New York City
  draft riots (1863), 118–119
  poverty statistics, 50–51
  welfare policy changes
    effects, 56
  See also specific places
New York magazine, 148
New York Times, 119, 128,
  132, 140, 142, 145, 146,
  147, 150, 154–155, 309
Nigger Heaven (Van Vechten),
  123
Nixon administration, 47, 48,
  53
North, Oliver, 127

Ogbu, John, 115–116
Osofsky, Gilbert, 118, 130, 133

Palestinian refugee camps
  Balata camp, 285
  favelas comparison, 278
  inferior status of, 285
  informal economy, 277, 285
  locations/history, 277, 285
  occupants, 277
  statistics on, 267
  transformation to ghetto,
    277–278
  UNRWA and, 267, 277,
    281 (fig.)
Park, Robert E., 9, 20–21, 226,
  284, 295, 296, 308
Pataki, George, 146
Patras, Greece encampments,
  268-269, 269-70, 85
Pattillo, Mary, 303, 311, 313–
  315, 313 (fig.), 317, 319
Payton, Philip A., 122

Perales, José Raúl, 209
Perlman, Janice, 193, 204, 211, 212, 296
Philpott, Thomas, 306, 307, 308–309
Pilat, Ignatz, 117
Piñera, José, 209
Place on the Corner, A (Anderson), 311, 313 (fig.)
"Places of stigma," 160, 178, 185
See also specific types
Porter, Michael, 57
Poverty
  blaming victims, 130–132, 181, 201–202, 203, 215, 216, 217, 248–249, 310
  "culture of poverty," 130–132, 181, 201–202, 203, 216, 310
  desire to develop models/stereotypes on, 198
  life chances and place of residency, 1, 15, 161, 183, 184
  in places that are not ghettos, 13–14
  using to enforce "good" citizenship, 56
  See also specific places
Powell, Morris, 129
Price, Gordon, 172
Prison
  analogy with ghettos, 24–25
  detainment of foreigners and, 282
  effects on ghetto resistance, 53
  as heterotopia, 280, 281 (fig.), 282
  statistics on African Americans/Latinos, 53

Race riots
  Northern-style race riots, 118, 119
  Southern-style riots, 118–119
  See also specific riots

Racism, 35, 40, 44, 59–60
  See also Ghettos; *specific types of ghettos*
Randolph, Philip, 87
Rasmussen, Karl, 133
Reagan administration, 49
Reckless, Walter, 301
Redlining
  Bedford-Stuyvesant, 140
  Fillmore neighborhoods and, 84
  See also Discursive redlining
Refuge
  definition/description, 265–266
  encampments overview, 267–268
  as heterotopia, 280, 281 (fig.), 282–283
  as self-described "ghettos," 270, 271
  transformation to ghettos, 266–267, 284
  See also Self-settled encampments; *specific types*
Refugee camps
  construction/changes, 269
  as ghettos, 24–25
  housing construction, 269–270
  as "jungle," 269
  Kenya, 274–277
  legal status of "refugee," 287
  locations overview, 267
NGOs, 274
  occupants of, 268–269
  organization in, 275–276
  Petras, Greece, 268–270, 285
  as self-described "ghettos," 270, 271
  statistics on, 267
  Sub-Saharan Africa, 274, 275, 267, 274–277
  turnover/length of stay, 270
  UNHCR and, 275
  See also specific camps
Relational isolation, 103, 104

Renoir, Jean, 165
Reservations, 3, 14, 24, 162
Riots
  of 1960s, 46, 48, 68, 113, 141
  following Johnson/Jeffries fight, 119
  northern-style vs. southern style, 118–119
  See also specific riots
Roberts, Bryan, 196
Robinson, Jackie, 145
Rockefeller, John D., Jr., 120
Rockefeller drug laws (1973), 47, 49, 143
Rohff, 172, 174 (fig.), 179
Roma people ("Gypsies"), 19–20 (fig.), 172–173, 283
Roosevelt, Franklin D., 87
Rosenwald, Julius, 120, 307–308
Rotival, Maurice, 167
Rustin, Bayard, 87

Salcedo, Rodrigo, 214
Samuel, Craig, 150
San Francisco
  black population (1940–2009), 90 (fig.)
  See also Fillmore, the (San Francisco)
Sánchez, Gonzalo, 213
Sarkozy, Nicolas, 20 (fig.), 164, 170, 180
Sawyer, Eric, 145
Segregated communities. *See* Ghettos; *specific types*
Segregated (voluntary) communities
  in cities, 15, 38, 60
  "gated communities," 15, 38, 60, 164, 198, 213, 214, 217, 287
  "gilded ghetto" term and, 15
  reasons for, 15
Segregation defined, 41
Self-settled encampments
  architecture, 270, 271
  description, 267, 268

favelas comparison, 271–
272
names for, 270, 271, 285
national borders and,
268
in northern Morocco, 270,
271
social order/organization
and, 270–271, 272–273
transformation to ghetto,
271–278, 283, 284
transformation to IDPs
camp, 268
See also Calais, France
encampments; Patras,
Greece encampments
Sellier, Henri, 166
Selling the Race (Green), 304–
305
Sennett, Richard, 127, 227
Shange, Sikhulu, 113, 129
Sharpton, Al, 129
Simmel, Georg, 161
Simone, AbdouMaliq, 320–
321, 322–323
Situational avoidance, 103–
104
Slim's Table (Duneier), 311–
312, 313 (fig.)
"Slums" official definition, 89
See also Ghettos
Small, Mario, 2, 133, 319, 320
Smith, Roland James, Jr., 129
Social boundaries
comparisons, 184–185
identification and, 160–
162, 161 (fig.)
making, 160–162
as shifting, 159
symbolic boundaries
definition, 160
Harlem Renaissance, 13,
45–46, 123–124, 132–
133, 140, 147
roots of, 45–46
See also Civil rights
movement (United
States)
Soweto, 42
Spanish Harlem (El Barrio),
New York City, 111–
112, 113–114, 182–183

Spatialized oppression
colonial relations and, 38
Israeli wall and, 38
See also specific types
Spear, Allan, 293, 296, 305–307
Squatter settlements
racism and, 38
spatialized oppression
with, 38
Sri Lankan exiles in
detainment centers, 279
Steinberg, Stephen, 132
Stella, Frank, 142
Stewart, Michael, 126
Stokes, Charles, 205
Suggs, Willie, 146
Survey Graphic, 124
Sweet Daddy Grace, 129

Telles, Vera da Silva, 247
Thiers, Adolphe, 165
Time Out New York, 150
Torres, Alvaro, 214
Truly Disadvantaged, The
(Wilson), 309, 314
Turner, John, 204

Une Partie de campagne
(film), 165
United Nations Conference
on Human Settlements,
248
United Nations High
Commissioner for
Refugees (UNHCR)
IDPs and, 268
Liberian refugees and,
270–271
statistics on refugees, 267
sub-Saharan African
refugees and, 275
United Nations Relief and
Works Agency
(UNRWA) for Palestine
Refugees in the Near
East, 267, 277, 281 (fig.)
Upper Manhattan
Empowerment Zone
(UMEZ), 146, 148–149,
152
Urban Outcasts (Wacquant),
2, 50, 294, 311, 318

Van Kempen, Ronald, 194,
213
Van Vechten, Carl, 123
Venkatesh, Sudhir, 229–230,
231, 241, 294, 312, 313
(fig.), 319
Vergara, Camillo, 37
Vietnam "boat people," 278–
279
Villas miserias, Argentina, 14,
164, 200, 235
Voting Rights Act of 1965
(United States), 48

Wacquant, Loïc
Chicago ghettos and, 50–
53, 294, 310, 311, 312,
313 (fig.), 318, 321
ghetto concept, 37, 132,
178, 179–180, 191, 194,
231, 231–232, 283–284,
287, 319, 321
ghetto conditions/life
opportunities, 293
ghettos' increasing
degradation, 50–53,
182, 228, 230, 231, 240,
241, 286
Walsh, Michael, 127
War on Poverty, 48, 49, 59
War on Terror, 52
Warner, W. Lloyd, 304
Watts riots of 1965, 46, 48
Weak ghetto, 35, 40, 42, 59–60
Weber, Max, 10, 12, 118, 133
Welfare-to-work legislation,
56
Welfare/welfare cuts, 56, 69,
70, 71
Western Addition. *See*
Fillmore, the (San
Francisco)
When Work Disappears
(Wilson), 294, 309–
311, 314, 322
White, Alfred T., 120
Wilder, Craig, 140
Wilkerson, Isabel, 119
Wilson, Robert, 196
Wilson, William Julius
black middle class and,
131

Wilson, William Julius
   (*continued*)
   Chicago ghettos and, 294,
      309–311, 312, 312
      (fig.), 313–315, 317,
      318, 319, 320, 322
   ghetto concept and, 14, 71,
      130, 132, 313–315, 317,
      319, 320
   ghetto living
      conditions/life chances
      and, 293, 309–311, 322

Wirth, Louis
   Chicago ghettos, 20–21,
      197, 226, 227, 293, 295–
      296, 308
   ghetto and ethnic cluster,
      3–4
   ghetto concept, 3–4, 9,
      131, 132, 197, 226, 227,
      228, 274
Womack, Bobby, 111
Wonder, Stevie, 114
World Bank, 208

World Social Forum charter,
   36

Yiftachel, Oren, 38

Zinn, Howard, 48, 48–49
Zukin, Sharon, 37, 60, 133